URBAN PLANNING AND CULTURAL IDEN....

The RTPI Library Series

Editors: Cliff Hague, Heriot Watt University, Edinburgh, Scotland
Tim Richardson, Sheffield University, UK
Robert Upton, RTPI, London, UK

Published in conjunction with The Royal Town Planning Institute, this series of leading-edge texts looks at all aspects of spatial planning theory and practice from a comparative and international perspective.

Planning in Postmodern Times
Philip Allmendinger, University of Aberdeen, Scotland

The Making of the European Spatial Development Perspective
No Masterplan
Andreas Faludi and Bas Waterhout, University of Nijmegen, The Netherlands

Planning for Crime Prevention
Richard Schneider, University of Florida, USA, and Ted Kitchen, Sheffield Hallam University, UK

The Planning Polity
Mark Tewdwr-Jones, The Bartlett, University College London

Shadows of Power
An Allegory of Prudence in Land-Use Planning
Jean Hillier, Curtin University of Technology, Australia

Urban Planning and Cultural Identity
William J.V. Neill, Queen's University, Belfast

Forthcoming:

Place Identity, Participation and Planning
Edited by Cliff Hague and Paul Jenkins

Public Values and Private Interests
Heather Campbell and Robert Marshall

Indicators for Urban and Regional Planning
Cecilia Wong

URBAN PLANNING AND CULTURAL IDENTITY

WILLIAM J.V. NEILL

Routledge
Taylor & Francis Group

LONDON AND NEW YORK

First published 2004 by Routledge, 11 New Fetter Lane, London EC4P 4EE
Simultaneously published in the USA and Canada by Routledge, 29 West 35th Street, New York, NY 10001

Routledge is an imprint of the Taylor and Francis Group

© 2004 William J.V. Neill

Typeset in 9.5/13.5 Askidenz Grotesk by Wearset Ltd, Boldon, Tyne and Wear
Printed and bound in Great Britain by St Edmundsbury Press, Bury St Edmunds, Suffolk

British Library Cataloguing in Publication Data
A catalogue record for this book is available from the British Library

Library of Congress Cataloging in Publication Data
Neill, William J.V.
    Urban planning and cultural identity / William J.V. Neill.
        p. cm. – (The RTPI library series; 6)
    Includes bibliographical references and index.
        ISBN 0-415-19747-3 (hardcover: alk. paper) – ISBN 0-415-25915-0 (pbk.: alk. paper)
    1. City planning. 2. City planning–cross-cultural studies. I. Title. II. Series.

HT166.N4218 2004
307.1′216–dc21

2003008576

CONTENTS

PREFACE

I would like to thank the many people who gave generously of their time in interview and who extended hospitality and advice, particularly in Berlin and Detroit. In Belfast, influences are harder to disentangle. In Berlin I am grateful in particular to Dr.-Ing. Günter Schlusche, Building Co-ordinator with the Foundation for the Memorial to the Murdered Jews of Europe. Dr Hanns-Uve Schwedler, Director of the European Academy of the Urban Environment, kindly facilitated the exploration of some of the identity and planning issues explored in this book at a joint symposia between the cities of Berlin and Belfast in February 1999 and December 2001. Funding assistance from the Anglo-German Foundation and Northern Ireland Community Relations Council is acknowledged, as is the help in so many ways of Jenny Johnson, also with the European Academy. The following individuals were interviewed in Berlin at various times since 1996: Christina Laduch, former Director of Planning for Berlin Mitte; Lea Rosh, leading campaigner for a Berlin Holocaust Memorial; Wilhelm V. Boddien, leading campaigner to rebuild the Berliner Schloss; Cornelius Hertling, Chair of the Berlin Chamber of Architects; Dipl.-Ing. Herbert Zimmermann, Berlin planner and former chair of the European Council of Town Planners; Detlef Will, former Building Director in Berlin Steglitz; Wolfgang Schäche, author on Third Reich architecture; Dipl.-Ing. Bernhard Schneider, author on public space and museum architecture and consultant to various Berlin Ministries; Tom Bremen, architectural restorationist working on the Museum Insel; Andrea Gärtner, Culture Department of Prenzlauerberg; Karin Nottmeyer and Frau Paesler in the Senatsverwaltung für Bau- und Wohnungswesen und Verkehr; Philip Meuser with the Berlin Stadt Forum; Peter Martin, Director of Commercial Marketing with Partner für Berlin; Gunnar Pantel, Head of Planning with Rummelsburger Bucht, Berlin, and Wilhelm Schultz, Head of Regional Planning, Land Brandenburg.

For help with German sources I must acknowledge contributions from Sabine and Juliane Engelhardt, Sigrid Reiter whose memory endures, and Andrea Fiddy and Keith Johnston, especially for many enjoyable discussions around Savigny Platz. The translation services of Susanne were invaluable and her tolerance, for the most part, of my introspective musings when I was neglecting other things can probably not be repaid.

In Detroit personal thanks for help and hospitality are due to former colleagues in the Michigan Department of Commerce, Office of Community

Development, Kathy and George Mechem and Tom Nicholas. The following individuals were interviewed in the summers of 1999 and 2001: Revd Wendell Anthony, President Detroit Chapter NAACP; Gloria Robinson, Mayor's Executive Office and former Planning Director, City of Detroit; Paul Bernard, Planning Director, City of Detroit; Paul Tait, Executive Director, Southeast Michigan Council of Governments; Ed Hustoles, former Director of Planning for SEMCOG; Eric Lupher and Paul Goode, Citizen's Research Council of Michigan; Mary Kramer, Editor, Crain's Detroit Business; David Blaszkiewicz, Detroit Renaissance Inc; David Newman, Chief of Staff to Michigan Representative, Samuel Buzz Thomas III; Professor Mary Andrews, Associate Dean, Human Ecology, Michigan State University; Professor Robin Boyle, Associate Dean, College of Urban Affairs, Wayne State University.

In Belfast the influences on one's understanding of how identity is embedded in place are too numerous to mention, let alone unravel. Emotional distance is more difficult when excavating through the sedimented memories of home where personal remembrances like my sister Christine 'going into town' interweave with collective experiences and constructions of the past. My involvement with the Irish Branch (Northern Section) of the Royal Town Planning Institute has, over the years, provided a valuable window on the world of planning practice. Frequent intellectual sparring sessions with planning consultant Dr Patrick Braniff, Senior Research Fellow at Queen's University, Belfast and, like myself 'Belfast-born and bred', has reassured me that empathy across difficult cultural divides is far from impossible and can be fostered by common roots in place.

Thanks are due to the Institute of Governance, Public Policy and Social Research at Queen's University, Belfast for granting me the breathing space of a Sabbatical Fellowship to complete this book and to Karen Agnew for producing the final manuscript with much care and good humour when mine was flagging. Two referees provided valuable feedback and for that I am also most grateful. The responsibility for making sense of it all remains, of course, mine.

ACKNOWLEDGEMENTS

The author would like to express his thanks to the following organizations and people for permission to use copyright material in this book.

Figure 2.2 Partner für Berlin/FTB-Werbefotografie, Gesellschaft für Hauptstadtmarketing; Figure 2.3 Fotobestand W. Schäche; Figure 2.4 Landesarchive, Berlin; Figure 2.10 Photo Landesarchive Berlin. Published with friendly permission of the Stiftung Denkmal für die ermordeten Juden Europas, Berlin; Figures 3.3, 3.4, 3.5 Berlin Ministry for Urban Development (Land Berlin); Figure 3.6 Landesarchive, Berlin; Figure 4.4 Tony Spina, Chief Photographer, *Detroit Free Press*. Reprinted with the kind permission of Francesca Spina; Figure 4.3 South-east Michigan Council of Governments; Figure 5.5 Professor F.W. Boal; Figure 5.7 and Figure 5.10 Laganside Corporation, Belfast; Figures 5.8 and 5.9 courtesy of Tom Neill, Co-ordinator Shankill/Drogheda Schools Project. Permission to quote from the poems *from* Conacre and The coasters in Chapter 5 has been generously given by the Blackstaff Press Ltd, Belfast.

For Susanne

CHAPTER 1

KNOWING YOUR PLACE: URBAN PLANNING AND THE SPATIALITY OF CULTURAL IDENTITY

There is within us only that dark divine animal engaged in a strange journey – that creature who, at midnight, knows its own ghostliness and senses its far road (Loren Eiseley, *The Night Country*, 1971: 54).

As Americans say, if life serves you up a lemon, make lemonade. Whether being born into an Ulster Unionist identity position in Northern Ireland makes it justifiable to liken one to a bitter fruit of dubious value is a matter of real debate. It is one of a number of questions of identity and its relationship to spatial planning that are considered in this book. What is not in question, however, is that 'one thinks of identity whenever one is not sure of where one belongs' (Bauman, 1996: 19). When one's cultural identity is challenged at its roots it can cause a defensive lashing-out from what Castells has called the 'trenches' of 'resistance identity' (Castells, 1997: 8). This is indeed an apt spatial metaphor at a personal level, since the real trenches of the Somme burn deep in the identity-consciousness of Ulster Protestants. Alternatively, when one's identity is questioned, it can cause one to think. To be off-balance and insecure in some primary or core identity can be, to use the terms currently in vogue, to occupy a position on 'the edge', an ill-defined 'borderland' from which the socially constructed nature of other identities wrestling with the problems of 'Us' and 'Them' can be better appreciated. This creates the possibility of proactively turning identity into a 'project' (Castells, ibid.) where it can be remade anew. This book examines the contestation over identity-building and the spatial constitution of this in particular in three different contexts, dealing respectively with German national identity in Berlin, racial identity in Detroit and ethnic identity in Belfast. It takes on board the well-made exhortation that the study of place in the planning field must put less emphasis on the notion of space as a 'surface on which things happen, a two-dimensional Euclidean "mosaic"' (Madanipour *et al.*, 2001: 7; Graham and Healey, 1999) and more on the meanings that are given to particular qualities of specific places. The selection of the three cities is based on places where the author was born and has worked or which have fired the imagination. As the philosopher and travel writer Alain de Botton has expressed it, 'it seems we may best be able to inhabit a place when we are not faced with the additional challenge of having to be there' (De Botton, 2002: 23). The case studies are united by a concentration on the 'city of the imagination' and the messy lived-in place world with which the planner is confronted. As such, the exploration of space unavoidably raises more questions for planning practice than can be answered in this volume but, based on the author's own personal and professional ethical stance, judgements are offered along the way. Maybe, like architects, who are not afraid to reach for the city of the imagination, planners need to nail their own colours more forthrightly to the mast. All the cities presented reflect a general dilemma (in an era of increasingly multicultural cities) of how to balance acknowledgement of cultural difference with a civic sense of what is held in common and what unites. As Thrift has recently pointed out, the myth that 'one city tells all' and that 'it all comes together in Los Angeles' or some other 'celebrity' city is a dangerous one. No one city can bear such a heavy interpretative load (Thrift, 2001: 34–5). It is likely to distract planners and planning theorists from addressing the particularity of place. Before examining how the spatiality of identity has entered into the urban-planning tales of the three cities selected and what we might learn from this as pulled together in a concluding chapter, a foray into the dense literature dealing with cultural identity, difference and spatiality is unavoidable. The object is to delineate some broad, orientating contours in a vast interdisciplinary literature without doing violence to the subtleties of what, at times, can be complex debates. As is often the case, the planning academic attempts to harvest concepts and insights from intellectual labours in less applied disciplines in order to adapt them for relevance to the world of practice.

IDENTITY IN QUESTION

To say that individual identity is possible only in relation to a cultural context is to state a truism. As put by Benhabib:

> Culture is the context within which we need to situate the self, for it is only by virtue of the interpretations, orientations and values provided by culture that we can formulate our identities, say 'who we are', and 'where we are coming from' (Benhabib, 2000: 18).

Hence, whilst Jenkins in his recent book on the social construction of identity cautions against the very use of the term 'cultural' identity because of the multiplicity of contested meanings to which the word 'culture' is attached (Jenkins, 1996: 179), the term nevertheless can be said to have valency because it calls attention to the fact that collective cultural identities imply a much greater sense of meaning for the social actors involved than the traditional sociological concept of 'role' (Castells, 1997: 6–7). As stated by Inglis: 'identity is constituted in terms of what is ultimately important to an individual. It situates a person in moral space' (Inglis, 2001: 8). A common-sense starting point for getting to grips with identity is suggested by

Hall when he describes identification as 'constructed on the back of a recognition of some common origin or shared characteristics with another person or group, or with an ideal, and with the natural closure of solidarity and allegiance established on this foundation'. Hall is quick, however, to point out and endorse the view that identity must not be reduced to some 'essentialist' and unchanging core but rather that it is always discursively formed and always in process (Hall, 1996: 2–3). This social construction of collective identities, which is always taking place in a context marked by power relationships, uses varied cultural building materials from history, geography, religion, sexuality and so forth (Castells, 1997: 7), not the least of which (and of particular concern to the planner) are the socio-spatial resources and potentialities considered later in this introduction. Identity is importantly 'marked out by difference' (Woodward, 1997: 9), implying the marking of symbolic boundaries and the generation of frontier effects. It requires what is left beyond the boundary, its 'constitutive outside' as Hall calls it (Hall, ibid. 3). Differences marking the boundaries of identity may be small or great. Sameness can indeed threaten our individual identity and cause us to hate. As Kohler puts it: 'the more strongly we sense how like us the other person is, the more threatening it seems that he is close to us' (Kohler, 2000: 24). Ignatieff in his study of ethnic hatred in the Balkans drew attention here to Freud's notion of the 'narcissism of minor differences':

> The common elements humans share seem less essential to their perceptions
> of their own identities than the marginal 'minor' elements that divide them. What
> Marx called 'species being' – our identity as members of the human race –
> counts for relatively little (Ignatieff, 1999: 48).

The chasm of difference between identities can also be great, as epitomized by the events of 11 September 2001 giving credence to the thesis of Samuel P. Huntington that the global future will consist of ethnic and religious, Us–versus–Them, cultural clashes between civilizations (Huntington, 1993). In this context, Edward Said has referred to the inflamed collective passions of the United States pursuing Osama bin Laden 'like Captain Ahab in pursuit of Moby Dick'. 'Demonisation of the other', Said adds, 'is not a sufficient basis for any kind of decent politics' (Said, 2001). September 11th and a subsequent degree of polarization of Western and Islamic outlooks on the world illustrate the point that what concept of difference matters most depends on the social circumstances:

> In conditions of peace, considerable blurring of ethnic boundaries may occur.
> People center their identities on their individuality, rather than on their ethnicity.
> They become husbands or wives, lovers or friends and members of a group
> second (Ignatieff, 1999: 52).

Lurking in the background, however, may be what Hall refers to as 'cultural identity' in the sense of 'a shared culture; a sort of collective "one true self" hiding inside the many other, more superficial or artificially imposed "selves", which people with a shared history and ancestry hold in common' (Hall, 1997: 51). Likewise, Castells conceives of 'primary identities', which for most social actors have a primary role in the organization of meaning and which frame other identities that people have (Castells, 1997: 7). Before considering the vexed question of the tension between understanding individuals as 'culture takers' or 'culture makers', and hence the matter of social agency now likely to be characterized as the 'structuration' debate (Giddens, 1984), it is appropriate to reflect on why culture has featured prominently on the academic radar screen long before the collapse of New York's twin towers.

CLAMOUR OVER IDENTITY

The fact that identity has been a topical subject both in- and outside academia for some time now can be crudely related to the collapse of the cold war and to globalization on the one hand, and on the other to the influence of what might loosely be called post-modernist theory, social movements and an associated identity-politics. Castells has referred to the paradox of an increasingly local politics as people strive to create meaning in a world structured by increasingly global processes (Castells, 1997: 8). In Europe we see the reassertion of national identities after the collapse of the attempt to create new identities under the umbrella of Soviet hegemony, and a pan-European identity project championed by political élites seems as yet a pale substitute for the very much alive national narrative of nation states. Ignatieff underscores the link to globalization:

> Globalism scours away distinctiveness at the surface of our identities and forces us back into ever more assertive defense of the inner differences – language, mentality, myth and fantasy – that escape the surface scouring. As it brings us closer together, makes us all neighbors, destroys the old boundaries of identity marked out by national or regional consumption styles, we react by clinging to the margins of difference that remain (Ignatieff, 1999: 58).

In seeing 'globalization' not merely as an economic process but also as a set of events that confronts cultures with each other and links them together, Kohler outlines three possible future cultural scenarios. The first, continuing Americanization, is counterposed against the possibility of global 'jihad' evoked by the writing of Huntington already mentioned. Here Ockman refers to 'the fatally interdependent

dialectic of "jihad versus McWorld" which played itself out with such dire consequences in September 2001' (Ockman, 2002: 19). A third possibility, which
would require working for a political culture of tolerance, could anticipate an
increasingly hybridized or creolized world culture with mixtures of cultural elements
and traditions (Kohler, 2000: 25–6).

The Pandora's box of difference has also been prised further open by post-
modernist theory and a wide variety of social movements. The post-modern critique
of grand narratives has been much commented upon. The various blends of post-
structuralism, deconstructionism and anti-foundationalism evident in the works of
Baudrillard, Lyotard, Derrida and Foucault and crudely classified as 'post-modern
theory' all, at least in different ways, 'criticized the universalist claims of the meta narratives of the Western Enlightenment' (Featherstone, 1995: 78). The critique of the
mission of modernity to impose order on disorder and its totalitarian nature in this
respect by squeezing out notions of 'differences' is traced by Allmendinger to the
1944 work *Dialectic of Enlightenment* by Adorno and Horkheimer. This has its roots
in Nietzsche's reservations about the Enlightenment project (Allmendinger, 2001:
16). Freud had gone some way towards intimating the nature of the problem of the
human power to annihilate through regulatory order when he commented in 1908:

> Experience teaches us that for most people there is a limit beyond which their
> constitution cannot comply with the demands of civilisation. All who wish to be
> more noble-minded than their constitution allows fall victims to neurosis; they
> would have been more healthy if it could have been possible for them to be less
> good (Freud, quoted Donald, 1996: 188).

A prominent theoretical casualty in post-modern critiques of attempts to provide
unitary general explanations of society and history has been the meta-narrative of
Marxism. While class remains as a conceptual necessity for understanding the
dynamics of society, as Anderson points out, we 'need to understand plural
sources of oppression or antagonism in contemporary capitalist societies' (Anderson, 1998: 202). It is more difficult to defend the notion of class as a 'master cat-
egory' in explaining social structure:

> Identities based on 'race', gender, sexuality and disability, for example, cut
> across class affiliations ... it is no longer sufficient to argue that identities can
> be deduced from one's class position (Woodward, 1997: 26).

One writer goes so far as to suggest that now current theories of difference are an
attempt to break from the stranglehold that class theory has exercised over the perceived constitution of social identity:

Subaltern theorists of all sorts – feminists, African Americans, post-colonialists, gays, to name but some – have all argued for the separation of processes of gender, racial and sexual constitution from processes of class definition and formation. While arguing for an interaction between these aspects of identity, there has been a sensitivity to the distinctive autonomy of these processes (Gibson, 1998: 307).

Whereas the Enlightenment impulse was to overcome differences through whole-ness, thus evading the sheer fact of difference (Sennett, 1992: 78), the impulse of post-modernism has been away from universalistic ambitions and notions of total-ity, system and unity towards 'otherness' and difference, fragmentation and local knowledge (Featherstone, 1995: 44). Optimists see the latter as making room for a wide variety of social movements and voices arguing from a range of identity posi-tions and creating a more healthy and less monolithic 'cultural politics of identity and difference'. Various planning writers see the possibilities of human agency in confronting various forms of oppression and discrimination in creating from such struggles 'sites of resistance' where people can redefine their identities anew. Soja endorses the distinction made by bell hooks, for example, 'between the marginality which is imposed by oppressive structure and that marginality one chooses as site of resistance, as location of radical openness and possibility' (hooks, quoted, Soja, 1996: 98). With similar optimism, Sandercock, also drawing inspiration from the African American feminist, theorist and cultural critic, bell hooks, empathizes with those who contribute to the creation of theory by occupying and reworking insur-gent spaces of difference 'on the borderlands' (Sandercock, 1998: ch. 5). While both Soja and Sandercock would undoubtedly be swift to acknowledge that the processes that work to construct identities and which frame the context for agency are always embedded in frameworks of power that lead to 'unevenly empowered differences' (Jacobs and Fincher, 1998: 6), it is sanguine to reflect that sometimes the space for insurgent radical openness may be considerably constrained. The spatial metaphor of 'the borderlands' of possibility, for example, as applied to the context of Ulster Protestants living on the actual borderland of County Fermanagh over the last 30 years, would have been regarded by many until recently as conjur-ing up the radical choice between staying in a landscape of fear and changing place. At a general level, however, a tension between optimism and pessimism can be discerned at the heart of critical writing on late capitalism. As Dubiel comments regarding the history of the Frankfurt School, which has been one of the seminal arenas for such debate:

> In a slogan-like manner, the schism in the Critical theory of late capitalism could
> be equated with the opposition between pessimism and optimism, between

defeatism and naïveté, between a 'Grand Hotel Abyss' and an unpolitical euphoria about communication (Dubiel, 1994: 130).

Since the current hegemonic paradigm in planning theory takes its persistently optimistic major cue from the second-generation Frankfurt School philosopher Jürgen Habermas, as a counterbalance it may be appropriate to consider reasons for pessimism among other writers who have reflected on matters of difference and identity. In the face of many reasons for pessimism and after a consideration of the role of memory and place in identity-construction, this introduction concludes with a reflection on the concept of 'citizenship', which has been a preoccupation of Habermas, as a necessary if optimistic 'civic glue' within which difference can embed. The striving and need for such 'glue' is a common aspect of the case studies in the following chapters. In the last instance, however we have little choice but to impose order on difference.

THE GRAND HOTEL ABYSS

Sitting in the lobby of the Grand Hotel Abyss it is possible to contemplate the death of visions of positive social change, the death of the traditional Cartesian subject and, latterly and most alarmingly, the death of 'human nature' itself. Richard Rorty, the American philosopher and a follower of John Dewey's liberal pragmatism, sees the current fixation on 'identity and difference' as the 'result of a loss of hope – or, more specifically, of an inability to construct a plausible narrative of progress' (Rorty, 2000: 50). The dangers of cultural relativism inherent in postmodernism have been well noted (Eagleton, 1996: 134). As harshly put by one critic, when authentic expression is demanded on the basis of 'pluralism, individualism and difference':

> Culture can quickly become a mere assertion of values that defines the
> battlefield on which the only causes are honour, faithfulness and death – and
> certainly not problem-solving, learning and getting on with things ... A self that
> no longer wants to be tied to a work ethic or a political project looks for
> resonance and reflection in the soft and all-embracing medium of culture (Bude,
> 2000: 38).

In the academic world, one American writer on difference and identity notes that conference attendees locate themselves publicly along a series of 'identity axes' to the extent that the question, 'How does your work reflect the politics of your (racial/gendered/sexual) positionality?' has overtaken the inquiry, 'What is your theoretical approach?' (Awkward, 1995: 4). For writers who link post-modernism to the cultural face of turbo consumer capitalism the outlook for human agency can be bleak indeed. Identity can be seen as 'sold' and reduced to the pre-packaged lifestyle choices satirized in the movie *American Beauty*, where life is shallowly constructed on the maxim 'I am what I consume'. In the film *Fight Club* the deadening suffocation of this corporate programming is brutally rejected as male identity is sought in the authenticity of bodily fear, pain and danger in the here-and-now. However, as one critic points out. while '*Fight Club*'s political analysis may have been brilliant . . . it offered no way forward' (Bunting, 1999). The popular book *No Logo* by Naomi Klein, reacting against the fear that the most powerful collective identities may be those that we buy, with our longings and desires pathetically projected onto lattes or trainers, does try to map out some space for rediscovering our identities as citizens rather than just consumers (Klein, 2000). While Klein is not a resident, more brooding critical theorists in the Grand Hotel Abyss are likely to see the task as considerable. For Fredric Jameson, a once 'semi-autonomous' and authentic culture has been transformed in 'the cultural logic of late capitalism' (Jameson, 1991) into a hyper-reality of depthless culture which has been 'set to work as the fuel for the now semiotic motor of capital accumulation' (Jacobs, 1998: 254). Jameson's work draws on the writing of Jean Baudrillard, with its nihilistic characterization of late modernity as a state where all referentiality and meaning are lost (Allmendinger, 2001: 41). This is depressing enough for a humanist sensibility which endeavours to cling to the notion that there are certain aspects of being that people share by virtue of their common humanity. However, post-modernist theory, with its emphasis on the constitution of subjectivity and sense of self linked firmly to the positions that we take up and identify with (Woodward, 1997: 39), can seem to squeeze out the possibility of a Cartesian sovereign self altogether as identity is theorized as constituted within regimes of symbolic representation with the 'death of the subject'. Powerful here has been the notion of 'interpellation', used by the structuralist Marxist writer Louis Althusser to explain the way in which subjects are 'hailed' or recruited into subject positions through recognizing themselves – 'yes that's me' (Woodward, ibid. 42). Althusser had drawn on the work of Jacques Lacan and his version of Freudian psychoanalysis. As opposed to a focus on subject recruitment at the psychic level, Michel Foucault has been a prominent French philosopher and social constructionist theorist, impossible to omit from any debate on identity, with his focus on identity construction through symbolic systems or discursive practices and their implicit power relations which insert individuals into subject positions. When 'baits feel like desires, pressures like intentions, seduction like decision making' (Bauman, 1996: 27) the notion of the subject as the centred author of social practice can seem rather threadbare. It is here that Grossberg rightly points to a paradox:

How can the individual be both cause and effect (an old question), both subject and subjected? Or in other words, how and where does one locate agency? This problem has animated the large body of contemporary political and theoretical work on the production of subordinate identities and the possibilities of resistance, whether in the name of the subaltern, feminism, anti-racism or post-colonialism (Grossberg, 1996: 98).

In that post-modernist theorists tend to be deeply sceptical about the proposition that subjects have an interiority (Eagleton, 1996: 71), Eagleton likens such anti-humanism to that of recently discarded structuralism, an approach to the study of human culture which claims that individual phenomena have meaning only by virtue of their relation to other phenomena as elements within a systematic structure (Milner, 1994: 76). People move from the controlled cogs that Thompson famously lampooned (Thompson, 1978: 99–102) to imprinted subjects. Both, for Eagleton, behave 'as a kind of technocracy of the spirit, the final penetration of the rationaliz-ing impulse of modernity into the inner sanctum of the subject' (ibid. 131). Com-ments such as the ego is nothing but 'the superimposition of various coats borrowed from the bric-a-brac of its props department' (Lacan, quoted Donald, 1996: 184) can sound chilling. There may be some comfort in the fact that, despite the notion of 'a messy interiority which drove Michel Foucault up the wall' (Eagle-ton, 1996: 71), in his later writings he came to address 'the existence of some interior landscape of the subject'. This opens up the possibility of understanding, for example, why some people are interpolated while others resist and requires an understanding of 'the suturing of the psychic and the discursive' in the constitution of identities (Hall, 1996: 16).

There is a final reason for humanists to seek comfort at the bar of the Grand Hotel Abyss. The titles of two recent books give a new twist to aspects of identity that provide fresh focus for academic debate. The book by Gregory Stock entitled *Redesigning Humans*, which welcomes the use of genetic engineering to go beyond what may be essential human nature, may be counterposed to the more circumspect views of Francis Fukuyama, who moves beyond the 'end of history' to contemplate *Our Posthuman Future* (Stock, 2002; Fukuyama, 2002). With the possibility of gene-mixing from other species and the creation of genetic élites, a situation may arise where a shared humanity is lost. With the possibilities of artificial intelligence the dilemma is compounded. In his concept for the film *AI*, Stanley Kubrick endeavoured to portray artificial intelligence 'not as a threat to human identity ... (but) robots as our future' (Maitland, 2001). The scriptwriter on the film, however, expresses doubts:

The culture I live in has taught me to overvalue a highly constructed and unnatural idea of 'the natural' to the point that I would rather be dead, as a species, than risk a computer generated future. My intellect is with the post-modernists, with the reality of the 'virtual' and the idea that there is no 'natural' but only constructions of language and the imagination. But my heart is not (Maitland, 2001).

In relation to such new frontiers it has been well said that 'citizenship will require some moral philosophy over the next decades' (Bunting, 2000).

MEMORY AND IDENTITY

If discourses are part of the means by which subjects come to be known and to know themselves, central here must be discourses involving the construction of memory. At the level of the self, a repository of cultural resources may be seen as being organized biographically in the form of memory (Jenkins, 1996: 46). Speaking at the level of collective identities, as Dolores Hayden reiterates, 'identity is intimately tied to memory' (Hayden, 1997: 9). Indeed it is the present assault on memory, with the constant bombardment of commercial images eroding a sense of continuity between past, present and future, that can lead to pessimism concerning the possibility of the construction of meaningful identities. Identity requires a narrative of continuity. Since the following two chapters highlight the contestation and negotiation wrapped up in collective memory discourses involved in urban planning in Berlin post-1989, this dimension of identity-building will be discussed in more detail in that context. It is worth remembering, however, that memory is not something abstract like history, that it cannot exist outside those people who do the remembering and that it is not 'a passive receptacle or storage system, an image bank of the past'. Rather, 'memory is historically conditioned changing colour and shape according to the emergencies of the moment' (Samuel, 1994: x). Collective remembering can take various institutionalized, cultural and ritualized forms. It is also constituted spatially and, therefore, of major significance for urban planning.

PLACE AND IDENTITY

In her book *The Power of Place*, Dolores Hayden points out that social scientists have frequently avoided the messy concept of 'place' in favour of more quantifiable research with fewer epistemological problems. Yet the concept of place is powerful:

> If place does provide an overload of possible meanings for the researcher, it is place's very same assault on all ways of knowing (sight, sound, smell, touch and taste) that makes it powerful as a source of memory, as a weave where one strand ties in another (Hayden, 1995: 18).

This book examines contested, 'conflicted' and unfolding memory narratives in three cities where identity is wrapped up in the uniqueness of place. Other places have their own stories but in Detroit, Berlin and Belfast identity sensibilities are raw. While one must be careful in 'mapping' cultures crudely onto places, given that multiple cultures and identities frequently inhabit a single place and contribute to its character, the focus on such cities throws up the big questions of what it means to be black in Detroit, German in Berlin and Irish and/or British in Belfast. These are important questions for while 'landscape is made in the image of capital this is not its sole image' (Keith and Pile, 1993: 8). Such case studies can locate themselves as part of a growing literature which studies space as a cultural product. Here space may be distinguished from place in that the latter involves the assignment of symbolic meaning to objects:

> Whereas space is open and is seen as an abstract expanse, place is a particular part of that expanse which is endowed with meaning by people (Madanipour, 1996: 158).

Indeed it is difficult to think of space that is not a place of some kind, since it will be designated with meaning of one sort or another within some cultural frame. Keith and Pile put the matter succinctly by saying that work in social science is increasingly taking on board the basic notion that spatialities are 'to be understood as a constitutive element of the social' although they rightly point out that Walter Benjamin's ruminations on the place-character of his native Berlin and of Paris in the 1920s evoked the relationship between spatialities and identity with the increasingly spatialized vocabulary of social theory therefore, not entirely novel *account insight* (Keith and Pile, 1993: 9). Whatever the historical genealogy of the insight, however, the basic point is that identity must be theorized as a socio-spatial phenomenon. Soja, who views Henri Lefebvre's book *The Production of Space* (published in French in 1974 and in English in 1991) as 'arguably the most important book ever written about the social and historical significance of human spatiality' (Soja, 1996: 8), puts it this way:

> We are becoming increasingly aware that we are, and always have been, intrinsically spatial beings, active participants in the social construction of our embracing spatialities (Soja, ibid. 1).

Given the commonly accepted significance of Lefebvre as foundational to spatial theory such that it is common now to see the term 'spatial practices' used in a general way to refer to space as a cultural production (Liggett and Perry, 1995: 6), and given the focus in the chosen cities of study on the importance of the symbolism invested in place (a major concern of Lefebvre) to the constitution of identity, some key spatial distinctions evoked in *The Production of Space* are worthy of brief mention. Reviews exist elsewhere (Soja, 1996; Madanipour, 1996; Liggett and Perry, 1995) but from the standpoint of the investigatory focus in the following chapters it is Lefebvre's concept of 'representational space' that is especially productive. This is to be distinguished from the notion of 'spatial practices' or the spatial patterns of everyday life and abstract 'representations of space' common in professional practices such as urban planning. Representational space involved in the overall cultural process of 'place assembly', as Liggett puts it:

> is heavily loaded, deeply symbolic and embedded culturally, not necessarily entailing conscious awareness. It calls on shared experiences and interpretations at a profound level ... representational spaces are the loci of meaning in a culture (Liggett, 1995: 251).

When the same locational representational space is invested with different profound cultural meanings, as is the case with the Dome of the Rock in Jerusalem, a single place can be a lightning rod for disaster. While Ariel Sharon's visit to the Temple Mount in the summer of 2000 may not have been the cause of the second Palestinian intifada, it was the spark that lit the fuse (Makiya, 2002: 152). Before moving on to consider some other useful concepts for getting to grips with the meaning of places for people, it is worthwhile pausing to consider whether in an increasingly global and cyber age local place will continue to matter to people at all. Here there is a clear tension in the literature on place. Cyberspace can be thought of as a de-territorialized 'place' with rooms and locations where people can experiment with the plasticity of identity. Castells pointed some time ago to how the meaning of places for people was disappearing in the 'space of flows' as 'the logic of dominant organizations detaches itself from the social constraints of cultural identities and local societies through the powerful medium of information technologies' (Castells, 1991: 6). In their recent book on *Splintering Urbanism*, Graham and Marvin point out that geographical proximity within cities is no guarantee of meaningful relations or connections as places become bound up in global-local or 'glocalized' interactions (Graham and Marvin, 2001: 197). In a splintered local urbanism, with the use of modern technologies, globally distant places can be intimately connected, joined together by 'customised network spaces' (ibid. 101). The result is 'the fragmentation of the social and material fabric of cities (ibid. 33). On the other hand, Graham and Marvin concede that 'the continuation of public mixing in cities means that spaces continue to exist within which strategies of resisting secession and urban splintering can be constructed' (ibid. 392) and that such struggles of resistance may revolve around 'questions of representation, meaning and identity' (ibid. 397). Indeed there is reason to believe that globalization has led to heightened attempts to draw the boundaries between the self and others, provoking reactions that seek to discover particularity and difference rather than acquiescing in a dissolution into a global 'Gemeinschaft' which transcends physical place (Featherstone, 1995: 117). The philosopher Edward Casey puts the matter in more existential terms in referring to place as 'the bedrock of our being-in-the world':

> To lack a primal place is to be 'homeless' ... being without any effective means of orientation in a complex and confusing world ... I shall accord to place a position of renewed respect by specifying its power to direct and stabilise us, to memoralise and identify us, to tell us who and what we are in terms of *where we are* (as well as where are *not*) (emphasis original) (Casey, 1993: xv–xvii).

In such a perspective, while there can seldom be one reading of an urban landscape when identity is wrapped up in place, 'meanings may become more important than facts in policy deliberation' (Hillier, 2001: 71). This is overwhelmingly the case in the three cities shortly to be checked for identity, and yet it is a reality with which planners are not always comfortable. For more intrepid planners venturing into the messy world of 'place' some other conceptual points of reference are available, many of which have been nurtured in the discipline of architecture but which have a saliency that goes beyond the confines of urban design. Important here are notions of 'genius loci', 'dwelling', 'home' and 'place-making', all inevitably picked up in the following tale of three cities.

As Harvey observes, drawing on the work of Norberg-Schulz, it can be helpful at times to talk in terms of contestation over the 'genius loci' where the latter 'spirit of place' is defined as the 'meanings which are gathered by a place' (Harvey, 1996: 308). The absence of active political controversy over the genius loci can be seen as a sign of the domination of some hegemonic power. This contest is important because 'to release a different imaginary concerning the past is to release a different imaginary as to possibilities in the future' (ibid. 309). The power of symbolic places in cities holds major sway over the imagination and, therefore, they can be sites of struggle in the same way that images representing the city as a whole can be disputed because of the power which they bestow (ibid. 322). Willis reminds us that the city is also a place of the imagination. It is not simply appearance which counts but 'rather the sum total of all we imagine it to be'. Cities must 'be as founded in the imagination as securely as they are founded upon the earth' (Willis, 1999: 9). The notion of *genius loci*, which endeavours to capture this ultimately illusive character of place, can in turn be linked back to Heidegger's concept of 'dwelling'. With acknowledgement to

Heidegger, Norberg-Schulz defines 'dwelling' and existential foothold as synonymous:

> Man dwells when he can orientate himself within and identify himself with an
> environment, or, in short, when he experiences the environment as meaningful
> (Norberg-Schulz, 1980: 5).

Having roots in a place, belonging to a place, and grounding oneself in the everyday meaningful world of significance keeps at bay the ultimately unsettling groundlessness of experience, or 'Dasein' in Heidegger's terminology. Place provides the
basis for individual identity as always embodied, having the possibilities of seeing,
feeling and smelling 'the other', for example, not provided by the Internet (Bouchet,
1998: 126), and thus opening up the world of the phenomenology of place that
was explored at a micro level by Gaston Bachelard (Bachelard, 1994). 'Dasein',
the German word for being alive, literally means 'being there'. In short, dwelling in
place protects us from the void. Nothing is more primal here than the notion of
'home'. Here, in the 'dynamic rivalry between house and universe', Bachelard talks
of how the former provides the inhabitant with 'counsels of resistance' (Bachelard,
ibid. 46–7). We can never plan, however, for a cosy 'cotton-wool' concept of
home. Dorothy in *The Wizard of Oz* acts out the two archetypal contradictory long-
ings that people have always felt: the desire for freedom and the wish to make a
place one's home. With what Willis calls these 'two polar activities of the heart' we
can never be totally content with any place, no matter how perfect. We are 'conflicted creatures forever trying to find a balance between weight and lightness,
flight and return . . .' (Willis, 1999: 98–9). In ongoing efforts to capture such frus-
tratingly elusive but fundamental characteristics of place, the concept of 'habitus'
as associated with the French social scientist Pierre Bourdieu has recently been
press-ganged into possible service (Hillier and Rooksby, 2002) to capture the
notion of habitus as 'a sense of one's (and others') place and role in the world of
one's lived environment . . . an embodied, as well as a cognitive, sense of place'
(Hillier and Rooksby, 2002: 5). While, as Friedman points out, however, given that
the focus of Bourdieu's theory was not primarily spatial, the concept is perhaps 'of
only limited use for the city-building professions' (Friedman, 2002: 314), a more
useful concept is arguably that of 'place-making'. In 1980 in a paper entitled 'Architecture as Identity', presented to the Semiotic Society of America, Chris Abel
endorsed the interpretation of architecture 'as a purposeful, place-making activity'
necessarily imbued with meaning in a deep sense since architecture itself 'is a way
of being just as science, art and the other major culture-forms are ways of being'
(Abel, 1980). Discussion of 'place-making' as an interpretative frame of reference
is postponed until Chapter 4, where it is the major interrogative tool used to get to

grips with identity issues and urban planning in Detroit. It is sufficient here to note two points. First, a collaborative approach to 'place-making', which brings into focus 'the way people think about place and the meanings they give to it', has gained some prominence as a proposed overarching normative direction for planning practice (Healey, 2001: 278). The new motto of the Royal Town Planning Institute is 'mediation of space-making of place'. Second, it may be difficult in Western place-making to be truly open to identity and difference. Sennett argues here that Western urban planners are in the grip of a Protestant ethic of space. This regards the inner life as the most important and, being fearful of the pleasures, differences and distractions of the 'outside', it has had a controlling and neutralizing effect on the environment (Sennett, 1992). It is in Christian cities that Sennett finds the root of the desire for what can be a deadening legibility and the imposed organization of difference celebrated as necessary by Lynch in his influential book *The Image of the City* (Lynch, 1960). A cursory brush with some desolate soulscapes in Belfast, especially on a wet Sunday, would only reinforce Sennett's insight.

CITIZENSHIP, IDENTITY AND DIFFERENCE

As Inglis observes, it is a much-commented-upon difficulty with liberal politics that it embodies a deep contradiction:

> On the one hand cultural differences must be respected and preserved; on the other culture is subordinate to a political theory of universalism in which difference is transcended in the doctrines of equality and human rights (Inglis, 2001: 17).

In looking at discourses on the spatial constitution and contestation of identity in three case-study cities, where 'everything does not come together' but which nevertheless stand obdurately in their uniqueness, the following chapters reflect in various ways the basic tension to which Inglis refers. The possibilities and difficulties involved with reaching a tolerable accommodation between 'difference' and common shared values of citizenship will be discussed in the final chapter, which focuses in particular on the notion of 'environmental citizenship' implicit, for example, in the concerns of Local Agenda (now Local Action) 21. These are matters of central preoccupation to Jürgen Habermas, seeking through processes of dialogic democracy to create common meaning. To take such a course can draw the criticism that identity is being taken too seriously and obfuscating questions concerning the state and 'the politics at work in all this: the role of power'

(Niethammer, 2003: 89). One recent critic of identity politics criticizes its 'ideological absorption' in laying claim to public validation, going so far as to express the frustration that:

> so long as talk about identity dominates the public sphere, practical conclusions and intellectual agreement are impossible (ibid. 88).

Identity becomes equated with a form of false consciousness, 'a fog' from which the invitation is extended to emerge to confront the 'heterogeneity of the actual collectives in question', when we will be able to obtain 'a less distorted look at everything that wears a human face' (ibid. 91). To this it might be countered that meaning should surely be negotiated and should not be the product of a vain quest to peel away 'magical formulas of identity' to find an underlying reality beneath. Or, in the words of the Zen Master to his pupil:

> The secret is that there is no secret. If you meet the Buddha on the road, kill him! (Kopp, 1972: i).

CHAPTER 2

PLANNING, MEMORY AND IDENTITY I: ACKNOWLEDGING THE PAST IN THE CITY OF REMORSE

'The greatest test of post-modernism, or for that matter of any other political doctrine, is how it would shape up to (fascism)'

Terry Eagleton, *The Illusions of Post-modernism*, 1996: 134.

Capital cities 'reverberate with symbolic power' (Sennett, 1990: 51). It is in the capital city of a country that the relationship between urban planning, architecture and evolving conceptions of national identity is likely to be most direct and most closely under political influence. Suggestions that the environs of Buckingham Palace should be opened up and turned into a public place or that statues of forgotten generals should be removed from Trafalgar Square witness to a desire of London's Mayor, Ken Livingstone, to celebrate monarchy and past imperial glory less in the construction of national identity. A new monument to RAF Battle of Britain pilots on the Embankment in London will identify the nation with the spirit of 'the Few'. In Washington, DC the decision to construct a Holocaust Museum and not a museum of African American history on the Washington Mall speaks loudly, for example, as to what is currently deemed acceptable in the United States' construction of its national narrative of invoked identification, soon to be accompanied by a bonding September-11th memorial in New York. The African American project, which would have been an acknowledgement of America's own historical crimes, was finally killed in 1994 by Senator Jesse Helms of North Carolina (Finkelstein, 2000: 72). Jerusalem, a city closely associated with the 'collective soul' of Jewish identity (Wiesel, 2001), is caught in a competing claim from Palestinians to make it their capital city. Here Israel can use the 'moral capital' derived from the Holocaust *inter alia* as legitimacy for its case (Novick, 1999: 156). In contrast to Jerusalem, Berlin stands in a different relationship to the Holocaust. It was the power seat of the perpetrators. This chapter, largely based on interview sources and the review of relevant literature, traces the manner in which Berlin, in the physical planning of the city, has dealt with the dilemma of how the Holocaust should be acknowledged in the texture of the new capital, how moral capital can be replenished, and how the parallel debate on what the Holocaust means for German identity has influenced this. Seldom can planners and architects, two closely allied professions in Germany, have been drawn into such an emotionally charged cultural cauldron where the city is the locus of such intense debate over the meaning of place. In general, while planners can propose in this context, politicians dispose.

The chapter proceeds by way of a discussion of current civic-nationalist and ethno-nationalist claims on German identity. Berlin as a setting for these claims is then reviewed in general terms within the context of wider European economic and political transformation, which is also redefining Berlin's role and image. The spectre of Albert Speer's ethno-nationalist Germania which haunts the *genius loci* of the German capital is then considered, showing how Hitler was certainly no stranger to an understanding of the relationships between spatiality, identity and power. The relationship of Holocaust memory to German self-understanding sub-sequently provides a backdrop for how the burden of the Nazi period in German history has been acknowledged in the move of the federal government from Bonn to Berlin, with the consequent planning of a new urban landscape of political power on the heavy cultural legacy of the old. The political decision to build a vast memorial to the 'Murdered Jews of Europe' close to the heart of the new government quarter receives particular attention, cast as it is within a much wider memorial landscape which tries in various ways to engage with an unforgiving and unforgivable past. The dark shadow that this throws on how Germans define themselves and relate to others cannot be lifted by any quick-fix resolution in the foreseeable future.

ETHNO-NATIONALISM AND CIVIC NATIONALISM

The historian Norman Davies describes how nationalism, one of the most elemental and resurgent identity-building processes of modern times, came from the late 18th century and 19th century onwards in two opposing variants: civic nationalism and ethnic nationalism. The former was initiated 'at the top' among a political élite which sought to project its values downwards into society at large. The latter started 'at the grass roots', seeking to attract mass popular support for the notion that the proper forum for the exercise of the general will was the national or ethnic community, not the artificial frontiers of existing states (Davies, 1996: 812–15). Ethnic nationalism, in its concept of 'nationhood', emphasizes mythical notions of ethnic identity, language, culture, poetry, history and romantic feelings about the land. Civic nationalism is based on political institutions (Buruma, 1998). Britain as a nation state based on civic nationalism leads citizens to look to the state 'as a source not of poetry but of institutions that protect rights and liberties' (Buruma, ibid.). Or, as another writer puts it, the British national identity, forged and deliberately constructed by political élites especially from the 18th century onwards in a context of empire-building, had as its 'first pillar' the notion of a 'nation held together by its central institutions' (Leonard, 1997: 25–6). Recognizing that the civic/ethic dichotomy is an ideal type-distinction, and that the nationalism of every nation has romantic as well as constitutional and political elements, Buruma poses an important question: 'Where do we place more weight – on culture, or on shared political institutions?'

In constructing a sense of shared belonging and identification out of cultural and civic elements a 'national narrative' is essential to any nation state. Here collective memory, open to contestation, selects from history what is emphasized, remembered and forgotten. While Maurice Halbwachs, the French sociologist, pointed out in the 1920s that it is present concerns that determine what of the past we include in collective memory (Novick, 1999: 3), Easthope reminds us (not without significance for identity preoccupations in Germany) that, since the function of a national narrative is to confer a sense of identity on members of a nation, this is only possible if the national narrative retains a considerable degree of stability. The national narrative bestows a sense of 'being a people', a 'large scale solidarity' with a 'perceived integration of past and present in an envisaged future' (Easthope, 1997: 4). Stories are ongoing. The traditional 'British story' is presently being reworked to better bring into the picture ethnic minorities. The inevitable integration of the events of 11 September 2001 into the American national narrative will be no less deep because civic nationalism in the United States sees national identity as rooted in common citizenship and attachment to a shared set of political values and practices rather than in common ethnicity. However, as Ignatieff points out, while most major Western nation states now define their nationhood more in terms of common citizenship than by common ethnicity, one prominent exception, until recently, has been Germany (Ignatieff, 1994: 4).

GERMAN IDENTITY

In Germany, ethnic nationalism was the invention of the Romantic intelligentsia at the end of the 18th and beginning of the 19th century:

> The German intellectuals rose up against the French Enlightenment's vision of political society as a society of contractual equals, and they exalted Germanness as the universal culture of feeling against the cold mechanical individualism of the French. In so doing, figures like Novalis, Schiller, Fichte and Müller self-consciously constituted themselves as the true voice of the nation (Ignatieff, 1994: 63–4).

In a controversial but only half-facetious review of German nationhood at the dawn of the new millennium, A.A. Gill, columnist for the *Sunday Times*, recently referred to the forest as 'the spiritual, mystical heart of Germany':

How you feel about a silent birch forest at twilight says more about your blood and kin than your passport. The Germans are children of the woods, people of the dappled half-light, the secret glade, the silence and camouflage (Gill, 1999: 22).

Here Gill could point to the mythical role of the hero Arminius in the German national narrative, who emerged with his followers in the Teutoburg Forest in AD 9 to slaughter three Roman legions under the command of Quinctilius Varus. There are few German schoolchildren who are not aware of this great tragedy that befell the Roman Empire and of the cry of Emperor Augustus when hearing the news: 'Varus, Varus, give me back my legions!' That Gill is only half facetious is underscored by the knowledge that, during the Third Reich, no less than 100 researchers were employed simply to look at the role of the forest in German culture (Wood, 1999). *Scene of event   importance*

It is towards Berlin as a locale for the reassessment of the meaning of German nationhood and identity that passionate debate seems inevitably channelled. *echo* This parallels and reverberates with debates on appropriate urban planning for the restored capital. While Berlin is historically associated with a cosmopolitan openness extending back from Weimar decadence to Prussian qualities of liberalism, toleration and enlightenment (Craig, 1991: 300), and while almost three out of four Berliners voted against Hitler in 1932 (Read and Fisher, 1994: 197), Berlin is irrevocably associated with the failure of a nation state under the Nazis that was based on a most extreme and grotesque form of ethno-nationalism. In the words of Daniel Libeskind, designer of the new Jewish museum in Berlin, who lost most of his family to Hitler's gas chambers:

> The Holocaust is not just another event in the time line of Berlin. It's an axial redefinition of Berlin (Libeskind, quoted Range, 1996: 116).

When Richard Holbrooke, the former American ambassador to Germany, recently referred to 'unquiet ghosts' in a city where 'every decision of the planning authority, every new building or monument, triggers an argument based on conflicting views of history', it is to Berlin as the former 'undisputed capital of evil' to which he refers (Holbrooke, 2001: 33). In Hitler and the Holocaust, the German national narrative was shattered in a way not permitting of easy suture. While it is possible to omit, for example, the behaviour of Oliver Cromwell at Drogheda in Ireland from the British national narrative, the 'break in civilisation', as Habermas calls it, during the Nazi period cannot be easily dismissed from the German theatre of memory (Habermas, 1998: 25). As expressed by Alexandra Richie in her recent and highly acclaimed history of Berlin:

The legacy of the years 1933 to 1945 still presents enormous problems for
Berlin as a whole, and it is not an exaggeration to say that the way in which its
citizens face the past will help to shape both the future of the capital and the
very identity of the new Germany. And the rest of the world will be watching
(Richie, 1999: xlvii).

The spatial expression and constitution of German identity-angst is sedimented in
the plans, bricks and mortar of the new Berlin. This is not a simple matter of superficial urban representation, with Berlin presenting an appropriately acceptable built
image for Germans and to the world. The ongoing questioning by Germans of who
they consider themselves to be (common to all identities but particularly intense in
Germany) is, in a real sense in Berlin, acted out spatially. Liggett, drawing on the
work of Lefebvre, reminds us that making space is also about making meaning
(Liggett, 1995: ch. 9). In this process the contestation over the creation of
meaning in the built environment has put Berlin planners and architects in the
cockpit of urban semiotics on the grand scale. The context is that of coming to
terms with the German legacy of ethno-nationalism in an increasingly multicultural
city and society.

In Germany, in 2002, 7.3 million foreigners made up 9% of the population.
The city of Berlin itself has a population of 3.5 million, of whom 12% are
foreigners from over 180 countries (Fessenden, 2002: 39). Perhaps more import-
antly, Berlin is the world's fifth largest Turkish city (Berlin in Brief, 1996: 2001;
Hooper, 2000). Berlin's district of Kreuzberg has been given the nickname 'Little
Istanbul'. In Frankfurt, 30% of the population is foreign-born (Ignatieff, 1995: 60).
Immigration could dramatically increase, as in common with other EU states a low
birth rate and an ageing population will require further inflows to maintain the
present balance between the retired and working population (Steele, 2000).
With Germany then already a long way from being a mono-ethnic Volk, the
question is how can this be squared with a national identity based on ethno-
nationalism?

The so-called 'Leitkultur' (leading culture) debate in 2000 provided an important focus for this still-unresolved question. The trigger was a decision by Chancellor Gerhard Schröder to invite 30 000 foreign computer specialists to work in
Germany. Some conservative politicians, led by Friedrich Merz, parliamentary
leader of the Christian Democrats, put forward the view that if such foreigners
wanted to integrate they should adapt to an albeit ill-defined German 'leading' or
'defining' culture (Boyes, 2001; Finn, 2000). This contributed to this exclamation in
2000 by France's Interior Minister, Jean-Pierre Chevènement, which he might not
have uttered had it been after Le Pen's strong showing in France's presidential
elections two years later:

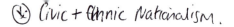
Civic + Ethnic Nationalism.

Germany has a conception of the nation that is one of das Volk [the people], in other words an ethnic conception. It must be helped to form another idea of the nation, the nation of citizens, in order to have a better dialogue with France (Chevènement, quoted Henley and Hooper, 2000).

Given that the Red-Green coalition under Schröder had in fact made a start on overhauling Germany's ethnically restrictive citizenship law, the jibe from Chevènement was perhaps slightly unfair. In what has been called a 'milestone' event, since 1999 naturalization has been made easier for long-term foreign residents and their children (Fessenden, 2002: 38–9). Children born to immigrant parents now have an automatic right, for example, to a German passport, provided one of the parents has lived in Germany for eight years. The carrying of dual nationality by adults, favoured by many Turks wanting to keep economic ties and identity connections with Turkey, continues to find disfavour with most Germans, who feel it would inspire divided loyalties and work against integration. It remains a reform too far. However, a bridge has been crossed. As expressed by one commentator who believes 'Germany has become less German':

> Germans who only sixty years earlier took the most brutal measures to preserve the purity of their so-called Ayran race now were passing laws and taking personal action to dilute their German blood (Kempe, 1999: 229).

A more pessimistic viewer, however, might point out that, while more Turkish residents in Germany can acquire a German passport, this means belonging only to the German state, not the German nation (Ignatieff, 1995: 68). It does not necessarily mean acceptance. In the words of one Turk who was born and lives in Berlin, has a German passport and speaks fluent German:

> We're an integral part of German society but we're still regarded as foreigners. Even if you have a German passport and speak fluent German, you're always a Turk in German eyes (Range, 1996: 116).

Such feeling and experience has led to many Turks choosing not to integrate themselves in a manner many Germans would like. Since 1993 in particular, which saw the burning to death of five Turks in the town of Solingen by right-wing extremists, the Islamic Community for a New World Vision (Milli Görüş) in Germany has grown rapidly by comparing Turks to Jews and charting out a non-integrationist path. A major voice among German Turks favouring integration, that of Cem Özdemir the former Green Party parliamentarian, expresses the opinion that the momentum behind Milli Görüş can be stopped 'but only if Germany strengthens the Turks' feeling of belonging here' (quoted, Kempe, 1999: 239). Against this background, various voices in addition to the outburst from France's Interior Minister can be heard appealing to Germany to redefine identity and belonging more in terms of common citizenship. Boris Becker has called for a 'cosmopolitan Germany' (Kundnani, 1999). Ignatieff calls on Germans not to pass beyond nationalism into bland Europeanism but instead 'to move from the ethnic nationalism of its past to the civic nationalism of a possible future' where identification is not so much with the nation and the idea of the German 'Volk' but more with the state (Ignatieff, 1995: 76). Likewise, Richie endorses the view that Brussels is not a substitute for history and that spiritual security should be sought in 'a nation which its citizens believe in and want to protect' (Richie, 1999: xxxvi). The German-born British Labour MP, Gisela Stuart, recommends that German nationality should abandon the principle of *jus sanguinis*, the primacy of bloodline, which enables her and her children to be regarded as German even though they are British citizens. She recommends that Germans bury the notion of the 'Volk' and redefine themselves by territorial boundaries and democratic and inclusive institutions bound by the constitution (Stuart, 2000). It is, however, Habermas, the inspiration for communicative planning theory, who has perhaps done most in his writing on citizenship to reconnect German post-reunification thinking on identity to the by-passed civic nationalist strain in German engagement with the issue of nationhood. As Ignatieff points out, ethno-nationalism did not go uncontested. The 1848 Frankfurt Parliament accorded German citizenship not just to those who were ethnically German but 'to all those living in Germany . . . even if they are not so by birth or language' (quoted, Ignatieff, 1995: 65).

In the opinion of Habermas, it was to this tradition that post-war West Germany looked in an effort to define itself, albeit an effort never fully permitting of healthy national pride. Habermas and the former President of the Federal Republic, Richard von Weizsäcker, argue that 8 May 1945 – 'Null Stunde' (Zero Hour) – is the only possible beginning for the construction of a new definition of Germanness. It is 1945 that is seen as a crucial turning-point in German history, when West Germans began a process of rediscovering 'the muted legacy of humanism and the Enlightenment in their own tradition'. Here Habermas conjures up the image and dangers not of the forest in 'the German tradition' but of the equally suspect 'fetid German swamp', a slipping back into which cannot be ruled out unless the concept of a nation of citizens is embraced as opposed to the notion of a 'community of fate shaped by common descent, language and history' (Habermas, 1998: 45–9). Rather, democratic citizenship establishing 'an abstract, legally mediated solidarity between strangers' is sought, which would ideally nest within an enhanced, European-level, civic identity-building project, culminating ultimately in a

European constitution based fundamentally on the mutual recognition of diversity (Habermas, 1998: 15–23).

In understanding German identity politics, it is useful to contrast these views of Habermas with those of former Chancellor Helmut Kohl. In the opinion of Kohl it is the year 1989, not 1945, which is to be emphasized in the broad sweep of German history as it represents a return to normality and normal history in Germany. The year 1989 marks the return of a common past to East and West Germans, with Kohl's new German Historical Museum in Berlin showing this history by taking the Germany pieced together by Bismarck in 1871 and giving it a coherence, continuity and nobility going back centuries. This is a position which has been criticized as seeing the Nazi period as 'only' a 'bad tributary' in Germany's past compared to the 'mighty current' of German history where the Nazi past was something that happened to 'victim Germany' (Kramer, 1995). In defence of his position Kohl can point to the 'Leitkultur' figures in Germany's proud cultural legacy in literature, philosophy, music and poetry – figures such as Goethe, Schiller, Bach, Beethoven, Nietzsche and Hegel, many of whom are linked with the other place most closely associated with what Kohl has called 'the heart of Germany': the city of Weimar (Kohl quoted Keohane, 1997: 4). Weimar is also evoked by Kohl as 'it stands for ... Germany's democratic tradition' (ibid.), however, one which, despite the success of the Bonn years, Kohl does not fully trust. In an interview in 1990, Kohl candidly admitted that Germany needed to be anchored in Europe as a protection against the romantic temptations of its worst self, lest it become a danger to other nations (Selbourne, 2001).

BERLIN: THE PROMOTIONAL REPRESENTATION OF PLACE

The development process through which the built environment is being delivered in Berlin, while having local peculiarities, shares common characteristics with that of other major European cities seeking to secure and maintain niches within the competitive urban hierarchy. Within a complicated institutional and political context and facing strong commercial imperatives, a city image has been constructed which is based on frothier ingredients but which endeavours unconvincingly to float free of the past. A pervading feeling from Hubertus Siegert's recent film on the reconstruction of the city after the fall of the Wall (*Berlin Babylon*) is of urban planning and architecture running blind to build and embrace a future pursued by a fear and sadness in looking back. The institutional and political context involved embraces the fact that Berlin is at the same time a city and a federal state (Land) that until recently was divided into 23 districts (Bezirke), which since 2001 have been reduced to 12. The districts can be compared with cities in other states, although the Bezirke have less authority and fewer legal instruments at their disposal (Schwedler, 2001: 31–2). The city of Berlin completed the production of a land-use plan (Flächennutzungsplan) for the whole of Berlin in 1994 which provides the legally binding framework for the local building plans (Bebauungspläne) prepared by the districts. Given that throughout most of the 1990s Berlin was governed by a Grand Coalition between Social Democrats and Christian Democrats (replaced in 2002, in the wake of a budgetary crisis, by a Red-Red Coalition between SPD and PDS) and that until the end of 1999 the two most important city departments concerned with urban planning – 'Building, Housing and Traffic' and 'Urban Development and Environmental Protection' – were directed by ministers from different political parties, the considerable potential for conflict over urban-development issues, including 'coming-to-terms-with-the-past' issues, is apparent. The potential for conflict and disagreement is heightened by other factors. The Federal Ministry for Regional Planning, Building and Urban Development, overseeing the relocation of the nation's capital from Bonn to Berlin, brings to bear the potential for federal versus city place-making tensions as far as the acknowledgement of the past is concerned. With large tracts of Berlin having been parcelled up since the fall of the Wall and made subject to elaborate urban-planning and architectural competitions, with local citizen-initiatives making their bottom-up inputs into a memorializing process, and with an active Berlin Chamber of Architects (Architektenkammer Berlin) as a focus for professional planning and architectural commentary on sensitive developments where 'the burden of history' is concerned, the city's considerable number of environmental journalists have had no shortage of opinions to draw upon in discussing the relationship of Berlin's built form to Berlin and German identity. Moreover, the former as desired by Berlin politicians and mayor has not always been in conformity with the demands of the latter. Here the city of Berlin's own commercial and fiscal imperatives and place-marketing needs are to the fore.

The city of Berlin is the largest city in Germany. With urban extensions into the surrounding state, Berlin/Brandenburg is the second largest German agglomeration after Rhine-Ruhr, with a GDP larger than that of Ireland or Greece (Mäding, 2000: 3). However, this is in a dynamic context of competitive economic positioning within the hierarchy of European cities, a task which played only a minor role for both West and East Berlin while, as 'Front Cities', they were representing their respective world powers (Schwedler, 2001: 24). In the face of the city's decline as a production space with the demise of old industrial structures in the East and the withdrawal of government subsidies for development in the West, Krätke traces the emergence of a new entrepreneurial urban policy in Berlin and an associated growth coalition meshing city government and important firms, private investors and real estate companies (Krätke, 1992; 2000). The intention is that the reborn

Berlin metropolis will be economically defined less by its industrial production structure and more by its new role as a centre for trans-regional finance and management functions, and especially as a major centre for the co-ordination of East–West relations in a European Union set to expand vastly to the East. Severe and persisting fiscal problems in Berlin, caused predominantly by the withdrawal of 'Berlin Aid' (cold-war federal subsidies to the city), have added to the development imperative. This commercial imperative in some cases has given short shrift to identity-angst, emphasizing more what Walter Benjamin, a native of Berlin and an early explorer of place-character and -identity, called 'the dream sleep' of capitalism (quoted Gilloch, 1996: 104). Here in an all-consuming present the city forms the space of 'the enthronement of the commodity and the glitter of distraction' (quoted Gilloch, ibid. 119). In the reborn **Potsdamer Platz** and plans for **Alexanderplatz**, two of the most historic public spaces in Berlin, Benjamin would have recognized, in the realized and proposed architectural forms, a direct line of succession from the Berlin arcades and department stores of his 1920s' memories to the modern shrines to the commodity in whose worship the post-war German collective unconscious has found distraction from the historical burdens of the recent past.

POTSDAMER PLATZ

Potsdamer Platz in pre-World-War-II days was the 'Times Square' at the heart of Berlin, the congested traffic 'crossroads of Europe'. During the cold war it had become a derelict, moon-landscape border territory on the 'death strip' between East and West. In his 1987 film *The Sky over Berlin* the director Wim Wenders, in a context where the place had literally disappeared, has one of his characters who is roaming close to the Wall exclaim: 'I won't give up searching until I have found Potsdamer Platz.' The re-founding of the centre of Berlin, however, has been criticized by one of Berlin's leading urban planners for being based less on contemplative and democratic thinking about the special place occupied by Potsdamer Platz in the German political and architectural imagination than on 'the violent imposition of undesirable monuments to world trade' (Hoffmann-Axthelm, quoted Caygill, 1992: 13–14). To accelerate Berlin's metropolitan economic transition, Krätke describes how the major project of Daimler-Benz (now Daimler Chrysler) to build a large-scale office and business complex on Potsdamer Platz was 'railroaded through without public discussion and without careful planning' (Krätke, 1992: 216). Berlin's SPD Mayor Momper, in July 1990, used the full power of his office to ensure the sale of 67 hectares of land to the Daimler-Benz subsidiary, Debis, at a knock-down price of less than one-fifth of its market value in order to facilitate its spectacular large-scale plans (Caygill, 1992: 11). The subsequent rush to an architectural competition, with the major developer incorporated from the beginning and with little public discussion on the future use of Potsdamer Platz and whether indeed it should be primarily a commercial centre, was criticized by Dieter Hoffmann-Axthelm, who was subsequently given the job of coming up with an urban design plan to suture together inner-city East and West Berlin, as 'lackeying to Daimler-Benz' (Caygill, ibid. 11). A decade later, on what was until recently the biggest building site in Europe, Berlin has a new corporate heart. Prestige corporate architecture has been provided by some of the world's leading architects. Renzo Piano has designed the new Debis HQ. As commented upon by one German architectural critic:

> It is ironic that, in spite of the democratic and liberal spirit of unification, Daimler-Benz, one of the world's most prominent armaments manufacturers, should have such a strong presence in the centre of Berlin (Rave, quoted Clarke, 1990).

However, it is not the architect and designer's intent that those enjoying the 110 shops, 30 restaurants, bars and cafés that are also part of the Daimler-Benz development be burdened with such concerns. Alongside the Debis HQ and also closing the gap in the centre of Berlin is Sony's European headquarters, again constructed on land sold by the Berlin government at much less than market value. The German-American architect Helmut Jahn, in addition to providing a 26-storey office tower, has furnished Berlin with a landmark building much represented in city promotional literature. The 'Forum', a 4000-square-metre elliptical arena cinema and entertainment complex covered by a fibreglass membrane, provides a striking addition to the Berlin skyline in celebrating the new and novel. In contrast, another part of the Sony development site nostalgically includes a remnant of the Esplanade Hotel (a famous meeting place of the Golden Twenties which survived the war), most notably the famous Imperial Hall (Kaisersaal) and breakfast rooms, which have been restored 'as a kind of architectural museum' (Sony, 1998: 184). Here the past can literally be shifted to create a new spectacle. In a complicated and highly publicized event, these rooms were moved 75 metres over a new concrete bed, using compressed air (Phillips, 1997: 180). With other famous architects such as Giorgio Grassi and Richard Rogers having contributed to additional corporate-led Potsdamer Platz projects, visitors and residents of the apartments and international penthouses on the reinvented public square can be seen as interpolated to their identity positions as on-site consumers providing *in situ* legitimacy for the concentrated economic power so obviously made spatially manifest.

ALEXANDERPLATZ

Plans for Alexanderplatz, while mostly unrealized because of a cooling of the property frenzy in Berlin after the euphoria of the early nineties, have likewise not been overly preoccupied with historical hand-wringing. Made famous as a place of the imagination in Alfred Döblin's 1929 novel *Berlin Alexanderplatz*, which evoked the lives of ordinary people in a big-city milieu, the actual space has been through various incarnations since the 19th century as meeting place, traffic crossroads, scene of World War II destruction and until 1989 the centre of GDR aims to present, in a soulless modernism, the triumphant ideas of socialism. The winning entry to an urban design competition, sponsored jointly in 1993 by a plethora of speculative investors and the city of Berlin and which was also to form the basis for planning for the area, was by the architect Hans Kollhoff. This design evoked references to a mini-Manhattan, an 'Alex' as an 'echo' to the prestige architecture on Potsdamer Platz. Alexanderplatz would 'reach for the sky' with 13 skyscrapers two-thirds the size of the landmark 365-metre-high GDR TV tower. It is these new buildings and reference points that would be an 'enduring carrier' for a new collect-ive memory in the future (Kollhoff, interviewed by Kieren, 1994: 105). The architect permits himself a sentimental proposal in the form of reconstructing the Berolina statue on the reinvented Alexanderplatz. Erected in 1895, the 25-foot-high, armour-clad 'Berlin goddess' became an instant historical symbol for the German capital. In 1927 the statue was removed to make way for underground construction. In Döblin's book, Franz Biberkopf comments, with uncanny prescience:

> Berolina stood outside Tietz with one hand outstretched. She was a colossal woman and they dragged her off. Perhaps they were melting her down and turning her into medals.

Berolina was in fact rededicated in Alexanderplatz by the National Socialists in 1933, before in reality being melted down during World War II as 'raw material for the war effort' (Kiehn, 1997: 43; Kollhoff, 1994: 85).

The official place-marketing of a Berlin identity, with associated images and symbols, today proceeds without Berolina but with the help of the reassuring Berlin bear (Figure 2.1). However it is the instantly recognizable Brandenburg Gate, recent symbol of cold war division and now symbol of reunification, that is shared between Germany and Berlin as the master signifier. The main city marketing agency 'Partner für Berlin', charged with developing the distinctively Berlin brand-identity, is a public-private partnership between the city, real-estate and commer-cial interests which grew out of Berlin's expensive failure, in the heady days after reunification, to secure the Olympic Games in 2000. When applying for building permits for major development projects, as one commentator points out, it can be prudent to be one of the business partners in Partner für Berlin. In the city's growth coalition, 'one hand washes the other' (Rose, 1998: 144).

Early attempts to find a place-marketing identity for the city proved difficult. A

Figure 2.1 Berliner Bär, 2002

major promotional film costing over one million marks, produced by Partner für Berlin in 1995, was rejected by Eberhard Diepgen, the city's mayor, because it 'lacked a Berlin identity' (Rose, ibid. 152). Insipid images of smiling children in front of the Brandenburg Gate were not enough. Subsequent efforts have been more successful. Partner für Berlin has a considerable image-bank to draw upon in seeking to rebrand and establish a new identity for the reinstated German capital. The past frisson of the cold war lingers, as does the powerful imagery of 1920s' Berlin depicted in the Kit Kat Club of Christopher Isherwood, the basis of the film *Cabaret*. Such images are now likely to be considered 'entrenched clichés', with the thrust of image promotion concentrating on the 'birthing process' of a new city where the new and novel are juxtaposed with older stereotypes and hence cast them in a new light. Berlin's new defining trademark is the old Quadriga atop the Brandenburg Gate against the backdrop of the new dome of the Reichstag (Schneider, 1999: 175) (Figure 2.2). From another angle the illuminated membrane of the Sony centre also invites the viewer to think less of the past and more in terms of the future and a new beginning. Architecture, urban planning and even the building sites of the city have been garnered in various promotional projects sponsored by Partner für Berlin. These present the image of a 'happening place' where

Figure 2.2 Berlin's new trademark

the future is being built now. An exhibition in 1995 by *Stern* magazine at various locations in the city displayed in huge temporary pavilions what the future built face of Berlin would look like. A follow-up red 'info box' at Potsdamer Platz, which opened in October 1995 and where major Berlin investors present their projects, has become an instant city landmark in its own right. Christo's wrapped Reichstag, which was seen by over 5 million people between 27 June and 7 July 1995 (which helped to lighten its historical load) was also sponsored by Partner für Berlin (Rose, 1998: 145). This was followed by the successful promotion of the city in 1996/1997 by Volker Hassemer, the newly appointed director of Partner für Berlin and former CDU Senator for Urban Development, as 'Schaustelle Berlin' (Show-case Berlin). Here, in a major marketing exercise to both Berliners (who were invited to reclaim their city from the cranes, scaffolding and excavations) and vis-itors, the concept of construction-site tourism opened major development sites in Berlin to the public as 'show places'. The catchphrase 'Schaustelle Berlin' remains to date as a successful play on the word 'Baustelle' (building site), where visitors are invited to now substantially realized architectural projects to 'Discover the New Berlin' (Das neue Berlin erleben). The Berlin Architektenkammer (Berlin Chamber of Architects) in association with Partner für Berlin is, in fact, now in the front line of Berlin's image promotion as 'The City on Exhibition' (BAK *et al.*, 1999). The now officially sponsored 'Love Parade' has even brought the criticism that it is overly commercial and bland (Boym, 2001: 205).

There is little danger, however, of breaking Berlin's unique place-identity on the rack of official place-promotion. In his 1903 essay 'The Metropolis and Mental Life', Georg Simmel suggested that from any point on the surface of existence one may drop a sounding into the depths of the soul. This is a principle shared by Walter Benjamin, a youthful follower of Simmel. In his own essay 'A Berlin Child-hood Around the Turn of the Century', Benjamin begins by saying:

> Not to find one's way about in a city is of little interest. But to lose one's way in a city, as one loses one's way in a forest, requires practice (Benjamin, quoted Sontag, 1979: 10).

Berlin still leaves plenty of space for losing oneself and for dropping a 'plumb line' into the depths of its soul. The experience of the city at its best offered for Ben-jamin the promise of new things and new thoughts, excitement, a promise of adventure and a disorientation carrying trepidation but also the possibility of novelty, discovery and change. At its worst, however, the city offered boredom because, being a concentrated site of commodity fetishism, our dreams and long-ings are commodified and sold to us as goods or experiences (Gilloch, 1996: 157). In the new consumption palace of Galeries Lafayette on Friedrichstrasse, for example, Benjamin would have had little problem in dropping his plumb line and discerning the inability of consumption to make up for the lack of myth and meaning in the post-modernist condition. In his writing Benjamin sometimes affirmed the radical potential of the urban population. However, latterly he came to regard the dreaming, consuming collectivity as the mass out of which Fascism was made and from which he ultimately failed to escape (Gilloch, 1996: 147–8). Identity remains important because consumption is not enough. Ultimately the task of harnessing physical imagery for German and Berlin identity construction and projection is outside the commercial scope of Partner für Berlin.

URBAN PLANNING AND IDENTITY IN HITLER'S BERLIN

In *Mein Kampf*, Hitler had early expressed the belief that cities, as consuming places, suffered from spiritual malaise and therefore needed to embody and express cultural identity:

> Thus our cities of the present lack the outstanding symbol of national
> community which, we must therefore not be surprised to find, sees no symbol of
> itself in the cities. The inevitable result is a desolation whose practical effect is
> the total indifference of the big city dweller to the destiny of his city. This too is
> a sign of our declining culture and our general collapse. The epoch is stifling in
> the pettiest utilitarianism, or better expressed, in the service of money (Hitler,
> Adolf, 1971: 265–6).

When the National Socialists came to power in 1933, taking up residence on Wilhelmstrasse was not enough. Rather than being satisfied with the most prestigious political address in Berlin, equivalent symbolically to Downing Street, Berlin was to be spatially remade and reimaged to express boldly a triumphant, confident and purified identity in the invoked notion of Volksgemeinschaft ('people's community'). This ultimately produced a breach with the then Berlin city administration which has a certain symmetry with recent tensions between the city of Berlin and federal politicians over dealing symbolically with the legacy of this period. In 1937, by Hitler's decree, Albert Speer had been made Inspector-General of Building and the highest planning authority of Berlin. The city's planning and construction authority was thus emasculated (the Weimar-tainted head of the Berlin city planning department had been given a 'leave of absence' in 1933), culminating in the dismissal of the Mayor of Berlin, Julius Lippert, after a 1940 controversy triggered by the arrogance of Speer's demands (Bärnreuther, 2000: 201–3). From his city planning office in Pariser Platz beside the Brandenburg Gate, Speer would regularly work until the late hours of the evening assigning 'major commissions to those men I considered Germany's best architects' (Speer, 1995: 212).

The aesthetics with which Speer set about remaking the face of Berlin he called 'Our Empire Style' (Speer, 1995: 195). Hitler, who had aspired to be an architect, used architectural images and forms to give concrete embodiment to his political project. The task of prestige architecture in the Thousand-Year Reich was to express National Socialist ideology as 'words of stone', as Hitler had put it in a speech on culture in 1938 (Mesecke, 2000: 187). For this purpose the style of architecture could only be a derivative of classical. Classical architecture was linked to heroic figures of antiquity; it communicated order and symmetry as opposed to freedom and equality, certainty as opposed to the liberal reason and doubt of the Enlightenment, and moreover the Greeks and Germans, in the national narrative of Hitler's imagination, were racially linked (Balfour, 1990: 72). After 1933 Wilhelm-strasse was progressively to lose its modest architectural appearance. The first large, Nazi prestige building to be completed was an extension to the Reichsbank, followed by the Reich Aviation Ministry (completed in 1936) and, most importantly, the New Reich Chancellery on Voßstrasse, designed by Albert Speer and completed in 1939. The spare classical form with the great rising eagle above the entrance has been described as 'the quintessential expression of the order and character of National Socialism' (Balfour, 1990: 76) (Figure 2.3).

In 1937 Hitler gave Speer the task of effecting plans for the construction of a new Berlin 'pleasing to our sense of culture' (Balfour, 1990: 81). The grandiose plans for the capital of the new Germanic Reich – 'from Berlin to Germania' (Reichhardt and Schäche, 1998) – were later to be described by Speer himself, keen to distance himself from his crimes, as part of 'the terrible things (Hitler) perpetrated' and indicating on Hitler's part 'a kind of chronic megalomania' (Speer, 1995: 203–4). It is these plans of Hitler and Speer to remake Berlin for its future historical destiny that have proven particularly sensitive for the planners and architects redesigning and reimaging Berlin since 1989. Germania was to affirm the privileged cultural identity of the German Volk and imbue it with self-confidence and the capacity for individual self-sacrifice and surrender to the whole that was necessary for world domination. An East–West Axis, a 'Via Triumphalis', was built as part of Speer's plans for Germania. This ran from Unter den Linden and the Brandenburg Gate west through the city to Adolf-Hitler-Platz (now Theodor-Heuss-Platz) and involved the relocation of the Siegessäule (Victory Column) from the Reichstag to its present location. However, it was the planned North–South Axis that was the greatest source of Hitler's place-making passion (Figure 2.4). As early as September 1933, developing an embryonic idea proposed by an urban designer 16 years earlier, Hitler charged the Berlin city planning office with designing a new street that would run north–south to the west of the Brandenburg Gate

Figure 2.3 The Court of Honour (Ehrenhof) of Hitler's New Reich Chancellery, 1938

and Potsdamer Platz. This would connect with a newly planned Tempelhof airport and central railway station in the south. On this axis the colossal display of power was the primary objective. Gigantic new ministerial buildings would line the new boulevard but pride of place would go to two structures that had taken shape in Hitler's imagination when he was in prison writing *Mein Kampf*. Visitors would arrive at the South Station and look north through a vast Triumphal Arch, 117 metres high and 170 metres wide, towards where at the northern end of the vista on a bend in the Spree river a Great Hall was to be situated. In the final plan of 1942 the proposed 'Grosse Halle' would be the largest building in the world, a thousand feet high, with the capacity to hold up to 180 000 people who could assemble to be addressed by the Führer (Bärnreuther, 2000: 205). The rough sketches for these buildings, drawn in prison, remained with Hitler in his bunker until the end (Balfour, 1990: 71), testifying to the power of an imaginary city, only partially realized, to give expression to and make palpably graspable in the mind a political and cultural order, in this case of the most diabolical kind. The Great Hall would be at the centre of the new political and cultural order and the Triumphal Arch would honour those who had sacrificed themselves to bring it about. As Ignatieff astutely observes, however, such massiveness in architecture, overwhelming the viewer with the aesthetics of effect, can be read as a confession of doubt. It must intimidate in order to convince (Ignatieff, 1994: 53). Today, the giant cylinder

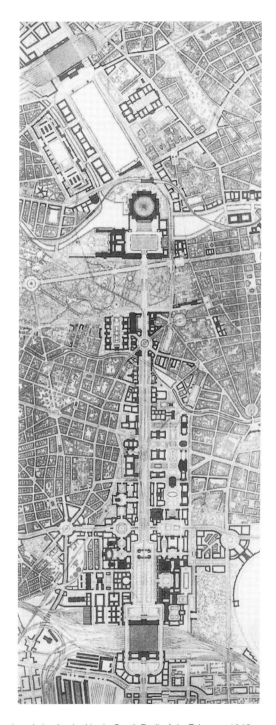

Figure 2.4 Final version of plan for the North–South Berlin Axis, February, 1942

of concrete that was poured in 1941 to form the base of the Triumphal Arch
stands abandoned and overgrown at the corner of Loewenhardtdamm and
General-Pape-Strasse.

THE HOLOCAUST AND GERMAN MEMORY

At the heart of 'coming to terms' with the Nazi period in German history and of (re)
constructing national identity stands the Holocaust. Here despite its self-
proclaimed anti-fascist credentials the German Democratic Republic confronted
the Nazi past only superficially (Habermas, 1998: 47), with the 'Day of the Victims
of Fascism' annually commemorated in the mythology of the GDR state with Jews
as victims and communists as the liberators (Bodemann, 1996: 196–205). The
significant rise of interest in Jewish issues among a wider West German public can
be dated to the beginning of the 1970s, when Willy Brandt had fallen to his knees
in the Warsaw ghetto. Bodemann refers to how Allied interventions and the 'justice
of the victors' thwarted to a degree a post-war German national discourse on the
Holocaust (Bodemann, 1996). This, of course, did not prevent major cultural reverberations in West Germany. Thus Ingrid Caven, wife of Rainer Werner Fassbinder,
emphasizes the importance of German identity to the film-maker's work:

> In his films, and in his life, until the most tearing and aggressive moments, he
> was looking for a form, for a beauty and joy based on the ruins of a Germany
> drained of life and soul (Hodgkiss, 1999).

Likewise Wim Wenders, another German film-maker, in having one of his characters in *Kings of the Road* say that 'the Americans have colonised our subcon-
scious' alludes to how in Germany one way of remembering and forgetting fascism
has been an involvement with other cultures (Morley and Robins, 1995: 95–6).

Bodemann, in dating the more active public invocation of Holocaust memory
in West Germany, singles out in particular a state ceremony in 1978 in the
Cologne Synagogue for the commemoration of Kristallnacht, shortly before the
airing of the American television series *Holocaust*. Bodemann also comments
importantly:

> Only when the bulk of the first post-war generation of politicians had begun to
> leave the political arena with their retirement (politicians who built their careers
> under Hitler, who were implicated in Nazism and continued under Adenauer,
> who were at least 30 years old in 1945), only when they began to withdraw
> from the political scene in the mid-seventies, could the commemoration take on

a broader political frame of reference and became an act of state, most visibly first in the Cologne synagogue ceremony in 1978 with Chancellor Schmidt and President Scheel (Bodemann, 1996: 211).

The *Holocaust* series and its media manufacture of raw material and discursive threads for the construction of memory and identity was watched by over 20 million Germans in 1979 (Morley and Robins, op. cit. 92). Commenting in *Der Spiegel*, one commentator wrote:

An American TV series, made in a trivial style, produced more for commercial than for moral reasons, more for entertainment than for enlightenment, accomplished what hundreds of books, plays, films ... documents and the concentration camp trials themselves have failed to do in the three decades since the end of the war: to inform Germans about crimes against Jews committed in their name so that millions were emotionally touched and moved (Hone, quoted in Buruma, 1989: 40).

The West German television series *Heimat*, broadcast in 1984 to an equally mass audience, was conceived by its creator, Edgar Reitz, as a German 'answer' to the American Holocaust series, which he argued had 'stolen our history ... taken narrative possession of our past' (Reitz, 1985). The same year also saw the ill-fated visit of President Reagan and Chancellor Kohl to the military cemetery at Bitburg where foreign media attention focused on the graves of Waffen-SS soldiers buried there and evoked associations with German wartime crimes rather than the intended joint celebration of Germany's 'liberation' in 1945. The controversy over Bitburg was fuel to the so-called 'war between the historians' in Germany in the second half of the 1980s over how the Nazi past should be remembered. Here the German identity question was to the fore, with the historian Michael Sturmer arguing that Germans should be given 'the chance to recognize themselves again' and with Jürgen Habermas responding that this would be to repudiate Germany's post-war generation's 'opening to the West' (Craig, 1991: 316–17).

The debate over memory and representation of the German past, wrapped up as it is with the politics of identity in Germany and the spatial manifestation of this, was therefore picking up pace even before the fall of the Berlin Wall in 1989. After a hasty reunification, which missed the chance (in Habermas's opinion) of a republican refounding of the Federal Republic based on a new national self-understanding, the negotiation of a new German past and identity has assumed greater urgency (Habermas, 1998: 51). With the political decision of the federal government to move to Berlin, the reinstated German capital may be said to have become an intensified 'theatre' forming a stage for contesting plays of collective memory. Such memory work has taken place against a background in recent years of foreign claims that most Germans were culpably implicated in the crimes of the Nazis (the charge in Daniel Goldhagen's controversial 1996 book *Hitler's Willing Executioners: Ordinary Germans and the Holocaust*) and the claim by the British historian David Irving that 'the gas chambers were a myth', as refuted in the book *Denying the Holocaust: The Growing Assault on Truth and Memory* by Deborah Lipstadt in 1993 (Lipstadt, 1993: 179). Irving, in an internationally publicized trial, was to lose a libel action against Lipstadt in April 2000 – and his professional reputation besides. With such eyes on Berlin, the spatial aspects of identity ruminations were at times since reunification to prove rather tortuous.

'DEMOCRACY AS BUILDER': THE CAPITAL MOVE FROM BONN TO BERLIN

In a famous speech in 1960, Adolf Arndt, SPD Senator for Science and Art in West Berlin, coined the phrase 'Democracy as Builder' (Demokratie als Bauherr) to describe the nature of the architecture in which the young democracy should recognize itself (Wilhelm, 2001: 8). This phrase was later picked up by Hans Stimmann, one of the most influential city planners in the reunited city, to describe the general values and intentions behind the physical dimensions of the federal project to relocate the German capital back to Berlin (Stimmann, 1996: 7). 'Democracy as Builder' in Bonn had reacted against the stone of National Socialist buildings. In sharp distinction:

> Glass surfaces and floating white walls with sharp contours became the synonym for democracy (Bartetzko, 1995: 11).

The Bundestag in Bonn with its glass transparency was a prime exemplar, with the circular and bright plenary chamber designed to exude an air of what Arndt had called 'Mitmenschlichkeit' (humaneness). Conspicuous imagery in Bonn was limited. The German federal eagle, also known as the 'Fat Hen', adorned the front wall of the Bundestag chamber and a statue of Henry Moore sat non-threateningly in the gardens of the Chancellery. As expressed by one commentator in Bonn, Germany 'stepped out of history and stepped into business' with the hard Deutschmark as the founding symbol of a post-war West German state which felt uncomfortable in projecting a political image of itself (Dürrenmatt, quoted *Spiegel*, 1998: 57). Michael Wise, in his recent book on the federal move to Berlin, has described Bonn as 'the capital of self-effacement', representing a reassuring sign of discontinuity for Germans with their troubled history. In the design of Bonn, with an historical eye on Speer's Berlin, there had been a conscious aversion to large-scale urban planning schemes, with a consequent haphazard placement of govern-ment buildings like 'cows in the pasture' of the provincial small town on the Rhine (Wise, 1998: 30). The selection of Bonn as a provisional capital in 1949 had been largely due to its lack of historical significance. In the words of Konrad Adenauer, West Germany's founding Chancellor: 'Bonn was a beginning, a city without a past'.

The closeness of the vote in the Bundestag on 20 June 1991 (338 to 320 votes) in favour of moving the capital back to Berlin indicated a considerable collective ambivalence among Germany's political class. Arguments against the move included the view that important 'real history' had happened in Bonn and that it had thus developed beyond being just a provisional capital (Blüm, 1991: 12). However, behind this undoubtedly lurked the apprehension in many politicians that returning to the epicentre of German history would mean facing up to the uncom-fortable task of dealing with the burden of the recent past, in the process putting questions of 'nation' and identity back on to the public agenda (*Spiegel*, 1998). Proponents of the move, while also pointing to the fact that having the capital in the economically weaker east would help to balance the federal structure of the German state, nevertheless overwhelmingly endorsed the move primarily on sym-bolic grounds. Moving to Berlin was a symbol of German reunification and soli-darity. It touched on how the new Germany would represent itself and project itself to the world. Willy Brandt, who came to prominence as mayor of Berlin in the 1950s and 1960s, thus implored that the Bundestag do what it had promised itself since 1949. In urging that the federal government should return to 'the cradle of German-Western friendship on the Spree', Brandt was pointing to the post-war symbolic power of Berlin as a beachhead of democracy secured by the Berlin Airlift (Brandt, 1991). It was in Berlin that President Kennedy had uttered the resounding words 'Ich bin ein Berliner', and where President Reagan perhaps with some prescience charged Mikhail Gobachev to 'open this gate'. The point was put most precisely by the CDU politician Wolfgang Schäuble:

> Over the past 40 years *the provisional capital Bonn* stood for freedom, democracy and the rule of law. It stood for all of Germany. But the *symbol* for this was Berlin (emphasis added) (Schäuble, 1991).

Berlin's chief urban planner (Senatsbaudirektor), Hans Stimmann, in the sub-sequent formative years of melding the motif of 'democracy as builder' into the his-toric centre of Berlin, was in direct line of succession to Albert Speer in planning for a united capital city. In subsequent negotiations between the city of Berlin and the federal Ministry for Regional Planning, Building and Urban Development, responsible for overseeing the physical federal relocation to Berlin, this historical lineage was naturally in the foreground of consciousness. Here urban planning and architecture on the grand scale has been at the heart not just of building a functional governing city, but also of endeavouring to articulate a modern German identity. This applied both to building the core of a new government quarter within the general curtilage of the Spreebogen (bend in the Spree) and to the reuse or otherwise of old Nazi buildings.

THE NEW GOVERNMENT QUARTER

Within a thousand metres or so of the Brandenburg Gate, the most important symbol of German nationhood, and extending northwards in the direction of the Spree, lies a site of unsurpassed concentrated symbolism and symbolic work in progress. This encompasses *inter alia* the renovated Reichstag, Band des Bundes (Ribbon of the Federation) and the new Federal Chancellery (Figure 2.5). The Brandenburg Gate, itself centrepiece of a 'critically reconstructed' Pariser Platz, has been through no less than seven symbolic incarnations. Inaugurated in 1791 and soon becoming a symbol of Prussian power, the removal to Paris of the crowning Quadriga by Napoleon in 1807 left the Gate as a symbol of military humiliation.

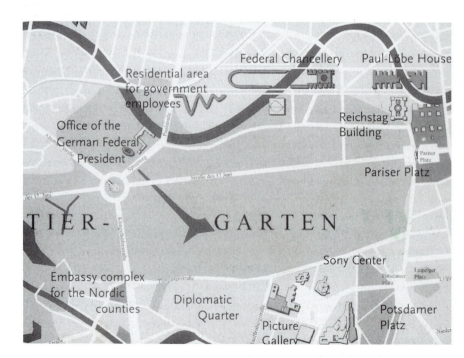

Figure 2.5 New Federal Chancellery north of the Tiergarten on the 'Band des Bundes' (Ribbon of the Federation)

The repatriation of the Quadriga in 1814 reclaimed the Gate as a symbol of Prussian nationality and civic solidarity. In 1871, with the formation of the German Reich, the Gate became the national symbol par excellence. Used symbolically by the Nazis, the gate subsequently became identified during the Cold War with the division of Germany. As put by the former German President, Richard von Weizsäcker: 'As long as the Brandenburg Gate stays shut, the German question will remain open'. Rebranded following 9 November 1989 by German people from both East and West dancing on top of the wall in front of the Gate and with pictures broadcast worldwide, the monument again stands as the symbol, above all others, of a reunited Germany (Zimmer and Paeschke, 1991; Cullen, 1998).

In contrast, the rebranding of the German *Reichstag* building required the aid of a Bulgarian artist and an English architect. Before its recommissioning on 19 April 1999 as the seat of the German parliament, the Reichstag building in its previous 105 years of existence had been described by an American historian of Berlin monuments as 'a symbol of parliamentary democracy rather than the place where democracy was practiced' (Cullen, 1999: 8). The inscription above the entrance, 'Dem Deutschen Volke' (To the German People), had been grudgingly tolerated by Kaiser Wilhelm II in 1916 (Cullen, 1999: 44) and the Reichstag fire of 27 February 1933 stands forever as a symbol of the Nazi takeover. The hoisting of the red flag over the Reichstag at the end of April 1945 was 'both a symbol of liberation from Nazi tyranny as well as the symbol for renewed tyranny' (Cullen, 1999: 8), and during the division of Germany the Reichstag standing beside the Wall in the west was for many people in East Germany a symbol of democracy. As summed up by *Der Spiegel*:

> The invisible aura that surrounds this monument and fuels the imagination conjuring up pictures in the mind is even more complex and explosive than the built reality (*Der Spiegel*, 1998).

It is the wrapping by Christo in the summer of 1995 that *Der Spiegel* argues reworked the identity of the building and set the scene for 'the suggestive power of the Reichstag's unifying symbolism'. The final decision on the future design of the renovated building had been made in April of that year as the culmination of a lengthy process of discussion between Sir Norman Foster and a federal Building Commission in Bonn set up in 1991 to take charge of practicalities associated with the capital move and reporting to a Parliamentary Advisory Committee in the CDU-dominated Bundestag. In June of 1993 Foster had won an international architectural design competition organized by the Building Commission for the redesign of the Reichstag building, but a sticking point had been the insistence of opinion, especially among CDU/CSU MPs in the Bundestag and against the wishes of

Foster, that a restored Reichstag without a cupola was a symbolic break with history taken too far (Mönninger, 2000: 393). The Reichstag dome in its previous incarnation, regarded by some as bombastic, had also given offence to Kaiser Wilhelm because it rivalled in height the dome on his Berlin Stadtschloss (city palace) (Cullen, 1999: 34). The new dome delivered by Foster likewise gives a symbolic nod in a democratic direction. In the words of a publication of the Bundestag in 1996:

> The intention is to erect an open transparent forum accessible for both
> representatives and visitors which will prove itself as a parliament and symbol of
> democracy in the next century (Kontext, 1996).

From inside the Reichstag's new glass dome, Germans and visitors can look down and see 'the state at work' in what has become the trademark of the new Berlin skyline. The dome, however, has not been the only representational problem hovering over the Reichstag. Relatively 'minor' matters have included the decision after the consideration of many alternative designs to keep the Federal Eagle in the assembly chamber in the form of the 'Fat Hen' displayed in Bonn. A leaner more dynamic version of the German national symbol was regarded as inappropriate by the country's parliamentarians. More controversial among German MPs was the decision to leave as an historical exhibit the anti-German graffiti of Red Army soldiers scrawled on the walls in 1945. With endorsement of this by the federal Building Commission, Der Spiegel commented that the Reichstag was being treated 'like an archaeological site' (Der Spiegel, 1998). Some MPs felt the graffiti was more appropriate to a public toilet than a parliament (Traynor, 1999). Equally controversial was the decision to display paintings provided by each of the victorious powers. The Russian artwork by Grischa Bruskin features a man bearing a bomb marked 'For the Reichstag' (Traynor, 1999). CSU Member Wolfgang Zeitlmann was thus to claim that Germany had 'kowtowed' to the allies and to ask: 'Why are we always worried about what others think of us?' (Cullen, 1999: 76). Again, sensitive to history, a controversy raged before the move of the Bundestag to Berlin in 1999 over what to call the new seat of the German parliament. Determined to sever links with any notion of empire, since 1997 a group of German MPs had proposed renaming it the Bundeshaus (federal house), thus literally taking the Reich out of the Reichstag (Conradi, 1997). A final decision endorsed the name of 'Bundestag im Reichstag', but not before the Berlin Tagesspiegel joked that the building should be called 'the speaking place of the German Bundestag which is not identical to the Reichstag' (quoted Cullen, 1999: 77). No such levity, however, has accompanied the debate over whether Bismarck's statue, which formerly stood in front of the west façade of the Reichstag, should be replaced. The proposal to do so has been advanced by the polemical playwright Rolf Hochhuth, who once argued that Winston Churchill was a war criminal. Gathering a swell of popular and political support, the question of the degree to which Germany should rehabilitate the Bismarck of 'blood and iron' is back on the public agenda. Arguing that 1989 'ended Germany's half-century of holiday from world history', Bismarck's great-grandson Prince Ferdinand von Bismarck not surprisingly supports putting his ancestor back on a pedestal. Others disagree. The historian Golo Mann argues that the legacy of Bismarck is not sympathetic to the values of democracy and par-liamentarianism embraced by Germany over the last half century. Likewise the author Klaus Harprecht echoes the sentiments of Habermas:

> Our nation is not the continuation of Bismarckian Germany. The break that occurred in 1945 ran too deep. It is final. Bismarck does not belong in front of the Bundestag.

Harprecht instead endorses the placement in bronze of Adenauer, Willy Brandt or even Helmut Kohl ('Bismarck in a cardigan') in front of the Reichstag building. The rifts over how Germans conceive their identity and how they constitute it spatially run deep. Harprecht's idea of a statue of Kohl inspired many protest letters in 2000 to the *Süddeutsche Zeitung*. One reader wrote:

> We should put the Bismarck monument in front of parliament and thus accept our history with all its mistakes and weaknesses (quoted Boyes, 2000).

Two years later the latter sentiment, that Germans should approach their past with less of a spirit of apology, is increasingly influential. Günter Grass in his 2002 novel *Crabwalk* focused on the victimhood of German refugees fleeing from East Prussia in 1945. Jörg Friedrich in his book of the same year (*The Burning: Germany in the Bombing War 1940–1945*) also stressed German suffering, drawing the criticism that Dresden was being compared to the Holocaust (Ullrich, 2002). In 2002 it was not just the rehabilitation of Bismarck but that of the 'banned' state of Prussia itself, banned following an imposed law in 1947, which was on the public agenda. A government minister in the state of Brandenburg, Alwin Ziel, has broken with taboo and proposed that any future union of Berlin and Brandenburg, possible after a likely referendum in 2006, should create a new Land called Prussia. While other Berlin/Brandenburg politicians have been hostile to the idea, backers of the plan include the novelist Martin Walser and the poet Hans Magnus Enzensberger, both with liberal even radical pasts (Hooper, 2002).

While the symbolism connected with the Reichstag and Brandenburg Gate has raised questions of the re-empowerment of existing national icons, other buildings and designs slightly further north in the Government Quarter of the Spreebogen have raised questions over the representation of German identity in the new-built fabric of the city. Again, controversy and the presence of the past have been to the fore. In terms of building a new *Chancellery* for the executive branch of government and parliamentary office space to serve the needs of the legislature, attention turned in the early 1990s to the Spreebogen area, where the Spree river bends in Berlin. Close to the Reichstag, the area had the advantage of being cleared and available. The one fly in the ointment was that the clearance had been carried out by Hitler as the setting for his Great Hall and Führer's Palast at the northern end of the planned North–South axis. Few of the over 800 entrants to the international urban design competition for this site who submitted proposals in 1993 could have been unaware of the symbolic potency of this National Socialist *tabula rasa*. Despite this, the architectural critic Charles Jencks has lamented the fact that none of the entries represented 'an architecture that symbolised a new dawn', and (in the words of one of the jurors) that there had emerged 'no brilliant or distinctive proposal that would provide an image for the new Germany or the city of Berlin ...' (Jencks, 1995: 19). The eventual winner of the first prize was the design by the Berlin architects Axel Schultes and Charlotte Frank. Officially described as 'planning with symbolic character', the core idea is the *Band des Bundes* (Ribbon of the Federation). This 'clasp' across the Spree is described as

> a symbol (which) ties together the two halves of Berlin which have been separated for decades by incorporating the functions of parliament and government on an east–west axis of 1½ kilometres (Bundesbaugesellschaft, Berlin, 1996: 11).

The theme resonates with the aspirations of Willy Brandt when looking over the ruins of the Wall in 1989 that 'now something would grow together which belongs together' (*Der Spiegel*, 1998). Partially inspired by the separation of powers as spatially visualized on the Mall in Washington, DC, the Band des Bundes joins Bundestag office blocks (named after respected democratic politicians of German history[1]) with the Federal Chancellery. These are linked in the middle by a connecting piece known as the Bundesforum, 'a kind of auditorium for the citizens' (Schubert, 2001: 9). The intended overall motif is that of balance and co-operation between the various arms of the state with the *Civic Forum* providing a symbolic common focus as an 'agora of the Republic' (Mönninger, 2000: 392). Most importantly, however, the East–West axis is at right angles to the North–South axis of Speer, thus having the double symbolism of uniting East and West but also setting the Berlin Republic apart from its predecessor on the Spree. While this fact was not lost on jurors aware that the rest of the world was looking over their shoulders, *Der Spiegel* was unimpressed with this gesture towards coming to terms with the past:

> This clasp is architecturally impressive but is powerless as a symbol. It is a new chapter in the endless history of failed attempts to end the discussion about the past. It goes without saying that a line through the Nazi axis can no more be drawing a line under the past than a Holocaust memorial can be a full stop behind the coming to terms with Auschwitz (*Der Spiegel*, 1998).

Other critics of the symbolism of the Band des Bundes have noted with disapproval that the central spine of government buildings is presented in 'a severe Prussian Functionalist block-geometry' (Jencks, 1995: 19). In the proceedings of the Berlin Stadtforum (City Forum) which, since its establishment in the early 1990s, advises on city planning matters, Max Welch Guerra goes much further in arguing that 'the motif of German unity' associated with the 'ribbon of development' has the function, in conjuring up a return to normality or a new beginning, of permitting 'the Germans to appear to be the victims, not the perpetrators, of 20th century history' (Guerra, 1998).

The competition of concepts won by Schultes and Frank in 1993 provided the guidelines for the architectural competitions that followed, above all for the one for the new Federal Chancellery. When one of the joint first prizes in the competition was set aside in 1994 because of some unintended similarities to the planned Palast des Führers, which was to have stood on the same spot (*Der Spiegel*, 1998; Guerra, 2001: 4), the way was left open for a design by Axel Schultes and Charlotte Frank, but not before revision and final approval by Helmut Kohl himself (Meyer, 1999: 45). 'Demokratie als Bauherr' is seen in the Chancellery Building as finding a 'Third Way' between an early-1990s Berlin architectural dispute between proponents of anti-monumental glass architecture and on the other hand a 'block-type stone and brick mentality' (Meyer, ibid. 32). As an official commentary on the new Chancellery and Ribbon of the Federation development expressed the matter, the use of stone was of extreme symbolic importance:

> (The) aesthetic coalition between the members' offices and the administrative sections of the Chancellery visibly echoes a Bonn tradition which recognised simple, transparent functionalism as the architectural symbol of democracy and established this in the public consciousness. At the same time, the steadfastness of massive stone-faced walls expresses the new confidence of the Federal Republic ... this has set the tone for new construction in Berlin as the architectural symbol for a recovery in self-esteem (Bartetzko, 1995: 15).

The Chancellery and the entire length of the Spreebogen complex is 'perforated with incisions, conservatories and a series of comb-like outward-facing courtyards which aim not so much for glass-like transparency as for a three-dimensional porosity of the entire complex' (Mönninger, 2000: 391).

At the ground-breaking ceremony for the new Chancellery on 4 February 1997, Helmut Kohl expressed satisfaction with the result:

> This is an important day for the capital, Berlin, and for the reunited fatherland . . .
> The construction radiates relaxed self-confidence combining modesty with
> dignity. Like no other place, this immediate area symbolises Germany's recent
> history. It embodies the brilliance and the hubris, the destruction and the new
> beginning (Kohl, quoted Traynor, 1997).

Criticisms of Kohl's depiction of the symbolism of the new Chancellery have included the accusation that, while for the first time in the history of German democracy both parliament and Executive will have direct control at one place, nevertheless in terms of 'Democracy as Builder' the Kanzleramt is too presidential, having 'spatial and formal dominance over the Reichstag', and lacks Mitmenschlichkeit (humaneness). It thus perhaps indicates that, as Guntar Hoffmann put it in *Die Zeit*, 'a slow process of deparliamentarisation has begun' (Wilhelm, 2001: 8). As Schubert points out, others have been less polite, referring to it as a 'megalomanical colossus' recollecting Hitler's chancellery on Voßstrasse (Schubert, 2001: 9). The dominance of the building has also been read as 'politicians watching the people' (ibid.), a semiotic interpretation which tracks its origins to an earlier design by Schultes which incorporated a large circular façade and was quickly christened 'the eye of the Chancellor'. Owing to Big Brother Gestapo and Stasi associations, crescent-shaped arched recesses were cut into the heavy walls instead, but the nickname persists (*Der Spiegel*, 1998). A related criticism pertains to the fact that despite Kohl's association of the Kanzleramt and the government quarter with 'light transparency and greenness' the whole complex can be represented as a self-contained separate world linked by an underground tunnel and with potential intruders kept at bay with omnipresent CCTV surveillance (Wilhelm, 2001). Even Hans Stimmann has recognized that in this context 'Democracy as Builder' will only be realized in a limited form (Stimmann, 1996: 9). In a context where architectural interpretations of the design by Schultes and Frank abound (for example, that they are really Wagnerians 'trying to revive the Teutonic and Scandinavian mythology of the primeval horde'(!), quoted, Mönninger, 2001: 391, exclamation added) one piece of symbolic omission from the Band des Bundes concept stands out. The decision not to proceed for the present with the Citizen's Forum – described as the formal central element and linking piece of the whole Schultes design

(Stimmann, 1996: 8) – leaves a conspicuous gap in the federal ribbon. Without the Civic Forum symbolizing the underlying democratic source of state authority (Guerra, 2001: 4), the government district, as one critic has put it, 'is not complete' (Meyer, 1999: 19). The question of civic identity, both literally and symbolically, remains unfinished business at the heart of Germany.

REUSE OF NATIONAL SOCIALIST BUILDINGS

In former East Berlin under Soviet and GDR control, major angst was not usually expended over the survival or reuse of Nazi-tainted architecture. At the end of the war Hitler's Chancellery was unceremoniously bulldozed by the Russians, with the building's marble cladding carted off for their war memorial in Treptower Park (Clarke, 1990). Shortly before the 'Wende' the GDR had built anonymous apartments on part of the site but without disturbing most of the underground bunker complex notoriously associated with the Voßstrasse edifice (Thieme, 1998: 104). Since the GDR had characterized itself as an anti-fascist state, it officially exculpated itself from responsibility for National Socialism and thus had no hesitation in reusing the old regime's buildings. With Nazi ornamentation removed, for example, Göring's Luftwaffe building had even served as an interim People's Chamber of the GDR (*Der Spiegel*, 1998). For the federal move from Bonn to Berlin such uncritical lack of compunction was never likely to be a possibility. In December of 1992 Bonn had publicly announced that buildings from the Third Reich (and GDR) were to be demolished, being simply 'beyond the pale' as addresses for Berlin ministries. New buildings would be constructed in what Helmut Kohl called 'the extinguishing of the unloved witnesses of history' (Kohl, quoted Guerra, 2001). Protest immediately ensued, with many voices delivering the same message, that such physical erasure of history from memory was 'no way to come to terms with the past' (Guerra, 2001: 4). As expressed by one proponent of the importance of place to memory in Berlin:

> Access to history through people and places is important to young people. It is fascinating to find the location in the Tiergarten where Hitler declared World War II. The fleeting film image cannot provide this. Rather the material substance helps to get to grips with the past ... In this context demolition is censorship (Abriß ist Zensur) (*Der Spiegel*, 1998).

This conflict ended only in 1994 with the announcement by Federal Finance Minister Theo Waigel that, for financial reasons, over 80% of the estimated ministerial space requirements in Berlin would be met from existing buildings (Levine, 1994: 8–9). This pragmatism, while not universally accepted, opened up in turn a process of lengthy discussion and fundamental reflection on how these 'unloved witnesses of history' could be adapted for reuse as an alternative to building a new Bonn on the Spree. Klaus Töpfer, the Federal Minister for Regional Planning, Building and Urban Development and with overall responsibility for the Berlin move, argued that buildings with major Nazi associations be presented as 'places of inescapable memory', which would stand as a warning that 'perpetrators could never again seek refuge behind their desks' (Töpfer, quoted Der Spiegel, 1998). Whether the building conversions accomplish this task remains an open question. The buildings involved have taken criticism for outwardly not signifying a bold enough break with the past and not making themselves look and feel sufficiently accessible to the public (Schlusche, 2001: 20). Given the visage and history of the buildings, this is perhaps a tall order, leaving one official responsible for the recommissioning pro-gramme to express relief that the allied bombing legacy and the communist bull-dozer had removed some of the most sensitive ministerial buildings from the Hitler era (Conradi, 1997). In the 'musical chairs' allocation of federal departments, Göring's Aviation Ministry on Leipziger Straße is the location of the new Finance Ministry. The building, with the solidity of its overpowering orderliness and cold-ness still capable of striking fear and foreboding into the human soul, is now renamed after the assassinated Detlev Rohwedder, former manager of the Treu-hand trust agency, which oversaw the privatization of East German state-owned enterprises. The 1930s numberings in the long corridor of the building continue to be used: Göring's bunker below has been demolished. A rebranding on the north-facing gable wall by the GDR, depicting the standard scene of smiling agrarian and industrial workers, was in turn trumped in 2000 by a new piece of officially spon-sored art. This invites the viewer to reflect in a pool, constructed in the exact dimensions of the mural, on what has taken place here, including the workers' revolt on 17 June 1953. It is the original meaning of the building, however, that continues to dominate. The Reichsbank, now the seat of the new Foreign Ministry, was approached by renovating architect Hans Kollhoff with the concept of 'making history visible' (Der Spiegel, 1998). This has not just involved acknowledging Third Reich history, where on top of being the first monumental building of that era the basement was the repository for plundered Nazi gold. It involves GDR history as well. In 1959 the building had become the seat of the central committee of the SED and thus the heart of power in East Germany. In 1990 the Volkskammer of the GDR met in the building and voted the communist state out of existence. Of the two other major Nazi buildings, the former Reich Interior Ministry now houses the computer facilities of the Bundestag and the Propaganda Ministry of Goebbels on Wilhelmstrasse is the new Federal Ministry for Labour and Social Affairs. From other office buildings used if not built by the Nazis, one stands out.[2] The Imperial Navy Office dating back to the Kaiser Reich had been the home of the Wehrmacht Supreme Command. Graf von Stauffenberg was executed in the courtyard of the east wing after the failed attempt to assassinate Hitler on 20 June 1944. Today, in the same yard of the building, now the Federal Defence Ministry, there is a memorial to the German Resistance.

In terms of the reuse of Nazi architecture in Berlin and of the problem of dealing with associations firmly imprinted on the historical record and collective imagination, the 'rebranding' of the *Olympic Stadium* deserves special mention. As part of a larger Reichssportfeld complex, and headquarters of the British military forces in Berlin until 1994, the Stadium is among the largest completed and still existing constructions of the Nazi era. With its massive pillars, soaring towers and sleek stone façade it is a quintessential example of Third Reich monumental architecture (Roth and Fragman, 1998: 103). At the 1936 Olympic Games it was put on worldwide display as the architectural showpiece of the Thousand-Year Reich. Modest rebranding has included the naming of a Jesse-Owens-Allee to the south of the Stadium, but the main entrance is still reached via Reichsstrasse, which, although dating back to the Kaiser Reich, is still associated in many minds, especially in East Berlin (where imposed street renaming has often been contentious), with the more notorious Reich. While the Olympic Stadium has been the home ground of Hertha BSC for some time, it is the opening and final games of the Football World Cup in 2006, to be played here to international audiences, which may go some way towards lightening the heavy *genius loci* of the site. While it is claimed that the extensive renovation now taking place for the 2006 events will 'retain the overall composition and lines of view intended by the Stadium's original architect, Werner March' (Rödiger, 1999: 38), this view is disputed by the leading scholar of National Socialist architecture, who claims that the renovation is being regarded as almost entirely 'a practical problem with discussion focusing on cost considerations and with scant attention given to the political heritage of the site and its importance as a locus of National Socialist sculpture' (Schäche, 1998). Rather, the charge is made that the renovation work is based 'on the highly questionable demands and principles of shirt sleeved sports functionaries and their populist stooges in political positions' (Schäche, 1998). The conclusion is reached that in this instance the stone heritage of the Nazis has been subjected to 'systematic mental suppression' (ibid.).

HOLOCAUST MEMORY AND MEMORIALS IN THE NEW BERLIN

Debate over how to 'come to terms with' (Auseinandersetzung) the National Socialist past has impregnated the construction of new-built landscapes in Berlin and the reuse of old ones. This debate, going to the heart of how Germans are reworking their sense of identity and wrapped up in the urban planning of the capital, has been of equal intensity in relation to a parallel memorialization process explicitly concerned with constructing sites of memory for the contemplation of crimes against humanity. This has involved a combination of local citizens' or Bezirke initiatives, and city of Berlin and federal memory projects. While an exhaustive inventory is beyond present scope simply because scores of sculptures and plaques evoke the theme of the Holocaust, nevertheless, certain selected sites of recent memory work can convey the enormity of 'dealing with' this open wound in a place which retains a tortured *genius loci*. While all memory sites are unique, a basic division can be made between the power of 'authentic places' where specific events and deeds happened and locales offering the opportunity for more general contemplation. In relation to the former, in 1994 the Berlin Department of Building and Housing published a unique and solemn document cataloguing the winning entries for recent artistic design competitions in various states of realization. The document is entitled 'Memory in Word, in Stone, in Light, in the Void' (Senatsverwaltung für Bau und Wohnungswesen, 1994). The head of the unit responsible for the report refers to opposition to such remembrance 'being strong if not always publicly articulated' (Nottmeyer, 1998). As described by Wolfgang Nagel, Senator for Building and Housing, all projects listed 'are concerned with the endeavour to make the authentic site and the historic event real through artistic means'. Further:

> these monuments are dealing with the most important subject in Germany since 1945. They cannot free us from the duty of dealing with the past but they can help us to understand connections. The bitter truth is that it was individuals who, step by little step, allowed the perfidy of implementing the murder of millions of people (Nagel, 1994).

A subsequent introduction to the projects explains that the ideas represent a ten-year intensive discussion about the limits and possibilities of monumental art in engaging with the subject of National Socialism:

> Monumental art confronts the artist with a challenge to give collective memory substance and form in a way that finds acceptance in society. It retrieves historical events and projects them in recognisable form into the mind ... Artists have tried to react with artistic means to the phenomenon of a crime which has surpassed all limits of rational understanding and which cannot be put into words ... Monuments cannot tell the whole story of an event or a place. They can only set signs, make you think or irritate. They can generate a picture that remains in the mind of the viewer and starts working there (Endlich, 1995: 6).

rarely

Seldom can urban planning, broadly understood, have been involved with such a sensitive process, where artistically inspired meaning has informed public debate and political 'memory choices'. Artistic works that have now left their mark on Berlin's memory trail of shame include:

- The empty library monument to the book-burning on *Bebelplatz*
- The light projection marking a satellite concentration camp on *Sonnenallee*, Neukölln
- Stone sculptures on *Rosenstrasse* marking the protest of women against detentions
- The monument to deported victims at Berlin's *Grunewald* S-Bahn station
- The *Spiegelwand* in Berlin-Steglitz.

BEBELPLATZ: MEMORY IN THE VOID

Designed by the Israeli sculptor Micha Ullman, an empty underground library has since 1995 lain opposite the main building of the Humboldt University on Unter den Linden, site of the notorious book-burning by National Socialist students on 10 May 1933:

> In the middle of Bebelplatz, a small window is set flush into the paving stones. Beneath the glass is an empty white room. The white room is lined with white shelves: an empty library, sterile and ghostly, a symbol of the books burned and the culture and knowledge lost (Roth and Frajman, 1998: 75).

To the left of the window into the library is a famous quote from the poet Heinrich Heine: 'Where one burns books, it is only a prelude; in the end one also burns people.' An earlier plaque, erected nearby under the East German government and still extant, constructs memory with a more direct and terser message:

> On this plaza Nazi brutishness destroyed the best works of German and world literature. The fascist book-burning of May 10, 1933 should be an eternal reminder to be vigilant against imperialism and war.

Vigilance against totalitarian censorship in other dramatic forms receives no mention.

SONNENALLEE SATELLITE CONCENTRATION CAMP, NEUKÖLLN: MEMORY IN LIGHT

Designed by the German artist Norbert Rademacher, a memorial was installed in 1994 near the spot of a satellite forced-labour camp associated with the outlying Sachsenhausen concentration camp. The site itself is now a sports stadium and urban allotment. The memorial consists of a laser light that is triggered to project an inscription on the pavement when someone walks by at night. The illuminated inscription is bluntly factual and far from poetic:

On this spot in 1942 the company National Krupp Cash Register Limited erected a forced labour camp for the armament of the National Socialists. Several hundred women were locked up here. From 1944 to 1945, 500 Jewish women from Poland were in this camp. During these years this was a subsidiary site of the KZ Sachsenhausen.

ROSENSTRASSE: BLOCK OF WOMEN: MEMORY IN STONE

Since 1995 a stone sculpture by the Berlin artist Ingeborg Hunzinger marks the Rosenstrasse Women's Protest, the single known occurrence of mass public protest during the Nazi regime. Outside 224 Rosenstrasse in March 1943 several hundred non-Jewish people, mainly women, protested, even when threatened by machine guns, against the detention by the Gestapo of Jewish men who until then had been protected because of mixed marriages. Behind the central figures of two mourning and protesting women the inscription reads:

> 1943: The strength of civil disobedience, the vigor of love overcomes the violence of dictatorship; Give us our men back; Women were standing here, defeating death; Jewish men were free.

Panicked by an unprecedented protest, the SS and Gestapo released the prisoners and actually brought back 25 men already dispatched to Auschwitz (Roth and Frajman, 1998: 119). However, the images conjured to memory at other sites of deportation have no fairy-tale ending. The Gleiss 17 memorial in Grunewald and the Spiegelwand in Steglitz are cases in point.

GRUNEWALD DEPORTATION MEMORIAL: MEMORY IN WORD AND VOID

Few memory sites in Berlin are more chilling than the Gleiss 17 Mahnmal (warning monument), where Platform 17 at the Grunewald station was the main deportation point for over 50 000 Berlin Jews who were marched openly through the streets. Emerging from the claustrophobia of what seems like an endless tunnel, the steps to Platform 17 are marked by a simple plaque erected in 1998 by German Railways:

> To the memory of those deported between 1941 and 1945 to the death camps by the trains of the German Reichsbahn.

Emerging onto Platform 17 itself as it stretches eastwards, one is left to imagine the fear of those herded onto transports. Installed in the early 1990s by the city of Berlin, a series of iron plates running along both sides of the old track (which is now overgrown), record with words of ledger-like banality the date, camp destination and number of Jews deported by each train. Not far away, recalling the motif of the new Libeskind museum, human-like voids disappearing into a vast concrete wall evoke the cold inhuman horror of the crimes perpetrated here (Figure 2.6). Beside this memorial, by the Polish artist Karol Broniatowski, is the inscription:

> To admonish us to oppose courageously and without hesitation every disregard to life and human dignity.

SPIEGELWAND STEGLITZ: MEMORY IN WORD AND LIGHT

7 June 1995 saw the unveiling, virtually outside the city hall in the southern Berlin Bezirk of Steglitz, of a very public and controversial Holocaust memorial. The memorial, beside the site of the former local synagogue, consists of a large reflecting wall of steel 3.5 metres high and 11 metres long, polished to a mirror finish. On it is engraved the seemingly endless Gestapo list of deported Steglitz Jews, with their full names and addresses. A sign on one side of the mirror wall, reflecting back to the onlooker everyday scenes of passers-by, asks the question: 'and today?'. This monument by Berlin artists, the result of an architectural competition organized by Steglitz at the instigation of a local citizen initiative group, hit the German national headlines in 1993/94 and drew international attention because of bitter disagreement in the Steglitz municipal assembly and in Steglitz more generally over its planned erection. In some ways a rehearsal and 'curtain raiser' for the

Figure 2.6 Human-like voids in concrete at the Grunewald station, Berlin, 2002

vigorous debate surrounding the planned erection of a national German Holocaust Memorial in Berlin several years later, much attention focused on the aesthetics of the artwork, in particular its provocative size. With the Christian Democratic Party (CDU), Liberals (FDP) and right wing 'Republicans' opposing the memorial and the Social Democratic Party (SPD) and the Greens in favour, the embarrassed Berlin city government intervened to complete the project (Will, 1996; Seferens, 1995). While the Steglitz Building Director points out that criticism of sensitive memorial projects can be misinterpreted and does not necessarily indicate anti-Semitism or an unwillingness to confront the past (Will, 1996), the main German chronicler of the Spiegelwand controversy is more judgemental:

> Even though primarily aesthetic arguments were brought to bear, it was patent that the opponents basically took exception to the meaning of the Reflecting wall ... the controversy is symptomatic of a slow but unmistakable change in the political climate of Germany. Calling for a new national consciousness, the political centre joints the extreme right in its foremost concern of relativising the crimes of the Nazi regime (Seferens, 1995: 96).

This, in a more general context, is perhaps too harsh. In this local contest over memory the result has been an outcome which is both contemplative and challenging (Figure 2.7). Other authentic sites in Berlin that bring to the forefront of

Figure 2.7 Spiegelwand, Steglitz, 1999

memory the genocidal abominations of 'the perpetrators' alongside the fate of the victims have also engendered debate over the most appropriate form of representation. Looming large here are the House of the Wannsee Conference, the Sachsenhausen Concentration Camp, and the Topography of Terror site near Potsdamer Platz, headquarters of the Gestapo and the office of the Reichsführer SS, Heinrich Himmler.

In the western Berlin suburb of *Wannsee* on 20 January 1942, Reinhard Heydrich, chief of the Gestapo and the SD (the security service of the SS), chaired a meeting of 14 top Nazi officials and SS officers in a lakeside villa. The agenda was to discuss and co-ordinate the 'final solution of the Jewish question'. Given that the first death camp at Chelmno was up and running before Wannsee and that mobile gas vans were already disposing of Jews in Poland, a recent scholarly study of the historical significance of the Wannsee Conference concludes that in some respects 'the deed of murder begat the idea of genocide as much as the other way round. Wannsee emerges as an important act of closure in the process of turning mass murder into genocide' (Roseman, 2002). The proposal to establish in the villa an 'International Documents Centre for the Study of National Socialism and its Consequences' dates back to 1965 and is the work of the historian Joseph Wulf, who brought the significance of the site to popular imagination. Despite advocacy for a documentation centre from the World Jewish Congress, support from the Berlin city government was forthcoming only with the 50th Anniversary of the Conference looming. On 20 January 1992 the house was formally inaugurated as a memorial and educational site (Haus der Wannsee – Konferenz Memorial, undated: 145–6). The visitor stands in the villa's large dining room, where the conference was held and which affords splendid views over the Wannsee lake, and imagines the waiters serving cognac after lunch as the awful fate of millions was sealed in such civilized surroundings. By contrast, it is just as soul-chilling an experience to walk at dusk along the dilapidated fencing and watchtowers of the *Sachsenhausen* concentration camp on the northern outskirts of Berlin. Sachsenhausen, because of its close proximity to Berlin, was a 'model camp', a training centre for SS camp guards before despatch to other even more infamous places, in addition to being a centre of forced labour and mass murder in its own right. From 1938–40 the commandant of Sachsenhausen was Rudolf Höss, later in charge of Auschwitz (Roth and Frajman, 1998: 96). The site was also home to the Concentration Camp Inspection, which administered and supervised all the other concentration camps (Krause, 1996). This is a memory space of past crimes of the first rank. The Brandenburg Memorials Foundation, which manages the only partially restored site, sees its role *inter alia* as 'to preserve the memory of terror ... [and] to recall the crimes of tyranny' (Krause, 1996: 3). This educational role has been carried on in the face of arson attacks on the preserved part of the site from

right-wing xenophobes, who in 1992, after a visit to Sachsenhausen by the Israeli
Prime Minister Itzhak Rabin, almost completely destroyed reconstructions of two
barracks used exclusively for Jewish prisoners. Reconstructed again and opened in
1997, charred walls from the arson attack are now memorialized as a part of the
history of the site, alluding to what it means to remember in a context of present-
day, neo-Nazi skinhead violence. In 2000 the Brandenburg Memorials Foundation
financed a symposium to consider what to do with the remainder of the vast site.
Subsequently Daniel Libeskind, architect of the new Berlin Jewish Museum, has
been working with the Foundation on a new-build design concept entitled 'wedge
of hope', having the intention of ideologically decommissioning some Sachsenhausen land for reuse. Prominently under consideration at the time of writing in
2002 was a proposal to use part of Sachsenhausen as a new training academy for
the Brandenburg police force. Whether the contrast between a democratic police
force and the former repressive state apparatus of fascism on the site is appropriate must remain open to some doubt.

One 'site of the perpetrators', however, above all others stands out at the
very heart of Berlin with its provocative challenge to memory, making any easy,
settled notion of German identity impossible. The site is irrevocably associated
with 'the most feared address' in the city (Dingel et al., 1996: 2). This was at
8 Prinz-Albrecht-Strasse, a stone's throw from Potsdamer Platz, the headquarters
of the Gestapo and the office of the Reichsführer SS, Heinrich Himmler. This building and its immediate environs, the control centre of the Nazi regime, were a place
of torture and death, and

> a site inhabited by so-called desk-bound criminals, who concentrated on the
> 'orderly dispatch' of processes, operations and proceedings while preferring to
> remain far from the areas in which the terror was being executed (Dingel et al.,
> 1996: 1–2).

This area in former West Berlin, right up against the Berlin Wall, for decades
after the war was described by one German historian as symbolizing 'a place not
considered acceptable for German history' (Scheffler, 1960, quoted ibid.). Early
demolition of ruins was followed by the blowing-up of the former Gestapo headquarters in 1956 and subsequent neglect. However in the 1980s, with the Nazi
legacy beginning to be discussed, the notorious site on Prinz-Albrecht-Strasse
moved to the forefront of memory debate. The first impetus for 'rediscovering' the
area's fascist historical significance had come at the end of the 1970s from the
architect and historian of architecture, Dieter Hoffmann-Axthelm (Berliner
Festspiele, 1998: 208), who was subsequently to be closely associated with master
planning for post-reunification Berlin, ironically concerned with the erasure of com-

munist history and described in the following chapter. In 1983, the Berlin Senate organized a design competition for a memorial which drew much criticism when it asked the entrants to 'reconcile the historic depth of the location with practical applications such as the establishment of parks, playgrounds, space for exercise, etc,' (*Berliner Festspiele*, 1998: ibid.). In December 1984 Berlin's Mayor, Eberhard Diepgen, decided not to proceed with such a questionable harmonization. With this episode best seen as a first crack in breaking a process of historical repression that had lasted 40 years, the West Berlin city government under the direction of the Senator for Cultural Affairs prepared a provisional representation of the site to coincide with Berlin's 750th Anniversary celebration in 1987. A provisional *'Topography of Terror'* remains in place, exposing the remains of the prison cell floors, eschewing any voyeuristic or shock representation of horror. The imagination is enough to conjure up a slight intimation of the fear, but also the courage, of those who suffered and died here. The official guidebook to the 'Topography of Terror' puts the significance of this site for German identity and self-understanding rather bluntly:

> The Gestapo prison with its prominent inmates but numerous unknown persons as well testified to the fact that there were people who refused to bend, who did not take the easy route of accommodation or of closing their eyes but who opted for resistance and did not hesitate to risk their lives in order to prevent, lessen or shorten injustice. To them who became victims and who, through their actions, stood for a different Germany, this place is therefore a memorial (*Berliner Festspiele*, 1998: 8).

A joint foundation formed in 1994 between the city of Berlin and the federal government presently oversees the construction of a permanent building to house an exhibition centre on the 'Topography of Terror' site. Designed by the Swiss architect Peter Zumthor, who won an architectural competition in 1993, the building was symbolically begun by a speech to the Berlin Senate by Ignatz Bubis, chair of the directorate of the Central Council of Jews in Germany, on 8 May 1995, the 50th anniversary of the German surrender. Completion of the building has proceeded slowly and in fits and starts because of financial difficulties and escalating costs. It is due to open in 2004. Along with the new Berlin Jewish Museum and the Memorial to the Murdered Jews of Europe, these 'grand projects of memory' have been referred to as a *Capital Triad of National Socialist Memory*. The trio is seen as collectively calling to memory in central Berlin destroyed Jewish history, the Jewish victims and the acts of the perpetrators (Stiftung Topographie des Terrors, Berlin, 2000: 33). The motif of the stark, concrete-and-glass three-storey building, arising on the site where one is conscious of the fact that so much of what happened was hidden from view, is that of 'stone made transparent'. The new exhibition is intended to facilitate on one authentic site of terror 'an intensive engagement with the causes and consequences of tyranny'. The purpose, in the words of the Foundation, is to learn and come to terms with the past (Auseinander-setzung) to better cement the values of a pluralistic democracy:

> there is no stronger argument for a free and democratic society than a glimpse
> of a political system which represented a radical negation of all human and civil
> rights. If you think long and hard about National Socialism and its crimes you will
> want to ensure the sound foundations of a state where law rules, power is
> controlled through free elections, the principle of the separation of powers is
> accepted and pluralism of ways of life respected. In a time of new horror from
> right-wing racism and neo-Nazi tendencies and violence, the Topography of
> Terror makes an important contribution to cementing democratic principles as
> foundations of our society (Stiftung Topographie des Terrors, ibid. 23).

Whether the future 'Topography of Terror' can fulfil this mission, rather than becoming one of the major stop-off points on a central Berlin Holocaust tourist trail, remains to be seen. One columnist with *Die Zeit*, for example, comes close to pandering to a Holocaust industry in suggesting that the memory triad will be 'an ensemble of great magnetism and will have to be seen as one of the main attrac-tions of the new centre' (Lau, quoted ibid. 34). As 'visitor attractions', Holocaust sites certainly sit uncomfortably within the standard brief of most city promotional agencies. Also in this regard, the remnants of Hitler's bunker just north of the 'Topography of Terror' so far remain beyond the pale in terms of being presented as a site for contemplating the memory of the biggest perpetrator of all. Here the views that it could become a shrine for neo-Nazi pilgrimages, that it sits on 'histori-cally contaminated soil' and should be erased, or is simply too macabre, sit along-side the opinion that not to open the bunker to the public is to 'tiptoe away from history' (Thieme, 1998: 104–5). One American historian who has controversially exhorted Germans to memory work has even suggested that the bunker be placed under the auspices of the United Nations World Heritage Committee:

> If neo-Nazis want to use this bunker as a rallying point, then let people see the
> contemporary evil, be horrified by it, combat it, and defeat it with a single minded
> purpose that did not exist 60 years ago. In secure democracies, one does not
> eradicate symbols of hatred. One rises in solidarity with those who are hated
> against those who hate (Goldhagen, 1999).

So far the only 'corner' of Berlin's grand 'memory triad' to be fully completed is the new *Jewish Museum, Berlin,* designed by Daniel Libeskind following an architectural competition organized by the city of Berlin in 1989. City marketing has so far resisted the temptation to 'over-sell' what is now one of the most popular tourist attractions in the city, unkindly renamed by one commentator as 'Jewrassic Park' (Lackmann, 2000). One architectural critic refers to how people 'experience the drama and emotional force of this extraordinary spatial configuration immediately and instinctively' (Schneider, 1999: 58), built as it is around a void representing the presence of the absence of what has been obliterated from Jewish life in Berlin. After Hitler came to power in 1933, more than 82 000 of the city's 160 000 Jews emigrated. Of those who remained, less than 6000 survived the war. The rest died in the Holocaust (Range, 1996: 116). The most intense experience in Libeskind's architectural creation is associated with the freestanding concrete Holocaust Tower:

> The austere space is dimly illuminated by daylight passing through a slit overhead and the sounds of the city are faintly heard. The closed, bare, empty and unheated space, its darkness penetrated only by a sharp beam from its single window, exerts an extremely compelling effect on anyone who experiences it (Schneider, 1999: 51).

This is an understatement. As the door to the Holocaust Tower falls heavily into place behind the solitary visitor, the overwhelming sensation is of rising panic and a consuming fear of an awful entrapment, that the door will not reopen, that there is no way back.

THE MEMORIAL TO THE MURDERED JEWS OF EUROPE

In the spring of 2003, on a 19 000-square-metre site just south of the Brandenburg Gate, construction started on the erection, by the Federal Republic of Germany, of a 'warning memorial' (Mahnmal) to the Murdered Jews of Europe; 2700 concrete pillars in a vast field of memory designed by the American architect Peter Eisenman will, in the words of the resolution passed by the German Bundestag on 25 June 1999:

> honour the murdered victims; maintain the memory of this unthinkable occurrence in German history and admonish all future generations to never again violate human rights, to defend the democratic constitutional state at all times, to secure equality before the law for all people and to resist all forms of dictatorship and regimes based on violence (Foundation of the Memorial to the Murdered Jews of Europe, 2000).

This third and most controversial component of Berlin's 'Grand Projects of Memory' has, over the past decade, been a focus for fundamental debate over German identity and self-understanding. A chronology of milestones on the road to the memorial, which dates back to 1988 and a Citizens' Initiative based around the journalist Lea Rosh, is provided in Figure 2.8. Over the ensuing years and especially since 1995, when Chancellor Helmut Kohl vetoed the design of a winning entry in a design competition for the project, national debate has involved politicians, historians, philosophers, novelists, journalists, artists, and architects among many others in what is a major place-making set piece in the urban planning of Berlin's government district. Those charged with officially documenting the process leading to the Mahnmal decision leave no doubt as to what has been at stake. The collected documentation is subtitled 'a cross-section through the soul of a nation'. While acknowledging that the Mahnmal debate has stretched the patience of the German public beyond endurance, the editors recognize that:

> the debate has become a central discourse on political and historical self-understanding in the reunified Germany. The project is a point of crystallisation for the precarious ambivalence between the still valid onus of history and the desire for normality. With hindsight the debate around the concept and the design of the memorial for the Murdered Jews of Europe will probably be seen as a sharp break (Zäsur) in how the Germans look at their history after Auschwitz and in the new understanding of their role in Europe and the world on the threshold of a new century (Heimrod, Schlusche and Seferens, 1999: 7–8).

In giving his imprimatur to the final design concept in March 1999 as 'the best alternative', Jürgen Habermas establishes the central function of the memorial as making Germans think critically about their identity half a century after the rupture in civilization (Zivilisationsbruch) represented by Auschwitz. The hope is expressed that the memorial will be a sign stretching far into the future of the possibility of 'a purified collective German identity . . . (where) the break in the continuity of our fundamental traditions is the condition to regain self respect' (Habermas, 1999).

The Berlin Mahnmal controversy has involved debate over why a memorial should be built, where it should be built and what it should look like. Concerning the first and most fundamental question of all, Lea Rosh, the leading campaigner who has seen the project through from inception to erection, is clear. The purpose of the monument is twofold. It is about Germans 'not forgetting but confronting the unique event in history involving the industrial murder of millions of Jews'. Second, 'it is a memorial erected by the perpetrators to their dead victims' (Rosh, 1999). Other major national memorials exist in central Berlin to recall the horror of war in general terms, such as the landmark remains of the Kaiser Willhelm Memorial Church dedicated as long ago as 1961. More recently, Chancellor Kohl in 1993 had rededicated the Neue Wache in Berlin Mitte with the installation, at his personal selection, of a sculpture, 'Mother and Dead Son' by the artist Käthe Kollwitz. Heavily criticized for being an overly sentimental and generalized memorial to 'the victims of war and tyranny', Kohl's 'gift to Berlin' has been seen as adding to the case for memorials to specific victim groups (Endlich, 1995). Rosh's arguments, however, for a specific memorial to the Murdered Jews of Europe have been met with honourable criticism. The question was inevitably raised as to why Germany should be unique in putting a national symbol of shame so publicly on display. As a forceful critic of 'the Holocaust industry' points out, there is no memorial in Washington to the millions who died in the slave trade or to commemorate the extermination of Native Americans. Attempts between 1984 and 1994 to build an African American museum on the Washington Mall, location of the US Holocaust museum, were abortive (Finkelstein, 2000: 72). As put by the liberal *Süddeutsche Zeitung*:

> Stone symbols are supposed to remind us of glorious moments in the past ... who wants to be reminded forever of the horror which will bind the descendants ad infinitum into a chain of collective liability (*SDZ*, 1998).

Equally acute has been the fear that such a memorial could become a place of forgetting rather than remembering. In 1998 this view was expressed by Michael Naumann, spokesman on culture for the Social Democrats. Rather than addressing the black hole in German self-understanding, Naumann suggested that a memorial would communicate the message that the past could be overcome once and for all. It would stamp on the past an official seal of 'closure'. In similar vein the urban-planning voice of Peter Marcuse, who with his family was forced to flee Berlin as a child, has criticized Kohl's support for a Jewish Holocaust memorial as involving the 'cleansing' of this part of German history (Marcuse, 1998: 335). Michal Bodemann, a prominent academic tracker of how Germans are dealing with the memory of the Holocaust, has likewise articulated the concern that the memorial could become a German 'holy site', which one enters to be healed (Bodemann, 1998).

On the second rationale for the Mahnmal put forward by Rosh, that the descendants of the perpetrators and heirs of a common culture should erect a memorial to the dead victims, there have also been reservations. Fundamental to these has been the uneasy sense that there is perhaps something quite absurd, if not distasteful, in such a project, given that a memorial in the land of the perpetrators would have a quite different meaning from, say, that of Yad Vashem in Israel, where the Jewish state is presented as a deliverance from the catastrophe of the Holocaust (Korn, 1996). While Lea Rosh claims one-quarter Jewish ancestry, the

August 1988	A private citizens' initiative is formed to raise money and to campaign for a 'Memorial to the Murdered Jews of Europe'. The group (Förderkreis zur Errichtung eines Denkmals für die Ermordeten Juden Europas) supported by Willy Brandt and leading writers (including Günter Grass, later to change his mind) has, as a leading spokesperson, the journalist Lea Rosh who in 1994 becomes Chair.
November 1992	The federal government and Berlin Senat agree on a 20 000 square metre site just south of the Brandenburg Gate as a location for the memorial and to finance half of the cost. The Förderkreis, federal government and the city of Berlin become a 'sponsoring group' for the memorial thus transforming the project from a private initiative to a part of German political history.
18 April 1994	An artistic design competition for the memorial is launched by the sponsor group which brings forth 528 entries by January 1995. Nine prizes are awarded with two first prizes going to Simon Ungers and Christine Jacob-Marks. Lea Rosh advocates the design by Marks.
30 June 1995	Chancellor Kohl, calling for more discussion, vetoes the design of Christine Jacob-Marks for a gigantic gravestone bearing the names of all known Jewish victims of the Holocaust. Ignatz Bubis, head of the directorate of the Central Council of Jews in Germany, had called the monument 'tasteless'. Berlin's Building Senator, Wolfgang Nagel, calls the episode 'shaming'.
January– April 1997	Three colloquia held in Berlin sponsored by the city's Department of Science, Research and Culture, to discuss why, where and how to build a suitable memorial. Much disagreement over this 'fresh start' is in evidence and publicized in the national press.
July 1997	A second design competition is held with 16 invited artists and architects in addition to the nine prizewinners in the 1994/95 competition. The 'Search Commission' of five includes the Director of the German Historical Museum appointed by Chancellor Kohl and James Young, American expert on Holocaust memorials; 19 entries are received.
November 1997	Jury shortlists four designs with a submission by Peter Eisenman and Richard Serra from New York favoured by Chancellor Kohl. The concept involves a vast cemetery-like field of stones.
18 March 1998	Eberhard Diepgen, Berlin's CDU mayor, breaks ranks with Kohl and speaks out against the memorial declaring that he does not wish Berlin to become a 'capital city of remorse'. Berlin has enough memory sites already.
June 1998	Peter Eisenman parts artistic company with Serra, who resists aesthetic modification, and in consultation with Chancellor Kohl and the jury comes up with a revised and scaled down memorial design.
August 1998	The memorial question enters national electoral politics. Michael Naumann, cultural spokesman for the SPD expresses doubt over the memorial. The monument, he says, would 'freeze memory' and would communicate the message that Germans had 'paid our last debt to history'. Chancellor Kohl remains in favour of the revised Eisenman design.

Figure 2.8 Berlin's Memorial to the Murdered Jews of Europe: a chronology

11 October 1998	Martin Walser, liberal novelist and pillar of the German intellectual establishment, very publicly criticizes the whole idea of the memorial complaining that Germans should not be made constantly to atone for the crimes of the Nazis and that Auschwitz should not be used 'as an instrument of moral bludgeoning'. An intensified national debate ensues which proves a final catalyst to action.
9 November 1998	On the 50th Commemoration of Kristallnacht Ignatz Bubis, leader of Germany's Jewish community, condemns Walser's comments that Germany should look away from the past. Walser is accused of attempting to suppress history and of 'spiritual arson'. Bubis dies 13 August 1999, a 'German citizen of Jewish faith'.
January 1999	Eisenman design modified in consultation with Michael Naumann, Culture Minister in the new Schröder administration. Schröder and Naumann, previously sceptical about a memorial, agree on a design incorporating a documentation centre. Cost 120 m DM.
February 1999	Amidst calls for a new design competition because the fairness of the selection process had been called into question by the intervention of Kohl and the aesthetics of the memorial had been compromised, Lea Rosh states 'we are becoming ridiculous'. In an interview in *Die Zeit* (Feb 4) Schröder states that 'post-Walser' to say no to the monument would be misunderstood and that 'those honourably against it should shut up'.
25 June 1999	By a vote of 314 to 209, with 14 abstentions, the Bundestag approves the building of the revised Eisenman design with documentation centre.
27 January 2000	On the 55th anniversary of the liberation of Auschwitz Chancellor Gerhard Schröder officially dedicates the memorial site. Berlin's mayor Eberhard Diepgen does not attend. Neo-Nazi protesters claim that the memorial is a 'stain on the Reich capital'. James Young, a Jew, points out that for them, 'identity depends on forgetting the crimes of their forebears' (Young, 2000: 194).
August 2000	Fund raising poster by the Citizens' Initiative supporting the memorial reads: 'The Holocaust never happened'. Amidst much controversy and with a split in Jewish opinion the shock effect posters are withdrawn.
30 October 2000	Wolfgang Thierse, Bundestag President, symbolically begins site clearance. Thierse declares that the debates surrounding the construction 'were part of a process of understanding how to deal with our past (and) an assertion of our historical responsibility'.
Summer 2001	Site preparation and testing of materials begins.
Mid/Late 2002	Controversy is caused by the choice by Lea Rosh of supermodel Claudia Schiffer to do a 'commercial' voice-over for the Förderkreis.
1 April 2003	Construction of the Memorial begins.
2005	Anticipated completion.

Figure 2.8 continued

clamour for such a memorial has not come from Jews in Germany, who quite naturally would find it awkward and have ambivalent feelings about asking the Germans
for a memorial. Ignatz Bubis, former chairman of the directorate of the Central
Council of Jews in Germany, never publicly supported the idea of Jews 'needing' a
memorial from the Germans (Rosh, 1999). Hence, while acknowledging that the
Holocaust for Germans is 'constitutive' for the Federal Republic as 'an ever
present origin comparable to foundation myths', one writer points to the dilemma
that memory must 'take place for its own sake, not just as a tool for self betterment'
(Ross, 1998) or, as Habermas puts it, while the memorial will inevitably affect
Germans' sense of identity, it is not the function of Auschwitz and the victims to
'help Germans feel better about themselves' (Habermas, 1999). Moreover, the
project of building a memorial specifically to the Murdered Jews of Europe has
raised the objection from Professor Julius Schoeps, head of the Mendelssohn
Centre for European Jewish Studies at Potsdam University, that a 'hierarchy of
victims' will be created (quoted Staunton, 1998). To this Rosh replies, echoing
Ignatz Bubis on the issue (Bubis, 1997: 26–7), that other victim groups such as
the Sinti and Roma and homosexuals[3] can legitimately expect memorials of their
own but to conflate the treatment of various victim groups is to belie the different
stigmas and gradations of treatment meted out by the Nazis to each (Rosh, 1999),
not to mention the fact that the Jews were the largest victim group marked out for
extermination. In an argument that takes the tension in spatial planning between
pragmatic incrementalism and comprehensiveness into a further dimension, one
prominent critic of the Holocaust Mahnmal in Berlin, the president of the German
Academy for Language and Poetry, argued that an *ad hoc* approach to sites was
an unacceptable 'continuation of isolated memorial planning' in a context of no
overall fundamental discussion of official 'memorial culture' in the German capital.
The result would be an incoherent patchwork quilt of memory in a context where
such memorials were important as part of a process of 'reminding ourselves who
we really are and how we want to start the Berlin Republik' (Meier, 1997).

The officially designated site for the Berlin Holocaust Memorial is a 19 000-
square-metre parcel of federally-owned land promised to Lea Rosh by Helmut Kohl
in 1992, lying just south of the Brandenburg Gate and formerly constituting the
gardens for government ministries (Figure 2.9). While close to the centre of Nazi
power, the site itself is not associated with any particular *genius loci* of its own.
Two major counter-proposals challenging the importance of this site for memory
work arose in the course of the memorial debate. In March 1999, in the lead-up to
the federal government giving the official go-ahead for the Ministerial gardens location, the directors of seven concentration camp memorials (Belsen, Buchenwald,
Dachau, Dora, Neuengamme, and Ravensbrück and Sachsenhausen on Berlin's
doorstep) rebelled against such a centralized focus of memory. In an open letter

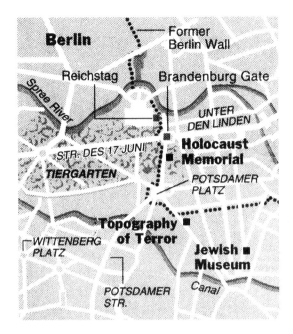

Figure 2.9 Location of Berlin's Holocaust Memorial

they stated that: 'Parliament is facing a fundamental decision – it is about how the Holocaust should be anchored in the cultural memory of Germany.' Resources, it was argued, should preferably be spent on the original camps so that visitors could see the real sites of the horror rather than an artistic representation (Boyes, 1999). The proposal resonated strongly with a much-discussed design entry in 1995 for the first Mahnmal competition. This came eleventh by proposing that a prominent bus stop would be an embarkation point to take people to Sachsenhausen and Ravensbrück. An objection of a different kind was raised by Salomon Korn, member of the governing board of the Central Council of Jews in Germany, in 1997. Korn, an architect with responsibility for articulating Jewish views on Jewish memorials, argued that the memorial site was not central enough. Being close to the former Chancellery and to Hitler's bunker, Korn argued, 'bound the planned memorial to the Nazi past instead of to the federal republic's present which would be the case on a site close to the Reichstag'. Even Lea Rosh, in rejecting the latter idea, is criticized as delivering the real message that 'the Holocaust Memorial is connected to past National Socialist history while the present centre of German history is untouched by the millennial crime, having to be kept clean for the future of the unified Germany' (Korn, 1996). Korn rather looked with favour on the radical idea beyond the remit of design juries of a deep trench in front of the main entrance to the Reichstag. This symbolism, recalling the

'Zivilisationsbruch' of Habermas, would remind German legislators in an inescapable way of the historically conscious new beginning that the reimaged Reichstag represented.

On the question of what Berlin's central Holocaust Memorial should look like, the aesthetic production of 528 entries for an artistic design competition in 1995 stoked a considerable furnace of national and international debate on how the awfulness of such an event could possibly be represented and made available for the necessary individual 'memory work of visitors', what one Holocaust memorial scholar has called 'the fundamentally dialogical, interactive nature of all memorials' (Young, 1994: 21). Whether the Holocaust is conceived of as a failure by Germany's political culture to adequately take on board the ideas of the European Enlightenment (Hohendahl, 1998: vii–xxiv), or in fact the reverse, a case of the worst expression of the narcissistic fantasies of omnipotence and superiority that haunt Western modernity, as argued by the French post-modern philosopher Jean-François Lyotard (Huyssen, 1994), the question of the artistic representation of the Holocaust has always aroused passionate views. While in the background lies Adorno's rightful wariness of aestheticizing the unspeakable suffering of the victims, one contributor to a study of Holocaust memorials, based on an exhibition organized by the Jewish Museum of New York in the early 1990s, pointed out how much is at stake and not only to Germans:

Fifty years after the notorious Wannsee Conference, at which the Final Solution was first given political and bureaucratic shape, the Holocaust and its memory still stand as a test case for the humanistic and universalistic claims of Western civilisation. The issue of remembrance and forgetting touches the core of a multifaceted and diverse Western identity ...

Perhaps post-modern culture in the West is itself caught in a traumatic fixation on an event which goes to the heart of our identity and political culture. In that case, the Holocaust monument, memorial and museum could be the tool Franz Kafka wanted literature to be when he said that the book must be the axe for the frozen sea within us (Huyssen, 1994: 10–17).

James E. Young, American author of a cultural history of Holocaust memorials (Young, 1994) and curator of the exhibition just mentioned, has been an advisor to the Berlin memorial 'sponsor group' since the mid-1990s. In his work Young describes the various artistic trends in Holocaust memorial representation (literal figuration, deconstructionist designs, anti-memorial memorials and so forth), a comprehensive portrayal of which is beyond present scope (Young, 1993). In general, however, Young argues that the Berlin memorial will 'succeed', as is the case with all other memory sites within the fabric of a city,[4] if it engages people in an active process of remembering. This process is always necessarily structured or steered in some way (the motives of memory are never pure, as Young puts it). Yet since it is the discreet memories of many individuals, the product of diverse responses to the exhibit on display, that are gathered together in common memorial spaces, Young prefers the term 'collected memory' to that of 'collective memory'. Collected memories in shared spaces 'lend a common spatial frame to otherwise disparate experiences and understandings' (Young, 1993: 6). Such 'collected memory' around national memorials can even invest such places with a nation's 'soul' (Young, 1993: 3–15). The German conundrum, as Young acknowledges, is how does a nation build a new and just state on the bedrock memory of its crimes which are to be memorialized in the heart of its capital city? (Young, 1994: 35). When Young accepted the invitation to join the competition jury he was aware of what the job entailed:

> Holocaust memorial work in Germany today remains a tortured, self-reflective, even paralysing preoccupation. Every monument, at every turn, is endlessly scrutinised, explicated and debated. Artistic, ethical, and historical questions occupy design juries to an extent unknown in other countries. In a Sisyphean replay, memory is strenuously rolled nearly to the top of consciousness only to clatter back down in arguments and political bickering, whence it starts all over again (Young, 1993: 21).

The memorial design finally selected and presently in the process of construction has been the result of a process, described with prescience by Young, stretching back to 1994 and involving two design competitions, three discursive colloquia organized by the 'sponsor group', extensive national debate and decisive political intervention along the way at the highest level. The first design competition in 1994/95 brought forth over 500 entries, the exhibition of which in central Berlin between April and May 1995 *Der Spiegel* was to call 'an embarrassing parcours of hackneyed symbolism' (*Der Spiegel*, 1997). Responding to the large size of the site, many submissions went for gigantic monuments acknowledging the enormity of the Holocaust but also evoking memory of the gigantism of Nazi architecture. A handful of conceptual artists proposed to build nothing. The shuttle bus stop to surrounding concentration camps has been mentioned. The submission by Rudolf Herz and Reinhard Matz wanted to introduce a speed limit on certain roads as a permanent remembrance of genocide. Of the two first prizes, that of Simon Ungers from Cologne involved the erection of a heavy, 85-square-metre steel sculpture intended to convey the feeling of an incredible burden and into whose 6-metre-high beams (forming the perimeter) would be perforated the sites of the death camps. Sunlight through the steel perforations would project the names onto the stairs leading to the monument. The second first prize awarded by the jury, and favoured by Lea Rosh, was even more gigantic. Submitted by a group headed by the Berlin artist Christine Jacob-Marks, this proposed a vast, 100-by-100-metre inclined stone slab in the style of a tombstone onto which would be engraved the names of all identifiable Jewish Holocaust victims. The proposed collection from the public of money by the Förderkreis to inscribe the names Ignatz Bubis described as enabling those with a bad conscience to buy indulgences. The personal intervention by Chancellor Kohl in June 1995 in rejecting such gigantism was to result in a second design competition organized by a new 'Search Commission' two years later, where again the intervention of Kohl was to prove decisive. Of 19 submitted designs from invited contributors, two were shortlisted by the Search Commission, those of Gesine Weinmiller from Berlin, and Eisenman Architects with Richard Serra from New York. Any notion that a fair set of procedures and assessment criteria could ever exist and deliver a consensus result was dispelled when the sponsor group involving representatives from Berlin, the Citizens' Initiative and federal government doubled the shortlisted designs for the memorial project, bringing in the entries of Daniel Libeskind of recent Jewish Museum fame and Jochen Gerz, noted for his pioneering work in designing 'anti-monuments' to the Holocaust which challenge the very premise of their being. A critic, writing under the banner of the Berlin Chamber of Architecture, was not overly impressed with the field of four. Weinmiller's motif of having a destroyed star of David set in a square of meditation was described as 'rather hollow'. Libeskind's entry was described as highly abstract and too 'self-referential' to the Jewish Museum. Jochen Gerz's concept was likewise 'disappointing'. The 'zone of instability' of the Americans Peter Eisenman and Richard Serra was looked upon more favourably as:

> an aesthetically impressive installation in which the visitors are led in a criss-cross way between huge columns. This is to generate a feeling of insecurity, irrationality, and even fear — but what if these emotions will not be stirred up? (Endlich, 1995: 164–6).

Following extensive debate in the media in late 1997, in January 1998 at a meeting between CDU Chancellor Kohl, Lea Rosh, Berlin's mayor Eberhard Diepgen and president of the Bundestag Rita Süssmuth, high-level political consensus began to gel around a design based on the broad principles of Eisenman and Serra (Conradi, 1998). This was dealt a backward blow on 18 March 1998 when Berlin's mayor spoke out publicly against the Mahnmal project, giving the clearest of indications that memory debate in Germany, in terms of views and feelings held, crosses party lines. Diepgen, never a strong supporter of the Steglitz 'mirror wall' or the Wannsee House memorial, expressed the view that Berlin, in doing too much of the Republic's memory work, should not be turned into a 'Capital of Remorse'. A more cynical view, expressed to the writer in interview by a Berlin official close to events, is that for electoral purposes Diepgen chose to identify with a strong undercurrent of public opinion in Berlin and beyond, which, unlike prominent voices in Germany's political class, would like to lay this aspect of the nation's past to rest. Following discussions between Peter Eisenman and Chancellor Kohl, a modified memorial design was to emerge in the summer of 1998. The disorientating 'waving' field of pillars with a cemetery motif was scaled down from 4000 to 2700 columns and the size of the slabs reduced from the former 7 metres to 4 metres and less, lest the sense of fear be too intense. The prospect of disoriented and panic-stricken visitors in an architectural field of fear almost adjacent to the Brandenburg Gate would do little for the image of Berlin. The change, Eisenman argued, would 'in no way diminish the idea of our monument' as 'a place one feels alone and abandoned, a place without a beginning or an end, with no direction' (Eisenman, 1998; Eisenman quoted Staunton, 1998). His collaborator Richard Serra disagreed, withdrawing from the project on the grounds that artistic integrity had been compromised. In a situation where no 'right' artistic solution can possibly exist, in August 1998 James Young, as a spokesperson for the Search Commission, endorsed 'Eisenman II':

> This memorial comes as close to being adequate to Germany's impossible task as is humanly possible. This is finally all we can ask of Germany's national attempt to commemorate the Nazis' murder of European Jewry.
>
> By choosing to create a commemorative space in the center of Berlin – a place empty of housing, commerce or recreation – the Chancellor reminds Germany and the world at large of the self-inflicted void at the heart of German culture and consciousness. It is a courageous and difficult act of contrition on the part of the government. Because the murdered can respond to this gesture with only a massive silence, the burden of response must fall on living Germans – who in their memorial visits will be asked to recall the destruction of a people once launched in their name, the irredeemable void this destruction has left behind, and their own responsibility for memory itself (Young, 1998).

With the Sisyphean 'memory boulder' previously identified by Young almost at the top of the mountain, on 11 October 1998 it was to come crashing down again, but for the last time. In a public speech accepting a peace prize for his latest book, the prominent liberal novelist Martin Walser spoke out against the Berlin Holocaust Memorial, linking it to the strain of past disgrace which Germany should now move beyond. Conscience, he argued, should be a private matter and

Germans should not foster a 'cult of past guilt' where a nation is blamed forever (Ross, 1998). Walser's comments in fact echoed the concerns of James Young that, while people should be 'permanently marked' by a Berlin memorial, they should not be 'disabled by memory' (Young, 1997). Highlighting the fact that a consensus relationship to the Nazi past is fragile in Germany, the Walser intervention may be seen as having the opposite of its intended effect. With such sentiments exploited by far-right parties and with a condemnation of the remarks by Ignatz Bubis on the 50th commemoration of Kristallnacht, Gerhard Schröder as the new Chancellor, previously sceptical about a memorial, was galvanized into supporting yet another variant of the Eisenman design, incorporating an information centre (Figure 2.10). Construction has started, with completion anticipated in 2005.

CONCLUSION

While market-driven cultural and physical suture, with its tendency to induce what Benjamin many years ago called 'the dream sleep of capitalism', is as strong in place-making processes in Berlin as elsewhere, Berlin is no ordinary place. Also

Figure 2.10 Artist's impression of the Memorial to the Murdered Jews of Europe

impregnated in place-making is the *cri de coeur* of what to do about the memory of a 'ground zero' event in Western culture with an epicentre in Berlin and shock-waves stretching to the gas chambers of Auschwitz. With so much at stake here in place-making, urban planners suggest and to a limited extent mediate but in general take a back seat. There is no collaborative dialogic planning process where a consensus memorializing response can be brokered. Habermas himself, the oracle for collaborative planning, argues his case in the general marketplace of ideas where misunderstandings, distortions of communication, genuine and deeply held differences of conviction and even some electoral manoeuvring have all played a part. The place-making agenda has naturally been driven by citizens' initiatives, historians, novelists, artists, politicians and so forth, with architects, planners and others facilitating informed discussion about the local spatial context within which memory suggestions can be implemented and helping to take matters forward once political decisions, however contingent, have been reached. The planning brief for the second design competition for the Berlin Holocaust Memorial thus pragmatically accepts Chancellor Kohl's call for less gigantism to guarantee the 'intensity of memory' and provides some suggestions on how practical site considerations such as traffic can be coped with (SWFK, 1997).

Ultimately, any assessment of how Germans and Berliners have coped with the necessary but impossible task of 'dealing with' the legacy of the Nazi past and the Holocaust in particular must remain subjective. However, while in some cases the moral imperative to 'never forget' takes an inevitable back seat to a market-driven future with its emphasis on spectacle and enjoyment in the here and now, for the most part the Nazi element of the *genius loci* in Berlin has been engaged with, in a reasonably transparent and honest, if inevitably unresolved, way. In the course of speaking to 'grief workers' in Berlin, the opinion of this writer is that the charge from some quarters that memorializing is part of a process in Germany of laying memory to rest and forgetting, and that relationships between objects in the built environment are being required to do the memory work of people (Kramer, 1999), seems too harsh. The process resembles more the reclamation of reason through recognition. The extensive spatiality of memory in Berlin makes it no less a social and personal process than if memory work was, say, centred more around the media of poetry and film. The nature of German identity wrapped up in memory work still remains 'work in progress', dealing as it must with the brute intractability of the legacy of the Holocaust. Here, in the potent spatiality of the German identity question weighing heavily on the German capital, the Berlin Holocaust Memorial when it opens in 2005 can be seen as posing an open question to the vacant space for a Civic Forum in the Band des Bundes. In the long shadow of the Holocaust evoked literally and figuratively by Eisenman's grave-like slabs, what does the Berlin Republic put first: civic identity within Germany or the ethnic identity of Germans?

NOTES

1   Paul Löbe, President of the Reichstag 1925–32 and subsequently jailed twice by the
    Nazis. An SPD member of the post-war Bundestag, in 1954 he was a founder member
    of the Committee for an Undivided Germany; Jacob Kaiser, a CDU esteemed
    contemporary of Konrad Adenauer; Marie-Elisabeth Lüders, one of the 'mothers' from
    the CDU of the post-war German Grundgesetz (Basic Law).

2   A catalogue of infamous addresses in Berlin from the Nazi period has recently been pro-
    vided by (ed.) Braun, Markus Sebastian. *Spuren des Terrors*, Verlagshaus Braun, Berlin,
    2002.

3   In 1998 federal level acceptance was forthcoming for a Sinti and Roma memorial on a
    site suggested by the Berlin Senate just south of the Reichstag in the Tiergarten. The
    Israeli artist Dani Karavan has been commissioned for the design. A campaign for a
    memorial for homosexual victims continues.

4   In some usages 'memorials' recall only tragic events and provide places to mourn while
    'monuments' are celebratory markers of triumphs of heroic individuals. In reality, as
    Young points out, the distinction becomes blurred. Young uses the term 'memory site'
    interchangeably with 'memorial'. Memorials can be temporal (memorial days, events) as
    well as spatial. Monuments in spaces which may or may not be works of public art, are
    in Young's usage always a kind of memorial (Young 1993: 3–4).

CHAPTER 3

MEMORY AND IDENTITY II: ERASING THE PAST IN THE CITY OF THE VICTORS

History is the version of past events that people have decided to agree upon.
Napoleon.

The previous chapter considered the socio-spatial process of remembering the Nazi period and the Holocaust in particular in national identity-narrative construction in Germany's capital city. This chapter examines how the memory of the GDR state is being handled in recent urban planning in Berlin. This is a complementary process, which proceeds in tandem and is largely about identity construction through forgetting. The judgement is made that erasure of the built legacy of the GDR is being taken too far. In 2002, for example, with the report of a federal and city of Berlin committee set up to consider the fate of the 'Palace of the Republic' (Palast der Republik), the most important symbolic building of the GDR in central Berlin, the crust of 'normal' history seems to be closing over the top of the molten lava of human possibilities, both good and bad, that should be kept in the watchful eye not just of academic historical seismologists but of public memory. This chapter places the debate over the future of Berlin's Palast der Republik, former home of the Volkskammer (People's Chamber) of the GDR, in a wider context. A victorious capitalism threatens to erase all memory of socialism, the other 'wayward child of the Enlightenment', to borrow a term from Günter Grass (Grass, 2002: 65). The denial by neo-liberalism, now without the historical counterweight of communism, that there is any alternative to the free market (Grass, 2002: 66) can be seen in the urban-planning tendency in Berlin to repress the notion that there was once the possibility of a different system and with it the realization of the ultimate arbitrariness of human social and economic relationships and its latent niggling threat to capitalist legitimacy. The chapter proceeds by way of a general consideration of the relationship of East and West Berliners to the memory of the German Democratic Republic. With the GDR, after the fall of the Wall, virtually annexed by the West, and despite the fact that the heirs of the SED, the Party of Democratic Socialism (PDS) are now in coalition government in Berlin, sentiment by former easterners for some aspects of their 40-year unique history is still likely to be dismissed by western Germans as 'Ostalgia'. Certainly the erasure of many potent symbols of physical division have rightfully gone unmourned. The Berlin Wall itself and its watchtowers and crossing points sit alongside the inevitable removal of many other communist traces and the reclaiming of places through renaming. However, this process of reclamation is arguably being taken too far in the case of present urban planning for the centre of the former GDR state. Here the recently approved urban design plan (Planwerk Innenstadt) to connect Berlin back to its 'normal' pre-World-War-II ground plan and plans to at least partially reconstruct, on the site of the Palast der Republik, the old Berlin city castle (Stadtschloss), home of the Hohenzollern, seem to be normalization by way of amnesia. Urban planning and design is being used as an instrument of selective collective memory-construction, emphasizing a common German past before troublesome difficulties in the 1930s and beyond. However, the questions posed by 'scar tissue' are perhaps preferable to a falsely reassuring reality of continuity presented by cosmetic suture. Indeed it is the presence of 20th-century 'scar tissue' that makes Berlin unique as a place of memory and reflection. As President George W. Bush put it in the sound bite of his speech to the German Bundestag in Berlin in May 2002: 'The history of our time is written in Berlin' (quoted Widmer, 2002). This being so, it should at least be legible.

GDR Memory and German Identity

The memory of the GDR continues to exert a strong influence on the difficulties involved in consolidating a common German identity between East and West. Here the attitudes of so-called 'Ossies' and 'Wessies' differ sharply, with the former likely to complain, with the euphoria of the fall of the Wall long gone, that their own unique identity and experience has been dismissed by the latter as just a transitory aberration. Not all in the former East are young, rich, educated and mobile enough to be absorbed easily into capitalist youth culture, with the mobile phone as the portable badge of identity of a transition generation (Miller, 2000). For 40 years and for the most part in the special spatial circumstances of confinement, a social experiment in identity construction took place in the GDR. This experience was both top-down and bottom-up. A first period of official identity construction, with its manipulation of history and memory, extended to 1974. In this year the constitution that had previously defined the GDR as 'a Socialist State of the German Nation' which strove to overcome 'the division of Germany forced upon the German Nation by imperialism' was changed. No longer looking to German unity on the basis of socialism, the GDR defined itself as a separate 'State of workers and peasants' (Craig, 1991: 308). In this first period, invoking a wider sense of German nation-hood, ironically all German cultural roots were relentlessly attacked. As expressed by Richie, 'the only thing East Germans had to be proud of was the fact that they had been liberated by the Soviet Union after the Second World War' (Richie, 1999: 728). The guilt of German fascism was purged from the East and transferred to the West, with East Germans expected to look to the Soviet Union and the international communist movement for heroes and memory figures. The dynamiting of the Berlin city castle by the GDR in the early 1950s vehemently spatialized this reality, with a parade ground, symbolizing order and aping Red Square, taking its place.

With this denial of history and suppression of memory the GDR during this period has been aptly referred to as 'an ideology in search of a nation' (*Economist*, 1989: 10). A second identity period followed in the 1970s, symbolized by the building of a new home for the Volkskammer (People's Chamber) of the GDR on the site of the former castle. The prestige building of the worker and peasant state was, in the urban planning of the capital city of the GDR, part of the new 'showcase for socialism', which reflected the growing confidence of the GDR regime. This was born in part from the acceptance of its legitimacy expressed in the West German policy of 'Ostpolitik' following the election of Willy Brandt as Federal Chancellor in 1969. The replacement of Walter Ulbricht as GDR leader by Erich Honecker, less tainted by the Stalinist era, eased the domestic severity of the East German state in the 1970s (Ardagh, 1995: 371), but the issue of how to build loyalty and an identification among the citizenry with the socialist project was ultimately to fall back on a rehabilitation yet substantial reinterpretation of German history and culture. Here Ardagh refers to how in the 1980s:

> Party ideologists sought to stress that the GDR emanated from the age-old peasant and worker traditions of the German nation, with its roots in the peasant revolts of the Middle Ages, the 1848 uprisings, and of course the teachings of Marx and Engels. More surprisingly, the Party even began to rehabilitate aspects of the old Prussian past that had no such leftist credentials.

Frederick the Great, formerly denounced under Ulbricht as a 'forerunner of Hitler', was thus restored to his old plinth on Unter den Linden, this time as 'Comrade Fritz' (Vesilind, 1982: 20). The urban planning of East Berlin thus began to pay slightly more attention to the restoration or reconstruction of historic buildings such as the Kronprinzenpalais and the German State Opera House and less to the socialist brutalism of wide streets, squares and industrial building techniques, not just to attract Western tourist revenue but also to try and root the tenets of Marxism-Leninism into the soil of cultural identity. Here, revised urban planning became the spatial counterpart to compulsory weekly classes in schools on socialist civics (Ardagh, 1995: 490). However, such a top-down approach to creating an official socialist state identity proved shallow when the moment of truth came in 1989. Ultimately backed up with Soviet tanks, Richie suggests that:

history became stale and lifeless; it had no relevance to people's lives – they
might have been happy to see the old familiar faces of Luther or Frederick ...
they might have been proud of the old Prussian palaces (but) for most people
that was as far as it went. The material was too sparse, the story too flimsy, to
make this sterile view of the past attractive or to create the sense of identity
which Honecker had tried so hard to create (Richie, 1999: 748).

A bottom-up identity had, however, emerged during the GDR years, based on
the common experience of living under the regime, especially after the reality of
Soviet tanks on the streets of East Berlin in June 1953 and on the streets of
Budapest in the summer of 1956. Ardagh refers to how 'the great majority had
come to terms with their destiny; they found life under Socialism grey and frustrat-
ing, but perfectly liveable and even with some advantages' (Ardagh, 1995: 368–9).
The corrosive activity of the Stasi notwithstanding, a degree of 'camaraderie' under
conditions of hardship, resembling that of British people during World War II, is
commonly acknowledged even by the severest critics of the regime, as people
inevitably 'looked for snatches of happiness away from the public domain'
(Maćków, 2001). A less materialistic outlook, social levelling, job security and
closer personal ties are aspects of the East German identity claimed by the PDS
(Hooper, 1999). Swept along in the drive by Kohl for speedy reunification in 1990
and enticed by the promise of a 'flowering landscape' in the East, with the latter
hope failing to materialize, bitter feelings among 'Ossies' leave Germany still a
divided country. The cries of 'we are one people' and 'Germany, one Fatherland' at
popular rallies in December 1989 (Ardagh, 1995: 428) for the present remain just
words. Habermas refers to an alienation in the East not entirely reducible to economic factors, of a hurt to self-esteem felt in the old GDR where in 1989–90 the
federal government relieved people in the East of meaningful participation in the
decision to go for rapid reunification. No refounding of the Federal Republic took
place with 'structural violence' done to the East where in the ex-GDR people did
not get a chance to engage in public discourse 'in their own home' (Habermas,
1996: 11–13). Likewise Günter Grass, a defeated advocate of gradualism, has
written scathingly of how the velvet revolution segued into what he portrays as
'colonial annexation' (Grass, 2000). In the words of one PDS politician:

After 50 years of completely different development, there was another culture
and this other culture is just not being recognised (Brie, quoted Hooper, 1999).

With the ruthless implantation of Western structures and values, Tamara Danz,
East Germany's most popular rock singer, expressed the frustration of many when
complaining that 'easterners have to apologise for breathing'. From rejoicing at the

fall of the Berlin Wall, Danz by the mid-1990s had turned her concerts into protests against the destruction of East German identity and the exclusion of easterners from the process of shaping the new Germany (Staunton, 1996). With the prospect raised of East Germany turning into a German Mezzogiorno, the combination of severe unemployment from industrial dislocation, the absence of rooted democratic traditions and lack of familiarity with foreigners under the previous regime has led to a search for identity by many in the intolerance and xenophobia of the extreme right, where the more sinister conceptions of German nationalism are evoked (Bonfante, 1998). At the other end of the political spectrum, with due recognition to the fact that the SPD and CDU account for the majority of votes cast in Eastern Germany, the reformed communist party, the PDS, with its roots in a disgraced regime, still remains a force to be reckoned with outside former West Germany. Polling 25% of the vote in former East Berlin in the 2002 federal government elections and over 22% of the vote in Berlin as a whole in city elections in 2001, the PDS at the beginning of 2002, 12 years after the fall of the Wall, found themselves back in power in Berlin's city hall as partners in government with the Social Democrats. That this 'Red-Red' coalition was presented by the parties involved as a symbol of the growing unity between the two parts of Germany and a breaking-down of the Wall in the head between the two parts of Berlin is undoubtedly political window-dressing (Fiedler, 2001). Opinion polls, admittedly before the empathy induced by floods in East Germany in 2002, suggest that westerners condemn the old GDR regime more than easterners (Steele, 2001). Resentment has its roots in West Germany in the brutal put-down by military force of a workers' revolt in East Berlin on 17 June 1953, subsequently commemorated annually by West Germans as the 'Day of German Unity'. With people in the East now ironically associated with the regime itself, resentment at the size of the fiscal transfer to the East amounting to 2000 million DM since 1990 (Maćków, 2001) spills into Western contempt, not reducible to budgetary arithmetic alone. Given that 2.7 million people had left the GDR between 1949 and the construction of the Wall in 1961, the acquiescence of the remainder had previously led westerners in a popular joke to rechristen the DDR as 'Der doofe Rest' (the dopey dregs) (Ardagh, 1995: 380). As to why this contempt has intensified, Steele has suggested that, now defunct, 'the GDR becomes a scapegoat on which blame for an earlier and much greater German failure can be piled' (Steele, 2001). By extension it can be suggested that the demonization and rejection of everything associated with the GDR intensifies identification with the capitalist victors in the Cold War. In one particularly scathing assessment of the GDR population, a recent writer in *Die Zeit* dismisses them as 'Soviet people' protected by West German financial transfers from 'the positive educational effects of the market' borne more directly by ex-communist regimes without a sympathetic big brother (Maćków, 2001). Meanwhile in Western Germany, which has bathed for a long time in the healing waters of consumer capitalism, identification has long been possible with the 'good guys' of history. Capitalist hegemony and national self-esteem in search of normality go hand in hand. Starting with the Berlin Airlift in 1948/49 and continuing through John F. Kennedy's famous 'Ich bin ein Berliner' speech in 1961, the West Germans, symbolized by Berliners in particular, stood in solidarity with the Allies and especially the Americans against the common enemy, communism. The presence of this demonized significant other enabled West Germans to relate to Americans 'no longer as enemies but as friends' as Berlin's mayor Reuter put it after the airlift in 1949 (quoted Christopher, 1994). This experience can be seen as formative in a reconstitution of post-World-War-II West German identity and cannot easily be shrugged off. If standing steadfast with the Allies against communist 'tyranny' provided some protection from 'an empty space of identity', there was no better symbolic representation of this than the Berlin Wall.

THE WALL

REPRESENTING THE WALL

Seldom in the history of urban planning can the spatial organization of a city have been so turned on its head as through the walling-in of West Berlin by the GDR military which began in the early hours of 13 August 1961. The subsequent fortification more than anything else represented for the population of the two German states their increasingly differing political, cultural and social experiences. Tearing gashes in the urban landscape and going through various phases of development from improvised barbed wire to the chilling technical perfection of surveillance, border fortifications of 155 km in length stretching 43 km through the city centre were masterminded by the architect and urban planner Ehrhardt Gisske. As Director General of Architecture and Building in East Berlin in the 1980s, Gisske described his working relationship with the head of the GDR state:

> It's very pleasant working with Comrade Honecker. We have a relationship of trust. The politburo always approves my plans.

The reasons for such trust are perhaps given in Gisske's autobiography:

> In the socialist planning world a director is an important and influential individual who is blessed with great ability: he processes the problems that come his way with cleverness and cunning to achieve great results. (These) can be judged in their complexity not by each individual but by the Government (Gisske, quoted Cowan, 1989).

The subsequent erection of 302 watchtowers, 22 bunkers, 127.5 kilometres of electrified fencing and 45 000 segments of actual wall, each weighing 2.75 tons (Flemming, 2000: 75), was represented by East Germany as an 'Anti-Fascist Protection Wall' necessary to head off Western invasion plans and attempts to undermine the building of the socialist state (Ardagh, 1995: 405) (Figure 3.1). The inscription on the memorial to the border guards killed in defending the Wall read: 'Your death is an obligation to us' (Sikorski and Laabs, 1997: 75). Such a representation was embarrassingly weak with the Berlin Wall forming the last segment in the building of the 'Iron Curtain' necessary to staunch the flow of refugees to the West.

In the West 'the wall of shame', as the Berlin Wall was frequently represented (Camphausen, 1999: 29), became the prime symbol of the division of Germany and of the Cold War itself. Here capitalism and communism attempted to face each other down. In a famous act of taunting defiance the publisher Axel C. Springer had received building permission to construct his new headquarters right next to the Wall between 1961 and 1966. This was answered with the erection, by the GDR, of apartment blocks on the other side of the Wall, blotting out the visual impact on East German citizens (Hampel and Friedrich, 1999: 71). In West Berlin, memorials to those shot while attempting to escape morally called to account the GDR depiction of the Wall. Most poignant here is the simple cross on Zimmerstrasse to Peter Fechter, who bled to death in agony on 17 August 1962 after almost making it to the West.

DEMOLISHING THE WALL

The main reason for the swift erasure of most of the Berlin Wall was the popular feeling that the symbol of division and even terror should disappear as soon as possible. Spontaneous demolitions began on the night of 9 November 1989, followed by millions of people from around the world who came to Berlin to chip off a piece of the Wall for themselves. Demolition had proceeded so rapidly that officials responsible for the protection of historic monuments could not keep pace (Trotnow, 1999: 11) and most of the Wall quickly ended up as aggregate for East German road-building. The capitalist West had triumphed, and with an outrageous lack of taste sections of the Wall were auctioned off in Monte Carlo in June 1990 as cold-war trophies to the illustrious and wealthy. The wife of an Italian publisher paid 27 000 DM for a Wall segment to put in the garden of her villa. A Zürich businessman invested in 11 segments. US Presidents and Cold-War warriors Ronald Reagan and George Bush each received their own piece of Wall (Flemming, 2000: 75). Axel Springer had a street named after him beside his headquarters, and only yards away the GDR monument to border guards was permanently removed from the Berlin memorial landscape.

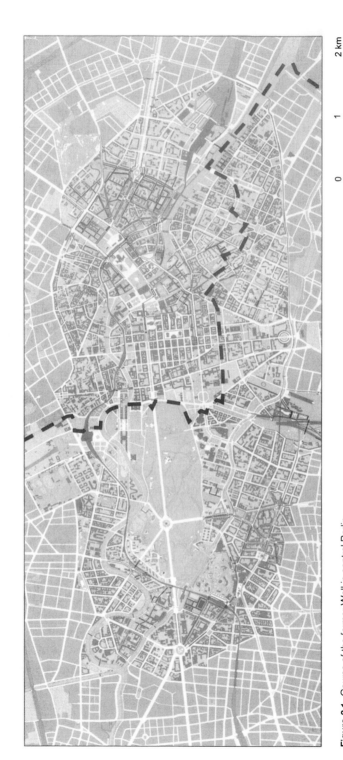

Figure 3.1 Course of the former Wall in central Berlin

0   1   2 km

REMEMBERING THE WALL

By 1995, six years after the 'Wende' (the 'turning' events of 1989/90), the Berlin Wall which had separated the city for decades had virtually disappeared. The notion that memory of the Wall should be built into the necessary urban-planning suturing of Berlin was promoted not only by Berlin's tourist industry, bemoaning the loss of the biggest attraction the city once possessed, but by the city of Berlin itself, concerned that the historical legacy of the Wall which had once split the world be treated in a contemplative way (Zander, 1995). On 14 June 1995 the Berlin Senate Department of Culture and Department of Building and Housing held a hearing to consider the question of 'memory and the Wall' (Senatsverwaltung für Bau-und Wohnungswesen, 1995). Prominent West Berlin urban planner Dieter Hoffman-Axthelm, closely associated with the master inner-city design plan for Berlin to be considered shortly, advocated that it would be enough to simply better signpost remaining Wall fragments (Zander, ibid.). East Berlin representatives expressed minimal interest in artistically marking the course of the Wall, holding the opinion that any such representations were likely to make the Wall 'tame' and would not do justice to how it made people feel. The majority view, however, coming from West Berliners, wanted some marking of the Wall route, to work against the forgetting of the oppression that the Wall symbolized (Nottmeyer, 1998). Two proposals in particular received a measure of cross-city consensus. A design by Gerwin Zohlens proposed to mark the course of the inner-city Wall with a 7-cm-wide copper band. The logic, according to the artist, was that 'copper connects', as in telecommunications cables, thus being counter-symbolic to the division represented by the former barrier (Zander, 1995). However, a second, more prosaic (and cheaper), proposal by Angela Bohnen, that the route of the Wall be marked out with a 7.5-kilometre double line of concrete cobblestones to remind viewers of the material of part of the Wall itself, was eventually implemented by the Berlin city government in time for the 9 November celebrations in 1999. The Senate Department of Building and Housing also sponsored an artistic design competition in 1996 for ideas on how to remember the seven border crossings in Berlin. The design brief asked participants to 'confront the topic of crossing in all its facets', recognizing that these locations had also, on 9 November 1989, been 'places of peacefully won freedom' (SBWV, 1996b: 5). A few of the designs have been realized. At the crossing point on Chausseestrasse, the artist Karla Sachse has sunk fist-sized brass rabbits into the pavement in a quirky reminder of the hundreds of rabbits that once populated the 'death strip'. At Checkpoint Charlie, symbol of the Allied military presence, the competitor Frank Thiel has designed a photo installation erected on a pole in the middle of the road, which has, back to back, a picture of a Russian soldier looking south along Friedrichstrasse and an American soldier looking north. Memory, however, does not come cheap. These two memory markings alone cost 360 000 DM.

The documentary film by Eric Black and Frauke Sandig (*After the Fall*, 2000) points to the speed with which the Wall was ripped from its foundations as an indication of an understandable if damaging desire to forget history. However, the fact that a complete removal of all authentic remains of the actual Wall was never achieved is due in part to citizen initiatives wanting to keep in memory evidence of this time as a warning to future generations. A 250-metre stretch of Wall thus remains along Niederkirchnerstrasse on the way from the former checkpoint to the Brandenburg Gate, owing to the campaigning work of an East Berlin citizens' action committee (Sorges, 1997: 21). The last remaining watchtower survives on Schlesische Strasse in Kreuzberg because of the direct action of a group of artists as memory workers who in 1990 persuaded guards to hand it over in order to preserve the memory of the stark division of the city. Subsequently the artists had to face down two attempts to raze the structure before successfully having it declared an historic monument, home to the work of artists who have lived under dictatorship (Museum der verbotenen Kunst, undated). By contrast, the raw material provided for memory by an almost exact and equally rare watchtower at Rüterberg, north-west of Berlin, speaks more of historical erasure. Painted pink and rebranded as the 'Pink Flamingo', enterprising entrepreneurs have created a holiday home where capitalists can now find repose in the sentinel outpost of a hard-line regime that once defied them (Hall, 2001). Indeed, the largest section of remaining Wall in Berlin, on Mühlenstrasse, the East Side Gallery, stretching over a kilometre in length, undoubtedly owes much of its survival to its tourist value, marketed as it is as the world's largest outdoor picture gallery. In 1990 over 100 artists had come to decorate it with their work. However, in 2002, even the famous kiss between Honecker and Brezhnev is fast fading as public interest wanes.

In one particular location in Berlin, proposals to preserve the memory of the Wall were met with hostile objections from former East Berliners. The stretch of Wall in Berlin Mitte along Bernauer Strasse was profoundly symbolic. Nowhere else had so many successful and desperate escapes to West Berlin been made. The erection of a border through the middle of an established residential street made the division of Germany palpably real. The picture of GDR soldier Conrad Schumann jumping over the barbed wire on Bernauer Strasse on 15 August 1961 has become an icon of the 20th century. On 28 January 1985 the image of the collapsing tower of a church on the death strip along Bernauer Strasse, blown up by the GDR to create a better field of fire, was seen throughout the world. Helmut Kohl commented the following month:

> This event is a 'symbol'. The demolition of the church shows us how long, how difficult and how uncertain the path before us is in order to overcome the division of Europe and the division of Germany (Kohl, quoted Fischer, 1999: 34).

Arguments against proposals by the united city of Berlin to memorialize in some way sections of Wall along Bernauer Strasse met with various objections, particularly from those who had lived on the wrong side of the Wall's shadow. The Berlin Wall Victims' Association, whose members include relations of more than 200 former East Germans shot dead trying to escape to the West, warned against presenting a Disneyland-style version of the Wall which did not convey the sense of threat that the death strip had evoked (Paterson, 1999). A common feeling among residents of the area was that, having been forced to live with the Wall for so long, it should be over with and all manifestations of separation obliterated. Moreover, other memories were involved. The Sophien Parish, whose church was dynamited and which had been forced to sell its cemetery grounds to the GDR, demanded the reinstatement of sacred ground. To this end in April 1997 direct action was taken by the district authority of Mitte supporting the Sophien Parish, with the removal of 32 segments of Wall in order to reclaim the graves underneath. Predictably, traffic planners had entered leaden-footed into the debate, wanting the expansion of Bernauer Strasse into a multi-lane relief road. After April 1997 the Wall on Bernauer Strasse existed as an original object of East–West German post-war history only in broken fragments (Camphausen, 1999: 19–21). A chronicler of the memory 'tussle' on Bernauer Strasse sees the demolition in April 1997 as a turning point, with more easterners realizing that evidence of their experience was in danger of being tipp-exed out of collective memory if not of history. On the symbolic 9 November of the same year, construction of a Berlin Wall memorial site sponsored by the federal government began on Bernauer Strasse, recognized as a focal point of international post-war political history. Taking the form of a 'mock-up' of the Berlin Wall around the cemetery of the Sophien Parish, the artistic design has been criticized for not being true to scale and for failing to recreate the terror of the Wall (Camphausen, 1999: 21). In 'memory battles', inevitably there is no one formula for correct commemoration. Heated debate took place over the inscription on a monument plaque unveiled on 13 August 1998. The plaque reads:

In memory of the division of the city from August 13, 1961 to November 9, 1989, and in remembrance of the victims of Communist tyranny.

A Berlin Wall Exhibition Centre and a small unpretentious chapel of clay and wood for reflection on the site of the demolished church, with the old altar retrieved and returned to its original location, complete 'The Wall Memorial Site Ensemble'. The most recent commemoration at this site is an indicator, however, of how East and West Germans are not unified in the sharing of common feelings about the Wall and what it represents. At a wreath-laying ceremony on 13 August 2001, to mark the 40th anniversary of the Wall's construction, representatives from the various parties made their visits at different times. Symbolic of the fact that a Wall continues to exist in people's heads, attempts by the Party of Democratic Socialism, the successors of the SED, to show grief over the hundreds of people shot by East German border guards were rebuffed on the basis that they had not said 'sorry' or made a meaningful statement on the most brutal symbol of their origins (Karacs, 2001; Steele 2001). Amidst scuffles and obscenities a wreath laid by the PDS was trampled on by members of a victims' group and flung into a dustbin. Two years previously, at the events to commemorate the 10th anniversary of the fall of the Wall on 9 November, PDS representatives had perhaps been understandably excluded but, as one commentator wrote at the time:

> the celebration has been brought close to a farce by the decision not to include a single leading East German civil rights leader or politician of the time, who have been virtually erased from the history books (Woodhead and Cleaver, 1999).

As expressed by Wolfgang Ullmann, Green MP and former East German human rights campaigner:

> The list of speakers betrays a complete lack of sensitivity and an extraordinary lack of historical awareness. Those who were imprisoned by the wall and then helped to bring it down should not be forgotten (Ullmann, quoted Patterson, 1999).

In similar vein, as put by another prominent Eastern critic of communism, the SPD politician Richard Schröder:

> It was the spadework done by the human rights activists that gave East Germans the courage to bring down the Wall. I sometimes think this historical fact is ignored by West Germans because they cannot take any credit for it (Schröder, ibid.).

EAST BERLIN ICONOGRAPHY: NO REQUIEM FOR FALLEN IDOLS

The fate of the urban iconography of a failed identity-building project has gone through various phases in Berlin since 'die Wende'. In a first phase, amidst the spontaneous removal of many smaller plaques and symbols, open *discussion* took place on what to do with larger artistic set pieces of socialist realism. With the failed putsch in the Soviet Union in August 1991, *demolition* moved to the fore-ground. After publication of a Berlin Senate commission report on the future of GDR political monuments in February 1993, some mobilization occurred around the *protection* of threatened public art works, especially the colossal Ernst Thäl-mann statue on Greifswalder Strasse in Prenzlauer Berg. Some measure of success was achieved by bringing the 50-ton Thälmann bust under the protection of the Berlin monuments office in 1996. Since then, like a Samson drained of its power, the former communist icon is mocked by graffiti artists and vandals who seem to be the only ones paying any attention amidst general indifference and other priorities (Figure 3.2).

DISCUSSION PHASE

By the summer of 1990 commemorative plaques and GDR symbols of various sorts had been removed, often by spontaneous local action. Stone and bronze backdrops bearing the inspirational words of Erich Honecker often disappeared, having been discreetly carried off by Bezirk park departments. In May 1990 East Germans no longer had to strain belief when Honecker's granite-etched words which had proclaimed 'The Berlin of today becomes ever more a symbol for the victory of socialism on German soil' (*Die Zeit*, 1990) were removed from Gendar-menmarkt. The hammer and divider, the state emblem of the GDR, would soon be removed from the entrance to the Palast der Republik, home to the people's chamber of this one-party socialist state. However, as one East Berlin building his-torian points out, despite some paint bombing in this early period there was no demolition or toppling of major set-piece memorial art works. The revolution had resulted in a change of power without violence (Elfert, 1993). Despite increasing calls in 1990, especially after currency union in July, for official demolition of various pieces of statuary including the 'usual suspects' of Marx, Engels and Lenin, there was no hasty removal 'in the interests of public interaction with history', as stated in a resolution by the council of Prenzlauer Berg in September 1990 (Elfert, ibid. 4–5). In August 1990, in an atmosphere of discussion, the art history depart-ments at the Humboldt, Free and Technical Universities combined to stage an exhi-bition entitled: 'Keep, Destroy, Change: Political Monuments of the GDR in East Berlin'. One reviewer for *Die Zeit* was unimpressed, referring to the display of 'false heroism of a dissembling state' (Berkholz, 1990). Following Berlin government elections in December 1990, the SPD/CDU coalition signalled its intention at some future date to deal with the issue by way of an expert committee. The gener-ally unloved relics were thus to remain drained of emotive power, awaiting their ulti-mate fate until events in Moscow in August 1991 energized them with renewed threat.

Figure 3.2 Ernst Thälmann, East Berlin, 2002

REMOVAL PHASE

The failed 'putsch' against Gorbachev sent Lenin monuments tumbling in places such as Riga, Tallin and Vilnius. In September 1991 the Bezirk of Friedrichshain, home to East Berlin's gigantic statue of Lenin, on the appropriately named Leninplatz solely designed for its occupant, recommended to the Berlin Senate that the Soviet idol be demolished. The Berlin Senator for Urban Development did not hesitate in accepting the invitation. Taking three months to disassemble at a cost of $\frac{1}{2}$ million DM, the removal of the Lenin statue, to be laid to rest in a gravel pit in Köpenick, was a popular 'happening event' (Gärtner, 1998). Following this, Leninplatz was innocuously renamed United Nations Square. The next offending GDR artistic monument to fall was an exalting memorial to a 'people's' paramilitary group which had helped to guard the Berlin Wall. A trio of the people's militia standing in solidarity with Kalashnikov in clenched hands was, as of December 1991, no longer to be tolerated in the people's park of Prenzlauer Berg. A resolution of the council, expressing identity with Germany as a whole, declared:

> The former fighting groups (Kampfgruppen) of the GDR were a paramilitary institution and as such an important instrument of the SED and its power apparatus. Their purpose and their duties were aimed exclusively against their own population. Their co-operation in the building and the guarding of the wall through our city and around our country ... must be ... acknowledged. The council of Prenzlauer Berg considers it unsupportable that such an organisation which served inhuman and undemocratic ends should continue to be represented by such a public monument (BW, Prenzlauer Berg, 1991).

In early 1992 the group was unceremoniously carted off in the back of a lorry and in May 1992 a Senate committee was finally established to make recommendations on the issue of such memorials more generally. In June 1992 the Berlin Chamber of Deputies, in setting the tone for this review, announced:

> Whenever a system of rule dissolves or is overthrown, the justification for its monuments — at least those which served to legitimise and foster its rule — no longer exists (quoted Calle, 1996: 7).

PROTECTION PHASE

The Berlin Senate's expert commission on the future of GDR monuments in East Berlin reported in February 1993. One member resigned, complaining that appointees were directly under the political control of the SPD and CDU

(Prenzlauer Berg, 1993: 23). However, such influence by the two leading parties on the sensitive issue of political art in the soon-to-become nation's capital is hardly surprising. More surprising perhaps in the recommendations of the commission are the large number of more innocuous, smaller-sized and further distant monuments that were put forward for retention. Statues saluting the contributions of ordinary building workers, GDR monuments to the victims of National Socialism, those condemning fascism and even the life-size bronze figures of Marx and Engels, side by side in the very centre of historical Berlin, were to be kept. Monuments in memory of border soldiers, the Spartacus movement and the November Revolution in Russia were to be removed. Most controversial was the recommendation to dismantle the huge bust and clenched fist of Ernst Thälmann, a prominent German communist politician of the Weimar years. In an exhibition by Prenzlauerberg museum in August 1993, close to the actual Thälmann statue, four positions were outlined on the fate of this latter-day GDR mega structure, completed only just before reunification. The SPD, the largest party in the Prenzlauerberg council with 31% of the electoral vote in 1992, recommended demolition and redesign of the whole area. For the CDU and FDP, with 16% of the Bezirk vote between them, this did not go far enough. Thälmann was to be removed and placed in a hall of shame alongside other sculptures of socialist realism. The preferred location was the site of the major Stasi detention and interrogation centre in Hohenschön-hausen, a place which under the GDR had no postal address and never appeared on any map. With cries of horror from the victims of the Hohenschönhausen centre that characters in the 'Honni-Horror-Picture-Show' should be remembered along-side the site of their suffering, the idea was a non-starter (Wiehler, 1992; Fischer 1993). With virtually no support in the Prenzlauerberg council chamber, unre-formed communists (KPD and DKP) desired the preservation of the Thälmann statue in its present form. This position differed from that of the PDS, successors to the SED, who argued for keeping the monument as an interim measure until a better form of artistic representation, which did not idolize Thälmann, could be found. Under the slogan of 'Justice for Thälmann', the PDS, with 25% electoral support in Prenzlauerberg, in one interpretation of history used to validate how public memory is shaped, pointed to the fact that the anti-fascist communist leader had been murdered by the Nazis in Buchenwald and to his famous speech in 1933 warning that 'those who vote Hindenburg vote Hitler and those who vote for Hitler vote for war' (PDS, 1993). Drawing on a differing interpretation of history to justify the erasure of Thälmann from any public memory is the view that in fact Thälmann helped bring Hitler to power. With derision for 'Ostalgia', in her recent book on Berlin, Richie refers to how Thälmann, as chairman of the German Communist Party between 1925 and 1933, rather than join with the moderate left, led a relent-less attack on the legitimate Weimar government:

In short, Thälmann was directly involved in bringing to power the very people who would destroy him. He is no German hero. The statue is not merely an ugly remnant of Soviet-German communism; it supports a deliberately doctored version of history and glorifies a man who helped to destroy the Weimar democracy (Richie, 1999: xliii).

In the event the Berlin Senate did not take the advice of its 'independent' commission concerning Thälmann and included the statue in 1996 in the city's list of protected monuments. In a worsening city fiscal situation, the sheer cost of removal was undoubtedly a factor. A contributing factor may also be the latent potential of the huge symbol to be invested with new meanings should dismantlers from the West arrive. In these circumstances, general Eastern indifference to the beached behemoth could turn to further anger over Western heavy-handedness and unfulfilled if unrealistic promises, as a unified German identity and sense of solidarity still remains out of reach. Meanwhile the Director of the Berlin State Monuments Office leaves us in no doubt that Thälmann is simply being tolerated with a stay of execution. In true Alice-in-Wonderland style she states:

> The monument list is not for eternity. The inclusion (of Thälmann) is only valid until a different decision has been made (Wolf, quoted *Berlin Kurier*, 1996).

Reclaiming by Naming

The Berlin Senate commission that reported in March 1994 on street-name issues left no doubt about the significance of place names for Berlin's identity, German self-identity and image abroad:

> A particularly sensitive element in the pattern of remembrance of a city are its street names ... They are part of the founding of tradition in a society. In contrast to the distance and commentary with which historical remembrance is treated in a museum, a street name will be seen generally as agreement. When you are dealing with prestigious parts of the city like the government area or historical city centre it may be presumed that inhabitants and visitors, not least state official visitors, will read the city names as a conscious testimony to the capital and the state (SVB, 1994: 4–5).

The GDR in its capital city had used naming as a prolific instrument of tradition-formation. This extended as far as distinguishing in official jargon 'democratic Berlin' (i.e. East Berlin) from the invented term 'Westberlin', written as a single word to portray a transitory and artificial phenomenon, a sentiment returned in the

use of naming to withhold legitimacy by the sign at Checkpoint Charlie: 'You are
now leaving the American Sector' (Friedrich, 1999: 17–18). By the beginning of
1998, no less than 250 streets in former East Berlin had either been named or
renamed (SBWV, 1998). To a large degree this had resulted from local action,
given the powers of street-naming residing at Bezirk level, although political pressure from above was also a factor (Paesler, 1998). Early casualties had been the
sweeping away of Ho-Chi-Minh-Straße and the restoration of Leninallee to Lands-
berger Allee. More controversial, and based on 'call-in' powers over naming residing with the city of Berlin, had been the early change in the heart of Berlin's
historical government quarter of Otto-Grotewohl-Straße back to Wilhelmstraße.
(An intermediate name of Toleranz-Strasse never caught on.) That the first president of the GDR should fail to be honoured in the future on what was once the
equivalent of Berlin's Downing Street is understandable. Resentment of the heavy-
handed nature of the name change, however, led to a 'demeaning row' with the
district of Mitte, contributing to the establishment in September 1993 of a commission by the Berlin Senate to examine and report on naming issues generally for the
centre of the united city and also where some especially prominent GDR heroes
and notables were concerned (SVB, 1994). With membership of the prominently
labelled 'independent' commission on street-naming agreed between the CDU and
SPD (SVB, 1994: 3) the Director of Urban Planning for the district of Mitte, the
locality most affected by the commission's recommendations, questioned the inclusive nature of the commission with even the CDU 'Ossi' mayor of Mitte at the time,
having difficulty, as she points out, with the central CDU party line on issues of
GDR 'heritage' (Laduch, 1998). Some recommendations, swiftly acted upon by the
Berlin Senate, could not have been in doubt. Clara-Zeitkin-Straße, running eastwards directly behind the Reichstag, has had the former name of Dorotheenstrasse
restored. At the heart of government, Clara Zeitkin, despite her acknowledged role
as a leading late-19th-century and early-20th-century campaigner for the legal and
social emancipation of women in Germany, has been deemed an unacceptable
public memory trace so close to the political soul of the nation. Because 'she saw
in Stalin's Soviet Union the political and social role model for Germany' she makes
way for the second wife of the Great Elector, a woman aristocrat who is associated in the view of the commission with the enduring Prussian values of tolerance
and duty and an 'exemplary cosmopolitanism' (SVB, 1994: 7). In fact the name
change had been a foregone conclusion with the personal intervention behind the
scenes of Chancellor Kohl himself (Paesler, 1998). Karl Liebknecht, a male
contemporary of Zeitkin, has been luckier. His name survives in central Berlin,
being closer to Alexanderplatz and not next door to the Brandenburg Gate. Rosa-
Luxemburg-Strasse and Karl-Marx-Allee likewise survive beyond Alexanderplatz.
Equally not in doubt was the restoration of the name 'Schlossplatz' to the area

surrounding the dynamited old city castle at the eastern end of Unter den Linden which, as Marx-Engels-Platz, had been the parade ground of East Germany. The commission, in restoring a name prominently associated with aristocracy and privilege, attempted to broaden the basis for the legitimacy of its decision by arguing that 'the renaming of Schloßplatz reminds us of the events of the revolution of 1848' (SVB, 1994: 15). Other casualties in the renaming deliberations of the commission have included the head of the GDR Council of State Wilhelm Pieck, whose street was restored to Torstrasse. The commission here 'took it as a principle that the second German democracy has no reason to honour politicians who contributed actively to the destruction of the first German democracy' (SVB, 1994: 5). Also at the suggestion of the commission, Georgi Dimitroff, associated with the forced Stalinization of Bulgaria, has disappeared from Berlin's streetscape. The Ernst Thälmann statue now stands bordered not by this GDR 'hero' but by the restored Danziger Straße, the result of a decision by the Berlin Senate in preference to the commission's suggestion that the opportunity be used to honour social-democratic politicians of the Weimar years whose memory had been distorted and ignored as a result of the GDR's 'playing politics with history' (SVB, 1994: ibid.). Going further along this line and strongly prefiguring urban design ideas for suturing Berlin together that emerged in the mid-1990s, the commission also suggested that street-naming in Berlin should stress strongly the 'common' German history of Weimar and, more broadly, names such as Hegel and Schinkel from a pre-1933 common intellectual and cultural history (SVB, 1994: ibid.).

URBAN DESIGN – PLANWERK INNENSTADT

On 18 May 1999, after an intense political debate lasting for three years, the Berlin Senate passed a resolution making an inner-city planning and design concept known as 'Planwerk Innenstadt', a standard to which the inner-city boroughs of Mitte, Friedrichshain, Kreuzberg, Schöneberg, Tiergarten and Charlottenburg are obliged to abide in partnership with the Berlin Senate itself. This 'standard' was endorsed by the Berlin House of Representatives on 27 May. Despite compromises along the way, this urban design framework, while not embedded in the presently legally binding Flächennutzungsplan for Berlin and the various local plans at Bezirk level (Bebauungspläne), forms a major reference point for future planning explicitly concerned with changing the identity and character of central Berlin. In the Planwerk Innenstadt the urban designer's pen is used on the grand scale to consciously erase and etch physical traces of memory into the built fabric of the city. In this exercise, both the place-identity of Berlin and the representation of German cultural identity have been at stake. In essence, in a project mobilized by Western politicians, architects and planners and where the lead has been taken by the SPD in

Berlin headed up especially by former Building Director Hans Stimmann and Senator for Urban Planning Peter Strieder, planning and design has been used as an instrument for reconnecting Berliners with a shared history from before 1933, when Berlin was a 'normal' and more classically beautiful city in the European tradition. While the Planwerk's 'identity areas' cover 30 million square metres stretching from Charlottenburg in the west to Friederichshain in the east, most of the designated planning zones are in former East Berlin and seek to tackle the legacy of socialist-modernist planning there. The first version of the plan, dating back to 1996 and meeting criticism especially from the eastern part of Berlin that it was an imposed, top-down, 'master plan' drawn up by westerners (Hain, 2001: 74), was to result in a process of legitimacy-building stretching over two years in the form of local workshops, exhibitions and discussion in the Berlin Stadtforum. The basic idea of the plan, however, has remained constant throughout. It is rooted in the design concept of 'critical reconstruction' much popularized by Hans Stimmann but dating in origin from the Berlin International Building Exhibition between 1979 and 1987. At this time Josef Paul Kleihues, Director of the IBA, a showcase for architects to build under the theme 'the inner city as a place to live', argued that modernism with its 'tabula rasa' approach to city development, denying that the city had evolved historically as a place of collective memory, was not enough. Development, Kleihues argued, should rather proceed in dialogue with history and tradition. Modernism was not rejected in favour of a liberated post-modernist architecture but rather on the basis of a return to critical engagement with centuries-old 'conventions developed for architecture and town planning that have universal character'. In this 'essentialism' the 'identity of the city ... is fatefully linked with the ground plan of that city', which could even be regarded as 'the permanent gene structure of the city' (Kleihues, 1990: 6–7). As Berlin Building Director, Hans Stimmann at an early stage after reunification had applied the concept of 'critical reconstruction' in an attempt to suture together both parts of a previously divided city. The concept left a significant mark on the redevelopment of Pariser Platz in particular beside the Brandenburg Gate, on Potsdamer Platz and on Friedrichstrasse. By privileging the urban ground plan and architectural principles of Berlin in the 19th and early 20th centuries, this limits the maximum permitted plot size to a city block. With reference to the Berlin Building Regulations of 1929, 'critical reconstruction' severely limits building eaves' heights to 22 metres. It favours mixed-use developments and requires that the historical street pattern of building lines and squares be respected or reconstructed (Stimmann, 1995). It is not without its fierce critics: one of the most famous modernist architects currently associated with Berlin, Daniel Libeskind, has described critical reconstruction as 'neo-fascist', with an approved cartel of architects building within a narrow Prussian tradition of simplicity and order and creating a stone-clad, cold new German capital that turns its back on unconforming but desirable architectural artistic despotism. Given the architectural diversity of the new Berlin this is perhaps an exaggeration, but the following comment by Libeskind in 1994 on the notion of 'critical reconstruction' around which the Planwerk Innenstadt was to be constructed alludes to an important point:

> Berlin doesn't stand for one history but for many, including the history of people who have been wiped out. This is a concerted attempt to write a revisionist history of the city in keeping with the new mood in Germany since reunification (Libeskind, quoted Staunton, 1994).

The Berlin Planwerk Innenstadt, the first draft of which was published in November 1996, while representing the more systematic application of critical reconstruction ideas writ large in central Berlin, has also been 'floated' as a planning concept supporting sustainable development in a more compact city. The proposed densification of socialist open spaces and excessively wide streets accommodating traffic has led to necessary compromises with the CDU, who were prepared to sacrifice, to a greater degree, 'the historic city' for a car-based city. However, the Planwerk remains something not far removed from a 'blueprint' for the place-identity of the historic core of Berlin and a representation of a presentable German cultural identity in stone. In identity and memory terms, the aspirations of the Planwerk are on the grandest of scales. Some selected extracts from the objectives make this clear:

• The Inner-City Plan is an attempt (at the) appropriation of the city through civic dialogue to reformulate Berlin's identity (SSUT, 1997: 78)
• No historical phase should be denied ... The aims are ... to pick up the thread of historical continuity and rediscover the historical plan of the city (ibid. 79)
• The Planwerk should not 'deny the city as a cultural form which has evolved historically and as a place of collective memory' (ibid. 79)
• The Planwerk is guided by 'dialogue with the features of place and memory ... not a rupture with history and tradition' (ibid. 79)
• The Planwerk should seek 'reinforcement of an identity which is typical of Berlin and of a European city' (ibid. 79)
• The Planwerk should 'be seen as an attempt to "take on board" the collected knowledge of the departing century, in other words without neglecting any of this experience' (SSUT, 1999: 185).

In essence and in some cases in quite painstaking detail the spirit of the historic ground plan of Berlin pre-1933 (Figure 3.3) will 'hover over' and guide changes in

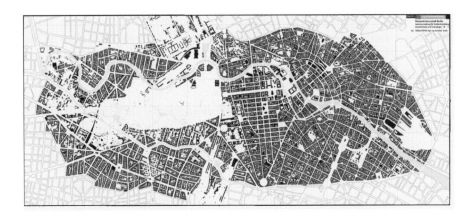

Figure 3.3 Central Berlin around 1940

the built environment in eight major designated areas for the foreseeable future. Rooted back to this street plan, densification will be based on selling off much publicly-owned land to developers who will be expected to build on small plots conforming to the appearance of Berlin as a city in the early years of the 20th century. This cannot fail to evoke some sympathy. In Berlin Mitte, for example, the GDR in the complete obliteration of Gertraudenstraße by an eight-lane road, had at a stroke, erased the origins of Berlin in the medieval heart of the settlement of Cölln (Bodenschatz, 1998: 18) (Figure 3.4). One aspect of returning to a common German past, however, proved a step too far for Peter Strieder, the SPD Senator for Urban Planning. In early versions of the Planwerk the critical reconstruction in the area centred on Karl-Marx-Allee had referred to the zone as 'Königstadt' (King's City). In deference to Germany's firm republican identity this is now banished from the final document (SSUT, 1999: 70–1).

Over the three years of public discussion of the Planwerk, criticism from East Berliners was considerable. The Director of Urban Planning for the borough of Mitte expressed the view in 1998 that the design plan represented taking 'a western steam-roller' to the history of the GDR:

> The Planwerk denies the epoch of East Germans. It does not respect East
> Berliners' identity. We should not pretend that forty years of history did not
> happen. Likewise Mitte is being merged as a borough with Tiergarten and
> Kreuzberg not just because of administrative efficiencies but to dilute the power
> of the PDS on the doorstep of the new federal Chancellery (Laduch, 1998).

Another East Berlin urban planner and member of the Berlin Monuments Preservation Committee has recently gone as far as to call the Planwerk Innenstadt

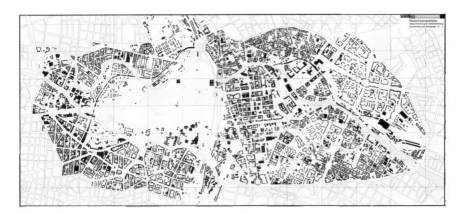

Figure 3.4 Central Berlin around 1989

'a declaration of war' against the east of the city (Hain, 2001). A Western capitalist colonization of the East is identified, based on the cheap selling-off of communal public space dressed up in the language of densification and sustainable development. Wealthy Western consumers are to be attracted to the new centre to underpin commercial development already there and to add cosmopolitan flair not provided by less affluent easterners. Especially aggravating for Eastern planners and architects has been the fact that the design team developing the Planwerk for East Berlin (and led by Dieter Hoffmann-Axthelm from the West) did not include a single Eastern built-environment professional (Hain, 2001: 77). While the final plan is based, in deference to Eastern sensibilities, on minimal demolition, the disrespect and even contempt shown for Eastern design traditions has rankled, adding to the frustration at the difficulties of having Eastern views on the development of East Berlin taken seriously and of being able to find outlets in a Western-dominated city administration (Hain, 2001: 74). While architects and planners associated with the dissolved Construction Academy of the GDR may well feel piqued at their marginalization from the development of the new Berlin, of more importance is the point driven home by Hain that behind the Planwerk is a victorious and divisive attitude towards the East, implicitly asking and answering the question: 'who *did* actually win the Cold War, you or us?' (Hain, 2001: 81). With much justification Hain argues:

> This plan (Planwerk) is based on a concept of history which sees the post-war historical period as abnormal, a-historical and ultimately destructive. It thus, in symbolic fashion, ignores forty years of an urban double existence – which was after all of major historical and international importance. Whenever reference is made to Berlin's identity, apart from the roots of the bourgeois city in the last century, it is always in terms of the former Western city at the forefront of the

Cold War, with its former shop window function, which the city acquired in the confrontation between the two rival systems. Rather, it could well be the urban design and socio-spatial legacies of those decades which we now ought to recognise and through monuments conservation policy pass on to future generations as opposing symbols of the social systems they represented (Hain, 2001: 80–1).

That the memory of Berlin's global importance in the post-war era should be preserved rather than swept away in aesthetic suture is a strong argument on its own. It attains additional force when the very notion of a founding, historic, city ground plan is called into question. The Berlin ground plan, Bodenschatz argues in reply to the Planwerk, has always been 'a patchwork' of different building eras whose modernization, with inevitable historical erasure, urban planners were arguing for in a rapidly developing city over a hundred years ago (Bodenschatz, 1998: 16–18). Because of serious city budgetary difficulties and peripheral residential pressure in Berlin's 'Speckgürtel' (literally, suburban 'fat belt') competing with the attractions of being a Western urban settler colonizing the prairies of the East, implementation of the Planwerk Innenstadt has been slow. Work currently proceeds on the narrowing of Leipzigerstraße (Figure 3.5). However, a plan resulting from a supposedly 'dialogic' consultation process with East Berliners but which many deem to have been in bad faith, remains in existence. Planwerk has the end goal of reinstating the 'normal city beautiful of history' in preference to more discordant spatial testimony to 20th century ruptures in the urban fabric. Leaving the evidence of the latter is perhaps more likely to induce critical reflection than comforting aesthetic pleasure. Nowhere are these conflicting tensions more intense than in the decade-long debate, now coming to a head, over what to do with Berlin's 'Palast der Republik'.

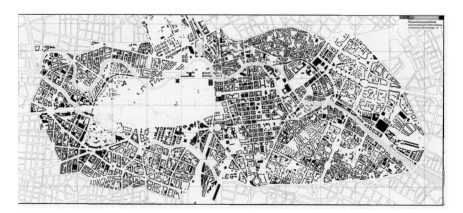

Figure 3.5 Central Berlin proposed in 'Planwerk Innenstadt' around 2010

THE PALAST STORY

As one commentator has pointed out, 'urban planning and the Planwerk Innenstadt have been circling the central area of the GDR state buildings between the television tower and the Palast der Republik as if it were a mined area' (Hartung, 2001). There are good reasons for this. Above all this is hallowed ground, a place of German historical self-understanding. The Palast der Republik occupies part of the site of the old Hohenzollern Schloss, restorable despite war damage but, nevertheless, dynamited by the GDR government in the early 1950s (Figure 3.6). To understand the debate over the future of the present Palast a grasp of the symbolic and design significance of the old Schloss is crucial.

It is argued by one architectural commentator that the demolition of the Berlin Stadtschloss and surrounding buildings in the 1950s ripped the heart out of old Berlin. The Stadtschloss, in particular, was uniquely identified with Berlin with the oldest wing of the building actually predating the city itself and added to by its occupants over many centuries (Siedler, 1991). A leading Berlin architectural historian refers to the view held in some quarters that 'without a Schloss, history has no heart' (Engel, 1992). The former Schloss has been identified with German nationhood itself. Without this building, a *Die Welt* editorial has argued that the 'symbolic centre of Germany' is missing (Guratzsch, 1996). The Schloss, as one

Königliches Schloß mit Schloßbrücke

Figure 3.6 Berliner Stadtschloss circa 1910

commentator in *Der Spiegel* has argued, was 'architecture that could move the heart' (Matussek, 1998) or, as Germany's Chancellor has put it, the Schloss 'gave something to the soul of the people' (Schröder, 1999).

In more straightforward urban design terms the Schloss was important for a number of reasons. First, the Berlin Schloss with its incremental construction was a map of Prussian architecture. It reached from the Renaissance, including Baroque, up to Classicism (Siedler, 1991: 87). Second, the Schloss is said to tie together the diverse architectural styles of surrounding buildings:

> The real function of the Schloss's architecture was that its existence could hold together something so diversified – the baroque power of the Arsenal, the English tamed Rococo of the Opera, the simple Palladianism of the Palais of Prince Heinrich and the pure lines of Schinkel's classicism (Siedler, 1991: 94).

Third, and most important, the entrance to the Schloss not only provided an end point to the boulevard of Unter den Linden but it was from the Schloss that all buildings in this historic centre of Berlin took their point of reference. The Altes Museum in particular, by Berlin's most famous architect, Karl Friedrich Schinkel, still looks onto the space of the former Schloss garden, known as the Lustgarten since the mid-17th century. Remove the Schloss, however, and the whole setting for Schinkel's redesigned 19th-century ensemble has been destroyed. German parades up Unter den Linden, celebrating reunification, end not with the imposing mass of the Stadtschloss but in a crooked street and the new Palast der Republik, which ignores the traditional urban design principles for this key area of Berlin public space (Guratzsch, 1996; Siedler, 1991). As one *Berliner Zeitung* journalist has pithily put it: 'The Schloss is not everything but without the Schloss everything is nothing' (Mönninger, quoted Matussek, 1998). This brutal historical erasure was a quite deliberate and symbolic act by the former GDR regime.

THE 'PALAST DER REPUBLIK'

The demolition and removal between 1950 and 1951 of the old Stadtschloss to make room for what was eventually to be the Palast der Republik was charged with symbolism. Disregarding worldwide protests and disagreement within the East from a citizens' movement, including Bertolt Brecht, the GDR government under the leadership of Walter Ulbricht issued the following statement in 1950:

> The centre of our capital, the Lustgarten and the area of the Schloss ruins, must become a large space of demonstration on which our people's will to fight and rebuild can find expression (quoted Engel, 1992: 9).

Rejecting the Schloss as a symbol of the old Germany, an empty parade ground aping Red Square in Moscow dominated both the centre of Berlin Mitte and the political centre of the GDR until work began on the new Palast der Republik over 20 years later. At the topping-out ceremony for the Palast in 1974, Erich Honecker, remembering that the Schlossplatz was the starting point for the 1848 revolt in Berlin, again endowed the site with meaning and claimed it in the name of a different German identity:

> The Palast der Republik will be a house of the people, a place of vibrant political and cultural life. This house stands on historic ground. Here Karl Liebknecht declared the socialist republic in November 1918. Here sailors of the People's Navy fought against the reaction. Here the revolutionary workers of Berlin declared their loyalty to the young Soviet power. Here Ernst Thälmann spoke to the proletariat of Berlin and from here he pleaded for the creation of a broad anti-fascist action (quoted Engel, 1992: 7–9).

When the Palast der Republik opened in 1976 at a cost of 1.2 billion Ostmark, it joined a new Foreign Ministry Building and Staatsratsgebäude (Council of State Building, office of the Chair of the SED) to define three sides of Marx-Engels-Platz (Figure 3.7). The ensemble, totally ignoring any reference to traditional Berlin street lines and to the architecture of what had gone before, endeavoured, with a socialist version of modernist architecture, to create a political heart and identity for the GDR state. The urban design would 'express in architecture and volume the victory of the socialist society and its superiority over previous epochs in social development' (SED Fifth Convention, 1958, quoted Engel, 1992: 28). The only reference to the demolished Stadtschloss was in the Staatsratsgebäude, where the main entrance incorporated the Schloss Portal IV from which Karl Liebknecht had declared a 'Free Socialist Republic' on 9 November 1918.

However, no building is so closely linked to the history of the GDR as the Palast der Republik (Figures 3.8 and 3.9). Clad in white marble sheets and bronze-coloured mirror glass, the five-storey, massive, box-like building is 180 metres long, 90 metres wide and 32 metres high. Described as a child of its time, perhaps no worse or better than many modernist buildings of the 1960s and 1970s (Thurn und Taxis, 1995), the Palast der Republik was home to the Volkskammer (People's Chamber) of the GDR, with a plenary hall seating almost 800 people and a multifunctional congress hall with seats for 5000. More important, though, to the way the building was used by East Berliners is the fact that the five grand foyers in the building led to or were home to 13 restaurants and cafés, two discos, several galleries, a bowling alley and a theatre. With typical Berliner 'Schnodderigkeit' ('lip'), combining a certain irreverence and yet genuine affection for the building, East

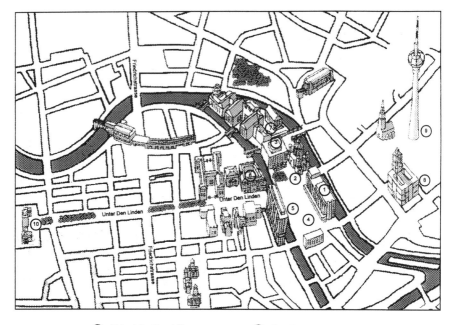

①	Palast der Republik	⑥	Zeughaus
②	Berliner Dom	⑦	Museumsinsel
③	Altes Museum	⑧	Rotes Rathaus
④	Staatsratsgebäude	⑨	Fernsehturm
⑤	DDR Foreign Ministry (now demolished)	⑩	Brandenburger Tor

Figure 3.7 Location of the Palast der Republik

Berliners linguistically appropriated the Palast and identified with it through the nickname of 'Erich's Lampenladen' (Erich's lamp shop). In the Palast der Republik, East Berliners and East Germans could forget plastic imitations and bask in the comfort of real leather chairs, surrounded by real wood and the lighting fixtures that were unavailable to buy in their own shops. Described as a place of escape from omnipresent bareness (Thurn and Taxis, 1995), people held weddings, birthday parties and other celebrations in the Palast. The Palast was, therefore, not simply the home of a rubber-stamp parliament and the symbol of a regime from which ordinary East Berliners felt isolated. A site for various social encounters, the building, as indicated by the nickname of Erich's lamp shop, elicited other 'readings' by people, according to their experience of it.

Figure 3.8 Berlin's Palast der Republik, 1997

WHAT TO DO WITH THE PALAST?

Four general positions on the future of the Palast der Republik have been put forward with various intensities since reunification: keeping the Palast, rebuilding the old Schloss (the position in political favour in 2002), erecting a new building and some hybrid solution. Attention will now be directed to who has been advocating each particular option, on what grounds, and against whom the argument has been made.

Attention is turned first to the position, now a forlorn hope, of those who advocated clean-up and **restoration of the Palast**. A focus for such opinion was provided in 1993 by the formation of a campaigning group calling itself the Spreeinsel Initiative. The catalyst for this had been the decision to demolish the Palast by the Berlin-Bonn Joint Committee set up to oversee the move of the federal government to Berlin. The excuse given had been the not inconsiderable problem posed by the 720 tons of sprayed asbestos contained in the Palast der Republik. That this, however, seemed an excuse was bolstered by the fact that the International Congress Centre in West Berlin was cleared of asbestos (albeit of the sheet rather than sprayed variety) in the early 1990s without much fuss (Neill, 1997: 186). Rather, the strong suspicion was created that the wreckers' ball

1950/51	Demolition and removal of the old Berlin Stadtschloss by the GDR to make way for a parade ground.
1976	Opening of the Palast der Republik partially occupying the site of the former Schloss. Home of the 'rubber stamp' People's Chamber of the GDR, the building was more importantly popular as a social gathering place with East Berliners.
1993	Formation of an Eastern campaigning group 'Spreeinsel Initiative' to thwart plans to demolish the Palast der Republik.
1993, summer	With sponsorship from Partner für Berlin a giant painted canvas of the Schloss is erected at the end of Unter den Linden rekindling a vision of what a return to this lost architecture would look like. A campaigning group led by Wilhelm von Boddien, called Förderverein Berliner Stadtschloss, takes up the cause of the Schloss as the central point of identity for the city of Berlin.
August 1994	Bernd Niebuhr a young German architect wins an international design competition for the Palast der Republik site with a modern building but the proposal fails to fire the imagination.
November 1996– January 1997	The Berlin newspaper *Der Tagespiegel* organizes a contest of ideas from over 20 architects to encourage reflection on the Schlossplatz and to lift it 'into the conscience' of Germans (Zimmermann, 1997). The entry of Norman Foster along with some other entries proposes an interim use with the avoidance of any hasty decision. Giant umbrellas, for example, on the space would enable sporting and other events to take place in the meantime.
September 1997	Prince of Wales' Urban Design Task Force convenes in Berlin to explore design solutions for the Schlossplatz. Keynote address by W.J.V. Neill stresses the importance of acknowledging the memory of the GDR on the site. The Task Force report emphasizes the baroque and medieval core of the city, the 'reintroduction of a tighter urban grain' and a new building with a dome echoing the presence of the Schloss (Thompson, 1997: 57). When a royal task force confronts a site where the equivalent of Buckingham Palace was blown up by communists the erasure of the Palast der Republik could hardly have been in doubt!
November 1998	Work begins on removing asbestos from the Palast der Republik. The building looks a sorry site in a desertified urban landscape.
February 1999	Chancellor Gerhard Schröder makes statements in favour of rebuilding the Berlin Schloss calling the Palast der Republik an aesthetic 'monster' (interview *Die Zeit*, 4 February).
September 2000	Following a storm of protest over Schröder's views a federal commission of 'wise men' is eventually appointed to deliberate and advise on the future of the Schlossplatz area.
April 2002	The International Expert Commission, chaired by the MEP, Hannes Swoboda, former chair of the Vienna Council's building committee, reports. The report recommends that the Schlossplatz be given a new identity with scientific and artistic usages, involving the partial restoration of the old Schloss all of which implies demolition of the Palast der Republik.
4 July 2002	The German Bundestag by a vote of 384 to 133 endorses the thrust of the Swoboda report. Unhappy with the decision Berlin's mayor Klaus Wowereit comments that if Germany wants a castle, the city cannot be expected to pay for it.

Figure 3.9 The Stadtschloss/Palast der Republik controversy: a chronology

would be used for ideological reasons. Although, for example, there has never been a simple party-political split on retention or demolition, both the CDU mayor of Berlin (Eberhard Diepgen) and Chancellor Kohl went on record in the mid-1990s as privately favouring the demolition option (Wiedemann, 1996). A leading role in the Spreeinsel Initiative was taken, until his death in 1995, by the major architect associated with the building of the Palast, Heinz Graffunder. Support among council members in Berlin Mitte for retention came not just from members of the PDS but from many who lived through the GDR regime across the new political spectrum. By April 1994, 38 000 petition signatures had been collected by the Spreeinsel Initiative and delivered to Bonn (Spreeinsel Initiative, 1994) and by mid-1995 no fewer than 52 demonstrations had taken place outside the Palast, demanding its retention (*Berliner Zeitung*, 1995). In August 2000, a decade after reunification, almost 50% of East Berliners still wanted the retention of the Palast – by then a miserable visual spectacle stripped to its innards for the removal of asbestos (Rauterberg, 2000) (Figure 3.10). In 1996, prominent names in the German architecture and urban-planning professions had lent their names to a petition objecting to any possible hidden political demolition strategy for the Palast. The signatories included the President of the Berlin Chamber of Architects, the President of the Union of German Architects and Engineers, the Chairman of the BDA (Bund Deutscher Architekten) and the Chairman of the Union of German Town and Country Planners (Vereinigung der Stadt-und Landesplaner Deutschlands).

Figure 3.10 Palast der Republik with Schloss excavations in the foreground, 2002

Among East Berliners the essence of the objection to the removal of the Palast der Republik revolved around the perceived demolition for political reasons of the most significant GDR building in Berlin Mitte. The strong suspicion lingers that, in the manner of a land annexation with the tentacles of the Planwerk extending into the symbolic core, the West wishes to rid the city of the memory of the GDR and to establish new functions and meanings as if the GDR had never existed (Flierl, 1994). This, it is argued, is insensitive to the meaning invested in the built environment by easterners, and to the built environment's role in the acknowledging of experience out of which identity is formed. As Brian Ladd has expressed it in his book *The Ghosts of Berlin*, the campaign for the Palast der Republik 'became an emblem for a fight to vindicate their former lives' (Ladd, 1997: 59). On top of this, an aesthetic-cleanliness mentality (ästhetische Sauberkeitsmentalität), whereby the city is sutured together with a unifying aesthetic such as critical reconstruction, can be regarded as a denial of history, leading to a less authentic city. Drawing on such arguments, Berlin Mitte, before its merger with Tiergarten and Kreuzberg, endeavoured to have the Palast der Republik declared a listed building. A building which for many in West Berlin symbolizes the wilful destruction of their city is for many in the East still a symbol of something softer. Not a Stasi building and not carrying the same baggage of political contamination as the summarily demolished GDR Foreign Ministry Building, which also stood on Marx-Engels-Platz, the Palast, while home to a rubber-stamp parliament, was also part of the everyday lives and spatial practices of many East Berliners for 15 years. However, while the separate identity of East Germans and East Berliners may eventually fade, a stronger reason to keep the Palast der Republik exists. While many have tried to make the Palast debate an aesthetic one, including Alexandra Richie in her recent book on Berlin when she states that 'the question of what to do with the Palast der Republik is an aesthetic problem rather than a political one' (Richie, 1999: xlii), this is so obviously untrue. More convincing is the argument by one recent writer for *Die Zeit* that a half-century of history simply cannot be undone with a return to an innocent 'before'. Germans cannot all 'meet again in the very far past with the erasure of all separating uncomfortable history' (Rauterberg, 2000). World events in a century of extremes reverberated on Schlossplatz, which more particularly as far as Germans are concerned calls into question their historical self-location. An alternative, albeit a flawed one, to capitalism once existed. To keep these facts in mind ought not to brand protagonists for the Palast as unreconstructed leftists as one writer for *Der Spiegel* has suggested, and nor need it convey the sentiment that an 'aesthetic monstrosity' should be borne by Germans as if they deserved masochistic memory work to expunge past guilt (Matussek, 1998).

Attention is turned, second, to those who wish to see the **rebuilding of the**

former Stadtschloss, former preserve of the electors of Brandenburg, kings of Prussia and finally emperors of Germany. An option along these lines, endorsed by the German Bundestag in July 2002, is popular among West Berliners and is usually articulated alongside the proposal to rebuild Schinkel's Building Academy (Bauakademie) on the site of the now-demolished Foreign Ministry Building. Supported by the Trust for Prussian Cultural Heritage (Stiftung Preussischer Kulturbesitz), the Berlin Historical Society (Die Gesellschaft Historisches Berlin) and a specially formed Förderverein Berliner Stadtschloss (Spreeinsel Initiative, 1994), this view finds most political support within the CDU, where Chancellor Kohl was rumoured to be in favour. In 1999 Chancellor Schröder caused controversy by aligning with this position because, as he put it, the Schloss was a 'beautiful building' (*Die Zeit*, 1999). This sentiment was not far out of line with opinion in the German Bundestag in mid-2000, where with the exception of the PDS, all parties were in favour of some sort of rebuilding (Rauterberg, 2000). Josef Paul Kleihues, father of 'critical reconstruction', leans in favour of a design solution based around some form of restoration of the historical Schlossplatz (Kleihues, 1998). In the summer of 1993 and with support from the city promotional agency Partner für Berlin, advocates of this alternative, to win Berliners over to the idea and to attract tourists, erected a giant façade of the Stadtschloss painted on canvas at the end of Unter den Linden. While arguments drawing on design rationales and the need to suture together a torn urban building fabric have been mobilized in support of rebuilding the old Schloss, the proponents of this position must realize that what is at stake is the meaning of the space for Berlin and for Germany as a whole. The space, which is the historical centre of Berlin and now the centre of Germany's capital city, necessarily raises the question of how to symbolize what Berlin and the state itself aspires to be. Here the desire to put aside reflection over more recent history in order to return to an older and more comforting German and Berlin past is prominent among those leaning towards some form of Schloss reconstruction. The rallying cry of the crusading Förderverein Berliner Stadtschloss, led by former Partner für Berlin Director, Wilhelm von Boddien, is urban pride in the fact that 'the castle was not situated in Berlin – Berlin was the castle' (Boddien, 1998). While the new Berlin Republic has expressed itself in political symbols around the Reichstag there are many who doubt that this is enough to express a sense of national self-understanding and act as a symbol of an imagined cultural community to which loyalty can be given. The right-leaning German newspaper *Die Welt* has called for a rebuilding of the Stadtschloss because 'at the symbolic centre of Germany a building is needed which represents the will of the German people to be a nation' (Guratzsch, 1996). The *Frankfurter Allgemeine Zeitung* has gone as far as to say that rebuilding the Schloss would be like a 'homecoming': 'it would be a signal to be able to return to German history' (*FAZ*, quoted Rauterberg, 2000). The Berlin

CDU Senator for Building in 1997 pulled together many of the threads of those leaning towards reconstruction, carrying in his omissions the stark reminder that rebuilding to remember can also be an act of forgetting:

Unter den Linden is the street with the greatest significance as regards city history and urban planning and it must again become an image-bearer ... The Stadtschloss belongs to Berlin's historical 'Mitte'. Whatever is built there, it is of great importance in the urban planning scheme. It will crown the Pariser Platz and Unter den Linden and must restore to the city centre its central point of reference. Particularly in the case of the Stadtschloss we must be conscious that the task involves an ensemble of European rank ...

Overall, regarding the design of Berlin Mitte it can be said: if we want to give it an identity, in the new reunited capital city, we must base this identity on the roots of our shared history. Not only German history but also European history. This also applies to urban planning. However, it must also be in the common awareness that there was a unified Germany in a shared Europe and a common development line before the division of our country (Klemann, 1997).

This is in step with Hans Stimmann, popularizer of critical reconstruction, who in relation to the Schlossplatz has expressed the opinion that 'the issue is national consciousness and nothing more than the normalisation of a European city centre' (quoted Rauterberg, 2000). Taking this a stage further, the Schloss has been recommended to the German people in the influential *Der Spiegel* as 'an electrifying appeal to pride and tradition'. East and West rebuilding the Schloss together would represent a 'common endeavour of national dignity in the rebuilding of a jewel' (Matussek, 1998). The new Schloss before long would be accepted by people as an original. Berlin would be prettier but at the cost of historical amnesia in the public realm and an invocation of a comforting memory time line of a city of the imagination which never existed.

Perhaps because a **new building** would raise the difficult question of appropriate symbolism on such an historic and meaning-impregnated site, no new building plan has been able to capture public imagination or overcome the legacy of the Stadtschloss or the existing built reality of the Palast der Republik. A DM 4.5-million international urban design competition for the part of the Spreeinsel containing the Palast der Republik, and sponsored by the Berlin Senate and the federal government, took place between August 1993 and August 1994. The ground rules that energized the countervailing Spreeinsel Initiative included the demolition of the Palast der Republik and the re-establishment of the structure of the old city ground plan. In the winning entry, by the young German architect Bernd Niebuhr, the Palast der Republik made room for a colossal new Stadthaus (Civic Centre), which was to incorporate a library, media centre, conference centre and exhibition rooms. With a large, internal, oval atrium and nicknamed 'the egg', the concept was stillborn because of federal budget problems and has failed in any case to ignite extensive popular support (Reinsch, 1994). An entry by the German architect Oswald Mathias Ungers was placed fourth even after challenging the rules of the competition and suggesting retention of the Palast der Republik:

> It is irresponsible to demolish such an important building in which reunification was decided and in which thousands of people got married (Ungers, quoted Reinsch, 1994).

In general, however, the idea of a completely new building on the site was one embraced by flag-bearers of modernist architecture, to whom the proposal to rebuild the Schloss was taken as a throwing-down of the gauntlet in an affront to their creativity (Matussek, 1998).

From 1996/1997 support grew for a fourth possible **hybrid** 'way out' of the Schlossplatz impasse. In 1996 the joint Bonn-Berlin committee dealing with the matter, headed by Berlin's mayor and the federal building minister, envisaged keeping the GDR Volkskammer, which would be integrated into any future architectural redesign of the space (Schweitzer, 1997). A plan of use for any new or restored building would involve a conference centre, hotel, library, shops and restaurants but such a commercial trivialization, perhaps indicating desperation over how to deal with the knots of German history entangled here, led to derisive descriptions by the President of the Berlin Chamber of Architects as 'capable of formulation by any Tom, Dick or Harry ("jeder Fritze") on the back of an envelope' (Hertling, quoted Wiedemann, 1996). Between 1997 and 2000 another international design competition, favoured by former federal building minister Töpfer, has, some would say mercifully, been passed over in favour of the appointment by the federal government of a Schlossplatz commission of 'wise men' to ponder and report on the situation. Asbestos removal commenced on the Palast der Republik in 1998 and recently Dieter Hoffmann-Axthelm, author of the Planwerk Innenstadt, proposed 'the retention of the Palast der Republik *at least in parts* (italics added) and ... a part reconstruction of the former Schloss' (Hoffmann-Axthelm, 2001: 68).

ENDGAME: REPORT OF THE INTERNATIONAL EXPERT COMMISSION ON THE HISTORICAL BERLIN CENTRE

The appointment by the federal government in September 2000 of an 'international' commission to consider the future of the Schlossplatz site firmly moved debate from Berlin to a national stage. In what was a penultimate step before a political decision was taken by the German Bundestag in July 2002, the prospects for retention and restoration of the Palast der Republik now look hopeless and any hybrid incorporation of the Palast into a future structure seems unlikely. The context in Berlin is a situation where, in an opinion poll conducted in August 2001 by the newspaper *Die Welt*, given a choice between a reconstructed Schloss and the Palast der Republik, 58% of Berliners voted for the former, with 36%, presumably made up of Eastern voters, still favouring the Palast. Little support existed for a modern building on the site (Boddien, 2001). What was particularly noticeable in the composition of the 17-member Schloss Commission, despite its heterogeneous inclusion of numerous architects and politicians, representative notables from the arts and history, some businessmen and three foreign participants (from America, Zurich and Vienna) was the relative absence of East Berlin voices. One notable exception was that of Bruno Flierl, a leading voice in the early-1990s Spreeinsel Initiative to save the Palast der Republik and since late 2001 Berlin's new PDS Senator for Culture and Sciences (Stache, 2000). The Commission has recommended that the Schlossplatz be reclaimed by way of use in the name of culture and science, which in itself will give the place 'a new identity'. A 'Humboldt Forum' will be established that will house important collections of non-European art and cultural artefacts now in the possession of the Foundation for Prussian Cultural Heritage, combined with important world-renowned collections concerning the history of science presently owned by the Humboldt University. The centre of Germany will be associated with art, science and learning of the highest order. As Peter-Klaus Schuster, manager of German State Museums, has put it, the site would become 'a visual place showing the inheritance of world culture, a place of the mind and the humane' (quoted Hartung, 2001). There is good historical precedent for this. The old National Gallery (Alte Nationalgalerie), reopened in late 2001 after refurbishment, sits just across the road from Schlossplatz, along with other famous museums including the Pergamon clustered on this part of Spreeinsel. This museum, as the dedication on the front beam signals ('To German Art 1871') (Figure 3.11), was marshalled to legitimize in high culture the unification of the German nation under Bismarck. As put by one historian of the Alte Nationalgalerie:

> The general humanist educational concept expressed in the Alte Nationalgalerie by Humboldt and Schinkel was moved in the direction of a deliberate patriotic politics of art (Lepik, 2000: 81).

Much has happened since 1871. While liberal Enlightenment ideals are worth defending more than ever, the question has to be asked if the Schlossplatz proposal is an act of cultural normalization, and whether something should not be

Figure 3.11 Alte Nationalgalerie, 2002

added to the *genius loci* of this place which brings to memory what we need to learn from more recent 20th century history. This is surely a place for doubt and with it possibility, not assertion.

The Schlossplatz Commission report recognizes the unavoidable in stating that 'the founding identity (of Schlossplatz) is not just about use but doubtless also about the built form' (Swoboda, 2002: 4):

> The architectural design of the Schlossplatz has to take into account the special historical and architectural importance of the place and fit into the existing urban area. This demand according to the consensus of the committee was not fulfilled by the Palast der Republik. There was largely agreement that the new building in the Platz would have to take its orientation from the structure and image of the former Berliner Schloss so that the existing vacuum is filled and the historical connection especially to the ensemble, Unter den Linden and Lustgarten is recreated. The majority vote of the Commission favours the reconstruction of the baroque facades to the NW and South ... (Berlin) needs a coming to life of its history and a built remembrance of one of the most important baroque buildings of northern Europe (Swoboda, 2002: 4–5).

The proposed building concept, while not ruling out some hybrid-type inclusion of parts of the Palast der Republik including the Volkskammer with its 'historical symbolism' (Swoboda, 2002: 44), was not regarded as compelling by a minority of commissioners. Three members, including Bruno Flierl and Peter Conradi, President of the German Architectural Chamber and member of the Bundestag, saw 'no compelling urban design reasons to demolish the Palast der Republik', with Flierl commenting independently that 'demolition and keeping of the Palast der Republik is not primarily a question of urban design', thereby implying that it was in fact a 'political and ideological decision' (Swoboda, 2002: 33). As one commentator on the deliberations of the Commission has observed:

> Even though architects were very much involved, the row over the Schloss was not an architectural debate. If it had been it would have been decided long ago (Hartung, 2001).

CHAPTER 4

PLACE-MAKING AND THE FAILURE OF MULTICULTURALISM IN THE AFRICAN AMERICAN CITY

'Can't Forget the Motor City...'
Martha Reeves and the Vandellas,
'Dancing in the Street' (1964)

Detroit is arguably the most important urban crucible in which African American identity will be forged in the 21st century. The prospect looms of a black homeland for African Americans who have given up on the possibility of integration with wider society. This chapter explores the degree to which African American cultural-identity conceptions have, in the last quarter-century, influenced the approach to 'place-making' in the largest black metropolis of the United States. More narrowly, the focus is on the physical aspects of city development falling within the commonly accepted purview of urban planners, even if such constricting professional horizons are presently subject to critique (Healey, 1999: 119). The relationship of planners in Detroit to the spatial constitution of identity under Mayor Coleman Young (1974–93) is contrasted with that under Detroit's second black mayor, Dennis Archer (1994–2002). In the face of prevailing racism and economic evacuation of the city Young felt pushed towards a more separatist conception of African American identity. This conception was also spatial and necessarily impinged on the horizons of planners working for the city. Under Archer, African American identity was presented in more integrationist terms. With the departure of Archer from office in 2002 this ship has now sailed. The interpretation of how the planning agenda has been shaped in Detroit by questions of black identity, and of what this says about how planners take their professional cues from forces over which they have limited control, is based on interviews with planners and policy makers conducted in South-east Michigan in the summers of 1999 and 2001. The interpretation is also seasoned by previous employment as an urban planner working for the State of Michigan in the 1970s and 1980s. Based in the State Office of Community Development this work concerned, in the main, policy matters pertaining to Detroit and the region. To some extent the interpretation presented is an attempt to make sense of why, for the most part, planners seem to stand impotent in the face of, or are accused of being implicated in the construction of, urban problems, which in the case of Detroit border on the catastrophic. The chapter proceeds by way of an initial discussion of the currently in-vogue concept of 'place-making' followed by a brief review of the wider regional economic and racial reality within

which and against which the shaping of the place that is the city of Detroit continues to struggle. For the most part, as far as Detroit is concerned, these are
forces not of place-making but of place-destruction. An overview of 'identity positions' and debates within African Americanism and the relationship of this to spatiality is then considered, to better illuminate the differing place-making and
urban-planning approaches of Coleman Young and Dennis Archer and the identity
tensions with which they were confronted, which they embodied and which remain
unresolved. Here Detroit sends out a warning about what can happen in a context
of unbridled sprawl where multicultural difference has little common civic identity in
which to ground itself. Creating 'place' by planners in such circumstances can be
but an impoverished affair.

PLACE-MAKING

The concept of 'place-making' is a useful one in capturing a sense of the local
importance of place to people and the constrained but still potentially significant
local pro-activity that can be mobilized in the face of the impersonal flows of global
economic networks (Castells, 1997: ch. 1). With an emphasis on the embeddedness of localized life-worlds, 'where we come from', place-making involves the
double-faceted quality of the development of a consciousness of place among
local stakeholders, going beyond outward competitive place-marketing in the
global economy to an inward-looking concern with local identity and a feeling of
belonging (Healey, 1997: 62). Bearing in mind the need not to fetishize place but
to see place-construction as a social process (Harvey, 1996: 320), and with due
acknowledgement of the fact that people in places are increasingly part of various
'relational webs' extending beyond the local confines of space, nevertheless, three
broad and overlapping aspects of city place-making can be identified. Local 'stakeholders' may feel various degrees of material, civic and cultural embeddedness and
well-being in place. The first of these involves the functional city of jobs and services extending to environmental well-being. It is strongly influenced by economic
positioning and social class. Civic identification and the feeling of stakeholding
involves expressions of 'pride in place' and has a relationship to how local place-
making decisions are made. Such processes can entail varying degrees of fairness,
equality and inclusiveness. Cultural attachment to place goes beyond the city as a
container or 'theatre' for social activity. It involves an emotionally charged spatial
imagination extending from the personal to various collective manifestations,
including spiritual and symbolic identifications. This often involves the endowment
of space with deep meaning (Lefebvre, 1991). In any 'reading' of Detroit it is difficult to avoid the conclusion that racial-identity issues have impregnated material,

civic and cultural aspects of place-making, including physical development and area-based concerns traditionally central to the urban planning profession. An understanding of this, without which it is impossible to make sense of what passes for urban planning in Detroit and its region, is best approached through a brief socio-economic profile of Detroit and of recent theorizing, in general terms, on African American identity.

RACIAL AND ECONOMIC EVACUATION: DETROIT – A BRIEF PROFILE

In the space of 50 years the city of Detroit has traded the positive sobriquets of 'Arsenal of Democracy', 'All-American City' and 'the Motor City' for more recent, negative, labels including 'Titanic City' (Rusk, 1993), 'Pariah City' (Neill, 1995), 'City in Freefall' (Boyle, 2000) and 'Broken City' (*Detroit Free Press*, 2001). Dramatic decline is measurable against a broad range of indicators. The population of the 139 square miles of the city of Detroit peaked at approaching 2 million people in the mid 1950s, falling to under one million in the year 2000. Meanwhile the African American population of the city has increased from 16% to over 80% but in a context where the city's population has now fallen to less than 25% of the core regional total (Figures 4.1 and 4.2). Since both New York and Chicago have larger

	Tri-County 'Core' Region	Remaining SEMCOG* Counties	City of Detroit	City as % of Tri-County Region
1930	2,177,343	204,852	1,568,662	72
1940	2,377,329	236,515	1,623,452	68
1950	3,016,197	328,596	1,849,568	61
1960	3,762,360	418,994	1,670,144	44
1970	4,199,931	532,460	1,514,063	36
1980	4,043,633	638,498	1,203,339	30
1990	3,912,679	677,789	1,027,974	26
2000	4,043,467	790,026	951,270	24

* The counties comprising the South-east Michigan Council of Goverments consist of the core counties of Wayne, Oakland and Macomb in addition to Monroe, Washtenaw, Livingston and St Clair.

Figure 4.1 Population change in South-east Michigan, 1930–2000

Source: US Census Bureau

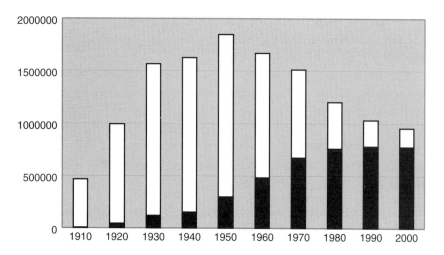

Figure 4.2 African American population, City of Detroit, 1910–2000

black populations, of over 2 million and nearly 1.5 million respectively (Earle, 2000: 130), it is thus not so much the total number of African Americans living in the city of Detroit that underlies the city's claim, in the words of one of its congressmen to be 'the black capital of the United States' (Crockett, quoted Chafets, 1991: 121). It is rather that in Detroit African Americans are more overwhelmingly in charge than in any other major US city.

However, political power has not translated into economic viability in an American institutional context of strong home-rule local government where *in situ* tax-based revenue is vital to the provision of basic city services. At the height of the American economic boom at the end of the millennium, poverty and unemployment in the city of Detroit remained high in absolute terms and especially in relation to their levels in the surrounding suburbs (Farley *et al.*, 2000: 250). Recent research funded by the Ford and Russell Sage Foundations concluded that Detroit's retail and wholesale trade sectors 'remain almost non-existent' (ibid. 250–1). Manufacturing employment linked to the auto industry still marks the Detroit region out as one of the most prosperous in the United States, but with a couple of hard-fought-for exceptions (the General Motors Poletown plant and the Daimler-Chrysler Jefferson plant on Detroit's East Side) new manufacturing investment has taken place in the Detroit suburbs dubbed 'the birthplace' of 'Edge City' (Garreau, 1993). In 2001, the two northern suburbs of Troy and Southfield taken together had double the office space of the city of Detroit in newer buildings with a much lower vacancy rate (Blacks Guide, 2001). General Motors, while recently having moved its world headquarters to the Renaissance Center on Detroit's waterfront, has left vacant its previous premises in Detroit's 'New Center' area, with the city's hopes for a service-jobs revival hinging on the decision of the Compuware computer firm to relocate its headquarters from the suburbs to Detroit's beleaguered central business district (CBD). Meanwhile, much of the city of Detroit, in the midst of regional prosperity, resembles a desolate and abandoned landscape that perhaps even Michael Harrington would have regarded as extreme (Harrington, 1962). However, it is not so much economic decline that singles Detroit out as unique among major US central cities, but rather the degree of metropolitan racial segregation. Only Greater Atlanta competes with Detroit for the distinction of being the most perfect 'urban doughnut': black in the de-industrialized centre, lily-white on the job-rich periphery (Davis, 1993: 17), such that the residential racial separation in Greater Detroit has been referred to as 'hypersegregation' (Massey and Denton, 1993: 76). In the light of the year-2000 US census confirmation of continuing spatial apartheid in the nation's most segregated region, the *Detroit Free Press* in an editorial spoke with a sense of foreboding:

> More than anywhere else in the nation, black and white children in metro Detroit walk different streets, live in separate neighbourhoods, attend different schools … In this region, most black and white children live in areas that are 90% their own race (*DFP*, 2001).

With Detroit's black middle class moving to major suburbs such as Southfield, which is, according to the 2000 census, 54% African American, longer-term integration with middle-class whites is not assured. Research shows that whites start packing when blacks make up more than 20% of the neighbourhood and Southfield, 32% black in the 1990 census, is expected to be 75% black by 2010 (*DFP*, 2001). Recent survey data from the 1990s indicates continuing white distrust of blacks and black distrust of whites, with many Detroit-area whites still holding negative black stereotypes. Detroit-area employers can be reluctant to hire black workers and whites generally do not want to live with more than token numbers of black neighbours (Farley *et al.*, 2000: 248). The perpetuation of racism through former stark discriminatory practices in Detroit's automobile factories and union movement has been the subject of considerable research (e.g. Meier and Rudwick, 1979; Geórgakas and Surkin, 1975; Babson, 1986), as has been the active role of spatial practices and the complicity of planners in creating and protecting difference and privilege. Within the city of Detroit, until the building of freeways from the 1950s onwards, the use of outright violence and racial intimidation, restrictive covenants on properties, and racist codes of practice by realtors kept blacks largely restricted to the crowded 'Paradise Valley' area on Detroit's Lower East Side. As whites moved to the suburbs, taking advantage of a federally subsidized suburbanization dynamic involving the building of freeways and stoking the furnace of post-war economic growth (Neill, 1986), blacks were able to move into previously white neighbourhoods. The memory of Paradise Valley still lingers, however, with black Detroiters having harboured resentment that this freeway construction had cut disproportionately through black neighbourhoods (Farley et al., 2000: ch. 6; Sugrue, 1996: ch. 2). In the developing Detroit suburbs of the post-war era, suburban officials conspired with realtors to convey the message that blacks were unwelcome and nowhere more so than in Dearborn, headquarters of the Ford Motor Company (Farley, 2000: 156). Planning and zoning in the United States is well known in such matters as being used to serve local interests to the detriment of broader interests (Krumholz, 2001). In Detroit's suburbs, for example, the involvement of planners in large-plot-size exclusionary zoning, thus keeping out lower-income groups, has been well documented (SEMCOG, 1976; Davidoff and Brooks, 1976). Today, partially propelled by the desire for racial separation and segregation and with only modest population growth, the Detroit ex-urban fringe sprawls further outwards onto greenfield sites in a scattered low-density form at the rate of ten thousand acres per year (SEMCOG, 1994, 1999) (Figure 4.3).

At this stage, before considering the relationship between feelings of racial identity and place-making in the city of Detroit under black political control, it is useful to consider some general aspects of African American identity debates and expressions in the United States. The voices of Detroit blacks are part of this wider cultural conversation.

AFRICAN AMERICAN IDENTITY AND SPATIALITY IN THE UNITED STATES

The starting point for any consideration of cultural self-understanding among African Americans in the United States must be an acknowledgement of the plurality of possible 'identity positions', albeit mediated to a white audience (including academics) through the writings of public black intellectuals. There is not just 'one way to be black' (Awkward, 1995: 10) and, as pointed out by Henry Louis Gates Jr, 'the facts of race don't exhaust anybody's human complexity' (Gates, 1997: 43). The same might be said for, say, Ulster Unionists, or any other ethnic group for that matter. In the words of the Michael Jackson song, and extending to bodily presentation in rejecting any essentialist notion of race: 'I'm not going to spend/My life being a colour' (quoted Awkward, 1995: 185). In the 2000 US census a full 8% of young blacks chose a multiracial characterization of their ethnic identity as opposed to only 2% of blacks over 50 (Sullivan, 2001). Certainly the organic experience of racial solidarity that existed in the 1960s, when '(Martin Luther) King had his day at the Lincoln Memorial', has passed (Gates, 1997: 50). A class divi-

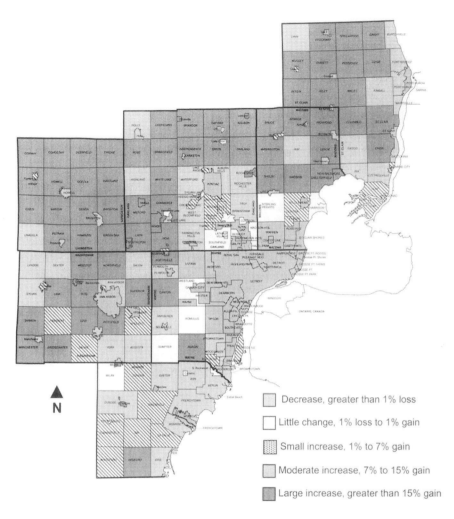

A N

☐ Decrease, greater than 1% loss

☐ Little change, 1% loss to 1% gain

▦ Small increase, 1% to 7% gain

☐ Moderate increase, 7% to 15% gain

■ Large increase, greater than 15% gain

Figure 4.3 Population change in South-east Michigan, 1990–8

sion in particular has opened up between the largest black middle class in United States history (which has benefited from affirmative-action policies now in retreat) co-existing alongside a large black underclass where 45% of all children are born at, or below, the poverty line (Gates and West, 1997: ix–xii). A bond, if tinged with guilt on the part of middle-class blacks, still exists between these two groups because, as one Detroit African American academic points out, 'racism is not destroyed through higher class location or enhanced social status' (Dyson, 1997: 186). The glass ceilings (limited promotions) and golden cuffs (big position and good pay with little or no power) remain in place for most blacks in corporate America (West, 1997: 110). Amidst a generally successful multiracial experiment in America with high rates of ethnic intermarriage, the intermarriage rate for black women with males from another ethnic group is still only 13%. This has led to a conclusion on the part of white liberal opinion that America has less a race problem than a 'caste problem': it contains a group of once enslaved people, segregated and isolated with seemingly entrenched systemic and historical aliena-tion (Glazer, 1997: 158). Likewise a notable intervention in the US 'race debate' from an African American perspective also sees blacks as conveniently fulfilling for whites the role of 'a subordinate caste'. They provide a comforting status floor below which white people cannot fall (Hacker, 1992: 217). Acknowledging the dangers of essentialist thinking in seeking the immutable essence 'of black culture' (Dyson, 1997: 87) rather than emphasizing its continually evolving and socially constructed nature (Awkward, 1995: 175), it is, nevertheless, difficult not to put the very spatial matter of the existential pain associated with rupture from place at the heart of African American identity ruminations and constructions. A collective memory exists of a people extracted from their homeland by force, brought to the United States in chains and renamed as property. This is a reality articulated in the novel *Beloved*, by the African American Nobel-Prize winning writer Toni Morrison. It reflects a sensibility where concern for place-making, in a deep sense, is central. As expressed by Cornell West speaking of Morrison's work:

> The search for black space (home), black place (roots) and black face (name) is
> a flight from the visceral effects of white supremacy (West, 1997: 88).

In relation to the legacy of slavery it can be strongly argued that certain back-ground unifying cultural reactions exist within the African American population. Here Dyson refers to 'the irreverent spirit of resistance that washes over black culture', related to the strong suspicions blacks possess of unqualified loyalty to a country where they were brought in chains (Dyson, 1997: 158–60). Beyond this, but still seeking to generalize about black American identity positions, it is difficult to escape the 'hoary old assimilationist/separatist divide' within African American culture (Gates, 1997: 36) and the different relationships to place that this entails. The assimilationist/integrationist camp, while encompassing a broad spectrum of opinion including that of black conservatives who argue that blacks should abandon a 'victim-focused identity' (Steele, 1991: 170), is most closely associated with the public faces of Colin Powell, current US Defence Secretary, and the Rev-erend Jesse Jackson. It traces its lineage back through Martin Luther King to the integrationist writings of W.E.B. Du Bois in the early 20th century (Gates, 1997: 33–4). Whereas Powell has been linked to black desires to 'transcend race' (Dyson, 1997: 154), something accomplished for a time by O.J. Simpson before his trial revealing the racial fissure running through the United States, Jackson is associated with a hybrid black identity recognizing African and American roots and feeling no need to suppress its particularity (Dyson, 1997: 193). It is an African American identity committed to overcoming racism and to the achievement of greater social equality through the building of a 'Rainbow Coalition' with others while maintaining historical cultural differences alongside a common civic identity (Castells, 1997: 59).

On the other side of the 'hoary divide', while the most public face of 'separatism' is that of Louis Farrakhan, this general stance again covers a broad swathe of identity positions which are united, nevertheless, by a belief in the necessity of group uplift associated with an 'accommodation' with white society involving group-imposed cultural and even spatial separation. It is a view tracing its lineage back through Malcolm X to Elijah Muhammad of the Black Muslim movement and the earlier 20th-century writings of Booker T. Washington (Gates, 1997: 33–4). It is a view also incorporating in a loose sense various Afrocentric identity positions which argue that Eurocentric culture has been imposed on black people in the US and that Africa should be the dominant cultural and spatial reference point for African Americans, lest black identity be lost through integration into dominant white culture (e.g. Asante, 1988, 1998). While from this standpoint the Black Muslim identity espoused by Louis Farrakhan can be criticized as not Afrocentric enough, the contrasting of Farrakhan and Powell by one African American Detroit writer as 'symbols of the divided mind of black America' (Dyson, 1997: 154) seems to go to the heart of black identity tensions inherent in place-making in the city of Detroit. The following question recently posed by the same writer cries out for an answer in the streets of Detroit:

> With the recent emergence of Colin Powell and Louis Farrakhan as credible
> black leaders, the nagging question of what route black folk should take into the
> next century – one of separation, or one of solidarity with other Americans –
> has renewed itself with foreboding intensity (Dyson, ibid. 149).

Prior to an exploration of this crossroads as it affects place tensions in Detroit it is worth considering more generally assimilationist and separatist black orientations to place.

RACE AND PLACE

Relationships to place are part of multidimensional cultural processes that invoke collective memory in the quest for cultural identity. How groups remember and contend in various ways in the marketplaces of power and culture where collective wills and interpretations can be in collision is a central issue in the study of historical memory (Blight, 1994: 52). Black identity in such contention is constructed

Phrase

and carried through various 'vehicles'. The rhythms and idioms of black language are crucial means by which blacks shape their social identities, with Black English described by one writer as the syntax [*structure*] of black survival (Dyson, 1997: 227). This fuses with 'body language' and clothing where it has been observed that black culture is a 'body-centered culture' (Dyson, 1997: 87). African American writers have questioned American national symbols such as the Statue of Liberty and Ellis Island by confronting them with the history of slavery and segregation (Sollors, 1994: 111). The naming or renaming of people (Malcolm X) and places (Malcolm X Boulevard, Marcus Garvey Park in Harlem) can map out bearings in space and time (O'Meally and Fabre, 1994: 10). Jazz, the blues and gospel music attest to the important place of music in African American identity, with the latter musical form fusing with the social institution of the black church, 'the visible womb of black culture' (Dyson, 1997: 85). Latterly Awkward refers to how Morrison has identified 'the Afro-American novel's destiny to replace the celebrated forms of Black expressivity (blues, jazz, spirituals and folktales) as a primary locus for pre- [*area where something*] serving and transmitting African-American cultural wisdom' (Awkward, 1995: 137). The reason given by Morrison is that 'we don't live in places where we can hear those stories anymore...' (Morrison, quoted Awkward: ibid. 137–8). This relationship of culture to place as the setting for events or as the locus for certain 'lieux de mémoire' (sites of memory) varies along a black assimilationist/separatist continuum. The term 'lieux de mémoire' usefully refers to landmarks of the past where 'memory crystallises and secretes itself' and invests persons, dates, events, artwork and so forth with particular symbolic meaning (Nora, 1994: 284) and in relation to place evokes the notion of Lefebvre's 'representational landscapes' of deep symbolic meaning (Lefebvre, 1991).

Even among African Americans leaning more towards assimilationist and integrationist positions and thus putting a greater premium on 'shared places' including residential integration, there is still an appreciation of the fact that collective memory and identity is held together by the confidence derived from association (Blight, 1994: 52). Here Maya Angelou, acclaimed African American novelist and civil rights worker with Martin Luther King, writes of the importance of black places to black security and identity in her childhood:

> In the evenings on the way home (from school) the sensations were joy, anticipation and relief at the first sign which said BARBECUE or DO DROP INN or HOME COOKING or at the first brown faces on the streets. I recognised that I was again in my country (Angelou, 1984: 209).

With such 'local lifeworlds' breaking down in general terms in the face of less bounded relation-building processes or relational webs in which we live our lives and create meaning (Healey, 1997: ch. 2), separatist African American positions nevertheless continue to lay great stress on the power to be derived from place relationships and association, albeit sometimes in the knowledge that just the appeal to the impractical realities of separatism from white America creates black solidarity and self-identity in itself (Dyson, 1997: 153). While many gradations of separatist feeling exist, four strands in such black identity articulations can be identified, having as they do place-making resonances in the city of Detroit. First, an Afrocentric Black Nationalist position argues that blacks in the United States are part of a more general North and South American diaspora. Africa's New-World descendants are seen as both placeless and misplaced. Africa is looked to as the major spatial referent and centre of blacks' existential reality, being as it is an ancestral home (Asante, 1998: x). In the words of one of the leading proponents of the 'Afrocentric idea', 'we exist in a borrowed space' where African Americans need a 'place to stand' (Asante, 1998: 8–13). Rejecting Eurocentrism, which is imposed, it is argued, on a multi-ethnic American society, such a view turns away from Greece and Rome, the reference points for the European world. Major representational spaces become Thebes in Africa and the sacred ground of Jamestown in the United States, where black slaves first came ashore (Asante, 1988: 4). Black concentration in places such as Harlem and Watts at 'both ends of America' is celebrated (Asante, 1988: 119), lest blacks succumb to being a lost people, 'zombies in the midst of stone and steel cities of the Americas' (Asante, 1988: 106). While Afrocentrism has been criticized for historical distortions in its quest to construct mythical pasts and imagined homes (Walker, 2001), its appeal nevertheless extends to liberal African American intellectuals such as Henry Louis Gates Jr seeking black roots in a homeland of Nubia among the ancient people of the Nile (Christy, 1999). This is seen as helping blacks in America ('neo-Nubians') take their place as cultural equals in a pluralistic, multicultural society.

From an Afrocentric standpoint other culturally separatist projects are seen as not Africa-centred enough. The anti-integrationist Black Muslim movement now headed by Louis Farrakhan is criticized for its submissiveness to the religion of Arabs (Asante, 1988: 2–3). Within the Nation of Islam tradition the separatist thrust was pithily communicated in place terms by Malcolm X in his autobiography when he commented: 'We didn't land on Plymouth Rock, my brothers and sisters – Plymouth Rock landed on us!' (Malcolm X, quoted Sollors, 1994: 110). From an Afrocentric perspective, black Christian churches espousing culturally separatist views and going under the label of 'Shrines of the Black Madonna' are regarded as transitional affairs on the road to true Afrocentric consciousness but, nevertheless, welcome departures from the powerful Baptist and Methodist black mainstream voice with which all pretenders to black power must still reckon (Asante, 1988: 71–8). A fourth 'black voice' articulating feelings of hostility towards wider

American society is wrapped up in what Cornell West has referred to as 'the bat-
tered identities rampant in black America where nihilism pervades black communities leading to a self-destructive disposition' (West, 1993: 13–14). Voices from 'the
street', often deemed in popular culture 'the repository of all that is real, that is
"black"' (Gates, 1997: 21), here speak in the intimidating language of the gangsta-
rap genre of hip-hop, albeit for the moment attenuated among major artists since
the events of 11 September 2001 (Lynskey, 2002). With white kids adopting the
dress, diction and menacing demeanour of urban black youth (Dyson, 1997:
113–16), is a voice rooted in a hunger for identity, meaning and self-worth but
which white suburban America is keen to contain. Nowhere is the crossover to
white culture so notorious as in the form of white Detroit performer in the 'gangsta
rap' tradition, 'Eminem'. Wielding a chainsaw and wearing a hockey mask, with
lyrics such as: 'I think I was put here to annoy the world and destroy your four-year-
old boy or girl...', Eminem has not been endearing to white Detroit suburbanites
(Harlow, 2001). He is the demonized identity of 'the other' come home and calling
out for exorcism and separation and acting as a lightning rod for a racism that was
also to see the downfall of US Senate leader Trent Lott in late 2002 after expressing sympathy for racial segregationist views (Watson and Monaghan, 2002). The
remainder of this chapter now explores the tension between assimilationist and
separatist leanings in place-making in the city of Detroit under black political
leadership, how this has structured the 'action frame' of planners and how planners
have reacted. What emerges in the overall story is less a cadre of experts and professionals mediating the construction of place on anything like an open and equitable basis and more a group of local state functionaries severely constrained and
dictated to by the politics of race and class. In relation to these powerful social
forces and their devastating effect on regional social cohesion, planners sometimes have become a scapegoat.

PLACE-MAKING IN DETROIT UNDER MAYOR COLEMAN YOUNG 1974–94

That Detroit's City Council building was recently renamed in honour of former
Mayor Coleman A. Young, who died in 1997, is hardly surprising. As Detroit's first
black mayor, elected in 1973 and serving for 20 years, Coleman Young in many
African American eyes became the very personification of the place that is the city
of Detroit (Figure 4.4). On his death the *Detroit News* described him as 'a torch of
hope and an ember of lingering anger' for a generation of black Detroiters
(Hodgson, 1997). When Diana Ross sang at his three-day inaugural celebration in
January 1974 there was no doubt that blacks now felt they were in charge and had

Figure 4.4 The personification of a city: Detroit's Mayor Coleman Young, 1989

elected one of their own, and looked to him for a new sense of material, civic and cultural stakeholding in Detroit (Rich, 1989: 104–5). Described by one writer as a 'Messiah Mayor' and 'racial champion' (Thomas, 1997: 149), Young, a former union organizer with a tough line in macho street talk, was a product of Detroit's segregated 'Black Bottom' and 'Paradise Valley' districts on the city's Lower East Side. In the aftermath of the 1967 'urban rebellion' in Detroit, when black frustration and resentment was sparked into violent revolt by the actions of the overwhelmingly white Detroit Police Department, the defeat by Young in the race for mayor in 1973 of the former Chief of Police, symbol of white power, was seen as no less than the defeat of an 'army of occupation' (Geórgakas, 1975: 189). Seeking not to unnecessarily alienate whites in the city, with black voters only slightly in the majority, Young distanced himself from more extreme militant black separatist rhetoric (Rich, 1989: 83), but the involvement of black nationalist organizations promoting racial separatism played a key role in his election. Primary here was the role of the Shrine of the Black Madonna, founded in the late 1960s in Detroit by the Reverend Albert Cleage, who has subsequently Africanized his name to Jaramogi Abebe Agyeman. Believing that Jesus was a black political figure, the organization, described as 'a place where church and statecraft intersect', rejects integration as a pipe dream, believing along the lines of Black Muslims that blacks must gain economic and political power to liberate and defend themselves from white oppression (Chafets, 1990: 114–15). The tension between identifying with a racially integrated society and the need to emphasize racial solidarity in a place-context where the former vision was to be repeatedly thwarted was to be 'resolved' at the end of Mayor Young's tenure with a firm swing towards racial solidarity and separatism. This can be charted in the approach to 'place-making' where, under Young, professional planners were at best seen as an irrelevance, as technical functionaries or, at worst, as part of the problem of racial oppression itself.

MATERIAL STAKEHOLDING

The thwarted material aspirations of Detroit under Coleman Young have been documented elsewhere (Neill, 1995). All Young could ultimately offer to many blacks was civic and cultural identification with and belonging in the city. Despite some high-profile projects Detroit, even before the 1967 'civil disturbances', has never been able to mobilize a strong 'growth coalition'. Such coalitions with the private sector to boost the city's economic prospects have always been public-sector-led with a hypocritical and recalcitrant business sector dragged behind. Prairie planning has long beckoned to the corporate sector and Detroit's CBD has never been a mid-west regional magnet for corporate headquarters and financial services. The high-profile Detroit Renaissance Inc., formed in the wake of the 1967 riots as a group of élite business leaders committed to effecting a physical and economic revitalization of Detroit, has been aptly described as providing the 'rhetorical cover' that enabled many of those same corporations to get out of town (Chafets, 1990: 22). Add to the urban cocktail the fact that whites do not wish to live beside or have their children educated alongside blacks, and the emotion, anger and frustration that caused Detroit under Young to 'turn in on itself' as a separate black place becomes easier to understand.

CIVIC STAKEHOLDING

It was in the opening-up of 'civic space' for African American identification with city government that the place-making achievements of Young rest on stronger ground. Under Young, the city administration was seen by blacks as fairer and more inclusive. By 1980 African American incumbency at city managerial and professional levels had increased to approaching 40% owing to political appointments and affirmative action (Fainstein and Fainstein, 1993). Most important of all, since people cannot identify with and give loyalty to a civic authority that is perceived to police them oppressively, was the fact that by 1980, owing to affirmative action, 35% of the Detroit Police Department was black with a black Chief of Police and a high proportion of officers above policeman also black (Time, 1980: 26). By 1990, the Detroit Police Department had the most integrated force of any major city in the US, with more than half of its senior officers being black (Chafets, 1990: 39). With a turnaround from the 1960s, when Detroit's policemen were almost all white, the integration of the Detroit Police Department (the getting of 'black into blue') was in fact regarded by Young as his proudest achievement (Hodgson, 1997). Under Young the use of black firms for city contracts was also considerably expanded but was accompanied by accusations by the President of the City Council of cronyism and the rewarding of political supporters. The claim that institutionalized white racism in city government prior to Young was replaced by black cultural exclusiveness and a measure of corruption, thus shutting out the possibility of a multi-ethnic Detroit civic culture, was a criticism to which Dennis Archer later felt compelled to respond in pushing the Detroit racial pendulum, against the odds, back towards integration.

CULTURAL STAKEHOLDING

Detroit as a place is also impregnated with black cultural associations and meanings significant to the place-making agenda under black political control. Detroit has close associations with black freedom, is a foundational place for black separatism and has been a 'womb' for black culture. Featuring prominently on the wall of the Michigan State Office of Representative Samuel Buzz Thomas III of Detroit is a mural depicting Detroit as the final station on the underground railroad for slaves fleeing to Canada. This significance is marked by a plaque at the north-east corner of Griswold and State Street in downtown Detroit, site of a depot for the last stage of the journey. Whilst racism has a long history in Detroit, with race riots dating back to 1833, these are not the only memories sedimented here. Slavery never officially existed in Michigan, which was part of the slave-free Northwest Territory, and, while some wealthy whites for a while flouted this, blacks had lived as free people since the days of the earliest settlement. Detroit was a frequent meeting-place for abolitionists and, 50 miles north of Detroit, the Republican Party had been founded by people with strong anti-slavery sentiments (Geórgakas and Surkin, 1975: 185). In 1955, Rosa Parks, now a long-time Detroit resident, had galvanized the civil rights movement by her refusal to move to the back of the bus in Montgomery, Alabama. She moved to Detroit in 1957 as a place where she did not have to 'Uncle Tom to white folks' (Babson, 1986: 163–5). Martin Luther King's famous demonstration and 'free at last' speech in Washington in August 1963 had been preceded in July by an unprecedented freedom march of 200 000 people down Woodward Avenue in Detroit. Black Detroiters, as Babson points out, were well suited to a leadership role in the civil rights movement because they had gained experience in the city's union movement unmatched by that of any other urban concentration of blacks. Rights fought for and won on the job reinforced demands for full equality (Babson, 1986: 164). Not much more than 50 miles to the north-west of Detroit, in Lansing, is the neighbourhood where a Malcolm Little grew up before changing his name, when he worked in Detroit, to Malcolm X. Detroit has long had strong associations with the black nationalist philosophy embraced by Rosa Parks herself as the civil rights struggle intensified in the 1960s (Brinkley, 1999). The Black Muslim movement was founded in Detroit in 1930 when preacher W.D. Fard hired a hall and renamed it the 'Temple of Islam'. One of his earliest assistants was Elijah Muhammad, and under his leadership Malcolm X organized and preached in Mosque Number 1 in Detroit in the early 1960s, being subsequently replaced in a leadership role in the movement by Louis Farrakhan (Games and Nicoll, 1998; Watson, 1994). In the words of Malcolm X for those in the Black Muslim movement Detroit is 'the Mecca', the 'origin' and 'focal point' (Malcolm X quoted Smith, 2000: 143). Influenced by Malcolm X, the shrine of the Black Madonna founded by Albert Cleage in Detroit in the late 1960s has already been mentioned in relation to its support for Coleman Young. It is also referred to as the Pan African Orthodox Christian Church and as a militant alternative to white-oriented Christianity; like the Black Muslim movement it espouses Black Nationalism and racial separatism. With major churches now exported to Atlanta and Houston the movement remains a force in the politics of Detroit. Indicative also of a separatist leaning in black identity is the New Bethel incident in 1969. A confrontation between the police and members of the Republic of New Africa, a black nationalist group, at the New Bethel Church, resulted in a policeman being killed and hundreds being arrested. After this, blacks planned in earnest for black political control of Detroit (Rich, 1989: 82), where for some time a militant separatist black tradition had been cradled.

Cradled also have been vibrant black artistic and musical traditions, lending to Detroit other cultural meanings available in the construction of African American identities. The womb here was Paradise Valley and Black Bottom where, hemmed in geographically in Detroit's East Side and repressed occupationally, a cauldron of identity formation was created in the 1940s and 1950s akin to Chicago and Harlem with their black concentrations (Conot, 1974: 378). Conot evokes the feel of Hastings Street at the heart of Paradise Valley in the 1940s where, in the absence of decent accommodation, the bars, streets, movie houses and pool-rooms were crammed with black people with shared memories of slavery, oppression and the migration north and seeking respite from the harsh realities of work in the auto plants.

> At midnight, Hastings Street in Paradise Valley was still carpeted with people. Jazz and boogie-woogie intermingled with the aroma of frying food and drifted like mist over the small neon signs. Darkness veiled the shabby, tawdry street with a patina of mystery (Conot, 1974: 380).

Jazz greats such as Fats Waller, Duke Ellington and Louis Armstrong were frequent visitors to Paradise Valley, but for many the riffs of John Lee Hooker and his
'foreboding moaning' came to epitomize the sound of Detroit, to which Hooker
had migrated from Mississippi in the early 1940s. Paradise Valley was lost to the
transportation-planning bulldozers in the 1960s but the meaning of the place
lingers. For being associated with such a heavy-handed reshaping of urban space
planners were to pay a heavy price in terms of the curtailment of autonomy and
influence under Coleman Young, no stranger to the various haunts and invoca-
tions of home associated with Paradise Valley. Indeed, to some extent under
Young Detroit became a kind of Paradise Valley writ large. The name 'Paradise
Valley' had, after all, always been an ironic comment on black hopes unmet
(Sugrue, 1996: 36).

In the 1960s it was to be the 'Motown Sound' that became synonymous with
black music. This sound, with its gospel harmonies and Afro-American rhythms
which can be traced back to the haunting chants that rumbled through the holds of
slave ships, expressed hope and aspiration and a clean-cut image aimed at mainstream culture (Walker-Tyson, 1980: 86). The Motown label and recording studio
founded by Berry Gordy at 2648 West Grand Boulevard in Detroit, now a museum
(Figure 4.5), launched the careers of Diana Ross, Marvin Gaye, Stevie Wonder and
Michael Jackson before its demise after being displaced by angry black rap and its
rejection of integrationist values. However, one musical name from the 1960s
above all others is associated with Detroit. The Queen of Soul, Aretha Franklin,
began her singing career at the Detroit New Bethel Baptist Church. As expressed
by one commentator, 'her songs became anthems – the soulful sound of a movement that increasingly seemed propelled by black pride and power rather than
"dreams" of racial integration' (Smith, 1999: 210).

Not only African American meanings and memories, however, are wrapped
up in the physical place that is Detroit. Middle-aged and older whites from the
comfortable and affluent suburbs can indulge in warm, nostalgic feelings about
childhood meetings with Santa Claus in the now-demolished downtown Hudson's
department store or rendezvous with friends under the nearby clock on the Kerns
block. Remembered trips to baseball games in Detroit's old and abandoned Tiger
Stadium can evoke more positive feelings among whites than among blacks, for
whom the stadium can be seen as a symbol of racism. Major-league baseball did
not integrate until 1946 and the Tigers were the second-last team to do so
(Rashid, 1994: 147). In a city from which whites have walked away (or, more literally, driven away) rather than seek accommodation, the question of 'Whose City?'
in 2001, as Detroit celebrated the 300th anniversary of its founding, hangs in the
air. Huge statues of former white mayors such as Hazen S. Pingree and
streets still named after former wealthy Detroit slave owners such as Joe Campau

Figure 4.5 The home of 'Motown': 2648 West Grand Boulevard, Detroit, 2001

(Ewen, 1978: 110) continue to convey an image of a city recently evacuated and where the remaining residents have greater preoccupations than claiming by naming territory that has been abandoned if not yet forgotten. Here it is perhaps instructive to be reminded that it took some time after Harlem began to be populated by blacks (from 1915 onwards) for a situated affirmation of the lived experience of people to manifest itself in changes in street names and other spatial expressions of orientating cultural memory. Here Dixon (1994: 20) points out how in Harlem through the naming and renaming of streets and public places 'people have taken charge of their lives and their identity as African Americans. Not only do these names celebrate and commemorate great figures in black culture, they provoke our active participation in that history'. In Detroit under Young this process began. Most dramatically, in 1987, a large black fist swinging inside a triangular frame appeared outside the City Council offices opposite Detroit's waterfront (Figure 4.6). A tribute to Detroit boxer Joe Louis, the statue makes a more separatist statement than the adjacent official statue and symbol of Detroit devised under white control. Here an Adonis-like figure holds aloft in one hand a globe, as a symbol of unity, and in the other cradles a Caucasian family group. Street-name changes under Young included Rosa Parks Boulevard, prominently displayed above a freeway overpass as one approaches downtown, C.L. Franklin Boulevard commemorating the father of Aretha and his involvement in the civil rights movement, and, of course, Martin Luther King Jr Boulevard.

PLANNERS AND THE PHYSICAL DEVELOPMENT AGENDA UNDER YOUNG

The core of the physical development agenda under Young went beyond the important need for jobs and a local tax base and the projection of a competitive entrepreneurial image of place, important as these all were. As but one aspect of 'place-making', the city's physical development agenda was haunted by the question: 'Who are we and how are we going to express ourselves?' Paralleling musical developments, Young's development posture started out with the hope of integration, as expressed in Motown, only to end up with the embrace of separatism, as expressed in the anger of gangsta-rap. This identity tension can be illustrated with reference to planning policy towards the Central Business District, transportation policy in the city and neighbourhood policy.

CBD

That the balance between integration and separatism in Mayor Young's conception of black identity was finally tilted in favour of the latter was due in no small measure

Figure 4.6 The 'Detroit attitude'

to the failed promise of a downtown development strategy symbolized by the flagship Detroit Renaissance Center. A towering office, hotel and specialist retail
development, modelled on Atlanta's Peachtree Center, the moving force was
Henry Ford II. While plans for the RenCen had been put in place in the wake of the
1967 Detroit 'civil disturbances', before Young came to office, the mayor readily
associated himself with the project, holding out as it did the hope that shared economic power and prosperity could accompany black political power in the city. The
Renaissance Center, built like a fortress, like a city within a city, conveyed an
ambivalent message to black Detroiters from its inception. It appeared, sheltered
behind a massive two-storey berm, to be in the city but not of the city. More importantly, in a story that has been told elsewhere (Darden et al., 1987; Neill, 1995),
despite major public subsidy from the city for various civic, apartment and office
developments, no major economic development flotilla followed in the wake of
RenCen. This perceived betrayal hurt black pride. The smiling face of Coleman
Young as he shook hands with Henry Ford II, leader of the white corporate establishment, at the opening of the Renaissance Center in 1977 had been replaced a
decade later by more bitter separatist manifestations of black identity and solidarity, recognizing the reality of regional racial division and uneven economic development unimpeded by the hindrance of any meaningful curbs on ex-urbanization. It
was primarily in 'Edge City' that the Detroit region met the Japanese competitive
challenge during these years. Detroit was expendable. In a notorious television
interview in 1986 Young declared that he was not in favour of the unilateral disarm-
ing of the people of Detroit while the city faced 'hostile white suburbs armed to the
teeth' (Chafets, 1990: 155; Mackie, 1987). Increasingly, Young was to see the city
as an 'island of black self-determination in a sea of white racism and hostility'
(Chafets, 1990: 29). Physical place-making became inseparable from such a conception. It became important to positive African American self-assertion under
Young that blacks were not just seen as running an abandoned plantation. Young
was sensitive to suburban or state interference in the running of 'captured' 'trophy
places' and 'jewels of the city', such as the Detroit Institute of the Arts and Belle
Isle Park, thus conveying a sense of 'we are the masters now'. Perceived slights to
the emotionally charged physical place-making agenda at the end of Young's
tenure included the insinuation that, like that of a 'post-liberation African leader',
Young's development agenda consisted of grandiose 'showcase projects'
(Chafets, 1990: 177), that the city was a 'vast archaeological site', a 'living
Pompeii' of ruins after the Vesuvian eruption of the 1967 race riots (Cornwell,
1995), and that old downtown skyscrapers should even be mothballed and turned
into a giant ruins theme park or 'American Acropolis'. Such a memorial to throwaway cities would be a macabre tourist attraction, elevating white meanings of a
lost Detroit above current black ones for the Detroit that remains (Vergara, 1995:

215–25). With the added problem that 'throwaway cities' implies throwaway people, Young was understandably hypersensitive to any exploitation of a ruins theme in a place-making agenda. Unfortunately this extended to demolishing part of the so-called Heidelberg Project on Heidelberg Street off Gratiot Avenue on Detroit's East Side. Here an artist and street resident, Tyree Guyton, in the midst of neighbourhood abandonment and overgrown lots, began a visual performance artwork in the 1980s. This has consisted of using discarded and painted objects such as shoes, baby dolls, tyres and so forth to decorate the fronts of houses, sidewalks and trees along a city block. A large proportion of the area and works is painted with multi-coloured polka dots as the signature motif. The project has been deservedly referred to as 'a miracle of exhilaration, a festival of lunacy and colour in a kingdom of despair' (Cornwell, 1995). That suburbanites were tempted into Detroit to gaze at this comment on the city's troubles, and, worse, that the artist received sponsorship from the white-run Detroit Institute of Arts, was sufficiently ruffling to Young's sense of pride in a black city to cause the bulldozers to be despatched. Fortunately part of the artwork survives (Figure 4.7).

TRANSPORTATION

Thomas, in a recent book, has rightly referred to the 'racial tension' that underlies all regional planning issues in Detroit (Thomas, 1997: 214). Nowhere was this more apparent than in relation to the so-called 'subway saga' during Young's term

Figure 4.7 Identity among the ruins: Heidelberg Street Project, Detroit's East Side, 2001

in office. With the possibility of federal funding support for a subway, or at least a light rail system, in Detroit's major Woodward corridor linking city and suburbs, Young was to champion the idea. The catch was that federal support required regional consensus. This proved to be an impossibility. On the one hand, as presented by Young, a subway became a symbol of black self-esteem and assertion rather than being defended on 'mere' economic development and transportation grounds (Neill, 1988). On the other hand, in the opinion of a senior transportation planner in Detroit, to suburbanites a subway had conjured up images of graffiti and marauding violent blacks being given access to whites beyond the city limits (Neill, 1993). Already in 1981 Young had referred to suburban opposition to a subway as 'racism and bigotry by suburban politicians seeking favour with their constituents' (McClure, 1981). There was good reason for this. In that year the Oakland Press, covering Oakland County north of Detroit, issued a special anti-subway supplement. This included racist letters stressing the dangers of such a physical connection to Detroit's demonized 'other'. As one letter put it: 'Who wants any part of Black Detroit?' (Thomas, 1997: 214–15). The price paid for the regional transport policy stalemate during the Young years has been the legacy of one of the most poorly developed public transportation systems in the United States. The Detroit People Mover monorail project, pushed through to completion by Young at considerable cost to a financially pressed city and linking the scattered elements of Detroit's CBD, is small recompense for this (Neill, 1995: 132–3).

NEIGHBOURHOODS

Frustration with development policy under Young inevitably came from Detroit's neighbourhoods. Despite some degree of increased civic and enhanced cultural identification with the city by African Americans, economic stakeholding was more difficult, with most of Detroit's 139 square miles remaining untouched by any development renaissance. With a shrinking property tax base Detroit was deprived of the ability to provide essential neighbourhood services. A radical neighbourhood policy was suggested in 1993 by Detroit's Ombudsman. This proposed that residential abandonment and population thinning was so bad that the city should close some neighbourhoods down. With people relocated to viable neighbourhoods and the cost of basic city services reduced, blighted areas would be landscaped and parts of the Motor City returned to pasture (Usborne, 1993). With the possibility of this being seen as a stark acknowledgement of failure by a black administration in its efforts to turn the city around, the idea, while having a certain cold logic, met with consternation in the mayor's office and was stillborn. In those same neighbourhoods Young's streetwise image of machismo struck a chord with young black nationalist sentiment as expressed increasingly through the sometimes nihilistic-sounding lyrics of rap music (Henderson, 1994: 96–8). However, while rap music at least implies some artistic and creative engagement, the Detroit neighbourhood 'tradition' of 'Devil's Night' is difficult to interpret as other than a particularly stark example of nihilistic disengagement from mainstream society. One author described Devil's Night thus:

> In 1983, for reasons no one understands, America's sixth largest city suddenly erupted into flames. Houses, abandoned buildings, even unused factories burned to the ground in an orgy of arson that lasted for seventy-two hours. When it was over the papers reported more than eight hundred fires. Smoke hung over the city for days. What at first appeared to be a bizarre outburst turned into an annual tradition. By 1986, Devil's Night had become a prelude to Halloween in Detroit in the way that Mardi Gras precedes Lent in New Orleans, or the Rose Bowl parade ushers in the New Year in Pasadena (Chafets, 1990: 3–4).

Amid Detroit's hollowed-out neighbourhoods, drug-related violence involving cocaine, crack and heroin led to an ongoing struggle by the city to avoid the label of 'Murder Capital USA'. While Detroit's competing gangs do not have the same 'impressive' lineage as those in Chicago or Los Angeles, membership and associated criminality is still bound up with a search for identity and a sense of belonging (Taylor, 1990: 108–12). It is a tortured relationship to place and the search for 'home' to which powerful emotional appeals can be made. Voicing the cry of separatism, Farrakhan has called black gang members to membership as 'born warriors for true liberation' (ST, 1995).

POLITICS AND PLANNERS UNDER YOUNG

Under Young, planners in Detroit did not find themselves orchestrators of a place-making agenda or anything so grand as 'selective organizers of attention to real possibilities for action' (Forester, 1989: 4). In a situation where class and particularly racial division were framing the possibilities for place-making action, planners found themselves working in a city loaded with a powder keg of place meanings and where they were to be marginalized. In 1972, Detroit councilman and former planner Mel Ravitz had pointed out to a meeting of the American Society of Planning Officials in Detroit that

> America's urban regions ... have been shaped far more by basic cultural and social forces than by the skills and perceptions of their planners ... (and that) attitudes of the White, middle class majority about race and poverty – not the concepts of the planners – decide how the American urban region grows and changes (Ravitz, quoted Thomas, 1997: 143–4).

As if such claims were not enough to dent professional self-image, planners under Young were to be regarded in one of the following ways:

- Lackeys associated with past racism
- Obstructionists
- Dreamers
- Useful technocrats
- Naïve advocates
- Followers of fads.

Thomas has described Young's distrust of planners, who in the words of one black planner were seen as 'people who cleared areas where Black folks lived' (Thomas, 1997: 184). This characterization as **lackeys** arose by courtesy of past associations with urban renewal projects in Detroit that had torn down black neighbourhoods and more particularly because of the planners' association with freeway building in the city in the 1950s and 1960s, when vast gouges were cut through abstract space on transport planners' maps in Detroit, ignoring the deep meanings in the 'representational spaces' such as 'Paradise Valley', where black people lived (Liggett, 1995: 248). The Detroit Metropolitan Area Traffic Study of 1955/56 and the follow-up Detroit Transportation and Land Use Study (TALUS) of 1969, both backed up with federal funding from the Interstate Highway Act of 1956, involved regional place-making in the image of the private automobile, which defines the race- and class-fractured Detroit city and ex-urban reality to this day. Freeways, which it was naïvely hoped would also ease congestion and keep people in the city (Neill, 1988), facilitated the departure of whites and jobs. Conot captures the reality well:

> As the expressways channelled through the city they tapped the pool of middle-class whites long chafing at their urban entrapment. Like water they poured into the channels and out of the city (Conot, 1974: 436).

This was a spatial agenda that was lobbied hard for in Washington by Detroit's automobile industry allied to a broader asphalt and petroleum constituency (Leavitt, 1970; Davies, 1975; Walker, 1981), from which, with the notable exception of Louis Mumford (1964), the planning profession, with the aid of new computers mobilizing vast databases to support 'trend planning', did not demur. That blacks, as a consequence, were to inherit the 'remains of a city' that whites left inevitably led to planners being characterized by Young as tinged with partisanship. They were not perceived as facilitators of a rationally derived place agenda, a technical role conception in the 1970s, increasingly difficult to sustain as the notion of comprehensive rationality in pursuit of the public interest came under critical scrutiny as a sound basis for orientating professional practice (Hemmens, 1980; Healey et al., 1982).

Being seen by Young as past lackeys had consequences for planners and for the city. While planners were marginalized within the city's Planning Department, the leading city development agency under Young was the Community and Economic Development Department. Under an 'aggressive African American director' appointed by Young (Thomas, 1997: 183), this agency worked on a pragmatic project-by-project basis to energize Detroit's increasingly enfeebled public-sector-led 'growth' coalition with the private sector. That planners argued for a more integrated place-making strategy less dependent on short-term development opportunism was regarded by the mayor as **obstructionist**, as interfering with getting things done on an *ad hoc* basis (Neill, 1995: 153). Suspicion of grand planning strategies was also much in evidence when Young reacted unfavourably to the report of the Detroit Strategic Planning Project in 1987. This was a private-sector-financed initiative going beyond physical place-making to incorporate recommendations on race relations, education, economic development, crime and city image (DSPP, 1987). While the mayor's sour reception was also due to the perceived arrogance of private-sector meddling in policy in a city which it, through investment decisions, had virtually written off, the suspicion of comprehensive planning (especially when not under firm black political control) was also a factor (Neill, 1991). To a considerable extent, however, under Young, planners were also indulged as **dreamers**, which in itself is a form of deliberate marginalization. Here Thomas has described how, under one planning director, politically appointed without any formal or informal training in the field of urban planning, the Planning Department was to produce a draft three-volume master plan for the city with 20 background supporting studies. These are criticized for lacking a 'firm grounding in reality' and for making 'recommendations ... so vague that it was difficult to envision implementation' (Thomas, 1997: 188). However, planners could also be **useful technocrats**, provided professional autonomy was minimized and kept on a strong political leash. Planners working in the CEDD would work on specific development projects. As stated by a former city council member:

> The mayor perceives planning to consist of a developer deciding that he wants to build something wherever he wishes and then of the mayor assigning his Community and Economic Development Department to work out the steps to make it happen (Ravitz, 1988: 164).

The conclusion is reached that 'the planning process – at least in Detroit – is basically political, not professional' (Ravitz, ibid.). Towards the end of Young's tenure the

Detroit Planning Department was to come under the political control of Ron Hewitt, a black nationalist and follower of Jaramogi Abebe Agyeman, founder of the shrine of the Black Madonna. Hewitt was later to become an outspoken critic of the political leadership of the city under the more integrationist Dennis Archer. Under Hewitt, the technical skills of planners were hitched to the open promotion of the idea of the city of Detroit being in a post-colonial situation after liberation from white occupation following the 1967 insurrection. Like many of Young's closest associates identifying readily with Africa and the Third World, the city's planning director had lost his son in the 1980s to Detroit street violence (Chafets, 1990: 177–8). This was not an environment where the promotion of planning as an inclusive, dialogic, consensual regional process was remotely possible. On the contrary, an attempt by the South-east Michigan Council of Governments (SEMCOG) to do exactly this had failed miserably. A 'Regional Development Initiative', launched in 1990 on the basis of extensive trend analysis and research, attempted to chart what a 'business as usual' spatial future would look like for the Detroit region in 2010. Showing that this would most likely lead to, *inter alia*, continuing racial polarization and crime, and worsening sprawl and traffic gridlock, discussion workshops were held in municipalities throughout the region to try to agree a consensual alternative on the basis of the common knowledge base provided (SEMCOG 1991). No such agreement proved possible, with business as usual continuing to rule. In the words of a recent city planning director in Detroit: 'SEMCOG was burnt by RDI' (Robinson, 1999). With the danger of SEMCOG losing local membership from what is a voluntary association of governments, the organization under a new director and head of planning takes a more cautious and circumspect stance on issues of regional co-operation and ex-urban containment. The bold approach by previous **naïve advocates**, promoting the RDI in looking for a step change in policy involving a more compact region, is now dismissed by SEMCOG's current director with some embarrassment. The RDI was meant to be 'educative only' (Tait, 1999). An attempt at dialogic, inclusive decision-making arising out of progressive and reformist leanings in planning's educational tradition came up against racial division, cut-throat intra-regional civic entrepreneurialism and America's 'love affair' with the private car. In the RDI planners were tilting at windmills. Coleman Young and Ron Hewitt could have told them so. The RDI joins many failed attempts over the years to foster a more 'regional ethic' in the planning of Greater Detroit (Mathewson, 1975). No regional planning effort, however, failed so abysmally – and justifiably – as a study of urban spatial form in Greater Detroit, completed in 1970 in the wake of the 1967 civil disturbances. In what must be regarded as the high point of rational comprehensive planning pretensions manifest in an ekistical incarnation, a 'scientific study' was made of the city and its metropolitan environs. Under the direction of Constantios Doxiadus, it was supported by the Detroit Edison Company, seeking locational advice on its utility infrastructure investments. The question was posed as to 'what alternative courses of action are available for the development of such a complex urban system?' The incredible answer given by planners following this particular **professional fad** was that in the computer-aided study 'it was found that 49 million(!) alternatives could be outlined. These were compared in a systematic way and the best and most representative ones were selected for further elaboration'! (Doxiadus, 1970: Volume 3, 161). With Detroit's spatial future shaped ever more since 1967 by racial tension and economic division, such professional flights from reality into extreme ungrounded 'representations of space' can have done little in Detroit to bolster professional planning credibility. In the words of the city of Detroit comptroller of the time, in the mayor's office the study was regarded as 'somewhat of a boondoggle' (Klein, 1980).

PLACE AND IDENTITY TENSIONS AT THE END OF YOUNG'S TENURE
One view of the place created under Coleman Young compares Detroit to Israel:

> Israel like Detroit, is a place where people with a history of persecution and dependence finally gave up on the dream of assimilation and chose to try, for the first time, to rule themselves (Chafets, 1990: 29).

With the feeling expressed by one Detroit city planning director that 'people in the suburbs want us to fail' (Hewitt, quoted Chafets, ibid. 178), it is not surprising that representational images of the city became a sensitive subject under Young. After losing his temper on a national television programme where 'Devil's Night' was discussed in November 1990, Young led a delegation to television executives in New York, demanding more positive image coverage for his city (DFP, 1993). Hollywood had inflicted the negative 'Robocop' image on Detroit in films, depicting random urban mayhem. This added to the national image of Detroit in 1993 as 'a dangerous wasteland' (Roush, 1993). Sensitivity to Detroit being perceived by its inhabitants as a black city was revealed in the dissatisfaction with a poster produced by Detroit Renaissance Inc. to market the 1993 Detroit Grand Prix. The poster juxtaposes Georges Seurat's pointillist painting of French leisure, 'Sunday Afternoon on the Island of La Grande Jatte', with Indy cars and Detroit's skyline. The people in the poster are all white, which drew black claims that it misrepresented the city's image. The Executive Director of the Race Relations Council of Metropolitan Detroit commented:

> It happens all the time. It's a slap in the face. It builds walls. It's sending a message that you're not important even when it's done without ill-intent (Parish, quoted Atkins, 1993).

One prominent black business leader also commented:

> Subliminally it's saying to white folks, 'We aren't looking for a bunch of black folks to be here, either, so come on down. You're safe' (Coleman, quoted Atkins, 1993).

The schizophrenia involved in marketing Detroit that was brought out by the poster issue was remarked on by one Detroit media consultant:

> These people never admit that it's a black city. They always look for some symbolism. The RenCen is not Detroit (Mongo, quoted Bratt, 1993).

However, the haemorrhaging of the black middle class to the suburbs was indicative of a less than universal African American willingness to identify positively with 'the black city of Detroit'. In the words of one black critic of Coleman Young in 1988:

> The participants in the 'black flight' will not hesitate to tell you that they are leaving because the elected black political leadership has failed to provide protection for them and their families ... at some point black politicians must be held accountable ... if the office of the mayor of Detroit were held by a white mayor under the circumstances of today, there would be wall-to-wall blacks marching around the City Council Building with clenched and upraised fists demanding the mayor's head (Dillard, 1988: 566).

This latter claim from some blacks that victim status was perhaps being overplayed, especially in the latter part of Young's tenure, was reflected in the two black mayoral electoral candidates available in November 1993. In a swing to a more integrationist black identity position, the winner of the contest, with the black vote split but with support from remaining whites within the city, was Dennis Archer. Reflecting the separationist stance and with the support of the outgoing Young, Archer's opponent Sharon McPhail implied that her successful opponent was an 'Oreo' candidate, black on the outside but white on the inside, and a 'tool of suburban interests' (Walker, 1993; *Economist*, 1993).

PLACE-MAKING IN DETROIT UNDER MAYOR DENNIS ARCHER 1994–2002

TOWARDS A MULTICULTURAL CITY?

As he was campaign manager for Coleman Young in his 1977 re-election campaign, it would be too strong to say that Dennis Archer later disassociated himself from the stewardship of his predecessor. In a meeting with Young in 1991 he pointed out that he was working on a new vision for Detroit but that he still 'felt like a son . . . telling a father that I have admired a lot of things you've been able to do and accomplish inside the city of Detroit' (quoted in Bohy, 1991: 50). Although he had spent part of his childhood in Detroit's African American community, Archer, as a former member of a top law firm and Michigan Supreme Court Justice, was not a 'street man' in the mould of Young. At the root of his vision for Detroit was adherence to a view that to stabilize and revitalize the city required bridge-building, negotiation and compromise with the suburbs and the white business élite. It is a vision that sees cultural separatism as an economic dead end for African Americans. The vision has been the assertion of the possibility of a multicultural city in a regional context where persistent racism makes this an uphill task, risking the personal charge of being 'a silk-stocking elitist', a synonym for 'the white man's candidate' (Bohy, 1991: ibid. 51). The tone of the two Planning and Development Department directors appointed under Archer was far removed from the outlook of the separatist Ron Hewitt. The first, Gloria Robinson, an African American and professional planner by training, points to how Archer had not played the 'victim card' in the manner of Young but also points to the 'difficulty of sending an inclusive cultural message to the suburbs when the mayor knows the reality of the real racism which is out there driving sprawl' (Robinson, 1999). Paul Bernard, her successor, also an African American planner and likewise exuding confidence and cultural pride, states plainly that the continued pursuance of a separatist identity for Detroit would have been a mistake. The aspiration is for 'a city where diversity is celebrated and different people can live side by side' (Bernard, 1999). The aspiration is for what the poet bell hooks has called a 'progressive multiculturalism' where people of colour unite not in order to separate from 'mainstream' culture but to claim an equal place within a multicultural democracy (hooks, 1995: 203). This expresses an optimism of the will over a pessimism of the intellect undoubtedly present at the heart of the Archer administration in Detroit. As hooks points out:

> More than ever in our history, black Americans are succumbing to and
> internalising the racist assumption that there can be no meaningful bonds of
> intimacy between blacks and whites (hooks, 1995: 269).

The result of collective black cynicism about the possibility of ending white supremacy is, according to hooks, the growth of nationalist separatist thinking. This cultural and political response is, however, rejected:

Many black people fear that white commodification and appropriation of blackness is a neo-colonial strategy of cultural genocide that threatens to destroy our cultural legacy. That fear is not ungrounded. Black people, however, are misguided in thinking that nationalist fundamentalism is the best or only way to either preserve our heritage or to make a meaningful response to ending racism (hooks, 1995: 260).

In an America where, particularly in an educational context, the term multicultural-ism has taken on negative connotations associated with the heavy institutionaliza-tion of and emphasis on cultural differences at the expense of integration and a common civic identity, the position of hooks in rejecting separatism is closer to, but still a long way removed from, the aspiration of one influential white American scholar of multiculturalism. Glazer argues that a voluntary attachment to a national civic culture is an appropriate ideal where citizenship is a transcendent status obtainable by all individuals who share a common membership in a democratic polity:

Let us agree that ethnic and racial affiliation should be as voluntary as religious affiliation, and of as little concern to the state and public authority. Let us understand that more and more Americans want to be Americans simply, and nothing more, and let us celebrate that choice, and agree it would be better for America if more of us accepted that identity as our central one as against ethnic and racial identities (Glazer, 1997: 159).

There is no immediate possibility of this 'ideal' coming to pass in Detroit. Under Archer 'race matters' continued to imbue the material, civic and cultural aspects of place-making in the city even if in a less up-front manner than during the latter years of the Young administration. These aspects will be considered in turn before a greater concentration on specific space-related aspects of place-making of more direct relevance to the work of planners.

ECONOMIC STAKEHOLDING AND REGIME-BUILDING UNDER ARCHER

The materiality of context, affected as this is by class divisions and economic competitive pressures, influences the cultural identity-positions to which people feel pulled or pushed. In considering the material well-being of Detroiters in relation to jobs, environment and services during the eight years of Archer's stewardship it is useful to make reference to regime theory. In relation to Atlanta in a major study of another black-led African American city, Stone has referred to the urban regime as the process of coalition-building and informal arrangements through which public office-holders have to come to terms with private interests in the governing of the city (Stone, 1989: ix). Stoker puts it as follows:

> In a complex, fragmented urban world the paradigmatic form of power is that which enables certain interests to blend their capacities to achieve common purposes. Regime analysis directs attention to the conditions under which such effective long-term coalitions emerge in order to accomplish public purposes ... Regime analysts ... do not regard governments as likely to respond to groups on the basis of their electoral power or the intensity of their preferences as some pluralists do. Rather governments are driven to co-operate with those who hold resources central to the achieving of policy goals (Stoker, 1995: 117–19).

In reaching out to Detroit's suburbs and white business élite the Archer administration can be seen as endeavouring to cement and strengthen what has been a very weak urban regime in Detroit. In Atlanta, a United States regional capital (which Detroit is not), a growth coalition committed to 'full throttle development' has been the linchpin of a governing coalition that has successfully wedded the interests of black middle-class leaders and those of white business (Stone, 1989: 159). To the extent that development in Detroit for over 30 years has, to say the least, been less than 'full throttle' and where the black middle class increasingly seeks its future outside the city, an Archer Strategy, on the basis of the limited successes outlined below, must be regarded as remaining vulnerable to a resurgence of electoral power in the form of solidarity based on more militant African American identity. The muted resonances of this were present in the Detroit mayoral election in 2001, considered presently.

In relation to the material aspects of place-making under Archer, the claim of the administration at the beginning of the year 2000 was that since 1994 $12 billion in commercial, industrial, institutional and residential development had either been completed in the city or was under construction. Of this, $5 billion had been invested in Detroit's 18 square-mile-Empowerment Zone, offering federal tax incentives for firms locating there and employing any of the some 100 000 zone residents. Over the same period the claim is that $80 million was invested in the much smaller (1340-acre) spatially fragmented Renaissance Zone, offering various state tax waivers to firms who likewise invest (City of Detroit, 2000: 91). These estimates have been questioned as presenting too rosy a view of any economic rebound by the city of Detroit, especially as measured against the vastly increased scale of development across the metropolitan region as a whole. The conclusion is reached that the city is consistently falling behind its regional competitors and failing to make up for earlier shortfalls and city-wide demolition. Based on these figures alone, Detroit is clearly a city in decline (Boyle, 2000: 15).

Likewise, one recent evaluation of Detroit's Enterprise Zone points out that in view of the fact that business abandonment has devastated Detroit's economy and communities for five decades there should be no surprise that participation by the corporate sector in Detroit's Empowerment Zone has been disappointing. Detroit Renaissance Inc., an organization of the 43 Chief Executive Officers of the region's largest businesses, has been a weak participant in Detroit's EZ. The promise of $1.9 billion in corporate EZ investment is seen as dubious, with few zone stake-holders expecting active corporate involvement. 'Commitments are made (by Detroit Renaissance) but City Hall is politely quiet when they are not kept' (Bock-meyer, 2000: 2436). In economic development competition with the suburbs, where balkanized local jurisdictions offer a wide array of financial incentives and where sprawl is seen by the State's governor as a positive sign of economic health, the difficulties of trying to recycle brownfield sites in the city of Detroit has been described by the Director of Planning and Development in the second half of Archer's administration as 'trying to run the one hundred metres race in combat boots' (Bernard, 1999).

More positively, against a national backdrop of economic prosperity, the unem-ployment rate in Detroit under Archer did fall from 12.5% in 1994 to 9.6% at the start of 2001 (McConnell, 2001). The opening of a new $260 million stadium for the Detroit Tigers baseball team in 2000 was heralded as yet another flagship sign that downtown Detroit was on the rebound (Backholz, 2000). With public funding of $80 million split equally between the city and Wayne County, matched by a grant of $55 million from the State of Michigan and with $66 million from Comerica Inc. who stamp their name on the new stadium (Roush, 2000), the Detroit Tigers have secured a cheap ballpark. Such a comment is perhaps ungracious. It is relevant to point out that the owner of the Detroit Tigers, Mike Illich, proprietor of the third largest pizza firm in the country and owner of the Detroit Red Wings ice hockey team which plays in the downtown Joe Louis arena, has since the late 1980s been a leading white corporate investor in the black city of Detroit. Against the trend of white corporate disinvestment from Detroit, including that of the Big Three auto-makers, the relocation of the headquarters of Little Caesar's Pizza to downtown Detroit from suburban Farmington Hills in 1988 was hailed by the city under Coleman Young as 'the first time a major company has moved into the city in more than thirty years' (City of Detroit, 1988: 77). The home of Little Caesar's sits on top of the renovated Fox Theatre, the largest remaining movie palace in the United States. The entrance to Comerica Park is now directly across the street from Illich's refurbished Fox on Detroit's main thoroughfare, Woodward Avenue. One might be forgiven for thinking that in remaking place, in this case through the beginnings of a sporting/entertainment hub in the north of Detroit's CBD, the city owes a lot more to the local 'Big Cheese' than to the local 'Big Three'. One cost, however, has been the loss of the name Tiger Stadium and its deep if not unproblematic associations with Detroit, where the terms 'Detroit' and 'Tigers' are intertwined. While the old Tiger Stadium remains abandoned, the new stadium is called Comerica Park – ironically named after a bank that in the early 1990s changed its name from Detroit Bank and Trust in order to disassociate itself from the negative image of Detroit (Neill, 1995: 148). In an effort to thwart such corporatization of stadium appellations and their efforts to claim legitimacy in space through the power of naming, a campaign exists in Detroit to find a more populist name for the home of the Tigers (Smith, 2000). In response the Comerica senior vice-president of corporate marketing, with official historical amnesia, retorts: 'I think the name Comerica really does mean something in this community' (Roush, 2000).

Adjacent to the new Comerica Park is a new and almost equally expensive domed football stadium, home for the Detroit Lions. Again with a major public subsidy, including $85 million from the city of Detroit itself (DEGC, 2001), the major private-sector 'place mover' has been William Clay Ford Jr, chairman and chief executive of the Ford Motor Company and vice-chairman of the Lions. The first family member in a generation to lead the car company, Ford describes himself as a Detroit man, albeit raised in the wealthy suburb of Grosse Point and with the Ford World HQ located in suburban Dearborn. Whether the newly named 'Ford Field' is a one-off symbolic gesture to the city (in the manner of Henry Ford II's key role in the building of the RenCen in the 1970s) remains to be seen. This new white corporate stake just outside the Detroit CBD shows, however, the vulnerability of places and their identities to the relocation decisions of major sporting teams run from business boardrooms. Detroit's considerable gain in consolidating the Red Wings at Joe Louis Arena, the Tigers at Comerica and shortly the Lions at Ford Field is set beside the loss of the Lions from the outlying Pontiac Silverdome, where they have played since 1974. The home of the Detroit Pistons basketball team continues to be in the far-flung 'Edge City' of Auburn Hills.

The acceptance by Mayor Archer in 1994 of casino gambling in Detroit after a voter referendum supported the idea has now brought to realization the operation of three casinos in the city: MGM Grand Detroit, Motor City Casino and the Greektown Casino, which opened in 2000. This was a concept long supported by the late Coleman Young to create jobs and bring a measure of fiscal independence to Detroit in the form of local betting taxes. The signs are that the casinos are a major commercial success, with Detroit's MGM Grand the second most profitable location for the company (DEGC, 2000) and with the city projected to earn $80 million from casino revenue in 2001 (McConnell, 2000). That Archer embraced the idea of such legalized gambling only reluctantly is related to the associational images that casinos bring, which will unquestionably directly affect the place-identity of Detroit and perhaps indirectly the collective identities in place expressed in the city. Detroit is now the largest American city with land-based casino gambling and offers an alternative to the brand identities of Las Vegas and Atlantic City.

In terms of the commercial development legacy of the Archer years, two other investments stand out. The first is the purchase at a keen price of the struggling Renaissance Center by General Motors for use as their global headquarters. A relocation, to be completed after refurbishment by 2003, will leave the old HQ in the New Center area three miles north of downtown vacant for hopeful reuse by the State of Michigan as a 'Government Center'. Given that the newly constructed US headquarters of Daimler-Chrysler is in Auburn Hills, 30 miles north of Detroit, keeping GM in the city is no mean achievement. The second major office invest-ment under Archer, which saw site construction get underway in 2001, is a reloca-tion of the headquarters of a computer software company, Compuware, from the suburbs (Farmington Hills in Oakland County) to the Detroit CBD. Following the example of Mike Illich, the CEO and founder of Compuware, Peter Karmanos, who grew up on Detroit's West Side and wants to do something for his native city, has declared that 'Detroit can be one of America's great cities again' (McGraw, 1999). The prize for the city will be up to 10 000 highly paid jobs, anchoring the city's plans to turn a 9-acre city-owned site known as Campus Martius, between RenCen and the new stadia, into a mixed-use shopping, loft-living and commercial hub. This is on the spot where the landmark, but long empty, Hudson's store stood before demolition in 1998. As summarized in a *Detroit Free Press* editorial:

> In the same way that GM's move downtown said very big things about the possibilities here, Compuware's vote of confidence gives the city a whole new cachet (*DFP,* 1999).

That Compuware is only the 14th largest company in Oakland County but its relo-cation will mean an increase of 13% in the jobs base of Detroit's CBD (Low, 1999; Waldmeir, 1999) is a measure of the uphill economic development task that the city faces. The conclusions of a 1992 study pointing to the 'inadequacies in rela-tion to regime-building in Detroit' remain valid today:

> The problems of co-operation between public and private leaders have only partially been overcome in Detroit ... In Detroit, the political capacity to respond to negative forces through public-private partnerships has been and remains limited and flawed (Orr and Stoker, 1992).

Reasons given for the inadequacies of regime-building included 'the lack of leadership and direction on the part of civic organisations' combined with 'the significant amount of electoral support Mayor Coleman Young has enjoyed' (Orr and Stoker, 1992: v). With the political shift of the city to the more accommodationist Archer, Detroit's public-private partnership seems, with the exception of GM, to have rested precariously on the civic actions of a few white Detroit 'home boys' such as William Clay Ford, Mick Illich and Peter Karmanos Jr, making gestures to the remembered city of their youth. One reason for this is that basic city services in Detroit, despite some improvement under Archer, fall far short of what can be provided by less fiscally challenged suburban jurisdictions. The potholes in many city streets, where rubbish remains uncollected and sidewalks are overgrown, tell their own story. Since 1994 Archer has returned Detroit to fiscal surplus with an improved city unlimited general obligation bond rating of A-, which, if Detroit were a developing country, would make the World Bank proud (Archer, 2000). The homicide rate has fallen from 554 in 1994 to 402 in 2000 (Gavrilovich and McGraw, 2001: 484) but still represents a murder rate that is the highest by far among the nation's ten largest cities (Josar et al., 1999). With the number-one visionary goal of Archer being to 'affirm Detroit as a safe city' (City of Detroit, 1995: 7) by 1998 the city had moved from six drug raids per day to 22, with a target of over 30 for the future (Archer, 1999). Equipment inadequacies in the city's Fire Department, snow removal problems and breakdowns in the City's Public Lighting Department have been ongoing. In June 2000 Detroit experienced the worst power cuts in its history and in January 1999 a snowstorm had closed the city down (McConnell, 1999). Failures in the Detroit Public Schools system precipitated controversial State intervention in 2000, which abolished the elected School Board. Racial sensitivity to such white interference will now be considered, *inter alia*, in the context of the gulf that emerged during the Archer years between keeping open a civic, inclusive, Detroit identity and tendencies towards a more exclusive, black cultural identification with the city.

CIVIC VERSUS CULTURAL STAKEHOLDING

The 'Detroit 300' tricentennial celebrations in 2001 showcased efforts under Archer to project an image of a multicultural city alongside a Detroit civic identity which offered an inclusive invitation to join to the rest of the metropolitan area. Celebrations reached a high point in July with a free waterfront concert by Motown recording artist Stevie Wonder, a Tall Ships visit and a musical 'concert of colours'. The publicity matter for the latter, part-sponsored by the *Detroit Free Press*, included the powerful logo: 'D is for diversity' (*DFP*, 2001). Banners extensively festooned from city lamp-posts proclaimed the direct message 'Proud People' (Figure 4.8). Suburban identification with this civic sentiment that could also be

Figure 4.8 Detroit's Tricentennial celebrations, 2001

read as a cultural statement was modest, as evidenced by a shameful reluctance to contribute financially to tricentennial events (Kurth, 2001). As put by one local politician from the suburb of Novi:

> For us to say no subjects us to criticism about a white enclave turning its back on a black community, and I'm sensitive to the charges (ibid.).

The Archer position of civic inclusiveness and equality of treatment for all citizens was to face a very public challenge in 1999 by a recall petition led by the Black State political arm of the Shrine of the Black Madonna and the New Marcus Garvey Movement. The regional chair of the Black State driving the recall was Ron Hewitt, the latter-day Planning Director under Young. The precipitating issue was the fact that of the three casino licences issued by the city none was to an African American business, despite the fact that a prominent African American Detroiter had experience in this area. The Archer position, as explained by Gloria Robinson, one of Archer's Planning and Development directors, was that 'the city was not interested in cronyism but in the best bids. The economic interests of the city were put ahead of race' (Robinson, 1999). While the recall failed, with an opinion poll suggesting that 65% of Detroit voters wanted to keep Archer (McConnell, 1999), the sentiment that the city 'should be looking after its own' is a powerful one and is a view shared by Wendell Anthony, high-profile Head of the Detroit chapter of the National Association for the Advancement of Colored People (NAACP). While identifying with a reluctance among blacks in Detroit to break solidarity and to vocally criticize the black mayor in charge – 'don't knock the brother', as a former Detroit councilman put it – (Cockrell, 1980: 82), nevertheless the view is expressed that 'black economic empowerment is essential as the cavalry is not coming. We must look to our own' (Anthony, 1999). Such black separatist cultural feeling, which falls short of outright black nationalism, has been stirred by other events in Detroit during the Archer administration. A perceived invasion by outside white authority in relation to the police system, criminal justice system and education system has led to a populist feeling on the streets that 'Coleman wouldn't have let it happen in our city'. In March 2000 the Michigan legislature lifted the residency rule requiring Detroit police officers, among others, to live in the city of Detroit. With a Detroit Police Department that is 63% black in a city which is 82% African American, the fear has been expressed by Wendell Anthony that 'without the residency rule, Detroit could go back to the days of an "army of occupation" when a largely white department policed a black city' (Anthony, quoted Hackney, 2001). The Detroit Police Department is already under investigation by the US Department of Justice and Amnesty International, who are focusing on allegations of excessive use of force and prisoner abuse, albeit dealing mainly with black-on-black civil rights abuses. In 1997 Detroit's Recorder's Court was folded into the Wayne County Circuit Court. The former, with juries only of Detroit residents, previously heard Detroit felony cases. The accusation now stands that African Americans do not get a jury of their peers when judged by suburban residents, who do not understand black Detroiter slang and dialect (Arellano, 2001). Likewise in 1997, in what was seen by many Detroiters as interference, Michigan's Republican Governor, John Engler, in pushing for the abolition of Detroit's elected School Board, succeeded in putting the administration of the Detroit Public Schools in the hands of non-elected administrators, albeit appointed reluctantly by the mayor.

Gloria Robinson, former Planning Director, is right to point out that Detroit is 'not a hotbed of Louis Farrakhan supporters' (Robinson, 1999). Nonetheless, the Archer message of racial accommodation and healing has been challenged by other voices and events arguing, even if indirectly, that his approach has 'not been black enough'. Reverend Wendell Anthony is keen to point in interview to the organizational summits for the 1995 One Million Man March on Washington, DC which were held in Detroit and the 75 000 men claimed as signed up from his church alone (Anthony, 1999). Afrocentric education has been growing in Detroit area schools. Before the disbanding of the elected board of the Detroit Public Schools, Detroit had pioneered 14 schools offering African-centred teaching (Allen-Mills, 1997). Advised by Molefi Kente Asante (Hopkins, 1993), the leading Afrocentric spokesman in the United States who has been heavily criticized for emphasizing racial separation rather than inclusion (Walker, 2001: xxxvi), Detroit now offers the possibility to black teenagers of enrolment in schools such as the Marcus Garvey, Paul Robeson or Malcolm X Academies as an alternative to being caught up in gangs, guns and drugs and to whom educational achievement can otherwise appear as selling out by 'acting white'. The Aisha Shule secondary school in Detroit is decorated with African flags and slogans in Swahili. Morning roll call is taken to the beat of African drums. At the end of the school day pupils recite the following anthem:

We pledge to think black, act black, buy black, pray black, love black and live black. We have done black things today and we're going to do black things tomorrow (quoted Allen-Mills, 1997).

Likewise the new Detroit Museum of African American History, which opened in 1997 and with funding put in place by Coleman Young, included Molefi Kente Asante among its consulting scholars (DMAAH, 1999) (Figure 4.9). With such a facility denied a place in the nation's capital on the Washington Mall, which in itself says something about how blacks fit into America's national narrative, the Detroit museum has been described as 'the jewel in America's black tourist crown'

Figure 4.9 Detroit Museum of African American History, 2001

(Allen-Mills, 1998). While it would be an exaggeration to describe the museum as wholly Afrocentric, the message that Africa is the spiritual centre of all blacks, (Figure 4.10), that a history of 'enslavement' is a unifying foundational experience and that 'African memory is a link to origins and history' is certainly strong (DMAAH, 1999). One exhibit claims that the struggle for black civil rights was won in courtroom battles by 'our lawyers' who 'outdid the best minds that white America could offer', overlooking the role played by many whites who joined the struggle. Such selective memory emphasizing cultural separateness led to the *New York Times* commenting: 'The main intention seems to be to create a mythology in which overall effect is more important than individual detail' (quoted Allen-Mills, 1998).

RACE AND PLACE UNDER ARCHER

Under Archer, the concept of black identity projected into the bricks and mortar of physical place-making was that of a city seeking a multicultural ethos within a common regional civic culture. Pride of place in this ethos was given to Campus Martius Park, the new physical jewel in Detroit's place-making crown. The park, at the junction of Woodward, Michigan and Monroe Avenues in Detroit's **CBD**, seeks historical continuity in the revival of the name of a public space on that spot in the early 19th century. The two-acre park will be fronted on one side by the new Compuware Headquarters and will have as a focal point the existing Soldier and Sailors

Figure 4.10 Afrocentric mural, West McNichols Road, Detroit, 1999

Monument. The latter sculpture, a civil-war memorial by Randolph Rogers, erected in 1872, commemorates, *inter alia*, 'Victory, Union and Emancipation' (Eckert, 1993: 30). The park was, with some hyperbole but laudable intent, described by Mayor Archer as 'the best public space in the world.' Campus Martius Park will 'attract people day and night to stroll, sit and meet friends. Beautiful gardens, artwork, and programming reflect and celebrate the great history and diversity of Detroit' (Detroit 300 Inc., 2001). Remodelling of the Renaissance complex, also underway, includes removal of the bunker-like Jefferson Avenue berms and the building of an inviting five-storey winter garden with new riverfront shops and residential units. Set alongside this, Detroit's existing 'jewel', the 960-acre Belle Isle Park in the Detroit river, is presently caught in a policy choice between being an open and inclusive 'people's park' and, on the other hand, the strong possibility of the need to charge a city entry fee to cover the costs of upkeep. While the provocative black fist of Joe Louis continues to swing downtown, thoughts were given by members of the Archer administration to its relocation, although this was eventually dismissed as being too controversial (interview with senior official, 1999). One area of strong policy and public-relations continuity with the Young administration, however, relates to the rejection of any association of the image of Detroit with the notion of 'urban ruins'.

In the last few years an extensive Internet site has grown up inviting the visitor to explore, in a matter-of-fact way, 'the fabulous ruins of Detroit'. In the Detroit CBD some trees growing on top of empty skyscrapers, warehouses and hotels reach, with no human help, the height of two storeys (McGraw, 2001). The city response has been one of acquisition and the offer of disposal at knockdown prices for unsentimental renovation or redevelopment. One city scheme envisages that the ruins north of the new Campus Martius Park can be turned into apartments in a 1500-unit, loft-style urban village (Greater Downtown Partnership, 1997). These 'ruins' are portrayed in a city reinvestment strategy, in an attempt to feminize the harsh image of Detroit, as making up the 'gems' on the strands of a loft-living neck-lace on 'Lady Detroit'. Grand Circus Park is the 'clasp' and Campus Martius the 'pendant'.

In relation to the broad thrust of economic development strategy generally it would be a mistake to overly exaggerate the difference between Archer and Young. As Boyle points out, Archer 'quickly re-embraced large scale project devel-opment, focused on the downtown, as the economic strategy for the city's recov-ery' (Boyle, 2000: 11). Here pragmatism was to reassert itself in the face of the limited willingness of the white corporate establishment to invest and a continued reluctance of people with choices, both black and white, to reside. Land specu-lation and the consequent difficulties of site assembly and integrated land-use planning continued, most significantly in relation to the eventual abandonment by Archer of the idea of clustering Detroit's casinos along the riverfront as part of a new 'Tricentennial Park'. This, complete with waterfall, fishing, boardwalks and new marina, could possibly have given Detroit's riverfront some of the long-awaited cosmopolitan feel of Chicago's Lake Shore Drive. Such a breakthrough, at least in Detroit's downtown image, cannot be ruled out. As part of a policy of containing crime in Detroit's neighbourhoods, the Detroit central business district is one of the safest places in the United States. In the words of city officials, 'officers from the 1st (Beaubien) Precinct know how to keep the 3.2 square mile area safe'. The Precinct Commander recently explained to a journalist that 'the downtown precinct puts officers on foot and bike patrols to maximise their visibility like nowhere else in the city'. In the first three months of 1999 there were no murders committed down-town, one reported rape, seven armed robberies and only one car-jacking. This safety record is aggressively marketed not just to outsiders but also to Detroit sub-urbanites, including those from Compuware considering a job relocation to within the city (Hackney, 1999).

In relation to **transport planning** the Archer years did see a thawing of the possibilities for co-operation between city and suburbs compared to the stand-off born of distrust during Young's tenure, with his insistence on a Detroit subway or light rail system and a separately run Detroit Department of Transportation. Some regional consensus began to emerge in 2001 for a new co-ordinating Regional Transit Authority, with the possibility of merged city and suburban bus systems and fixed-lane guided busways on major arterial and some cross-regional routes. A major impetus for such proposed integration and major augmentation of regional transit came from the corporate sector in the form of the Regional Chamber of Commerce. In a tight economy, potential Detroit workers without cars could not get to employment locations in the job-rich suburbs. In 2002, with unemployment increasing in the region, with no agreed regional funding mechanism, and with the Oakland County Chief Executive still lukewarm on co-operation, it seems likely that yet another regional public transport initiative in the automobile capital of the United States will come to nothing.

However, the major Achilles heel of physical planning policy under Archer remained, as it had been under Young, that of the condition of Detroit's **neighbourhoods**. If Detroit's CBD under Archer was a 'fear free zone' (Neill, 2001: 821), the same cannot be said of most of the 139 square miles of the city. Looking north along Woodward Avenue from its intersection with Interstate 75, which defines the edge of Detroit's three-square-mile 'safety zone', the observer of what looks like the overgrown remains of a city may be forgiven for thinking that those trapped in such an urban space are in a sense prisoners. Some new residential development has occurred in the city under Archer, but compared to the suburbs it has been pitifully small. Of the almost 26 000 new residential building permits issued in S.E. Michigan in the boom year of 1998, only 316 were within Detroit. This was a good year. In 1997 the total for the city was 95. In 1998 the city demolished 4500 residential units (SEMCOG, 1999: 1). The centrepiece initiative for the renewal of Detroit's neighbourhoods was managed by the City's Planning and Development Department and published as Detroit's Community Reinvestment Strategy in 1998 (City of Detroit, 1998). This visionary exercise, based on extensive neighbourhood consultation across ten 'cluster areas' making up the entire city of Detroit, has been criticized by one urban-planning academic as representing 'overly ambitious wish lists of every community in the city'. While the process was initially widely supported, disappointment quickly set in as the proposals were not grounded in fiscal reality and were presented in a 'planning vacuum' with no overall policy framework for physical development outside the downtown area (Boyle, 2000: 13–14). As an alternative the controversial 1993 proposal of Detroit's ombudsman is revived, with the suggestion again made that Detroit must realistically plan for decline, 'downsizing' and consolidation (ibid. 22–4). While this idea has clear rational merit in terms of the efficiencies of urban service provision, it nevertheless remains culturally loaded. The prospect of the African American city of Detroit returning major swathes of land to a fallow state, with parallel rampant development and growth on greenfield ex-urban sites, could be read as de facto acceptance of the continued reality of spatial apartheid accompanied by the rationalization of land use on a 'black plantation' stigmatized by association with the 'un-American' idea of 'decline' and the implicit insult that blacks cannot run a successful city. The African American head of New Detroit Inc., which runs various social programmes in Detroit, regards it as racist, for example, to suggest that Detroit cannot make it on its own (Thomas, 1997: 216). This is far removed from the concept of an inclusive multicultural city and region with the political will to redirect growth to the urban core. In the absence of such a regional policy consensus, neighbourhood achievements under Archer have been significant but modest. Halloween arson fires, for example, during 'Devil's Night', now renamed 'Angels' Night', have been reduced by youth curfews and volunteer neighbourhood patrols, from over 350 in 1994 to around 150 in 2001 (McWhirter, 2001). As put simply by Archer: 'Angels' Night is about pride, and the people of Detroit take great pride in their community' (Archer, 2001).

POLITICS AND PLANNERS UNDER ARCHER

Under Archer, according to one interpretation, planners were brought in from the cold and returned to active service with a political recommitment to the profession bordering on professional 'redemption' (Thomas, 1997: 198). Planners became identified as advocates for a city wanting to move in an open multicultural direction in a spirit of regional co-operation. City planners, whether working under Bernard or in the Detroit Economic Growth Co-operation at the hard end of deal-making and project finance or in the Greater Downtown Partnership, formed to focus redevelopment attention on central locations, all returned in this context to duty as partisan advocates for their municipality. Unfortunately, 'return to active service' is not synonymous with making a major qualitative difference. The institutional context is such that planners in Detroit under Archer took their place alongside many professional colleagues fulfilling partisan roles within the patchwork quilt of local governments making up the disunited region of South-eastern Michigan. Here Krumholz, a former Planning Director of Cleveland, Ohio, cautions that

> American politicians tend to support planning so long as the planners provide
> confirmation for whatever it is that the politicians want to do: when planners
> oppose political power or raise questions about its objectives, they are
> frequently overridden and sometimes disciplined (Krumholz, 2001: 97).

As under Young, place-making possibilities under Archer were again constrained by the regional socio-spatial realities of race and class division and private-sector economic evacuation. Planners could not wave a magic wand or mediate in the face of regional embedded power and prejudice to ensure more equitable metropolitan spatial outcomes. While more integrated, 'joined-up' spatial planning was attempted in the city under Archer, even this, in the face of fiscal realities and the need to take advantage of market opportunities that presented themselves, was understandably coloured by pragmatism. In 2001 the President of the British Royal Town Planning Institute after a visit reported his shock at the state of urban dereliction in the City of Detroit, the like of which, elsewhere, he had 'never seen'. The fundamental cause was put down to an absence of 'the worthwhile activity, town planning' (Davies, 2001). This is a misunderstanding. There is much town planning in S.E. Michigan. The problem is that it is used to serve local interests to the detriment of broader ones. In pointing over 25 years ago to the absence of racial integration and a regional civic consciousness, one campaigner for regional governance in Greater Detroit, borrowing from Arnold Toynbee's 1967 book *Cities of Destiny*, supported the view that the urban area, to become 'an association of human beings who have the feeling that they constitute a community ... must evolve at least the rudiments of a soul' (Toynbee, quoted Mathewson, 1975: 1). It is the absence of a regional soul rather than the absence of town planning that puts a serious lid on place-making possibilities in Detroit. And as Toynbee also said, as a useful antidote to evangelical professional planner pretensions: 'the town planner cannot do our spiritual work for us'.

WHITHER AFRICAN AMERICAN IDENTITY IN DETROIT?

While the election for Detroit's new mayor in November 2001 took place in the shadow of 11 September, when even Louis Farrakhan was eager to assert his patriotism as an American (Younge, 2001), both main candidates were to underplay bridge-building and rapprochement with the suburbs characteristic of Archer's election campaign eight years earlier. In a pre-election survey by the Detroit Urban League city – suburban healing had ranked low as a quality the next mayor should have (DUL, 2001: 3). The winner, with 54% of the vote from a poor election turnout, was the 31-year-old Kwame Kilpatrick, who presented himself as a 'son of the city' and to whom Coleman Young was a 'hero' (Elrick, 2001; Hill, 2002). With support from the Black Slate of the Shrine of the Black Madonna, which had given birth to the successful political careers of his parents, and with vocal support from Wendell Anthony, Kilpatrick had been minority leader in the Michigan House of Representatives. His defeated opponent, Gill Hill, the 70-year-old President of the Detroit City Council and former chief homicide detective in the city under Coleman Young, had additional 'street cred' from being Eddie Murphy's foul-mouthed boss in the *Beverly Hills Cop* film trilogy. Kilpatrick referred to Michigan as 'the Mississippi of the North' to distance himself from accusations (from Hill) of seeking white validation and approval in the State capital. Hill supporters had also attempted to identify Kilpatrick with the Detroit Schools' takeover and its rollback of black voting rights with the 'white power structure looting the black empowerment of Detroit' (Christoff, 2001). With both candidates able to present sufficiently 'black credentials', the outcome was to some degree one of age over experience, with speculation in Detroit that Kilpatrick's victory might herald a resurgence of the Shrine of the Black Madonna's political influence (McWhirter, 2001). With poorer economic and fiscal times probably ahead for the city, it is likely that Greater Detroit under Archer missed its last chance to embrace the concept of progressive multicultural regionalism. At his swearing-in ceremony at the beginning of 2002 Kilpatrick evoked the language of siege:

> I stand before you as a son of the city of Detroit and all that represents. I was born here in the city of Detroit, and I was raised here in the city of Detroit ... My entire family dwells within the walls of the city of Detroit. This position is personal (Hill, 2002).

In 2001, FBI statistics ranked Detroit as the nation's most dangerous city (Moses, 2001). At the end of 2002, in the yearly toll, 17 children under the age of 16 had been shot dead and nine others killed violently in Detroit (Schmitt and Hackney, 2002). In a State of the City speech in March 2002, Kilpatrick, looking inward, presented the choice for Detroit as one between 'community or chaos'. Planners should take their places for regional trench warfare as the pendulum in Detroit swings in favour of more cold-headed separatist feeling as opposed to the hot-headed variety under Young. Here the observation has been made that many African Americans, while not condoning, understand only too well the sense of anger and lack of voice that motivated the actions of 11 September 2001. Living in a parallel land, which James Baldwin in his 1962 novel called *Another Country*, many blacks inhabit a universe that has recently been described by one African American as a place where 'citizens are shadows, creatures glanced out of car windows, over the shoulder, tolerated, feared, despised ... an "issue", a thing to confront...' Many such citizens look at Ground Zero in New York and 'see not rubble but chickens coming home to roost' (Greer, 2001). At the end of 2002, Michigan's Governor preferred to 'blame the victim':

> It's frustrating. It just drives me crazy. And it is just a lack of acceptance of responsibility in that city. Look at the problems! Doesn't anyone want to step up? (Governor Engler, quoted Bell, 2002).

Against the odds it is to be hoped that the United States will wake up to the causes of hostile difference, not just abroad but at home. Detroit would be a good place to start.

CHAPTER 5

COSMOPOLIS POSTPONED: PLANNING AND THE MANAGEMENT OF CULTURAL CONFLICT IN THE BRITISH AND/OR IRISH CITY OF BELFAST

> Whatever political solution we eventually arrive at will be complex, and probably without international precedent; but that shouldn't worry us any more than it worried those who drew up the Paris and Rome Treaties that established the European community three decades ago (G. Fitzgerald, 'Irish Identities', 1982).

Amid current multiculturalism debates in Britain about the meaning and future relevance (if any) of British identity, the traditional English characterization of Northern Ireland as a 'place apart' (not unknown at Royal Town Planning Institute governing council meetings) seems bemusing. As the political scientist Richard Rose wrote some time ago:

> Englishmen are tempted to dismiss Northern Ireland as Neville Chamberlain dismissed Czechoslovakia in 1938: 'a far away country of whom we know nothing'. Such an attitude betrays gross ignorance of the foundations of the United Kingdom and of its contemporary government. The religious conflict in Ulster today can be traced back to one of the great events in English history: the decision of King Henry VIII to break with the Roman Catholic Church in the sixteenth century. Queen Elizabeth II reigns today because of military victories that her Dutch Protestant forebear, William of Orange, won on Irish soil in the late seventeenth century (Rose, 1976: 2).

This chapter argues that the history of urban planning in Belfast, framed as it always has been in a context of identities in conflict, speaks now to a wide audience of academics and practitioners about the management of cultural difference in cities. In a recent book, subtitled 'planning for multicultural cities', Leonie Sandercock looks forward to 'Cosmopolis', which is based on

> some kind of *civic culture* which embraces a shared/common destiny, an intertwined fate ... the possibility of 'togetherness in difference' (underpinned by) a set of values – dealing with social justice, a politics of difference, new concepts of citizenship and community, and a civic culture formed out of multiple publics (Sandercock, 1998: 198–9).

While with exuberant, adopted American optimism Sandercock posits 'Cosmopolis' as a laudable utopian target, a 'North star' in the direction of which planners should chart their course, with European and even Irish pessimism this chapter plots the difficulties of arriving in the 'land of Oz' at least in one concrete planning context. The local planning profession in particular, it is argued, is simply not up to the task.

The structure of the chapter is as follows. The next section confronts the basic question of whether the 'Northern Ireland conflict' is best conceived in colonial or ethnic terms. The answer to this question goes to the root of whether Protestant and Unionist identity can in a deep sense be considered as 'authentic' and, therefore, worthy of respect in its difference. The Good Friday Agreement, while based on the notion of 'parity of esteem' for both cultural traditions in Northern Ireland, seems just about capable of working practically in the short term with both these interpretations. The chapter proceeds to consider the appeal of Irish nationalism to Unionist identity in the longer term to embed itself within a multicultural, all-Ireland political framework. Conversely, the strong desire of Unionism to embed itself within a context of British multiculturalism and devolution inevitably puts Irish identity concerns full square at the centre of multicultural and citizenship debates in the United Kingdom as a whole. Lest this discussion be considered aloof from urban planning, the spatiality of identity conflict in Northern Ireland in general, and Belfast in particular, is briefly reviewed in historical terms. Put bluntly, territorial claims, with all their symbolic intensity, go to the root of identity conflict in Belfast and Northern Ireland. It is ground on which planners often fear to tread. The remainder of the chapter considers urban planning and the role of planners in Belfast since the 1950s, positioned as they have been within a state context where clashing cultural identities have gone to the core of the constitution of society as a whole. Belfast as a place 'coasted' along in the 1950s and attempted to modernize in the 1960s, but became a 'fortress city' in the 1970s. In the 1980s, what had become a 'pariah city' began to look forward to rebirth as the 'Emerald City' in the 1990s, a city to be reached fully at the end of the 'yellow brick road' of the peace process. In the Emerald City, capital of Oz, dreams come true for those who have endured the trials of the yellow brick road. In the year 2003 Belfast stands at a crossroads. Will the city be a site of 'culture wars', with the always-present possibility that this can again break out into real war, or can enough civic space be created for a shared city where difference is at least tolerated? While no 'Rainbow Coalition' emphasizing warm 'togetherness in difference' (Sandercock, 1998: 199) is about to come together to constitute 'Cosmopolis' in Belfast, planners nevertheless now face the choice, it is argued, of retreating from the challenges posed by the continuing spatiality of identity conflict, leaving this to politicians and other policy professionals (the likely outcome), or of a local professional regrouping that reappraises the knowledge and skills required in order to make a more proactive contribution to the present period of more peaceful conflict management.

THE NORTHERN IRELAND IDENTITY CONFLICT: COLONIAL OR ETHNIC?

NORTHERN IRELAND AS A COLONY?

The most fundamental challenge to Protestant Unionist British identity in Northern Ireland (the term 'North of Ireland' is usually preferred by those advancing the challenge in full awareness of the power that naming confers on place) comes from an Irish republican position which sees this presence and identity in the historical context of centuries of British imperialist involvement in Ireland. More particularly, the descendants of settlers planted by England especially in the 17th century are seen as resisting absorption and integration into Irish society and as a consequence are seen as never having shaken off a defensive settler consciousness. The creation of Northern Ireland through the partition of Ireland in 1921 is seen as the undemocratic British support for an illegitimate unionist statelet, thwarting the will of the Irish people in general for full separation and independence from a colonial power. The creation of Northern Ireland with a deliberately inbuilt Protestant-unionist demographic majority is seen as having institutionalized a culture of unionist supremacism with a Catholic nationalist minority deprived of full recognition of its cultural identity and even of equal citizenship. Protestant Unionist identity presented in this way, as characterized by an oppressor mentality, usually proceeds in tandem with a denigration of Protestant Unionist culture in general as the product of a false consciousness, less 'real' than nationalist culture, the basic project being to call into question the right of unionist cultural identity to exist. Rather, the 'invitation' is extended to unionists to see their future in the political union of Ireland, where they can lay claim to the rich Irish cultural inheritance that awaits them. This process would be speeded up by the removal of the colonial prop of British involvement in the North of Ireland, which blinds workers to their true class interests (Redmond, 1985: 69). The cross-class alliance of Unionism (Adams, 1986: 126) would supposedly fracture and accommodation with a united Ireland would inevitably follow. It is a position which, prosecuted militarily as a noble cause by the armed forces of republicanism in the course of 'the Troubles', would most likely be viewed by unionists, in Sandercock's terms, as delivering the 'togetherness in difference' of Cosmopolis at the point of a gun. In a post-Good-Friday-Agreement context, Sinn Féin, the political wing of the IRA, continues to publicly frame the Northern Ireland conflict in colonial terms. Martin McGuinness, MP, Minister for Education in the Northern Ireland devolved administration and chief Sinn Féin negotiator at the political talks leading to the agreement, speaks for many in the North of Ireland in declaring: 'I was born in a part of the island of Ireland that is occupied by a foreign power' (McGuinness, quoted in Logue, 2000). Another Sinn Féin Assembly member states bluntly:

As an Irish republican, I want to see a United Ireland, a reunified Ireland
that ends the injustices and conflicts partition created. I believe that the
British government has no right to be in our country either through their
physical presence or through the proxy of their settlers' descendants
(Kelly, 2002).

Much is at stake in framing the conflict of identities in this way. As put by one seasoned political commentator:

Once republicans start to see the primary focus of the conflict as inter-
communal rather than a fight against outside imperialist interference, then the
ideology which has sustained 30 years of violence and made revolutionary
solutions thinkable slips through their fingers and is lost (Clarke, 1999).

Some early academic explanations of conflict since the outbreak of the Troubles
were strongly couched within a colonial interpretative frame. Liam de Paor put the
matter in uncompromising terms in 1971:

The Northern Ireland problem is a colonial problem, and the 'racial' distinction
(and it is actually imagined as racial) between the colonists and the natives is
expressed in terms of religion . . . it is necessary to maintain the distinction in
order to maintain the colony as a colony (de Paor, 1971: xiii).

For de Paor, Great Britain, as a colonial 'interested party', could not hope to inter-
vene successfully as a peacekeeper or intermediary:

the exercise of responsibility in the affairs of other people, however well-
meaning, is the essence of imperialism . . . The responsibility for dealing with
Irish divisions, should, in my opinion, be returned where it belongs: to Ireland (de
Paor, ibid. xx).

A decade later, continuing a traditional Irish-Marxist genre which believes that the
Northern Ireland state is irreformable (e.g. Collins, 1985; Rowthorne and Wayne,
1988; Munck, 1992), a sociological study of a range of state policies in Northern
Ireland (including physical planning and locational decisions) rejected any characterization of the Northern Ireland state as 'above' the sectarian conflict. The Northern Ireland state itself was rather embedded in and constitutive of colonial relations
of subordination (O'Dowd et al., 1980). As such, given their location within such a
state, planners and other government agents could not in any sense be considered
as 'neutral' or as keeping the peace between two warring factions. More recently,

in similar vein, Miller claims that official community-relations work and research in Northern Ireland rules out conceptualizations that do not accept the inevitability or desirability of the Northern Ireland state (Miller, 1998: 23). On the whole, however, as Miller also points out with some regret, the vast bulk of literature on Northern Ireland does not treat the place as a colony of Britain and, as we move nearer to the present, references to colonialism become rarer (Miller, ibid. 3). One major exception to this is a recent collection of essays based on the argument that Northern Ireland is British in the sense that it is a colonial possession and that sectarian division is the result of this colonialism. This is seen as a counterweight to 'British propaganda, unionist ideology and revisionist "scholarship" (which informs) most contemporary discourse' (Miller, 1998: xix). All contributors to the 1980 sociological study previously mentioned are included, with updated contributions. The cover of the book depicts a provocative wall mural from the Falls Road in West Belfast. A hooded Ku Klux Klan figure on horseback is in the foreground, with a caption reading: 'Not all traditions deserve respect'. It can be confidently assumed that this does not refer to Catholic nationalist identity. From another colonialist/ Marxist reading one recent writer laments that ethno-national identity gets in the way of the formation of economic class loyalties and identity in Northern Ireland, with the virtual absence in fact of class-based politics. This is put down to the adeptness of the more privileged elements of the unionist community at 'fermenting ethnic division among the working classes'. The manipulated false consciousness of working class Protestants 'content to exist as subordinates within the unionist class alliance' is patronizingly dismissed as having 'a merely tenuous relationship with historical and contemporary realities'. The 'truth' of common class interests loses out to the more evocative but somehow less authentic appeal of ethno-national story telling:

> It is 'the Sash' or 'the Soldiers' Song' rather than 'the Internationale' that brings tears to the eyes of working class men as the end of the licensing hours beckons (Coulter, 1999: 93–5).

However, as John Whyte pointed out in his award-winning book, *Interpreting Northern Ireland*:

> the colonial parallel has not been so convincing that it has generally been adopted by writers on the Northern Ireland problem ... The colonial analogy is perhaps more apposite when applied to the whole of Ireland when under British rule before 1921. The majority of Irish people were indeed discontented with British government, and eventually, as has become the rule with colonies, threw off the metropolitan regime (Whyte, 1991: 178–9).

In contrast, Whyte posits an 'ethnic conflict-zone' model for the study of Northern Ireland, making the comment that 'a colonial situation can be ended by the departure of the imperial power, but an ethnic conflict may remain as long as the two groups exist' (ibid. 179). This move in interpretative research to an internal-conflict approach Whyte, in fact, regarded as 'not far from being a dominant paradigm' (ibid. 203). While within such an approach it is now common to refer to both 'cultural traditions' in the North, the academic characterization of the conflict as ethnic is preferred by many writers who point to the fact that the Catholic-Protestant split is so profound, going beyond religious observance alone to wider patterns of social (or more likely non-social) interaction and segregation, that the term is justified (Poole, 1997: 134). Thus Bruce, for example, states that:

> the first step towards understanding the political behaviour of the Protestants of Northern Ireland is to see them as an 'ethnic group'. They see themselves as the outcome of shared historical experiences and as the embodiment of a culture of a distinctive kind, with its shared traditions, values, beliefs, life-style and symbols (Bruce, 1986: 257–8).

PROTESTANT-UNIONIST IDENTITY

Rejection of the notion, historically powerful in Irish republican thought, that the separate identity of northern Protestants has been mainly rooted in material concerns, the result of manipulation by a cunning unionist bourgeoisie, is now regarded as facile and economistic by a considerable number of revisionist Marxist commentators (Whyte, ibid. 182–7). From a non-Marxist perspective, giving greater autonomy to cultural factors over class determination in the formation of group consciousness, Whyte writes:

> To stress economic divergence as the fundamental reason for the development of a different nationality in the north-east of the island from the rest of the country may be to place too little weight on cultural factors. If economics outweighed culture, one might have expected the Protestant farmers west of the Bann, whose material interests were much closer to those of their Catholic neighbours than they were to the workers and industrialists of the Belfast area, to have been drawn to nationalist Ireland, but in fact they were quite as staunch unionists as any other Protestants in Ulster (Whyte, 1991: 191).

While, as stated in the last chapter, there is not just one way to be a 'unionist' any more than there is one way to be black in Detroit, and while outlook and sense of identity are clearly also affected by class location, nevertheless a broad distinction can be made between those who, in defining unionist identity, lay more stress on religious affiliation and those characterizing unionism more in terms of political values and shared experience. Thus Bruce in his study of the politics of Paisleyism and his brand of evangelical Protestantism goes so far as to state that Ian Paisley 'represents the core of unionism' (Bruce, 1986: 262). David Trimble, leader of the official Unionist party, argues, rather, for an updated unionism on the basis that the Union:

> unites us all into a genuinely plural, liberal, democratic state ... Unionism is not based on any sense of elitism nor on personal religious belief, it is based on a sense of Britishness. This is at the heart of a shared psychological bond and a history of triumphs and sacrifices shared with the rest of the people of the United Kingdom (Trimble, 2001: 65).

However, if unionist identity can be framed in terms of what it considers itself to be, it tends with greater vehemence to present itself in terms of what it is *not*. Here unionist identity can be seen as constituted historically from the raw material of suspicion and fear in a context where sectarian strife was a much stronger tradition than unity (Stewart, 1989: 110), in opposition to the Catholic Gaelic cultural nationalism of the 19th and early 20th centuries. As a cultural minority on the island of Ireland but with return to Britain after hundreds of years not a practical or desired proposition, those of 'planter stock' have rightly been recently described as 'an unsettled people' (McKay, 2000), many of whom, as the cultural geographer Estyn Evans noted with bemusement 20 years ago, 'still obstinately refuse to call themselves Irish' (Evans, 1984: 12). Protestant foundation myths largely deriving from the 17th century are rooted in a sense of Catholic threat (the 1641 uprising and slaughter of planters and their families giving rise to a mentality of siege; the ultimately unsuccessful siege of Derry by Catholic King James II in 1689 giving birth to the enduring Protestant cry of 'No Surrender'; and the defeat at the Battle of the Boyne of James II by Protestant William III of Orange in 1690, which was to endure as a fount of unionist triumphalism up to 300 years later). One recent unionist Lord Mayor of Belfast has been active in the business of forging other foundational memories for Protestants from the interpretative possibilities presented by history. Seeking to go beyond a siege mentality, an origin myth is controversially sought in more ancient Irish history. In this production of heritage, the Plantations of Ireland in the 16th and 17th centuries emerge as the return of a Scots-Irish people who had been expelled from Ulster by invading Celts (Adamson, 1982; 1991). The search for a sense of myth and belonging not quite found, but rejecting a view of the past as providing through a siege mentality the assurance of meanings forever fixed, is to be found in the writing of Ulster's perhaps best-known 'planter poet', John Hewitt, described by Seamus Heaney as 'the conscience of the Planter tradition'. As put by one literary critic, 'Hewitt is inescapably an Ulster-man and for him Belfast is "irremediably home", and yet much of his life and his poetry has been a search for identity' (Warner, 1991: 6). In a quest for self-definition, 'perpetually unsure of one's place' in a province colonized by his ances-tors (Ormsby, 1979: 4), it is in a bond with the land that some peace is to be found:

> This is my home and country.
> Later on
> perhaps I'll find this nation is my own
> But here and now it is enough to love
> this faulted ledge this map of cloud above
> and the great sea that beats against the west
> to swamp the sun (Hewitt, 1943).

It was not, however, radical Protestant doubt that mobilized in the signing of the Ulster Covenant in September 1912, when 400 000 or so loyalists pledged them-selves, sometimes in their own blood, to use 'all means which may be found neces-sary to defeat the present conspiracy to set up a Home Rule Parliament in Ireland'. In reluctantly accepting partition and closing ranks as an ethnic identity it is difficult not to agree with the assessment of the historian A.T.Q. Stewart:

> In the long run the one decisive factor in partition is not the weakness of Irish
> nationalism, nor the guile of unionists, nor the chicanery of British
> statesmanship. It is the simple determination of Protestants in north-east Ireland
> not to become a minority in Catholic Ireland (Stewart, 1989: 162).

Such an assessment, however, does not necessarily confer legitimacy on the par-ticularity of this ethnic state-building enterprise. As Eagleton sensibly points out, 'people have a right to affirm their ethnic identities; but there is no reason in prin-ciple to suppose that they need to fashion their own political state in order to do so' (Eagleton, 1999: 45). However, Eagleton, while stating his preference for a United Ireland on grounds of democratic civic nationalism, concedes that 'there is nothing wrong in principle with part of the island being British' (ibid. 51).

CATHOLIC-NATIONALIST IDENTITY

The experience of 75 years of Irish partition and nearly 30 years of civil conflict have forged a discernibly Northern Catholic identity. As put by O'Connor:

> Northern Catholics in general traditionally saw themselves as denied full
> membership to society and forced by an alien and alienating state into

permanent dissent – a perception shared across the lines of class and political division by the better-off and the poor, republican and anti-republican alike (O'Connor, 1993: 365).

Foundational events such as Bloody Sunday in January 1972, when British paratroopers shot and killed 14 demonstrators in Derry, are seared into the memory of Northern Catholics, to whom a general sense of victimhood has been central in identity-formation. Here evidence for discrimination against Catholics in Northern Ireland under unionist administrations before direct rule is substantial, although there is disagreement about its extent (Whyte, 1991: 180). Some studies characterize sectarian practices (treating others negatively based on religion as a badge of identity) as the very lifeblood of unionism (e.g. Farrell, 1976). A not unnaturally-milder characterization of Catholic treatment was implicit in the image of place chosen by David Trimble in his Nobel Peace Prize acceptance speech in 1998:

> Ulster Unionists, fearful of being isolated on the island, built a solid house, but it was a cold house for Catholics. And northern nationalists, although they had a roof over their heads, seemed to us as if they meant to burn the house down (Trimble, 2001: 62).

A recent study of the Catholics of Ulster by an historian from a nationalist background goes some way to undermining the victim mentality, certainly justified in the past, which some nationalists have difficulty in relinquishing. This precludes, in the process, empathy with their ethnonationalist room-mates, who in turn are often introspectively preoccupied with their own corrosive siege mentality (Elliott, 2000). However, Catholic nationalist identity looks to a different house, going beyond an identity forged as a result of '50 years of Unionist mis-rule'. It looks to the island of Ireland as a whole as a place endowed with different historical readings and meanings. It is here that nationalists can still tap into a Gaelic-Catholic-nationalist Irish identity from whose exclusivity Northern Protestants feel alienated to the point of denying their own Irishness. This is a phenomenon that Martin McGuinness dismisses as a form of manipulated false-identity consciousness:

> Something I could never understand is how the British establishment were able to instil such detest of all things Irish in a section of our people that they deny their Irish identity (McGuinness, quoted in Logue, 2000).

A unionist answer would be that the raising-up and founding of the Republic of Ireland was based on a cultural nationalism and quasi-theocratic state from which Protestants had good cause to feel alienated. While Evans conclusively pointed out some time ago that the notion of a mongrel Irish people (none the worse for that) all having noble Gaelic ancestors is absurd (Evans, 1973: 59), the place-image of Celtic mists populated with warrior heroes nevertheless formed part of the romantic business of Irish nation-building (Graham, 1994: 145). The executed 'warriors' of the 1916 Irish 'uprising' take their place, through the pen of the poet W.B. Yeats, as foundation myth, at the centre of Irish collective memory and iden-tity. The anti-British sentiment so naturally wrapped up in the representational place-landscapes of the General Post Office in Dublin (site of the ill-fated uprising) and Dublin's Mountjoy Prison (site of the executions) finds limited fellow feeling among unionists. Indeed, what the historian Roy Foster has called 'the powerful determinist vision' of an oppressed but defiant Irish at odds with perfidious Albion has long gone to the core of the dominant definition of Irishness on the island of Ireland (Foster, 2002). This is, however, changing. Significant factors causing a re-evaluation of the meaning of Irish identity include European integration, the growth of the 'Celtic Tiger' economy in recent years, the secularization of society and the northern peace process itself, which has brought London and Dublin closer together. It is in this context, with the seeds present of a less ethnically myopic Ireland, that appeals can be more convincingly made to unionists, certainly no strangers to ethnic myopia themselves, to join a new, pluralist, all-Ireland state. Martin McGuinness, for example, looks forward to the inclusion of unionists in an Ireland that 'will be a multicultural, multiracial, multilingual secular society' (McGuin-ness, quoted Logue, 2000). The resonance is less with Gaelic-Catholic ethnic identity than with the tradition of a civic republicanism associated with its major proponent, Wolfe Tone (executed by the English in 1798), who argued for separa-tion from Britain based on a common Irish citizenship that accommodated 'Catholics, Protestants and Dissenters' (Kilmurray and McWilliams, 1998: 158). Leaving aside the issue, considered later, of how culture is still used as a divisive badge of identity in Belfast and Northern Ireland, there are reasons for unionists not to overestimate the strength of the pluralist tide in the Republic of Ireland. In the context of the Good Friday Agreement a recent Irish Foreign Minister has said: 'We've allowed you the Union. But we're damned if we'll allow you to be British' (Cowen, quoted Aughey, 2001: 69). Such perceived 'hollowing out' of unionist cultural identity in Northern Ireland sits alongside the opinion that Southern Protes-tants have had to dilute their identity in the search of a small religious minority for acceptance (Harris, 2000) and significant manifestations in Southern Ireland that 'Irishness' still remains stubbornly Catholic and ethnic. Thus, while a short Orange parade to mark the formation of the Grand Lodge of Ireland in Dublin (admittedly a controversial aspect of Protestant Unionist tradition) was called off amid protests in May 2000, a military guard of honour accompanied the religious relics of St Thérèse of Lisieux as they toured the capital. The Angelus (Catholic call to prayer) continues to be broadcast on RTE, a public-service broadcaster, and the equally powerful symbolic content involved in the state ceremonial reburial of ten heroes of the 1916 uprising in October 2001 created a scene depicted by one experienced Irish commentator as involving 'unionists looking out at an Ireland which is not theirs' (Ryder, 2001). Beyond symbolism, strong racism in the Republic of Ireland against those with black skin has been commented upon by individuals not particularly sympathetic to partition (Paulin, 2000) and a recent report on pluralism in the Republic commented that 'the state's acceptance and resourcing of majority religion medical ethics and denominational education have perpetuated the unjust way that non-Catholic interests and culture have been excluded' (BT, 2001). It is undoubtedly with such factors in mind that David Trimble in March 2002 rather bluntly referred to the Republic of Ireland as a 'sectarian, mono-ethnic, mono-cultural state', indicating his preference to embed Northern Ireland within 'a liberal, multi-national state such as the United Kingdom' (BT, 2002). While this drew the terse rejoinder from the Republic's Attorney General that perhaps Trimble was 'actually applying to the Republic sentiments which are to be found more aptly used closer to home' (ibid.), unionist intent to present their identity increasingly within the wider British multicultural arena is clear. As expressed by another Ulster Unionist MP:

> Like the Scots and Welsh we have a very distinct and unique culture, but we
> have always looked to the multicultural nature of the United Kingdom as the
> best home to accommodate our diversity (Donaldson, 2001).

Before consideration of Ulster unionist identity claims for a home within the wider context of British multiculturalism, some reference to the 'Good Friday Agreement' of 1998, which has radically changed the context for such overtures, is unavoidable. Attention will then turn to spatial matters, not least to urban planning and its links with post-war identity conflict and management in Belfast.

THE GOOD FRIDAY AGREEMENT: A FOUNDATION MYTH FOR NORTHERN IRELAND?

The 'Good Friday' political agreement of 10 April 1998, a subsequent referendum where it received over 71% support and elections to a new power-sharing Assembly, have changed the context not only for planning but for governance as a whole in Northern Ireland. Here the Agreement has aptly been referred to as a 'consociational settlement', novel in comparative politics, which avoids the integration of peoples but tries to manage ethnic differences equally and justly (O'Leary, 1999:

76). Common citizenship rights linked to an equality agenda and what can be seen as fair and held in common, stand alongside the institutionalized recognition of the differences between the two major cultural identities in the North, which are to be treated on the basis of 'parity of esteem'. While it cannot be ruled out that a deeper, tolerant, cultural pluralism will take root, there is a structural reason to be doubtful. It is unlikely that the Good Friday Agreement will take on the nature of a foundation myth, a story claiming allegiance from both cultural identities, because, while progressive unionism regards the Agreement pragmatically, rather than enthusiastically, as the best deal available, nationalism sees the Agreement as a transitional step towards full Irish political unification, which demography and increasingly persuasion is expected to deliver. In the latter case a North–South Ministerial Council is seen as the embryonic institution of a federal Ireland, and for unionists a weaker British-Irish Council bringing together no less than eight governmental entities from the islands of Britain and Ireland (Westminster government, Republic of Ireland, Scotland, Wales, Northern Ireland, Jersey, Guernsey and the Isle of Man) meets concerns for reciprocity of linkages. In short, the Agreement 'rests on a bargain derived from diametrically conflicting hopes about its likely long-run outcome' (O'Leary, ibid. 68).

BRITISH MULTICULTURALISM AND UNIONIST IDENTITY

If debate on the meaning of Irishness in Ireland is gathering momentum, the debate on Britishness within the United Kingdom is now in full flow. Unfortunately this is a discussion to which unionists are making little contribution. In fact they have for a long time not been invited to the conversation. As expressed by one disdainful observer:

> The unionists may identify with Britain but the problem is that their homeland is not particularly keen to claim them as their own. After all, what are they, these uncomfortable people in their sashes and bowler hats? They are not Irish. Despite their claims, they are not British either. There lies their profound insecurity and the tragedy of the province. Deprived of group attachments and their legitimate expression, people defend their ancestral myths with violence (Phillips, 1999).

The Belfast-raised poet Tom Paulin takes a similar view: 'Middle class Protestants are still clinging to a British identity, but nobody over here (Britain) wants them' (Paulin, quoted Wroe, 2002). Thus, while ethnic conflict in Britain is a major factor prompting the debate on multiculturalism, Northern Ireland as a 'place apart', despite the widely accepted ethnic basis of its 'Troubles', is rarely included in a discursive loop where 'academic and popular language in Britain largely coincide in using ethnicity as a polite euphemism for "race"' (Poole, 1997: 134). In November 2001 there was some sign, however, that Northern Ireland could perhaps sit down at the British multicultural table, with a spokesman for John Reid, the Secretary of State for Northern Ireland, articulating the view that:

> We want to reach a situation where it is not cool for young people to be sectarian and we want to put across the point that identifying Britishness with inclusiveness and multiculturalism is the best defence of the union (quoted Clarke, 2001).

Only a few months previously, with ethnic 'troubles' in Bradford, Burnley and Oldham, the *Sunday Times* 'Insight Team' even asked the question: 'Does Belfast hold clues to Britain's race crisis?' (*Sunday Times*, 2001). With television scenes of burning cars and stone-throwing youths from other United Kingdom cities giving a 'respite' from all-too-predictable similar images from the streets of Belfast, deeper common associations with residential ethnic segregation, 'turf' demarcations and separate schooling have been too blatant to ignore. That there is merit in bringing experience from Northern Ireland to bear on wider identity questions within the United Kingdom is indeed supported by the official 'Cantle' report of the investigation into the 2001 race riots in northern English cities. Calling explicitly for a national debate on a shared British identity and highlighting separate education, places of worship, cultural activities and communal organizations, the report concludes that 'many communities operate on the basis of a series of parallel lives', which is indeed an apt description of the extent of ethnic separation in Belfast and Northern Ireland (Cantle, 2001). So far, unionist participation in the wider debate on British identity has been limited. In the event that this becomes possible with a bedding-down of the 'peace process' and the Good Friday Agreement (an event that cannot be taken for granted), unionist voices in the conversation could usefully stress the civic aspects of unionist identity over the cultural. While some might see this as a tall order, given the defensive and provocative presentation of an embattled ethnic identity which has long been the dominant aspect of unionism in Northern Ireland (Longley, 2001: 24), it can be regarded as by no means impossible. Indeed, the conflict between anti- and pro-Agreement unionists has been characterized as a struggle between unionism as a form of ethnic (Ulster/British) nationalism and a civic understanding of Britishness (Longley, ibid. 25). One recent unionist writer, putting the case for civic unionism based on equal citizenship, represents the radical edge of such unionist identity-thinking in suggesting the traditionally almost unthinkable idea that new arrangements in Northern Ireland 'might also entail public institutions exhibiting British and Irish symbols, or even new symbols of Northern Irishness, to reflect our complex condition and to help purge these symbols of their exclusive sectarian connotations' (Porter, 1996: 182). For unionists, connecting positively with debates in Britain on British identity would mean going beyond rhetorical statements. It would mean not seeking defensively and belligerently to promote an ethnic concept of Britishness but rather the positive promotion of a shared British identity as something not to be brushed off at the tail end of empire but redefined to provide a common civic glue within which multicultural identities can co-exist and flourish. The challenge exists, if moderate civic unionism can muster itself to overcome short-term difficulties (not the least of which is a feeling of insecurity deriving from a political republican link to a still-extant private army), and can disassociate itself from still seemingly supremacist manifestations of narrow ethnic identity (most obviously present in some Orange parades), to connect positively with important, post-'cool Britannia', British questions of the moment. Making a civic sense of Britishness work in this corner of the United Kingdom and giving due recognition to questions of cultural identity might provide the basis for a useful exchange of experience of shared concerns. Crucial here is the recognition that balancing civic and cultural identity with the problems involved in this is an issue under heated discussion and presently writ large in the not-so-'United Kingdom'. This was a matter central to the report published in the autumn of 2000 on 'The Future of Multi-Ethnic Britain', better known as the Parekh Report.

THE PAREKH REPORT

The Parekh Report can be seen as a call for a reinvention of Britishness at a time when many academic commentators are predicting the eventual departure of Britain from the historical stage (Nairn, 2000). Prominent here has been the left-wing voice of Tom Nairn, who has referred to Britain as 'the empire's rump state' (Nairn, 2000: 79), embodying the increasingly ritual, empty and formal administrative structure of what is contemptuously called 'Ukania'. In the hollow shell of 'Ukania' Britishness is moribund, with the tenacity of island ethnicities (including that of the English) now asserting themselves. Britain, it is argued, can no longer sustain itself in the face of the redundancy of the post-imperial state and the drift towards a European identity where a rights-based legal system challenges British notions of parliamentary sovereignty on the one hand and where narratives of nationalism have once again become respectable (Aughey, 2001: 61). Other voices take a less pessimistic view of the durability, desirability and adaptability of British identity. The argument has been made that British identity existed before the Act of Union in 1707 joining England, Scotland and Wales, being in the making since the 10th century (Partridge,

1999: 10) and, as pointed out by Donald Dewar, former First Minister of Scotland, since 1707 a 'community of interest' and democratic solidarity has evolved (Dewar, quoted Aughey, 2001: 9). In the opinion of one academic reviewer of the 'Ukania' argument and former member of the Northern Ireland Community Relations Council:

> It does seem rather unlikely that Britain *only* had an imperial meaning and could survive only on the life-support system of empire if only because empire itself had no single meaning. Moreover, if one's identity is entirely defined in relation to what is external and different, then one has no identity at all. That is what the Ukania thesis does assert about Britain today. But that is surely a gross exaggeration. It fails to do justice to the solidarities and communities of interest which do, for the moment at least, depend on there being substance to the idea of Britain irrespective of imperialism (Aughey, 2001: 48).

The Act of Union of 1801 which created the United Kingdom, binding close a 'restless Ireland' and extending a single system of government over the whole 'British Isles' (Beckett, 1971: 128), has left, two centuries later, an 'imagined community', to use Benedict Anderson's phrase, in the North of Ireland, with a distinct sense of felt Britishness and common community of interest woven into its identity and facing a significant cultural 'other' whose felt identity comes from different emotional wellsprings and historical experiences. In his most recent contribution to the Ukania debate, Nairn, while castigating Ulster Unionism for an instinctive knee-jerk preference for old imperial Britishness (Nairn, 2001: 67), interestingly sees in the new political structures of the Good Friday Agreement (especially the new 'Council of the Isles' or British-Irish Council) the beginnings of new constitutional and administrative structures which could be new vessels for containing some sense of reworked Britishness after all:

> Our collective stake in the archipelago is far too high for most people to think of abandoning it (Britishness) *altogether* (italics original, Nairn, 2001: 62–3).

The 'Parekh Report' (FMEB, 2000) has set the backdrop for New Labour thinking on British identity and citizenship in the 21st century. The report, the product of a 23-member commission set up by the Runnymede Trust and chaired by the political theorist and working Labour peer Bhikhu Parekh, provoked controversy by putting a polemical question mark against the use of the term 'British', suggesting that it is associated with racial connotations of white colonialism. The report, in calling for a formal declaration that Britain is a multicultural society and in

its highlighting of racial and ethnic discrimination, has been described as a gener-
alization of the Macpherson Report of 1999, which had investigated the failure of
the police to pursue the perpetrators of the racist killing of Stephen Lawrence in
South London in 1993 (Barry, 2001: 57). The report and the discussion surrounding it leave considerable room for Ulster unionists to enthusiastically associate
themselves with a renegotiated, inclusive, British identity bringing together 'a
community of communities', which the report conceives Britain to be. In the words
of the commission, Britain should be thought of as a 'federation of cultures held
together by common bonds of interest and affection and a collective sense of
belonging' (Parekh, 2000). There seems, however, in principle, no reason why
'Britishness' should end at the arbitrary landmass of the Isle of Man, although this
seems an implicit bias in the report:

> People in Britain have many differences, but they inhabit the same space and
> share the same future. All have a role in the collective project of fashioning
> Britain as an outward looking, generous inclusive society …
>
>   A state is not only a territorial and political entity, but also an 'imagined
> community'. A genuinely multicultural Britain urgently needs to reimagine
> himself (FMEB, 2000).

That Ulster unionists have the opportunity of being part of this 'reimagination' is
accentuated by the fact that the report encourages, for example, organizations 'to
devise policies that promote diversity as well as equality' and argues for the establishment of an Equality Commission and a Human Rights Commission, an agenda
(it could be argued) that was prefigured in the Good Friday Agreement.

The Parekh Report is certainly not the last word in negotiating a new 'template' for British identity. One major debating point identified by a critic of the
report is that real problems exist in finding a secure basis for deciding where
respect for cultural diversity and associated practices ends and where adherence
to the content of the common civic nationality needed to integrate all members of
society begins. This is a problem not unknown in the present context of Northern
Ireland. Parekh in his academic writing on multiculturalism is critical of the ethno-
centricity of contemporary liberal political philosophers including John Rawls,
whose theory of justice and language of universal standards is criticized as not
leaving enough space for diversity. Parekh prefers the resolution of the possible
tension between specific cultural practices and the need for a common sense of
'agreed' Britishness to be based more pragmatically on 'the operative public values
of the wider society' (Parekh, quoted Barry, 2001: 64). As to why these values
should, in the last instance, trump the values of minority communities can thus be
seen as a failure of the report to explain 'why the majority's imposition of its values

on a minority is anything more than an application of the doctrine that might makes right' (Barry, 2001: 67). Because of this the report has been further criticized for not making enough of the expectations that minority ethnic communities can be held to as a condition of inclusion in the nation (ibid. 56).

In 2002 this was a nettle that British Home Secretary David Blunkett was not afraid to grasp. A government White Paper on citizenship suggested that, as a condition of seeking British nationality and to help newcomers to develop a British sense of identity, immigrants would be required to attend citizenship classes, learn English and take a loyalty pledge. Rejecting the notion that the requirement to learn English could be seen as an assault on human rights, the appeal is to a sense of Britishness based on the Parekh preference for public values in the wider society. Britishness for Blunkett is thus:

> Respect for laws we have developed in our country over centuries, that encourage norms of behaviour which we have to enforce (Blunkett, quoted Gerard, 2002).

The question of the minimum of adaptation that is to be expected of immigrant communities is a debate that takes place on a Europe-wide scale. It was brought dramatically to the forefront in the Netherlands with the murder of Pim Fortuyn in April 2002. In relation to the ongoing debate in the United Kingdom, Melanie Phillips, in an article in the *Spectator* in May 2002, rejecting any sort of lazy, academic, post-modernist cultural relativism, defined the minimum of adaptation as:

> welcoming Muslims, certainly; but, as with all minorities, it means expecting them to adopt a common civic identity which subscribes to overarching British values, under whose umbrella they can pursue their own culture and traditions – provided that the two do not conflict. When they do, the host culture wins (Phillips, quoted Ash, 2002).

One critic of the views of Phillips, while regarding them as too aggressive and lacking in sensitivity, nevertheless concedes that such debate is necessary provided that the minorities we are talking about are full partners in the debate (Ash, 2002). It is a pity that Ulster unionists on this wider stage are not sufficiently bringing their own recent experience to bear. On the local stage of Northern Ireland the Good Friday Agreement, still the best chance for peace, was couched, to the consternation of those preferring a simple colonialist analysis (Rolston, 1998), in the language of multiculturalism, but the accretion of common civic glue is still proving elusive.

SPATIALITY OF IDENTITY CONFLICT IN BELFAST: HISTORICAL CONSIDERATIONS

Whilst the arrival of town and country planning 'proper' in Northern Ireland is commonly taken to accord with the appointment of Professor Robert Matthew in 1960 to prepare a Belfast Regional Survey and Plan (Greer and Jess, 1987: 105), something of the essence of spatial planning in Belfast is lost if historical links to ethnic identity-constitution are not given central attention. It is difficult to disagree with the view expressed by the historian A.T.Q. Stewart that:

> topography is the key to the Ulster conflict. Unless you know exactly who lives where and why, much of it does not make sense (Stewart, 1989: 56).

Territory is not a neutral backcloth for conflict in Belfast and Northern Ireland. The conflict between the two identities is rather shot through with socio-spatial meanings that have long lineage. While some continue to see this lineage in the black-and-white colonial terms of supremacist newcomers who refuse to assimilate (Miller *et al.*, 1998), a more nuanced interpretation is likely to seek answers in the specificities of the 'Ulster problem'. As Stewart points out, within the context of the United Kingdom in the 19th century, unionism was created largely in reaction to the new forms that Catholic nationalism was taking. Underlining the view that 'the Ulster problem is, when all is said and done, only the Ulster problem' (Stewart, ibid. 161), David Trimble in his Nobel Peace Prize lecture in 1998 put it this way:

> I have, in fact, some fairly serious reservations about the merits of using any conflict, not least Northern Ireland, as a model for the study, never mind the solution, of other conflicts. In fact, if anything, the opposite is true. Let me spell this out. I believe that a sense of the unique, specific and concrete circumstances of any situation is the first indispensable step to solving the problems posed by that situation (Trimble, 2000: 54–5).

In terms of the specifics of urban planning and spatial identity-construction, a key occurrence in the North of Ireland was in the task given in 1608 to Sir Arthur Chichester, the King's Lord Deputy in Ireland, who was sent from Dublin to carry out a survey of Ulster and to report to London. Following the survey, the government's recommendations for the physical and economic development of Ulster included the planning of 23 new plantation towns, most of which were built (Evans and Patton, 1981: 20). The subsequent 17th-century plantation of Ulster, when England sought to consolidate control over the northern part of Ireland, marks the emergence of Belfast as a significant settlement attracting Protestant settlers and with an earth rampart constructed to protect the settlement against the Irish (Boal, 1995: 10). A sense of threat was implicit from the beginning. In the new towns, as Stewart points out, the castles, walled courtyards and fortified houses were not built for ornament (Stewart, 1989: 45–6). As the man with chief responsibility for directing the plantation of Ulster, Chichester was keen to set an example to others on his own grant of expropriated lands in and around Belfast (Bardon, 1992: 123). For over 200 years descendants of the Chichester family were to leave their proprietary mark on Belfast through street names and town-planning schemes before the age of such patronage-planning ended in the 19th century. Formative in the formation of settler identity during the early plantation years was the extensive massacre of newcomers in the 1641 rebellion. Stewart says this of the enduring legacy:

> The fear which it inspired survives in the Protestant subconscious as the meaning of the Penal Laws or the Famine persists in the Catholic . . . Here, if anywhere, the mentality of siege was born, as the warning bonfires blazed from hill top to hill top, and the beating drums summoned men to the defence of castles and walled towns crowded with refugees (Stewart, 1989: 49–52).

Residential segregation in Belfast and Northern Ireland dating back to the 18th century and beyond has been likened by the historian A.T.Q. Stewart to 'the disposition of opposing forces in a battle which has never ended' (Stewart, ibid. 56). In Belfast, because the native Irish were a small minority in a Protestant hinterland, they had been permitted to enter the city in the 18th century rather than being 'kept in their place' outside the walls, as in Derry (ibid. 59). In the 19th century, with rapid industrialization and a large Catholic influx of population, a pattern of segregated 'ethnic zones' in Belfast was to become established, recognizable to the present, where identity for many was firmly linked to locality and its defence. Incoming migrants, both Catholic and Protestant, imported intense territorial sensitivities well-honed in the rural landscapes to the west (Boal, 1996: 153). Here the urban geographer Professor Frederick Boal, who more than anyone else has mapped segregation in Belfast, points to the role of such spatial segregation in identity construction:

> It is easy to decry segregation. Undoubtedly it can lead to the reinforcement of stereotypes by reducing or preventing inter-group contact . . . on the other hand, where inter-group conflict is a dominant theme, segregation can perform a positive role. Concentration provides the basis for defence against physical attack; it provides a means of avoiding what may be difficult or embarrassing contact with strangers; it provides a basis for cultural preservation. It may offer an environment conducive to ethnic entrepreneurship, while forming an electoral

base for those members of the ethnic group who aspire to promote their group's interests in the political arena. In the worst-case scenario, segregated neighbourhoods provide an operations platform for the urban guerrilla (Boal, 1996: 155).

The spatial affirmation of identity, however, goes beyond the 'mere' occupation of territory to incorporate other symbolic claiming practices which planners in Belfast and Northern Ireland would sooner ignore. Before moving on to consider specifically the relationship of urban planning to post-war identity conflict and construction in Belfast, some of these are worth mention. They include the symbolic claims of the Stormont parliament building in Belfast and the spatial practices bound up with parades, murals, bonfires and place-naming not likely to find acknowledgement in any official plan ever produced for the city.

In Stormont, nationalist cultural identity confronts in spatial form an apex representational space symbolizing the Protestant-Unionist cultural identity of 'the other'. This space means very different things to both ethnic identities, which is related in turn to other planning issues in Belfast, even if unaddressed by professional planners, involving conflict over the spatial constitution of identity.

An official government publication introduces the building thus:

> The Northern Ireland Parliament Building stands on an elevated site at Stormont, about 5 miles from the centre of Belfast. The main approach to the building is by a broad processional avenue three-quarters of a mile long and rising some 180 feet, planted on either side with a double row of lime trees, and running through well-tended grounds of 300 acres. At the top of the avenue, a staircase of granite steps 90 feet wide leads up to the building itself, 365 feet long, 164 feet wide and 70 feet high, rising to 92 feet at the centre of the main façade (HMSO, undated).

In a similar neutral style, employing the detached language of aesthetics, Belfast's leading architectural historian describes the Parliament Buildings, designed in the 1920s by Arnold Thornley from Liverpool, as 'one of the most outstanding architectural sites in Ireland'. With a 'very dignified exterior', designed in the Greek classical tradition with a grand Ionic temple front, the building, opened in 1932, 'enjoys a magnificent and commanding situation to the east of the city' (Larmour, 1987: 110–11). With a façade of Portland stone above a plinth of granite from the local Mourne mountains, Stormont looks down upon what two urban conservationist writers have described as 'one of the most impressive man-made vistas in the Province'. This 'showpiece of the local conservation movement', it is suggested, could have a role in the creation of an 'image for Belfast' (Hendry and

McEldowney, 1987: 51). It is most unlikely, however, that such a contentious image can ever gain general acceptance in its meaning (Figure 5.1).

A closer examination of Stormont reveals that its construction was constitutive of a partially successful unionist project. It symbolized the fact that while southern Ireland had, despite Protestant opposition, left the Union with Britain, nevertheless the division of Ireland had given recognition and legitimacy to the unionist position of maintaining the link with Britain. The building, in short, symbolizes unionist self-assertion and the will to preserve their British cultural identity against the nationalist 'other'. From the top of Stormont, a large statue of Britannia, flanked by two guardian lions, looks out over Belfast's eastern suburbs. On the pediment below her, another group of statues 'represents Ulster presenting the golden flame of loyalty to Britain and the Commonwealth' (HMSO, undated: 3). This loyalist ensemble, firmly expressing unionism in terms of a British identity, in turn looks down upon a large bronze monumental sculpture of Northern Ireland's founding father, Lord Edward Carson, who rises up on a granite plinth at the end point of the processional avenue. The depiction of the unionist leader 'galvanized in rhetorical declaration' has been described as the 'expressive personification of the challenge which was mounted to an ascendant Irish nationalism' (Officer, 1996: 142). Panels around the base of the statue depict various scenes in the history of early Ulster Unionism, including the signing of the Ulster Covenant in September 1912. Stormont was deliberately conceived to physically constitute a grand

Figure 5.1 Parliament buildings at Stormont, Belfast

symbolic demarcation of difference and, impressive as it is, was actually scaled down on financial grounds from a more grandiose building with a grand dome.

The completion of Stormont, in the words of Hugh Pollock, a government unionist spokesman of the time, was the 'outward and visible proof of the permanence of our institutions; that for all time we are bound indissolubly to the British crown' (Pollock, quoted Bardon, 1982: 225). Seventy years on, and in the wake of the Anglo-Irish Agreement of 1985, the Downing Street Declaration of 1993 and the Good Friday Agreement of 1998, which explicitly recognize the legitimacy of two ethnic identities in Northern Ireland and contemplate Irish unity under certain circumstances, the indissolubility of the link to the British crown is precisely at risk in unionist eyes. Against this background, issues of representational space go to the heart of unionist cultural insecurity in Northern Ireland. In an astute observation by Graham, the implications of which have not been taken on board by planners in Northern Ireland, it has been pointed out that the single most important weakness of the unionist cause 'arguably lies in its failure to develop – through the creation of a specific heritage – a separate place consciousness' (Graham, 1994: 141). Stormont, at the apex of Protestant representational space, was intended as a symbol of defiance against Irish Catholic nationalism, not as an icon of Ulster Protestant nationalism (Boyce, quoted Graham, ibid.). No attempt has been made to produce a Protestant historic foundation myth. The greatness of the British past was a sufficient substitute (Coakley, 1990, quoted Graham, ibid.). In the words of Graham:

> British Ulster demonstrates the weakness and futility of a place in which the imaginary and symbolic world of identity is external to itself. The Unionist failure to recognise the centrality of laying claim and giving meaning to the landscape of Ulster, as distinct from grabbing territory, is part and parcel of the nationalist claim to 'the rhetorical high ground of moral advantage against the putative descendants of their oppressors' (Buckley, 1991) (Graham, 1994: 143).

Without an adequate representational landscape involving the construction of identity in symbolic spatial terms, northern Protestant Unionists continue to live in a state of embattled planter or settler-insecurity. If civic unionism is weak, ethnic spatial claims can appear to outside eyes to be weaker still.

From the perspective of the other ethnic identity in Northern Ireland, Stormont is a place that has always been anathematized by republicans (Officer, 1996: 130) and jars with the orientation to a different symbolic order on the part of more moderate Catholic nationalists. Brian Faulkner, a past Northern Ireland Prime Minister, describes how questions of symbolism were important to the Catholic SDLP party in formulating the operational practices in 1973 of Northern Ireland's last elected Assembly with executive responsibility. For example, the SDLP wanted the

Assembly to meet not at Stormont but in Ireland's ecclesiastical capital, Armagh. Westminster trappings and references to the Queen in procedures were disputed. Going to the heart of the matter, Faulkner writes: 'It was an argument over symbols, and to many Irish politicians symbols are the central issue in politics' (Faulkner, 1978: 202). While the experience of 75 years of Irish partition and nearly 30 years of civil conflict have forged a discernibly northern Catholic identity (O'Connor, 1993), nationalists still tap into a Gaelic-Catholic Irish identity (Figure 5.2), from whose exclusivity northern Protestants feel alienated to the point of denying their own Irishness. From the position of such relative cultural security, the hitherto unthinkable event of Sinn Féin ministers serving in a Northern Ireland Executive has now come to pass. This has, however, been symbolically represented as a frontal assault and occupation of a unionist citadel (Figure 5.3). In deference to such sensibilities the Queen in 2002 in her Jubilee visit to Stormont chose to speak to Assembly members in the building's foyer and not in the parliamentary chamber. While the agreement of Sinn Féin to meet in Stormont may be regarded as an unacknowledged symbolic prop to reformist unionism, other rebranding of Stormont's image has been helpfully in evidence. The hallowed ground of Unionism has been opened up to public concerts from, among others, Elton John, Pavarotti, Rod Stewart and the Eagles, and planning permission has been given to develop part of the grounds for environmental education purposes and playground space. Nationalism, in any case, can look to meanings invested in the enduring natural features of Belfast's Cavehill, which looks down on the city. Here in the late 18th century Protestant and Catholic 'United Irishmen' had climbed to the summit to give birth to civic Republicanism by the swearing of an oath committing themselves to subverting the authority of England over Ireland (Knox, 1997: 158). The power in the rock stays strong.

From Stormont, at the apex of contested representational space in Belfast, with its stone solidity and classical claims constituting in physical terms unionist legitimacy for the division of Ireland, other spatial reverberations flow. Four of these are briefly considered before the following section, which periodizes post-war identity conflict and spatial planning management in Belfast. Identity is contentiously spatialized in wall murals, parades, bonfires and place-naming.

WALL MURALS

The practice of marking territory through kerb-painting and, more creatively, wall murals continues in Belfast's Catholic and Protestant working-class areas. However, while republican wall murals can tap into powerful mythological Irish imagery, mobilized alongside military symbolism in the struggle for a future place-vision of the island, loyalist-unionist murals, in the main, tend to reflect the desire for a return to the *status quo ante* and an unequivocal link with Britain as

Figure 5.2 Irish republican iconography, Falls Road, Belfast, 1998

Figure 5.3 The rebranding of place, Belfast-style, 1998

depicted in the imagery of Stormont. There are signs that a crisis in unionist identity is producing murals that try to create a history for unionists as ancient as that claimed by nationalists but they do not really overcome what remains a central problem:

> Loyalism, with its central claim to maintain the past, does not switch easily to articulating the future; nor do its muralists easily find the themes and images of a future vision in the absence of that articulation (Rolston, 1995: viii).

PARADES

It is above all in relation to parades, or marches, in Belfast and Northern Ireland that clashes over the symbolic marking of territory and investing spatial practices with deep meaning have in recent years come to the attention of the international media. Spatial practices invested with a particular set of meanings by unionists can be interpreted quite differently by nationalists. Protestant marches, especially around the Twelfth of July, the commemoration of the Battle of the Boyne where in 1690 Protestant King William III defeated Catholic King James II, are seen by unionists as expressing their right to be Protestant and British in Ireland. As a unionist contributor to a government enquiry on the contentious issue of marches in Belfast and Northern Ireland put it, parades as exhibitions of celebration and commemoration 'attest to our survival as a community on this island' (HMSO, 1997: 44). Whereas for many nationalists a sense of identity is expressed through identification with the wider Irish community, the Catholic Church, the Irish language and so on, for unionists, the spatial constitution and affirmation of identity is central:

> In reality the Loyalist sense of identity achieves its positive valency (that is, being more than simply non-Irishness) in being actively paraded. That identity is dependent on the rehearsed myths, ritualised practices, and confrontations of the marching season. Indeed these symbolic practices in which the young play such a significant part today – the bonfires, the painting of kerbs, the erection of flags, arches and bunting, the marching bands and the parades themselves – are the specific means by which an exclusive Protestant identity is represented and renewed in the loyalist mind. Here primarily an embodied ideology is at work. It is the sound of the Lambeg drum rather than the resonance of political ideology which brings tears to the eyes of a Loyalist (Bell, 1990, quoted Bryson and McCartney, 1994).

From the standpoint of nationalist culture, where parades are not such a marked feature of identity formation, Protestant marches, rather than projecting the air of a unionist Mardi Gras, have communicated triumphalist messages. This is particularly the case when Orange parades, adhering to traditional routes, insist on marching through nationalist neighbourhoods. Referring to the political decoration of public space during the marching season, Rolston refers to the period before direct rule in Northern Ireland and the prorogation of Stormont when

> The Orange arches, erected over public roads, took on the significance of ancient yokes, reducing to the status of subjects all nationalists who could not avoid passing under them (Rolston, 1992: ii).

However, with the old assurances of Stormont symbolism gone, the role of parades in the constitution of unionist identity unfortunately seems more important than ever, representing to them not so much triumphalism as an affirmation of the right of a cultural identity to exist. With the rituals of the 'marching season' bands and banners symbolically occupy space and make ethnic territorial claims. Here Jarman refers to how Belfast

> was never just a collection of streets, factories, shops and buildings: it was always partly a place of the imagination, which could only ever really be realised in the act of movement ... (parading) also forms part of the process of mapping the city, inscribing an identity into the physical geography and reconnecting the fragmented parts into an idealised whole (Jarman, 1997: 88–9).

Under new conditions, however, such unreconstructed symbolic spatial practices can obstruct the process of civic identity-building.

BONFIRES

In their ethnic primordiality bonfires come close to the effect of the Lambeg drum in their symbolic appropriation of space. Bonding around a fire, especially when it involves the warding-off of threat, touches on the most basic human instincts. One cannot improve on the observation of A.T.Q. Stewart:

> (Bonfires) are among the most enduring signals used by either community to indicate a victory over the other. The red leaping flames, lighting up the wild and passionate intensity of gaunt Ulster faces, are a well remembered element in every Ulster childhood, even the most sheltered. It may be despised, condemned, arouse revulsion and even horror – but to an Ulsterman it speaks unmistakably of home (Stewart, 1989: 70).

PLACE-NAMING

Despite the fact that the name 'Belfast' is an anglicized version of the ancient Celtic name Beal Feirsde (loosely translated as 'approach to the ford'), unionists feel threatened by the Irish language as a symbolic marker of territory. As one liberal unionist has admitted, even having a benign view on the Irish language is politically damaging for any unionist (McGimpsey, quoted in Purdy, 1996). While a campaign by nationalists led in 1995 to the legalizing of Irish street names along-side English ones where residents want it, unionists in Belfast's City Hall remain hostile to the idea. A Democratic Unionist Party (DUP) councillor in the city has referred to Irish as a 'Leprechaun language' (Wilson, quoted Kachuk, 1993: 325), with his party claiming in the 1997 City Council election campaign that it was leading the resistance to Government plans to force ratepayers to fund the erection of street signs in Irish (DUP, 1997). This linguistic cultural war of attrition, where language is perceived and used as a marker of division, has been elevated to a new plane by the designation of what most regard as the dialect of Ulster-Scots as of formal equal-language status with Irish in the deliberations of the new Northern Ireland Assembly. Cultivation of this lunatic cultural fringe may be seen as dissipating energy from developing an updated civic unionism and dissipating major financial resources to boot. An Ulster-Scots Board (Tha Boord o Ulster Scotch) is now headed by a chairman who describes Ulster-Scots as 'almost certainly the fastest growing cultural movement in Europe' (Laird, 2002). Academic rigour is injected by the Ulster-Scots Institute at the University of Ulster (Clarke, 2003). The culture war is not without its wryly amusing aspects. In late 1999, Ulster-Scots road names were removed by loyalists who thought they were Irish (BT, 1999).

URBAN PLANNING AND POST-WAR IDENTITY CONFLICTS IN BELFAST

This section considers the most significant flagship plans for Belfast in the last five decades of the 20th century and the new Belfast Metropolitan Area Plan presently being prepared for adoption in a few years' time. Various major planning documents are considered in their relationship to the 'management' of identity conflict and the general characterization of urban policy in Belfast is periodized under various shorthand headings. This is summarized in Figure 5.4. Belfast *coasted* through the 1950s and began an overdue *modernizing* process in the 1960s before becoming a *fortress* city in the 1970s under the weight of violent ethnic conflict at its most intense. A *pariah city* in the 1980s attempted under the increasing imperatives of place-marketing and political conflict-management to implausibly

	General characterization of the city	Flagship plans	Approach to conflict management
1950s	Coasting City	Plannning Proposals for the Belfast Area – Second Report of the Planning Commission (1951).	A 'cold house' for Catholics under ethnic unionism.
1960s	Modernizing City	Belfast Regional Survey and Plan (The Matthew Plan, 1964). Belfast Urban Area Plan 1969 (Building Design Partnership).	Reformist civic unionism makes haste too slowly.
1970s	Fortress City	'Peace-wall' planning in Belfast 1969+ NI Regional Physical Development Strategy 1977.	Conflict containment and military intervention.
1980s	Re-imaged Pariah City	Belfast Housing Renewal Strategy (NIHE, 1982). Laganside concept plan 1987. Belfast Urban Area Plan – 2001. Preliminary Proposals 1987; Final plan 1990.	Normalization and equality agenda.
1990s	Looking to the Emerald City	2025 Belfast City Vision (2000). Shaping 'our' Future: Regional Development Strategy for Northern Ireland 2025. Draft 1998; Final 2002.	Search for cultural inclusion. (The promise of the Good Friday Agreement.)
2000+	Dual City	Belfast Metropolitan Area Plan 2015. Issues paper 2002. Final 2004. (Ostrich planning)	Ethnic poker.

Figure 5.4 Planning phases in Belfast, 1950 to present

remake its image by putting lipstick on the gorilla. In the 1990s an *Emerald City* began to appear at the end of the 'yellow brick road' of the peace process. With the illusions of Oz now dissipated, the question that hangs over planning in Belfast is to what degree the city will be *contested or shared*. This is a conversation in which planners in the main are unfortunately silent.

COASTING CITY: BELFAST IN THE 1950S

The Belfast-born poet John Hewitt, looking back in 1969 at the birth of 'the Troubles', published a poem entitled 'The coasters'. The subject matter was chickens coming home to roost from the lack of development of civic-minded unionism especially among the Protestant middle class, whose Unionist party representatives were amply reflected in the composition of the Belfast City Corporation which ran the city. The poem ends as follows:

> You coasted along
> and the sores suppurated and spread.
>
> Now the fever is high and raging;
> Who would have guessed it, coasting along?
> The ignorant-sick thresh about in delirium
> And tear at the scabs with dirty finger-nails.
> The cloud of infection hangs over the city,
> A quick change of wind and it
> Might spill over the leafy suburbs.
> You coasted too long.

While the coasting that Hewitt describes continued into the 1960s, the evoked image of complacency before the whirlwind has its roots in planning for the city in the 1950s. In physical planning for the city the ethnicity of spatiality was merely a passive backdrop and there was official reluctance to tackle physical infrastructural problems in general (Boal, 1967: 174). While one Belfast historian has described the 1950s as 'the most peaceful decade Belfast enjoyed in the 20th century' (Bardon, 1999: 105), the sores to which Hewitt refers include well-known and documented employment discrimination against Catholics in the labour market (Rolston and Tomlinson, 1988) and other unfair sectarian practices for which the term 'cold house for Catholics' may appear a euphemism. Amidst a 'backlog of neglect' in tackling housing problems in Belfast (Singleton, 1987: 154), a former chair of the Northern Ireland Housing Executive has referred to how

a first-class housing crisis was one of the principal contributory factors to the
Troubles ... In some areas there was more than a suspicion of conscious and
deliberate sectarian discrimination in the building and allocation of houses
(Brett, 1986: 36–7).

In 1942, the government of Northern Ireland had set up a Planning Commission,
from whose seeds the present-day professional planning in Northern Ireland has
grown. Reporting in 1951 on Belfast and its region, the Commission recommended a more strategic top-down approach to physical planning, among other
things to help modernize the economy and secure outside investment (HMSO,
1951). This idea, long discussed after the war, was to remain on the shelf until
the 1960s. Looking behind the lack of political will in the 1950s to change things
one critic lays the responsibility at the door of narrow ethnic unionism. The
changes required, Weiner argues, would have 'threatened the basis of the
Orange system':

> The influx of large industrial and commercial concerns would wipe out much of
> local industry and small scale retail trade, while the centralisation of
> administration would mean an end of local control and an end therefore of
> patronage, discrimination and ultimately of the protected position of the
> Protestant workforce (Weiner, 1980: 31).

In the 1960s, civic unionism got its chance but failed.

MODERNIZING CITY: BELFAST IN THE 1960S
Terence O'Neill, who as Prime Minister of Northern Ireland in the 1960s became a
standard-bearer for civic unionism, ultimately failed to face down the atavistic calls
of the past from ethnic unionism before 'the Troubles' engulfed them in 1969.
What Cooke refers to as the 'Janus-faced character' of the making of identities,
'keeping one foot securely in the past while placing the other in the uncertainties of
the future (being) actively produced' (Cooke, 1990: xii), remains problematic for
unionism under more difficult circumstances than those faced in the 1960s, but the
civic virtues of equality, fairness, justice and inclusiveness appealed to by O'Neill
maintain their relevance (O'Neill, 1969: 112–46). Economic and administrative
modernization, given an impetus by multinational companies knocking at Northern
Ireland's door, also had a physical planning face. The emphasis as O'Neill put it
would be on 'the improvement of communications; the provision of housing and
vital services; and upon a many-sided modernization of the local environment'
(O'Neill, 1969: 107). Under a new Ministry of Development a planning study was
commissioned from Sir Robert Matthew, the ghost of whose recommendations,

now commonly perceived to be ethnically insensitive, continue to reside in the
background of virtually all physical planning in Northern Ireland. The Matthew plan,
with the intention of demagnetizing the role of Belfast, proposed, drawing upon
growth-pole theory at the time, the promotion of development nodes which could
take some overspill population and help to protect Belfast's green belt. The growth
towns selected, however, were 'east of the River Bann' and therefore in predominantly Protestant space, the River Bann being a geographical divide in Northern
Ireland which also flows through people's minds. The naming of the major new
growth centre, the new city of Craigavon, after a former Prime Minister of Northern
Ireland who famously referred to Stormont as 'a Protestant Parliament for a
Protestant people' and the controversial location of a new university in Northern
Ireland near the Protestant town of Coleraine rather than in Catholic Derry compounded a feeling in the eyes of nationalists that civic unionism, whatever battles it
had to fight with its defenders of the *status quo*, was 'fine sentiment but little sub-
stance' (Osborne and Singleton, 1982: 177). A plan for the Belfast Urban Area
prepared by the consultancies Building Design Partnership and Travers Morgan
put forward proposals in 1969 to revamp physical space in Belfast within a
Matthew context, allied to major proposals for urban motorway construction.
Important abstract and codified categorizations of space, 'representations of
space' in Lefebvre's terms, devoid of the local meanings wrapped up in local 'representational spaces' (Liggett, 1995: 248), were quickly to show their brittleness
as the ethnicity of space reasserted itself with a vengeance in the 1970s.

FORTRESS CITY: BELFAST IN THE 1970S

Fortress aspects of planning during these years were reflected both in the pattern
of increasing residential segregation and in physical defensive measures to protect
the city centre from an IRA bombing campaign. Between 1970 and 1975 this campaign destroyed around 300 establishments in Belfast city centre and over a
quarter of the total retail floor space (Browne, 1985). Radical defensive security
measures ensued, including the 'ring of steel' security cordon at entrances to the
city centre where pedestrians and vehicles were searched. The government's
Review of Transportation Strategy in 1978 recommended the construction of a
high-grade motorway link running to the north and west of the city centre and
canyoned through part of its length. The road acted virtually as a moat, cutting off
the city centre from the Catholic and Protestant housing areas of the Falls and
Shankill. The spreading of riots emanating from within these areas into the city
centre was, therefore, made extremely difficult following the construction of this
'Westlink'. Where the road formed a flyover, or was at ground level, pedestrian
access to the city centre was guarded by heavily fortified police bases almost like
bastions in medieval walled towns. Planning and development in this protected city

centre would take on deep symbolic meaning in the 1980s, as a deliberate coun-
terposing by government in conflict management of the promise of prosperous normality with the destruction concomitant with extreme ethnic strife. It is, however,
the retreat into fortified residential camps, in many places demarcated with so-
called 'peace walls' in ethnic 'interface zones', that has left a more enduring spatial
legacy from these years (Figures 5.5 and 5.6). In the months of August and September 1969, amid intense inter-ethnic violence, a total of over 3500 families were
displaced in Belfast, an experience that burns deep into collective memory. In September 1969 the decision was taken to erect the first 'peace lines' between
Catholic and Protestant areas. Amid continuing fear, intimidation and arson, esti-
mates put the number of displaced families by February 1973 at somewhere
between 8000 and 15000 (Higgins, 2001: 28–9). In an already deeply segregated city, what Boal (1996: 152) has referred to as the 'segregation ratchet' was
racked up another notch in the 1970s (movement of the ratchet has historically
been one-way only), such that by 1981 over half of the population of Belfast lived
in highly segregated areas (Doherty, 1990: 28). Higgins makes a point that illumi-
nates the relationship between segregation and local identity in Belfast:

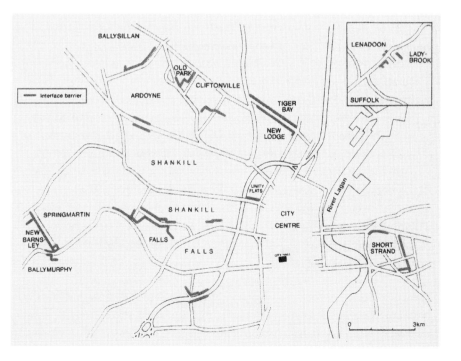

Figure 5.5 Belfast's peacelines

Figure 5.6 A door remains tentatively open on one of Belfast's peacelines

The displacement of these years led to a re-mapping of Belfast. Segregation, already a feature of the city, was consolidated and formalised in the erection of 'peace lines'. The politics of identity are most strongly asserted along borders and Belfast has created a series of borders along which fear, violence and the expression of ethnic identity code behaviour and shape private and communal life. The 'interface' areas are fortified, not simply by the erection of steel barriers, walls and gates, but also by a series of flags and symbols which mark out the identity of communities. Murals have become an important part of the claiming and reclaiming of certain areas. These spaces of public art are both political and historical in intention. They act as an internal dialogue and interpretation of the politics of the place and provide a public statement of the context and temper of Loyalist and Republican minds. In their assertion of local identity and the underpinning of paramilitary allegiance they can act as aggressive symbols of belonging (Higgins, 2001: 29).

The relationship of identity to the holding and defending of territory in Belfast was further illustrated in the 1970s by a planning and housing scheme to relieve over-crowding in west Belfast, where the majority of Catholic victims of eviction or intim-idation had taken refuge. A plan to build a new social housing estate at Poleglass in the greenbelt on the west Belfast boundary was strongly resisted by Protestants as an incursion into their space. The result, a scaled-back planning proposal, pleased neither side, with nationalists seeing in it discrimination in the face of need and Protestants seeing compromise as a concession of principle (Brett, 1986: 79). To the accusation from some quarters that the Northern Ireland Housing Executive, established in 1971 as a supra-public housing authority in the province, worked with the security forces to manipulate the physical sectarian geography of the city, one chairman gives short shrift (Brett, 1986: 137). Nevertheless, in the military management of ethnic conflict, the suspicion that urban-planning decisions involving roads and housing layouts, not to mention interface planning, involved direct security considerations still lingers. The view of the foremost ethnographic mapper of Belfast's divisions is that 'such considerations must have impinged' (Boal, 1990: 10). It stretches credulity to the extreme to think otherwise.

In terms of strategic planning the basic foundations, without outright acknowledgement, were subject to radical change during the 1970s. Planning, whether by acts of commission or omission, can be seen as a possible contributory influence on the outbreak of 'the Troubles'. In the 1970s, in a way which was to gather momentum in the 1980s, particularly in relation to Belfast, planning came to be seen as part of the calculus of management of ethnic conflict. In the mid-1970s a Regional Physical Development Strategy for Northern Ireland put forward for public discussion no less than six spatial options for the Province with relative degrees of laissez-faire, intervention, agglomeration and dispersal (HMSO, 1975). A 'district towns' strategy of relative dispersal was eventually adopted as official policy as opposed to the 1960s economic orthodoxy of relative development concentration taking advantage of agglomerations in the mainly Protestant East. Acknowledging the 'peculiar circumstances of Northern Ireland' (ibid. 32) the principal aim of the planning strategy 'would be to distribute population, development and activities of all kinds in such a way that irrespective of place of residence, everyone will enjoy at least reasonable access to a high level of employment opportunities and to services and facilities of all kinds' (HMSO, 1975: 26). In 1978, a relaxation of policy with respect to development in the open countryside added to a greater leaning towards settlement diffusion and away from the growth centre thinking of the 1960s. This ethnic spatial orthodoxy with the laudable aim of 'territorial equity' has been raised to the level of almost unchallengeable, taken-for-granted 'planning doctrine' in Northern Ireland. However, as will be discussed later in relation to current regional planning in the province, this unfortunately tends to foreshorten discussion of alternative spatial options and their associated costs and benefits.

REIMAGING THE PARIAH CITY: BELFAST IN THE 1980S

Physical planning in Belfast in the 1980s through the mobilization of development became related to the management of the Troubles in two major ways. A strategy to radically improve social housing in the city spearheaded an equality agenda and development in the city centre itself took on special symbolic significance in the non-military battle with political violence. In 1981 housing was elevated to the number-one priority among social and environmental programmes in Northern Ireland and, within this, special priority was given to the housing needs of Belfast (Singleton, 1987: 159). Unpopular tower blocks in Belfast were subsequently bulldozed, including most of the notorious Divis Flats complex, and Belfast in the 1980s saw new traditional terraced housing based on good-quality design standards come on stream. One reviewer commented in 1987 on how Belfast had been spared the harsh social policy rigours of the Thatcher years:

> Much has been achieved in alleviating the appalling housing legacy in Belfast during the last ten years. While new-build and other programmes have been drastically pruned in cities throughout Britain, in Belfast the largest ever public sector programme is now under way in the city and it is complemented by large scale rehabilitation and other related programmes aimed at tackling disrepair (Singleton, 1987: 167).

The planning and development of Belfast city centre in the 1980s and the meanings read into it complemented the British government's equality agenda with a parallel normalization agenda. An invitation was extended to common civic pride with the possibility of the pooling of difference in a shared identity wrapped up in consumption. The seeds of this policy can be detected in a package of measures 'to spell the rebirth of Belfast' announced by the British Secretary of State for Northern Ireland in 1978. The government looked forward to the spread of 'oases' through the central area and 'the creation of a new Belfast of which all its citizens can be proud' (NIIS, 1978). The city centre became an official symbol of a common prosperous future in opposition to the perceived wanton destruction of terrorism. The British Northern Ireland Environment Minister Richard Needham, who is most closely associated with this period, characterized himself in 'rebuilding Belfast' as 'battling for peace'. An objective was:

> to isolate the terrorists by proving that it was they in both east and west Belfast who were the villains, delaying progress and strangling investment . . . What we were attempting had to be part of a healing process and we had to provide a safe haven for all Belfast's people, haves and have-nots (Needham, 1998: 167–79).

In the publicly pump-primed development of Belfast in the 1980s the emerging place-promotion imperative of the time dovetailed with the political management of ethnic conflict. A new Castlecourt shopping centre, which Richard Needham 'demanded' should be faced in glass, threw down a gauntlet to terrorism as 'the defining landmark of the city's new confidence' (Needham, 1998: 171). A new development corporation was established to lead the physical transformation of Belfast's riverfront, renamed as 'Laganside' (Figure 5.7). A concept plan for the River Lagan in 1987 can be interpreted as extending an invitation to leave behind sectarian space with its antagonistic ethnic identities and to identify with the 'anywhere' of post-modernist space. A Belfast Urban Area Plan published in 1990 can again be seen as a consensus-inducing document holding up a vision of a future shared city. Here positive images of newly built or planned developments in the 'new' Belfast were projected, counterposed with anaemic-toned panoramas of the 'old' backward-looking city. Any reference to the sectarian divisions with which Belfast is ridden was avoided (DOE (NI), 1990). This reimaging of Belfast has been extensively documented elsewhere (Neill, 1993) and criticized on a number of fronts. First, in embracing almost any development as good, much third-rate architecture and design has been accepted in a city that deserves better. Second, 'lipstick on the gorilla' seems an apt metaphor for this planning period given its ultimately cosmetic approach and the failure to deal at a deeper level with cultural identity and meanings wrapped up in the city centre which cannot be naïvely interpreted as 'neutral space', however much diluted with newly-arrived corporate logos. Having an interest in the city as a shopper, in short, is not the same as an emotional stake where one's cultural identity is acknowledged under the common umbrella of citizen. A final major limitation of Belfast's reimaging and conflict management strategy in the 1980s (provision of social housing and even generous recreational facilities apart) was its property-led bias, since it failed to tackle other dimensions of urban deprivation in Belfast, particularly low incomes and unemployment in traditional working-class Catholic and Protestant neighbourhoods. This left intact a contributory factor to the harsher edges of inter-ethnic animosity and rivalry for resources (Neill, 1987: 52). In the urban-planning aspects of conflict management the main beneficiaries of Belfast's reimaging at this time were a relatively prosperous Catholic and Protestant middle class whose income in a weak regional economy was substantially underpinned by high public spending. Highly-paid civil servants, lawyers and consultants were the tip of an iceberg of people benefiting economically from the management of the Troubles and who could afford to eat, drink, shop and socialize in emerging new city centre and riverside facilities (Neill, 1995: 66).

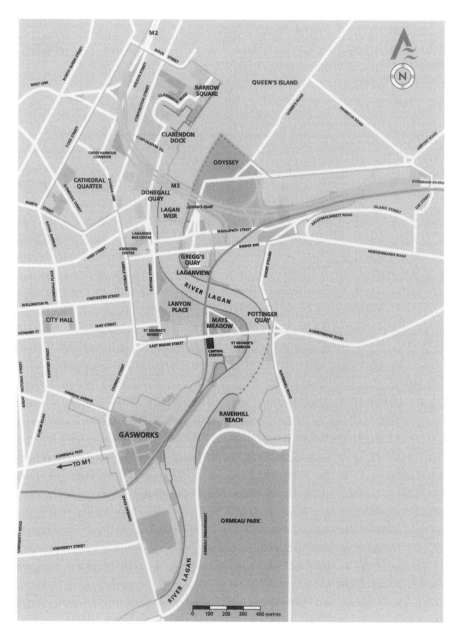

Figure 5.7 Belfast's river becomes 'Laganside': boundary of Laganside Corporation, 2002

BELFAST IN THE 1990S: LOOKING TO THE EMERALD CITY

Conflict management in Belfast and Northern Ireland took a major cultural turn in the 1990s and planning turned with it. The Downing Street Declaration of December 1993, which led eventually to the announcement of the first IRA 'complete cessation of military operations' in August 1994, stated in Article 4 that agreement in Northern Ireland would be sought based on 'full respect for the rights and identities of both traditions in Ireland'. While European Union and American funding through the International Fund for Ireland joined with the British taxpayer in endeavouring to target social need in Belfast as a contributory agent of conflict, cultural identity moved centre stage in what has now become known as 'the peace process'. In the 1990s the 'language of conflict' in Northern Ireland changed. On the one hand was an appeal of longer duration to the notion of 'citizenship' and a stress on what can be held in common where assimilation is possible. This is a language of equity and rights. On the other hand is a language of cultural pluralism. Influential here in promoting the locally-grown phrase of 'parity of esteem' for both identities was the formation in 1990 of the Northern Ireland Community Relations Council, core funding for which came from the British government and the US-financed International Fund for Ireland. The Good Friday Agreement itself can be seen as the institutionalized inclusion of cultural difference. Two major planning exercises affecting Belfast in the 1990s swam with the new tide of cultural diversity. These involved a 'vision plan' for the city and a new regional planning strategy for Northern Ireland, which obviously had Belfast as a cornerstone. These are now outlined, with the common criticism levelled that, laudable as these 'feel-good' plans are in the delicate process of peace-making, their vagueness has turned attention away from confronting actual difficult choices and trade-offs that have to be made in the real city not just of dreams but of compromises.

A New Place Vision for Belfast

In the 1990s, Belfast, along with many other cities, discovered 'visioning' as an approach to plan-making where planning merges even more closely with place-promotion in the competitive world of urban entrepreneuralism. Various problems associated with 'visioning' as a plan-making approach have been identified. The phenomenon on the positive side is in some cases loosening the hold of a rational technocratic culture in urban planning and replacing it with an enabling discursive one where the planning process tries to secure acceptable compromises from key actors concerning some future scenario called a vision (Hull, 1996: 262). However, as Hull points out, as acceptable compromises are difficult to reach, consensus around a vague and ambivalent vision is often the outcome. In a Dutch context, Needham has described how a plan for the province of Friesland 'was to win support by the attractiveness of the vision it put forward, not by showing how solid are the foundations on which that vision is based' (Needham, 1997: 185). Likewise, Healey has described how a unitary development plan for Birmingham is based on a 'vision' of the future city 'staked out' in relation to the 'key socio-economic forces that have acted upon the city', the vision then being expressed in relation to the city's role in the nation and the region and with respect to the city's citizens. However, the communicative strategy is criticized as being essentially about the management of ambiguity 'in a way which conceals the dilemmas faced, rather than presenting the richly textured nature of the tensions the council faces' (Healey, 1993: 88–91).

In Belfast in the 1990s, the communicative planning strategy of visioning was to be overhyped as a vehicle of inducing real consensus, with planners in the main, undoubtedly under political direction, keeping professional silence on contentious issues of socio-spatial resource allocation in a divided society for fear of rocking the boat of the wider peace process.

The communicative strategy involved in various visions has allowed a retreat to a hazy future, an 'Emerald City' capital of Oz where dreams come true for those who have endured the trials of the yellow brick road. Dreaming started with the announcement of a ceasefire by the IRA on 31 August 1994. This unleashed a wave of optimism and a flurry of planning activity in Belfast. First on the pitch was a private-sector think-tank established at the request of the government. It called for a rather ambitious 'visioning process' with the objective of 'positioning Belfast in the first division of European cities' (Business in the Community (BIC), 1995: 16). Belfast could now join the European city-region race and was to realize the vision of having its name 'equal with Barcelona, Brussels or Milan' by the year 2010 (BIC, 1995: 3). To encourage such optimistic aspirations towards joining the western European economic mainstream, the EU adopted in 1995 a Special Support Programme for Peace and Reconciliation with 240 million ECU allocated for community development and regeneration projects throughout Belfast and Northern Ireland (Adair et al., 1996: 528).

On 11 May 1995, Malcolm Moss, then Minister for the Environment in Northern Ireland, addressed a meeting of Belfast City Council, the first time a government minister had done so since the signing of the Anglo-Irish agreement a decade previously. This had given the Republic of Ireland a formal consultative role in the governance of Northern Ireland. In a seemingly thawing political atmosphere, the Minister appealed for civic leadership to formulate 'a strategic vision for Belfast which would provide the broad framework within which Government Departments, the City Council, major public bodies, the business and commercial sectors and the voluntary sector can work over the next 20 to 25 years'. The vision would seek to describe and define a way of moving towards 'the sort of city which we could proudly hand over to future generations' (Moss, 1995). A follow-up ministerial statement was just as vague, promising the establishment of a City Partnership Board to facilitate the creation of a Belfast Strategic Vision. 'Vision setting', this statement declared, required an act of faith:

> By stepping out into the future, say 20–25 years from now, envisaging what Belfast should look like, and working backwards from there, it can be possible to bridge the many differences and obstacles that currently hold back development (Moss, 1995).

This exhortative retreat to the future in a city that has difficulty advancing from the symbolic landscapes of the past was reflected in an important government discussion document on the sub-regional context for Belfast's city vision, published in January 1996. Articulating a vision for Belfast as 'a competitive, socially inclusive and sustainable city of the future' (Department of the Environment (DOE) (NI), 1996: 1), the document, recognizing 'the prospect of a permanent end to violence, and the hope of a sustained period of normality' (ibid.: 3), broke from past planning documents by at least openly acknowledging the harsh physical and visual realities of sectarian division. The document, majestically entitled 'The Belfast City Region: Towards and Beyond the Millennium', located itself within a broader process 'which goes well beyond land-use planning' (DOE (NI), 1996: 4). While drawing back from defining what this might mean at the level of the city or city-region as a whole, the invoked language of inclusiveness, discussion, negotiation, compromise and consent expressed the philosophy underlying the reorganization of inner-city regeneration policy in Belfast in the previous year. Six partnership boards in areas of most economic and social disadvantage were to draw up 'positive visions' for their local areas (McDonough, 1995: 7).

A massive IRA bomb at Canary Wharf in London on 9 February 1996, in reaction to the fact that inclusive political talks on the future of Northern Ireland had failed to materialize, for a while took the steam and euphoria out of micro- and macro-place-visioning in Belfast. With a reinstated ceasefire in 1998 and particularly with the signing of the Good Friday Agreement itself, euphoria was justifiably reborn. However, in the relaunch of Belfast's place-visioning exercise on 15 June 1998, a school choir and glitzy promotional videos could not hide the fact that the core issue of identity in this exercise continued to be avoided. It was reported that respondents to a questionnaire on how Belfast people felt about their city shied away from discussion on issues of identity, with the disappointing and naïve conclusion drawn that 'it will be necessary for the vision to demonstrate that it goes beyond issues of cultural identity to the core shared values which emerged for a future Belfast' (Belfast City Partnership Board, 1998: 3–4). This notion that there can be some escape into a transcendent civic or even cosmopolitan culture where values and meanings are held in common without confronting, negotiating and compromising over identity conflict rather than 'going beyond' or avoiding it seems well meaning but misplaced. The Belfast vision when published in June 2000 looked forward to a 'rainbow city':

> Moving beyond respectful tolerance of each other to a more common civic identity, we will celebrate the full range of our cultural affiliations. And enriched with such confidence, we will have enough goodwill left over to attract and embrace 'outsiders' . . . Such arrivals will add to our ethnic groups; Chinese, Indian, Jewish etc who will no longer exist at the margins of the city, relatively invisible. A more multicultural view of the city will be expressed at every level (Belfast City Partnership Board, 2000: 17).

The problem with such aspirations in the dimming afterglow of the Good Friday Agreement is that, to paraphrase Humpty Dumpty in *Through the Looking Glass*, they mean just what people choose them to mean – neither more nor less. Thus in March 1997 all political parties (including the more extreme Sinn Féin and Democratic Unionist Party) represented on Belfast City Council could agree on a joint city 'Vision Response' to government's thinking on the matter (Belfast City Council, 1997), while the following week the Democratic Unionist chair of Belfast City's Planning Committee could see no contradiction in admonishing a Protestant demonstration for its decision not to march uninvited through a nationalist neighbourhood in the city (Purdy, 1997). Likewise, in June 2000, the Northern Ireland Minister for Regional Development (whose Democratic Unionist Party opposes the Good Friday Agreement) gave his full support to the publication of Belfast's City Vision, seeing it in 'partnership with other initiatives such as the "Shaping our Future" document' (Robinson, 2000).

SHAPING OUR FUTURE: REGIONAL DEVELOPMENT STRATEGY FOR NORTHERN IRELAND

One of the early decisions taken following the election of a Labour Government in Britain in May 1997 was to develop a regional strategy for Northern Ireland as a whole (Dubbs, 1997: 2). June 1997 thus saw the launch by Northern Ireland's new Secretary of State, Mo Mowlam, of a process entitled *Shaping our Future: Towards a Strategy for the Development of the Region* (DOE (NI), 1997). The tone struck echoed the 'beyond land-use planning' ethos central to the soon-to-besidelined Belfast metropolitan strategy. It was visionary planning for Belfast writ large. The new Regional Strategy would 'reflect the views of the people of Northern Ireland and their aspirations for the future of the place which they share'. It was 'symbolic of a new era for the people of Northern Ireland and a unique opportunity to foster agreed values, aspirations and goals and to create a common vision of regional co-operation for growth and opportunity' (Mowlam, 1997: 1). This vision, defined in broad terms, stressing what is held in common, was carried through to a conference in November 1997 where a major discussion paper on *Shaping our Future* was presented by the Department of the Environment for Northern Ireland (DOE (NI), 1997). A reinstated IRA ceasefire in July 1997 added to the optimism of the occasion. A keynote speech from Monika Wulf-Mathies, European Commissioner for Regional Policy, attested to the 'European turn' in planning policy in Northern Ireland. Reference was made to the EU Peace and Reconciliation programme launched in 1995 and to the fact that she wished 'to assist in making PEACE irreversible in this violence-stricken region and in laying the foundation for a peaceful future' (Wulf-Mathies, 1997, emphasis original). The Commissioner admitted to being pleased to see the similarities between the *Regional Strategic Framework for Northern Ireland* discussion paper and the *European Spatial Development Perspective* drafted in Noordwijk in 1997 (Wulf-Mathies, 1997).

A major public consultation process got underway at the beginning of 1998, reporting in the summer in the wake of the Good Friday Agreement (Community Technical Aid *et al.*, 1998). A Draft *Regional Strategic Framework for Northern Ireland* was published in December 1998 (DOE (NI), 1998) with preparations following for an *Examination in Public* in the latter part of 1999. The Examination Panel reported in February 2000 (Elliott *et al.*, 2000). A response by the Department for Regional Development (NI) followed in April 2000 (DOE, 2000) with a final plan eventually agreed by the Northern Ireland Assembly in September 2001. This exercise has been criticized elsewhere for being overly general in dealing with potential conflict issues and for being, behind the feel-good haze, still very much a housing-land-allocation-led plan (Neill and Gordon, 2001). It is the former criticism that will be rehearsed here in abbreviated form. The new regional plan for Northern Ireland appeals in tone to both the civic and the cultural pluralism strands of the present phase of predominantly non-military conflict management. A folding in 1997 of the Belfast city-region planning study into a regional plan can thus be partly understood as offsetting the challenge that the Belfast planning exercise represented an over-strategic concentration on 'east of the Bann'. Likewise, an alignment with the vanguard of European spatial-planning thinking can be partially read as a normalization strategy stressing common European themes and transcending local identity conflict. With such European abstract spatial generalities as 'hubs, gateways and corridors', a gloss has been put on a substantial gulf between

aspirational rhetoric and the feasibility of substantive proposals in a regional strategy that carries the onerous weight of quasi-constitutional status, being explicitly
mentioned in the Good Friday Agreement of 1998 itself (Belfast Agreement, 1998:
19). A 'regional vision' including the following themes was put forward for discussion in November 1997.

VALUING PEOPLE

Goals identified in November 1997 under the theme of 'valuing people' included
'bridging the divided community', 'celebrating distinctiveness', 'targeting social
need', 'improving educational attainment', and ensuring that 'amenities are accessible to all sections of the community' (DOE (NI), 1997: 27). Public discussion of
this theme exhibited a certain confusion about its precise meaning (HMSO, 1998:
19), not surprising given that the implicit problems touched upon go to the heart of
conflict in Northern Ireland. Discussion did, however, focus on issues concerning
the importance of spatial equity and 'balanced development across Northern
Ireland', principles endorsed in the Draft Regional Strategy (DOE (NI), 1998: 22).
Peace walls could be removed over time on the basis of choice and integrated
public housing provided, again on the basis of preference. A proposal raised at the
public consultation stage by the Northern Ireland Community Relations Council
suggesting that settlement analysis in the regional plan should consider differential
sectarian geographies in relation to catchment areas for services and shopping
(HMSO, 1998: 29) was not picked up in the draft regional strategy or indeed subsequently. It was undoubtedly considered as shining too great a spotlight on division at a time requiring the rhetoric of healing.

IMPROVING COMMUNICATIONS

While aspirations have an obvious place in indicating the broad drift of public
policy, nevertheless, in a regional strategic framework for development, it might
seem a reasonable expectation that public investment projects and proposals
should be prioritized. Couched in the language of sustainable development and
emphasizing the need to co-ordinate transport and land use, to reduce the need to
travel through more compact settlements and to encourage the use of public transport, the draft regional strategy posited the desirability of an 'integrated regional
public transport system (both bus and rail)' at the level of an ideal (HMSO, 1998:
63). Key transport corridors were identified, linking east and west and the main district towns. However, given the constraints on public transport funding in Northern
Ireland, it is hardly surprising that the panel conducting the Examination in Public
pressed for more concrete proposals. However, perhaps the largest substantive
gap in the communications theme of Northern Ireland's regional vision is the
absence of any discussion of the changing information and knowledge flows of the

digital revolution, despite an acknowledgement of its importance for living patterns, work and leisure in the public consultation process (HMSO, 1998: 27). This is an omission carried through to the final plan, dancing around rather than confronting prickly ethnic sensitivities, and considered further in relation to a third aspect of Northern Ireland's vision: building prosperity.

BUILDING PROSPERITY

As it emerges from conflict, with an economy overly dependent on a public sector that can be anticipated to shrink in size, it is to be expected that Northern Ireland will join the race to build a strong, value-added competitive economic base. The regional strategic framework aligns itself with this objective and in particular with an economic strategy launched by the Department of Economic Development (NI) in March 1999. Commonly referred to as *Strategy 2010* (DED (NI), 1999), this document has received widespread criticism, not least from the Northern Ireland Economic Council (NIEC), an independent advisory body to government on economic policy (Trewsdale, 1999).

In a written submission to the Examination in Public, the NIEC noted that it was 'concerned about the degree of integration and consistency between the Draft Regional Strategic Framework and Economic Strategy' (NIEC, 1999: 11). The Council also recommended that the Public Examination should 'consider the broader issues of the importance of infrastructure and the spatial factor in economic growth as the economy becomes much more knowledge driven' (NIEC, 1999: 12).

This omission from Northern Ireland's regional strategy in the face of the well-established research literature emphasizing the links between spatiality and economic development and the relative importance, under changed conditions, of spatial agglomeration and diffusion in particular, is profound (Albrechts and Swyngedouw, 1989; Graham and Marvin, 1996; Hall and Castells, 1994; Porter, 1990; Sabel, 1989). The last Regional Physical Development Strategy prepared for Northern Ireland in the 1970s, which established present spatial-planning ethnic orthodoxy, did in fact put forward for public discussion no fewer than six spatial options for the province, with relative degrees of laissez-faire, intervention, agglomeration and dispersal (HMSO, 1975). A 'district towns' strategy of relative dispersal was eventually adopted as official policy as opposed to the 1960s economic orthodoxy of relative development concentration taking advantage of agglomerations in the east. With acknowledgement of the ethnic sensitivities involved when strategic spatial thinking can affect resource allocation and the desirability of spatial equity as an aspiration in contexts of cultural division (Neill and Schwedler, 2001: 209), it still remains unfortunate that professional planning silences should put orthodoxy beyond question under new economic and spatial

conditions. Remove theoretical rigour where spatial choices are weighed and eval-
uated and it remains difficult to see how the assertion can be maintained that economic development is 'a cornerstone of the Spatial Strategy' (Department of
Regional Development (NI), 2000). In the context of what is undoubtedly a
complex conflict-management environment, the Northern Ireland Economic
Council, as a local think-tank, has berated the regional plan process for steering
clear of controversial solutions let alone controversial recommendations (NIEC,
1999: 7). In the interests of competing in the global economy, for example, is an
Eastern seaboard development focus more appropriate? Can Northern Ireland
really support more than one major centre of economic growth? Why should policy
for economic reasons, for example, 'support the continued development of long
established rural communities' as opposed to urban ones? (HMSO, 1998: 53)
Should the 'genuine rural community' (HMSO, 1998: 41), a questionable concept
at best, curtail its more flamboyant housing-design predilections and tradition of
settlement dispersal in the interests, not just of efficiency, but of the lucrative rural
tourist gaze? In a cotton-wool approach to spatial ethnic management it would
appear that such questions in Northern Ireland are taboo. Rather the approach
taken is that Strategic Planning Guidelines in the plan identified as the 'expression
of the shared Vision, values and principles identified by the extensive consultation
exercise' remain aspirational, unprioritized and not connected to public expenditure
commitments (DOE (NI), 1998: 4). The generation of such rainbow-visionary ethnic
consensus through public consultation in a region where the rainbow is beginning
to fade also bears examination.

SHAPING 'OUR' FUTURE?

The legitimacy claims based on the *process* of preparation of Northern Ireland's
new regional plan are substantial. The public consultation exercise has consisted
of direct consultations by the DOE (NI) with district councils, political parties, other
government departments, business organizations and public sector bodies. In addition, and occupying pride of place in the consultation process, has been the work
of a government-appointed Consultation Consortium, which carried out consultations with no fewer than 477 voluntary and community groups, part of Northern
Ireland's 'institutional thickness' in civil society, grown as a reaction to the previous
absence of direct political democracy. The findings from these consultations,
informed as they were by an initial DOE discussion document, were then fed into
the preparation of the Draft plan. The Consultation Consortium, made up of local
academics and voluntary sector professionals, claims legitimacy for its work cast, it
is argued, within the methodological frame of 'planning through dialogue'. This is

seen as 'requiring from planners no small amount of willingness to listen, debate and understand' and provides a framework for 'harnessing (the) energy of contestation and for attempting to build a consensus of support' (McEldowney *et al.*, 1998: 111). Elsewhere the approach to participation adopted has been described as 'collaborative planning', which 'asserts people's collective capacity to transform the structures that they mould and are moulded by – offering open dialogue based on inclusive reasoning as a means of achieving this. As such, it provides valuable theoretical underpinning for the approach to public consultation undertaken in the *Regional Strategic Framework* for Northern Ireland' (McEldowney *et al.*, 2000: 4–5).

It is beyond present scope to critique the public participation procedures (meetings, focus groups, seminars, etc.) of the Consultation Consortium against some normative template for 'collaborative planning', even assuming that one were available. However, given the broad hopes of 'communicative planning' for helping to transform government cultures, for opening out a public conversation in which all affected parties can have a voice and be listened to, where the power of the better argument might prevail in a process of mutual learning, where power relations are not seen as set in stone (Healey, 1999), it is useful to consider where the consultation process, in broad terms, seems to have fallen short of the collaborative planning ideal, whether or not this approach in itself is seen as utopian (Tewdwr-Jones and Allmendinger, 1998). One is able to draw here, to an extent, from an auto-critique of one of the non-academic organizations involved in the Consultation Consortium (Rural Community Network (NI), 1999). The process or 'debate', and the legitimacy that is being based on it, can be criticized on the basis of the limited discussion of choices, perceived tokenism on the part of government and a political culture not yet ready to deal with 'planning as debate'.

The limited discussion of spatial and policy choices has been referred to already. Here the Rural Community Network (RCN) noted that 'consultations to date have not been deep enough' and that only 'limited prior information is provided thus restricting the development of informed responses'. In what is seen to be an 'extractive one-way process only' with information flowing from participants to government, 'consultation fatigue' and frustration is identified in the Network's review (RCN, 1999: 4). In addition, the review refers to 'tokenism' and the 'cynicism (which) exists in relation to the value policy makers place on people's input'. At the end of the day, 'it is largely the civil servants who draw the conclusions' (RCN, 1999: 6). In the report of the Consultation Consortium, the voices of almost 500 consultees are distilled into roughly 7000 words of text, including much repetition, a synthesizing feat which raises the question of whether the consensus sought was not that of a visionary retreat to the lowest common denominator. The Examination in Public which followed later can also be characterized as a soft

critique of the process and product, with a non-inquisitorial style facilitating participation but not rigorously interrogating it. Third, it must be questioned whether
Northern Ireland, in a situation of raw political sensibilities, presently possesses a
robust and mature enough political culture to enable a 'gloves-off', cut-and-thrust
debate on controversial planning issues. Here, nothing could be more controversial
than perceived spatial equity questions between the predominantly Unionist East
and the predominantly Nationalist West, in the province. With tourism-development
potential and the sustainable-development advantages of a more compact settlement pattern in mind, the initial discussion paper on the regional plan in November
1997, for example, was somewhat critical of a dispersed rural settlement strategy.
After mobilization, in particular from a West Rural Region of five district councils
employing planning consultants as advocates for their positions, policy was
amended in the draft regional plan one year later, this time endorsing the value of
the traditional rural way of life and its dispersed domiciliary practices (McEldowney
et al., 2000: 6). Whether this was a result of the 'power of the better argument' or
of an unwillingness on the part of government to mobilize even better arguments at
this delicate political moment in time, must remain an open question.

The final Regional Development Strategy for Northern Ireland, published in
September 2001 and endorsed with an introduction from a Minister for Regional
Development whose party rejects the Good Friday Agreement, contained few sur-
prises. As a result of lobbying in the local Assembly by environmental groups the
brownfield housing target in the province was increased but the general theme of a
'balanced' approach to development especially between East and West of Northern Ireland is reiterated and repeated *ad nauseam*. The plan in fact, with a goal not
made explicit in previous drafts or explored in any research-depth in terms of the
resource and economic-development implications involved, states that the spatial
strategy is designed 'to meet the wider variety of needs in a divided society' (DRD
(NI), 2001: 2). In an interesting twist to ethnic management, presumably meant to
keep the ghost of the Matthew plan firmly in chains, a new term emerges in the
final plan. In the future, policies of the Assembly will be subject to 'rural proofing'
(DRD (NI), 2001: 93), although the meaning of this, like much else, is left vague.
Such measures have to be seen alongside a criticism of the equality agenda in
Northern Ireland by Gerry Adams, leader of Sinn Féin. Here the suggestion is made
that the skewing of resources, infrastructure and job investment to the more
deprived areas 'west of the Bann and along the border' should be put on a statutory basis (Adams, 2001). At the risk of incurring disparagement for criticism of a
plan with laudatory aspirations prepared in the teeth of political instability, it is, nevertheless, important to point out that at some point such vision-planning must
come down to earth. Northern Ireland's *Regional Strategic Framework* has been
widely promoted as a model of best practice. One senior Northern Ireland planner,

for example, claims that 'the way it was prepared and tested is being hailed across Europe as the way to do things – a model regional development strategy that serves to link community development plans to national and international spatial development strategies' (Morrison, 2000: 8–9). Here 'planning spin' as an adjunct to the peace process should not be elevated to the holy grail of regional planning practice. Ultimately the 'collaborative' consultative planning process was inherently flawed because an adequate knowledge base was not provided to support it properly. The Strategy was not grounded in a model of the dynamics of the spatial organization of the economy and no alternative spatial scenarios were presented. Discussion of the important possibility that a trade-off might exist between economic efficiency and spatial equity, as recognized by regional planning in Northern Ireland in the 1960s, was avoided. Important issues involving the relationship of the two cultural identities in Northern Ireland to space should not be publicly avoided by planners just because they are controversial. It is all too easy to escape into a never-never-land where decisions can be postponed or, better, the drip feed of British and European public funds can assure the best of all possible spatial worlds. Here in his Nobel Peace Prize lecture David Trimble was rightly critical of what he called 'the kind of rhetoric which substitutes vapour for vision':

> Vision in its pure meaning is clear sight. That does not mean I have no dreams. I do. But I try to have them at night. By day I am satisfied if I can see the furthest limit of what is possible (Trimble, 2001: 61).

In preparing the Regional Strategic Framework, planners substituted clear sight for visionary vapours.

THE DUAL CITY: BELFAST 2000+

The general context for ethnic conflict management in Belfast at the beginning of the 21st century could be called **ethnic poker**, with both sides unrealistically upping the ante against the other. The result at the time of writing in March 2003 is temporary suspension of devolved government. Two cultural identities endeavour to continue to face each other down, albeit, for the time being at least, partially channelled and contained by the still-existing institutional framework of the Good Friday Agreement. This makes it difficult to construct and support a common civic identity which, in the circumstances, despite a raft of legal measures dealing with rights and equality issues, remains underdeveloped and brittle. On the one hand unionism, divided between a civic and still overly powerful ethnic strand, risks making impossible demands on Sinn Féin regarding the decommissioning of all weapons. The Democratic Unionist Party led by Revd Ian Paisley wishes to see a renegotiation of the Good Friday Agreement itself. On the other side Sinn Féin, increasingly gathering electoral steam as the main political voice of a more confident nationalism, continues to turn the knife in the pro-Union wound. At issue here is the continual highlighting and underlining by Sinn Féin that the Belfast Agreement is transitional and leading only to an inevitable united Ireland, which unionists should pragmatically prepare for. For many unionists this perceived unwillingness to make, even in the short term, a political success of Northern Ireland becomes translated into a direct attack on cultural identity when it is allied to a campaign to denude Northern Ireland of the symbols of British identity and United Kingdom sovereignty commonly accepted in Britain even under new devolutionary arrangements. With the curtailing of the flying of the union flag over public buildings and the removal of British symbols from courtrooms, the symbols issue came to a head in late 2001 over the design of an insignia for the new Police Service of Northern Ireland, successor to the Royal Ulster Constabulary. David Trimble protested in October 2001 that 'unionists have been pushed too far on the symbolism we hold dear'. Proposals for the new police badge he described as 'so neutral as to be meaningless ... the sort of thing you'd find on a police or fire engine in a toy store' (Trimble, quoted Gordon, *Belfast Telegraph*, 2001). After much wrangling, an acceptable compromise was eventually forthcoming. The new Police Board, from which Sinn Féin has so far excluded itself, agreed on a sunburst design incorporating the crown, harp, shamrock, a torch, laurel leaves and the scales of justice. Such issues in identity affirmation are far from trivial. People live and die for the meaning wrapped up in symbols. In June 2001, in the national British election, the more ethnically inward-looking wing of unionism in the form of the Democratic Unionist Party saw its number of MPs at Westminster increase to rough parity with the Ulster Unionist Party led by David Trimble. In its manifesto the issue of cultural identity was a central theme. Under the bold headline 'British Symbols and Identity under Constant Attack' the claim was made that:

> The symbols of the State are being torn down with the support of unjust laws. Everything Gaelic, republican and Irish is promoted while all that is British, unionist or Orange is derided and reviled.
>
> Parades are banned and the Union Flag can no longer fly on most days from government buildings. The Agreement is being used to undermine every expression of British identity (DUP, 2001).

Here it is difficult not to have some sympathy with the torch-bearers for civic unionism, attacked from within unionism itself as compromising too much in tolerating and respecting 'difference' and besieged from without by a republican tradition now using at least political and cultural salvos rather than real ones to challenge the identity of its prominent and troublesome significant 'other' on the island of Ireland.

The result of this cultural war of position is that the cultivation of a space of common civic identity remains fraught. Negotiated but brittle civic glue emerging from the Good Friday Agreement has led to the formal establishment of a Northern Ireland Human Rights Commission. An Equality House, home to a new Equality Commission dealing with all aspects of discrimination, is a new, refurbished addition to the Belfast streetscape. Necessary as such formal structures may be in a context of extreme cultural conflict, there is a danger that expensive bureaucratic proceduralism can militate against the building of trust. Significantly, in 2002 the Cambridge philosopher Onora O'Neill chose to give one of her series of Reith Lectures on the theme 'A Question of Trust' to an establishment audience at Belfast's Waterfront Hall. Rejecting the notion that the plethora of regulatory boards and watchdogs established since the Good Friday Agreement will create necessary trust between the two identities in Northern Ireland, O'Neill stated rather:

> I believe that human rights and democracy are not the basis of trust. Trust is the basis of human rights and democracy ... Rights are about the question, 'What can I get' rather than, 'What can I do'. We have to reorient our political thinking (O'Neill, quoted Walker, 2002).

Gestures of respect for the identity of 'the other' going beyond proceduralism and sometimes bearing the risk of rejection from within the identity-walls of one's own tradition are not absent in Northern Ireland. One SDLP nationalist councillor, for example, in the face of opposition from his party, expressed empathy with unionist cultural insecurity over the issue of symbols (McAdam, 2000). On a larger platform, in 2002 Belfast City Council elected a Sinn Féin mayor on the basis of some moderate unionists from the Alliance Party adding their weight to nationalist votes. The domination of unionism on Belfast City Council had been effectively broken in the 1997 local government elections in the face of a declining Protestant population base in the city. This loss of City Hall, the 'jewel in the unionist crown', was, in the words of one Sinn Féin councillor, of 'inestimable historic and symbolic importance to nationalists and unionists alike' (O'Muilleoir, 1999: 213). Sinn Féin had campaigned in the 1997 city elections on the slogan 'Our City Also'. Whereas a subsequent nationalist mayor removed some of the trappings of unionist heritage from his private office and a Sinn Féin deputy mayor frowned on the idea of attending Remembrance Day services (Walker, 1999), Belfast's Sinn Féin mayor adopted a different posture.

Referring to Belfast as 'a multicultural city' (Maskey, 2002, quoted Clarke) and as a 'shared city' (Maskey, 2001) the symbolic emphasis in the mayor's office was on balance rather than removal, in putting nationalist symbols alongside more traditional trappings. New symbolic ground was broken on 1 July 2002, when the Sinn Féin mayor laid a wreath on the city war memorial in commemoration of all those who died in the Battle of the Somme in 1916. With such an act, memories integral to unionist identity are acknowledged, thus giving a glimmer of hope to the possibility of common citizenship based on respect rather than cultural attrition in what still remains a grotesquely divided city. While meeting with a mean-spirited response from some unionists, one political commentator captured well the significance of this simple act:

> Let there be no doubt. The wreath laying was a giant step for Mr Maskey. It represented the lone crossing of a yawning divide. On the other side of it, among many others, lie those who, only eight years ago, would have rather seen him dead! (Waugh, 2002).

DIVIDED BELFAST

A study in 1986 noted that, of the 98 electoral areas into which Northern Ireland is subdivided, two out of every three had either very large unionist or very large nationalist majorities. Such strong segregationist instincts were exhibited in an even more pronounced fashion at finer spatial resolution (Kennedy, 1986: 32–3). A decade later, commenting on such segregated activity systems especially in education and kinship networks, Poole concluded that it was not simplistic to see Northern Ireland as a dual society. Integrated schools educate only 2% of children, with the remainder attending essentially segregated schools and with intermarriage between Catholics and Protestants accounting for merely 6% of all married couples (Poole, 1997: 134–5). A recent study has noted how separate estate agents, developers and solicitors service almost exclusive Catholic and Protestant housing markets (Adair et al., 2000). In Belfast more than half of the population presently lives in wards that comprise 90% or more of a single religious group (Blease, 2002: 11). A study in 2002 showed that internal sectarian partitioning in fact seems to be getting worse, with growing numbers of people wishing to live and work within the safety of their own community (Hughes and Donnelly, 2002). In this respect, nowhere is the challenge to the local planning profession to help attenuate the rawest manifestations of cultural conflict greater than in and around the so-called 'interface' areas in Belfast, where Catholics and Protestants live cheek by jowl with each other, often separated by peace walls. In the late summer of 2001 shameful pictures of young Catholic schoolchildren in North Belfast, running a gauntlet of Loyalist catcalls, stones and even a blast bomb to get to their local Holy Cross primary school, were broadcast by the international media. Loyalists, reacting to provocation, perceived or real but born out of sectarian hatred, attempted to prevent the Catholic children from walking through their territory to school, with nationalists refusing to take a longer route to avoid the trouble. While such behaviour cannot be excused, it must be understood. As a former Chief Executive of the Northern Ireland Housing Executive points out, 'social inequality linked to sectarian segregation makes whole communities unstable'. Over 240 000 people (15% of Northern Ireland's population) live in the 66 most deprived urban areas with high concentrations of unemployment, poverty, crime, vandalism, sickness and low levels of skills and education (Blease, 2002: 9). In such urban cauldrons, where people unavoidably confront, physically up close and personally, the presence of 'the other', territory can become imbued with intense meaning in the socio-spatial constitution of local identities. As a recently published report, commissioned by government to investigate the continuing causes of interface violence, points out, the wider context in Belfast is one where Protestants in such areas, especially in the north of the city, feel that a growing Catholic population has the desire, under the rationale of having their legitimate housing needs met, to move them out of the city and claim their space. In the circumstances, 'the boundaries, or interfaces, between these oppositional communities are the fracture zones where hostility and antipathy are maintained and renewed through violence and disorder' (Dunlop et al., 2002: 36–7). An important caveat is that the splintering of nationalist identity around sectarian interfaces is less than among 'loyalist' unionism. Paramilitary activists have been absorbed into the Sinn Féin political machine and a variety of projects funded by the European Union (Clarke, 2001), whereas, despite European peace and reconciliation money, among other things, providing refurbished offices for paramilitary leaders (Clarke, 2002), the militant ethnic extremes of unionism have become murderously fractured. The search for meaning and belonging has, in certain areas in an overall context where British cultural identity is seen as in retreat, turned, in its insecurity, viciously inward. Turf demarcations over the control of drugs and other criminal behaviour notwithstanding, the present mural iconography on Belfast's Shankill Road, the former 'heartland of Loyalism', tells a sorry story of a search for identity. Here the Ulster Volunteer Force (and its so-called Red Hand Commandos) dominating the middle Shankill appeals to the memory of the Somme for its validation (Figure 5.8). It defines itself violently not just in relation to 'the other' of republicanism but also in relation to the Ulster Defence Association, which, with its Ulster Freedom Fighters, controls the turf of the lower Shankill and appeals to the legacy of Oliver Cromwell in Ireland for its credentials in defending loyalist space (Figure 5.9). Here Bruce points out that,

Figure 5.8 The manufacture of heritage, Shankill Road, Belfast (1), 2002

Figure 5.9 The manufacture of heritage, Shankill Road, Belfast (2), 2002

while many among the unionist middle class might consider themselves in a sense 'West Britons', among the loyalist working class the identification with the territory of Ulster is more intense (Bruce, 1994: 70–1).

In 2002 interface violence across walls of hate in Belfast showed no sign of abatement and had spread to the east of the city. Between July 2001 and March 2002 136 houses in Belfast had been vacated due to the social unrest (Dunlop *et al.*, 2002: 21). In what can be seen as a militarization of urban planning, the thrust of policy response has been increased by CCTV surveillance, higher peace walls and electronic gates. The call from some politicians for a permanent police presence on both sides of peaceline flashpoints (Lowry, 2002) risks possible comparison with former Berlin Wall crossing points. Certainly, in parts of Belfast, signs displaying the warning that 'You are now leaving the British sector (or Irish)' would be regarded by many inhabitants as literally correct. In this fraught context a proposal is presently being considered by government to create a museum of citizenship in the former Crumlin Road Jail amidst the raw ethnic wounds in North Belfast. The desire expressed by the First Minister and Deputy First Minister is that this would be seen as a symbol of peace (Dunlop *et al.*, ibid. 83). While well intentioned, such an idea seems misplaced. In the context of the affluent middle class escaping to the relative safety of their sectarian patchwork-quilt apartheid-geography, reinforced with segregated patterns of social activity, the idea of placing a museum of citizenship on the front line of a cultural battle zone seems in bad taste and certainly a folly. The space for a common feeling of citizenship to grow seems more likely to come from mutual engagement and trust-building rather than exhortation, however well presented. Meanwhile, image-promotion in Belfast allied to urban planning continues to float free from underlying cultural identity conflict, having long ago, as in many other cities, cast off its moorings from the city of lived experience. Prominent here is the work of Belfast's Laganside Corporation, now charged by government with developing a cultural quarter adjacent to its work in visually transforming the city's riverfront (Figure 5.10). The questionable assertion has, however, recently been made by the urban planner and Chief Executive of the Laganside Corporation that the organization is not only in the business of physical change but is also handmaiden to cultural change. The claim is that young property buyers rejecting traditional unionist or nationalist areas are boosting apartment sales on the riverfront, especially on the 'neutral' east bank (Smith, reported Campbell, 2002). The east bank, home to the imported 'Belfast Giants' North American ice hockey team playing in a newly constructed Odyssey Centre, is undoubtedly a new and welcome shared place in Belfast. Whether this is breaking down older traditional allegiances is, however, suspect. It may rather be a segregated experience in an integrated space.

A report to the Northern Ireland Community Relations Unit in 2000 noted the

Figure 5.10 Shared identification with Belfast's newly arrived Salmon, 1999

assertion in some quarters that shared middle-class values and lifestyles were cutting across ethno-religious formulations of identity in Northern Ireland but noted 'the lack of research evidence on attitudes, values and behaviour that might give more convincing weight to the arguments' (Murtagh, 2000: 11). In 2002 survey work pointing to a hardening of traditional identities and segregational impulses over the previous two years (Hughes and Donnelly, 2002) must pour cold water on the hope that a transcendent identity in Belfast is a real possibility. Meanwhile the official place-marketing mask in Belfast continues to seem incongruous with underlying cultural reality. Mainstream city promotion, aided by a new post-Good-Friday-Agreement Convention and Visitors' Bureau, remains dominated by the impulse to banish apprehension and fear by appealing to a vapid but cosy transcendent cosmopolitan culture in whose reflection most city inhabitants would not be able to recognize themselves. A new City Council Development Department, another part of Belfast's new post-Good-Friday-Agreement promotional infrastructure, proclaims Belfast as 'Renaissance City'. The city has cast itself in the manner of a Cinderella come late to the city marketing ball and trying desperately to make up for lost time. Belfast with its 'metropolitan lifestyle' is hailed as 'one of the great Cities of Europe demanding to be explored' (Belfast City Council, 2000: 14). A bid was put in train to become European Cultural Capital in 2008, to emulate the example set by Belfast's nearest 'ugly sister',

Glasgow, in 1990. The bid document, produced by an offshoot of Belfast City Council calling itself 'Imagine Belfast 2008', resulted in an eclectically lyrical submission entitled: 'One Belfast: where hope and history rhyme' (Belfast City Council, 2002). In a context where to criticize the bid was misinterpreted as 'doing down the city', one brave academic was doubtful of the venture's legitimate credentials on the basis of 'high culture':

> How can a city which has no opera, no ballet, very little theatre, and which has produced few, if any, writers, painters, or composers of international note, aspire to be a cultural capital of Europe? (Kennedy, 2002).

While there may be some truth in this rebuke, the main criticism of the bid must be that the appropriate posture in a city with such an antagonistic and sometimes murderous gulf between the main local cultures should be one of shame, and not the hollow hyping of the mantra of 'creative cultural diversity'. Mercifully, the Belfast Culture Capital bid fell at the first shortlisting fence in late 2002. The cultural chasm yawns so deep that a recent report produced by Belfast City Council on the economic potential of cultural tourism entirely avoids discussion of two of the most 'colourful' expressions of identity in the city that are of possible interest to tourists. Here the Saint Patrick's Day Parade in a Belfast liberally festooned with Irish flags finds little favour with unionists and the worthwhile aim of a shared 12th of July parade celebrating unionist heritage remains a distant hope. Rather, one defensive reference to conflict cannot quite hide the cringing embarrassment that lies behind it. Key areas for attention are to include:

> working with communities to ensure that murals and other expressions of community identity that might be visited by tourists are contextualised, explained and presented in the best possible way (Belfast City Council, 2002: 37).

The challenge to cultural spin doctors posted to Belfast's interface zones would, however, appear to be considerable. As part of presenting Belfast 'in the best possible way' the city was treated between 20 and 26 August 2002 to a festival of international music to strengthen its bid for European Culture capital. In what is to become an annual event, citizens of Belfast experiencing the 'Rhythm in the City', as it was named by Imagine Belfast 2008, could enjoy the beat from Australia, Germany, Africa, Cuba, South America, Spain and even Southern Siberia. However, it is more likely that true tolerance and a relaxed cosmopolitan atmosphere will have arrived in Belfast only when nationalists feel unthreatened and can flow with the rhythm of an Orange parade and unionists can tap their feet to anti-British Irish laments with the knowledge that the past has been put in its place.

The strategic urban-planning response to the dual city that is Belfast in the year 2002 is a retreat to a position where the elephant in the living room is virtually ignored. A Belfast Metropolitan Area Plan with the task of getting to grips with concrete land-allocational decisions within the context of Northern Ireland's new Regional Strategic Framework is presently under preparation. An issues paper from which consultation proceeds provides little insight into specific spatial and public investment choices that might direct and inform fruitful debate (DOE (NI), 2001). Even more seriously, the issues paper for the plan casts the planning process in narrow land-use terms, with planners seemingly having a limited conception of their 'place-making' role. While calling for the *de rigueur* 'new vision' for the metropolitan area (DOE (NI) 2002: 6), the document contains virtually no discussion at all of the cultural and physical segregation which above all else scars and defines the region. Given that such division will shape so much of what is possible in the future – where people will work, recreate, go to school, shop and so forth, the retreat in Belfast by planners to the safer 'neutral' ground of private housing-land allocation has been criticized as signifying a lack of professional nerve (Neill, 2002). In a metropolitan area where fear influences where people are prepared to work, where travel often involves a mental map of safe and unsafe journeys, where people are often not comfortable or are intimidated out of using facilities and services in the territory of the other side (Smyth, 2002), an 'ostrich' approach to an unpalatable reality could perhaps be read as pragmatic realism, where the elephant is planned around rather than confronted. Segregated schooling, for example, brings its own costs in terms of infrastructural requirements but to raise this as a legitimate physical planning issue, for example, would undoubtedly stir up a hornet's nest of protest decrying fundamental questioning of how Belfast's two major cultural identities reproduce their division in socio-spatial terms. One sociologist who interprets the Northern Ireland conflict through an ethnic lens ultimately and rather bleakly concludes that the problem is without solution. The problem only has outcomes and policy cannot significantly reduce the ethnic divide (Bruce, 1994: 153). Planners here frequently step into the insufficiently theorized breach of practice when academics have given up. The remainder of this chapter considers the broad contours of ethno-spatial management in Belfast and Northern Ireland, the relationship of planners to this and some ideas for change in the light of the new 'vision' of the RTPI in 'mediating space' and dealing with 'the unique needs and characteristics of places' (RTPI, 2002).

Spatial policy since the early 1970s on the management of ethnic conflict in Belfast and Northern Ireland has been an amalgam of four types of approach. At a strategic level, planning, in moving away from the Matthew eastern development thrust of the 1960s towards a seemingly more proactive even-handed emphasis, has endeavoured to contribute to a resolution of conflict. A price paid for the premium placed on 'spatial equity' continues to be a certain amount of avoidance and obfuscation of what the economic and resource trade-offs are between spatial options involving relative degrees of concentration and dispersal. Other dimensions of the 'development in the interests of all' approach would include the large social housing programme now largely completed by the Northern Ireland Housing Executive and the considerable and ongoing efforts to entice all the population to identify with the new physical image of Belfast. A second approach to ethnic spatial management has involved emphasizing the neutrality of policy responses, although there is now some recognition that 'divisions are affected by Government policies and that, in turn, these policies are affected by the divisions' (DOE (NI), 2001). Neutrality, for example, has been the hallmark of the operational approach of the Northern Ireland Housing Executive, which allocates housing on the basis of need but from two de facto waiting lists. A recent community relations strategy of the organization highlights a core principle that integration in housing can only be voluntary and that everyone should have the right to freely choose their place of residence (NIHE, 1999: 3). Likewise, the Northern Ireland Planning Service, the major employer of planners in Northern Ireland, has a professional ethos that sees itself as responding equally to the needs of both sides by treating everyone fairly in the name of the public interest. Allied to this, market forces in their perceived 'neutrality' do not challenge but structure themselves around the reality of ethnic division. A third approach to ethno-spatial management can be called 'reactive ad-hocery'. Here the temporary can become permanent, as in the case of the proliferation of peace walls in Belfast and demands for more CCTV surveillance. The Northern Ireland Parades Commission, established following a review of the 'divisive remembering' embodied in parades in Northern Ireland (North et al., 1997: 6), can likewise be regarded as institutional ad-hocery in the management of controversial spatial practices that do not fall within the realm of more 'neutral' place-behaviour more acceptable to planners, such as the movement of cars instead of marchers in sashes. Again the Catholic Poleglass extension in West Belfast can be regarded as an ad hoc subversion of the usual 'laws' of territorial division in the light of nationalist population pressure at boiling point. A fourth form of ethno-spatial management is both visible and hidden. Watchtowers, listening antennae and fortified police stations represent the sharp end of the military management of conflict, now slowly disappearing in their intensity from the Belfast landscape. And as previously mentioned the active involvement of the military in more routine urban-planning decisions can by no means be discounted.

Given the considerable range of tasks and approaches involved in the spatial management of conflict in Belfast and Northern Ireland over the last 30 or so years it would be naïve in the extreme to suggest that this in any way could have come under the purview of one profession. The charge by one outside academic commenting on the role of planners and suggesting that the profession 'has retreated from its potential role in creating a strategic and comprehensive framework for ethnic management' (Bollens, quoted Boal and Murtagh, 1998: 18), thus seems exaggerated. Yet the feeling lingers that the profession could have been and should now definitely be more proactively engaged. This involves risking being controversial, having a voice, being less reactive and not always leaving it to others to rock the boat. A Belfast Metropolitan Area issues paper in 2002 should have held up a mirror to a dual city and showed the gorilla without the lipstick. It should have asked the question: 'What is to be done?' A reinvigoration of the profession in Northern Ireland under the reorientation of the mission of the Royal Town Planning Institute cannot be ruled out, but the obstacles in the way of planners moving to be more independent, modest 'resolvers' and mediators of conflict in Belfast and Northern Ireland remain considerable. Planners cannot 'solve' an ethnic conflict: only the protagonists can ultimately reach accommodation. The political context will remain fraught for the foreseeable future in Northern Ireland, with civic unionism struggling to assert itself. If it is to succeed, it must involve a distancing from the present obduracy of Orangeism. As one think-tank has pointed out, 'it would be helpful if the Orange Order would address some of the anti-Catholic material in its foundation documents, material which has remained unaltered for two centuries, which is insensitive or threatening to their Roman Catholic neighbours' (North et al., 1997: 6). Second, for the most part but with important exceptions in the private and voluntary sectors, professional planners in Northern Ireland are not comfortable with taking on a role that would nudge behaviour more deliberately in a tolerant, culturally pluralist, direction. A questionnaire survey carried out in November 1998 among senior members of the planning profession in Northern Ireland clearly indicated that not all in the profession are in agreement on how to even delineate a cultural-identity agenda, let alone on how to chart a modus operandi for proceeding (Neill, 2000). Those within the Department of the Environment (NI) Planning Service were the most conservative in their responses, tending to define the purview of the profession in quite narrow terms. 'Planners should not get involved in such controversy' was a typical response. The field of legitimate concern for planners (as opposed to 'just' being administrators of a statutory land-use planning system) opened out in the responses of the private sector, voluntary sector and academic-based planners. Even here, though, the view was expressed that planners might presently not have enough knowledge and background to 'thrust' themselves into cultural identity issues. In this situation it falls to Northern Ireland's University planning school and to the Royal Town Planning Institute in Ireland, working with the Irish Planning Institute, to help foster a new local professional ethos that can respond to the 'unique needs and characteristics' of Belfast and Northern Ireland. It is lamentable here that, while the Royal Institution of

Chartered Surveyors in Northern Ireland has responded with a statement of its mission based on the Good Friday Agreement, the planning profession in Northern Ireland through its local branch has not. Such an agreed statement might give planners firmer ground on which to stand, offsetting the possibility of retreating into narrow technicism to avoid being labelled as partisan Protestant or Catholic planners. It does not seem an unreasonable request that planners should see an important part of their responsibility as 'talking truth to power' (Benveniste, 1989), with part of that truth being informing public debate on ethno-spatial realities, costs, choices and trade-offs. There is surely a need for a planning voice sensitized to the complex meanings vested in places to add its own unique contribution to the equality agenda in Northern Ireland. This might in some cases involve showing the limits on this agenda, especially in the future when public resource constraints are more likely to be an issue. Finally, Belfast and Northern Ireland in general is crying out for planners who can sensitively explore the limits of the possible in community bridge-building across the ethnic divide.

CHAPTER 6

ENVIRONMENTAL CITIZENSHIP AS CIVIC GLUE?

We need myths that will identify the individual not with his local group but with the planet (Joseph Campbell, *The Power of Myth*, 1988: 24).

There is only one good way out of all this. A practical and possible general interest, which really does include all reasonable particular interests, has to be inquired into, found, negotiated, agreed, constructed (Raymond Williams, *Towards 2000*, 1985: 165).

It may seem odd in a book that focuses on the particularity of cultural identity to conclude with an overture on the desirability of planners playing a part in the creation of common meaning among difference. Indeed, to take such a normative stance is to lay oneself open to the charge of seeing the liberating potential of post-modernist thinking as negative and lapsing, thereby, into an 'indifference to the particularity and difference of various modes of otherness' (Featherstone, 1995: 79). Prior to a defence of such a position, which nests within the broad argument that planning should be a 'dialogic' process, some basic points on planning and the acknowledgement of difference are worth making, elsewhere referred to as 'planning for cultural inclusion' (Neill and Schwedler, 2001). Even in the face of what have been referred to as landscapes of 'unevenly empowered differences' (Jacobs and Fincher, 1998: 6) and bearing in mind that context does matter and that planners should 'know their place', it is worth stating a few general compass points. As in so much of life it is important, even in the face of resilient regimes of power, to stumble and push in the right direction, to move towards Cosmopolis even if the emphasis is on the 'towards'. This must be in the realization that the 'limits on the possible', which planners should always question, will necessarily vary from one specific urban working context to another. In relation to Holocaust memory the role of planners could be but modest. In relation to holding up a mirror to the costs of ethnic separation in Belfast, the role of planners could potentially be substantial.

PLANNING FOR CULTURAL DIFFERENCE

Planning with an ethic of cultural inclusion means acknowledging that it is acceptable to be different. It means planning for difference. Here the immediate qualifier has to be inserted that tolerance has its limits. Sometimes difference has to be confronted and the values and practices that are constitutive of it have to be faced down. As Inglis puts it, some ways of life, such as the Taliban's, are just 'plain horrible' (Inglis, 2001: 22). In his latest book, Ainitai Etzioni suggests that, 'in a world where imperfect choices must be made', paedophiles put themselves beyond the pale to the extent that they should be confined together in special towns (Etzioni, 2000). For those within the pale, with the boundaries of the pale decided through political and public debate, planning for cultural difference must involve an awareness on the part of planners that there is not just one reading of a place and that different cultural groups relate to space in various ways. There is a need to bring centrally into planning discourse the different representational landscapes of the city and the collective memory invested there. Here the limits of a 'colour-blind' approach by planners towards difference has been acknowledged in recent years (Ellis, 2000: 63). To treat everyone the same is not necessarily to treat them fairly and with sensitivity. The need for more nuanced and explicit place-readings for Belfast, where a vocabulary of ethnic conflict needs to be developed and used without embarrassment by planners, has been stated for some time (Bollens, 1999; Neill, 2000; Murtagh and Glendinning, 2001). Neither should planners in a situation of cultural difference and conflict contrive to pretend that less potential for division exists than is actually the case. In this context, the evasive resource-allocational fudge of Northern Ireland's recent Regional Development Plan was discussed in Chapter 5. Controversial but refreshing would be an exploration by planners, surveying the place-making horizon in the new Belfast Metropolitan Plan, of where planning for difference needs to stop and planning for common recognition of what is shared should start. Here the enduring acceptance of segregated education in Northern Ireland largely goes unchallenged, erecting barriers in the mind that are translated into barriers on the ground. In the United States, the equally blinkered crass insensitivity of the planning bulldozer to African American place identifications in the 1950s and 1960s, with the negative spill-over for the profession thereafter, was discussed in Chapter 4. In Berlin, planners on the grand scale need to be aware of the spatialization of discourses over Holocaust memory and, on the local scale, they need to understand, for example, the role of Turkish cafés or tea rooms as social focal points in the constitution of Berlin/Turkish male identity. The regrettable decision to rebuild Berlin's former Stadtschloss may be seen as a return to an Enlightenment impulse to impose an overly constricting order on difference where planners had little power to emphasize other important meanings, both local and global, working at the site.

PLANNING, INTEGRATION AND DIFFERENCE

The value to be placed on living together, engaging and mixing in cities of difference is the object of some dispute. Beyond the vacuous city marketing call to
'celebrate difference', which seems shallow post-11 September, lies a tension
between a perceived need for deliberate healthy indifference in cities and the value
placed on the mutual learning to be obtained from an active cosmopolitanism.
Allen, for example, argues, drawing on the writings of Simmel, that mutual forms of
distancing may be necessary to coexistence. Settings of indifference are not
necessarily bad:

> Because cities are places where all manner of different people live in close
> proximity, their relative 'strangeness' to one another may simply be a condition
> of city life. In other words rather than close themselves off to one another,
> different kinds of people may negotiate their social distance from others as
> part of going about their daily business and coping with whatever comes their
> way. Even though they may share the same spaces and facilities in the city,
> therefore, they may do so without there being a felt need to assert their
> difference (Allen, 1999: 91–2).

By contrast, Sennett has been a strong proponent of the argument that indifference
is a 'dead' relationship between diversities and that the stakes in cultural diversity
require a certain degree of confrontation (Sennett, 1999: 134). Indifference to
others in the city for Sennett is a problem, avoiding as it does verbal conflict, which
is 'a way of acknowledging other groups and taking a risk with the boundaries of
one's own identity' (Coser, quoted Sennett, ibid. 130). Whether this view would
survive exposure to the obscenities exchanged at Belfast ethnic interfaces at
closing time must be open to question. Sennett's point is a serious one. As
expressed by Hannerz:

> Cosmopolitanism is first of all an orientation, a willingness to engage with the
> other. It is an intellectual and aesthetic stance of openness towards divergent
> cultural experiences, a search for contrasts rather than uniformity (Hannerz,
> quoted Incirlioglu and Tandogan, 1999: 135).

In the face of the place-marketing cringing veneer of cosmopolitanism applied in
Belfast with liberal strokes of the European taxpayer's brush, the argument was
made in Chapter 5 that planners should be more proactive in at least spelling out
the costs, both psychic and economic, of cultural identities living in separate bell
jars. While the point of the city's major social housing authority is well taken that 'the

Executive does not believe that forced integration is any more desirable than a policy of deliberate segregation' (quoted Kennedy, 2002: 97), the narrow professional role-concept of planners in Belfast has cut the profession off from therefore often more impoverished debates on the management of ethnic space (Bollens, 1999: 106) and how perhaps 'bell jars' can be slowly lifted in the future. Place in Belfast is a complicated and messy construct, constitutive of identity but from which planners, despite scope to do otherwise, have ultimately retreated. If planners in Belfast have so far failed to widen the purview of their place-making scope and professional vision, Chapter 4 pessimistically concluded that the scope for planners in Greater Detroit to encourage racial integration appears to be severely limited, with the city of Detroit itself now steering on a de facto segregationist course in the wake of a failed attempt at multiculturalism. In the recent film *8 Mile*, mythologizing the African American city of Detroit's northern boundary with its mostly white suburbs, Eminem, as a white rap artist, seeks to adapt himself to a black identity south of '8 mile' in the now-black bell jar of the Motor City. The grim reality depicted will do little for Detroit's tourist industry. Indeed in such situations it can sound naïve to talk about the possibility of creating common meaning through citizenship-building, let alone 'environmental citizenship'. It becomes a matter of choice (and hope) here, despite many reasons for pessimism, to identify with what has been called the 'oppositional', 'alternative' or 'critical' post-modernist position of Jürgen Habermas, a perspective which acknowledges the deficiencies inherent in the modernist project but which argues that we should pursue it nevertheless (Ellin, 1999: 207).

CITIZENSHIP

In the face of a tension in modern nation states between the notion of citizens as rights-bearing individuals under a common rule of law and the demanded recognition of collective identities, Habermas, as one commentator on his work points out, pleads for 'a civilized dispute of convictions' as a way out, which is, however, dependent on the condition that none of the participating groups clings fundamentalistically to its position (Treibel, 1994: 144). Applied in a planning-theory context this viewpoint can be interpreted as 'theory of communicative action' writ small and is open to similar criticisms. Basic for Habermas in the difficult and almost stoical search for negotiated common meaning, even in the face of growing fundamentalism, is the need for 'solidaric empathy on the part of each person with regard to everyone else's position' (Habermas, quoted Treibel, 1994: 146), an aim whose plausibility as a humanistic ideal is certainly open to question as being heroic in the light of 'omnipresent ethnizations and particularisms' (Treibel, ibid. 146). As put by one recent writer, who accuses Habermas of 'wishful thinking' that precludes 'historical and philosophical comprehension of the real world':

> Acknowledgement that the 'idea of a just and peaceful cosmopolitan order lacks any historical support' does not deter Habermas from concluding that there is no alternative to striving for its realisation (Balakrishnan, 2003: 128).

Here Allmendinger and Tewdwr-Jones refer to how proponents of Habermasian-inspired communicative planning, which puts its faith in the belief that 'problems to democracy are best solved through argument' (2002: 13), are 'hemmed in by their commitment to modernist notions of progress' and as such open to the charge of being 'imperialist', having a 'strong resistance to post-modern thinking generally and its implications of a plurality of thinking' (ibid. 13). Indeed, to seek to find common cause among difference is to provoke the certain post-modernist rebuke of having some meta-narrative or other in the background. Harvey, for example, in advocating that 'we need to find a way to identify commonalities within differences and so develop a politics that is genuinely collective in its concerns yet remains sensitive to what remains irreducibly distinctive in the world today' (Harvey, 2000: 97), is with some justification dismissed by Featherstone as relying on a neo-Marxist meta-narrative with an 'inability to see culture and aesthetic forms as prac- tices in which their meanings are negotiated by users' (Featherstone, 1995: 79).

Despite the risk of naïvety and a potential intolerance to difference, Haber-mas is not alone in advocating a theory of 'deliberative democracy' based on making common sense and meaning together through discourse and going beyond a Rawlsian political liberalism with more emphasis on the procedural quality of formal rules inside which people pursue their own interests. As Benhabib puts it, deliberative democracy requires people to:

> articulate 'good reasons' in public, to convince everyone . . . societies in which such multicultural dialogues take place in the public sphere begin to articulate a civic point of view and a civic perspective of 'enlarged community' (Benhabib, 2000: 13).

Though not ultimately providing an answer to the wicked problem of fundament-alism as the enemy of tolerance, Kohler brings the matter back to culture and the need to try hard:

> A culture of mediation that does not level difference down but seeks to reconcile them (*sic*) with each other and beyond this to make them rewarding for everyone is thus a very demanding project; not something that could be had

for nothing and not something that could emerge without deliberate political actions. Thus the political culture of tolerance and understanding is always cultural politics; the expression of a joint idea of living together well that aims in the first place at securing certain standards and convictions socially (Kohler, 2000: 26).

Here, attachment to place can potentially be a binding factor in a territorially bounded civic solidarity that matures in the face of the flow of events. Depending on how this develops, for example, Bosnia will 'either come to represent a continuing cleavage along ethnic lines or a gradual re-establishment of a multi-ethnic society' (Robinson et al., 2001: 976). Seen in relation to bounded place, the notion of constitutional patriotism espoused by Habermas as the basis for a German identity can also appear less vapid and better able to answer the criticism:

> Could any set of institutional arrangements, however rational and just, really plug into structures of the self with the same peremptory authority as the claims of *nation* and *people*? Could they command our loyalty or solicit our desire? (Donald, 1996: 172).

Given that contemporary Europeanness is not an inclusive civic identity as Americanness is, the question has wider reverberations. Here Habermasian notions of deliberative democracy, while certainly not identical to it, strike a chord with a 'communitarian' concept of citizenship where the latter is very much about the preservation of identity and where the essential problem is not in agreeing a moral universalism but in the integration of self and other. For Charles Taylor, a prominent communitarian and philosopher of citizenship, citizenship is seen as having at its core the recognition of cultural difference in a context where the crucial feature of social life, as for Habermas, is its dialogical character (Delanty, 2002: 163). The fact that Habermas adheres to the view that when people co-operate with each other to reach a free consensus that convergence to a universalism is somehow inevitable, the philosopher of pragmatism Richard Rorty does not regard as very important when measured against the emphasis on communicative dialogical reason, with people making sense and meaning together (Rorty, 2000: 52). Such dialogic activity Rorty sees as giving grounds for social hope:

> The reason this kind of philosophy is relevant to politics is simply that it encourages people to have a self image in which their citizenship of a democracy is central. This kind of anti-authoritarian philosophy helps people set aside religious and ethnic identities in favour of an image of themselves as part of a great human adventure, one carried out on a global scale (Rorty, 2000: 52).

Citizenship studies has emerged since the 1990s as an incipient academic field, considering how cities and societies in the face of the globalization process can manage cultural differences and their associated tensions and conflict. A comprehensive review of this has recently been provided by Isin and Turner (2002). Taking a cue, however, from Richard Rorty, this book concludes with a consideration of the notion of 'environmental citizenship' as an aspect of the global human adventure that sorely needs attention and which arguably lies at the heart of planning as a globally inclusive place-making activity.

ENVIRONMENTAL CITIZENSHIP

In the aftermath of the rather disappointing outcome of the Earth Summit 2002 in Johannesburg, symbolized by the booing and heckling of US Secretary of State Colin Powell, talk of notions such as sustainable development and 'environmental citizenship' might sound like self-righteous waffle. Each year 2.2 million children under the age of five die because of a lack of clean water, more per day than were killed in the World Trade Center (Leake, 2002). It is useful to recall again the comment of Ignatieff:

> The common elements humans share seem less essential to their perceptions
> of their own identities than the marginal 'minor' elements that divide them. What
> Marx called 'species being' – our identity as members of the human race –
> counts for relatively little (Ignatieff, 1999: 48).

With an intense sense of foreboding about what lay ahead, the writer Martin Amis in the immediate aftermath of 11 September tried to look beyond the fears of the moment and came back to the concept in which Ignatieff had also struggled to find faith:

> Our best destiny as planetary cohabitants is the development of what has been
> called 'species consciousness' – something over and above nationalisms, blocs,
> religions, ethnicities (Amis, 2001).

Indeed some writers on citizenship go further, in arguing that citizenship, in its fullest expression, must be understood as encompassing the more-than-human community, a sense of belonging to a larger community of species (Curtin, 2002: 302). In the face of many reasons for despair, it seems an act of hope and an assertion of the optimism of the spirit over the pessimism of reason to articulate such possibilities for a peaceful cosmopolitan order. Voices doing so are, however,

by no means few. In the special report of *Time Magazine* to mark the Johannesburg summit in 2002 a featured article by a space-shuttle pilot described how she
regarded herself as 'a citizen of the planet' (Sullivan, 2002: 2). Kofi Annan in the
same issue talked variously of 'the human family', 'humankind' and 'world community' (Annan, 2002: 20–1). At a European level, in a recent essay Jürgen Habermas
has suggested that a common approach to environmental issues, which is certainly
at this moment distinctive in Europe compared to the United States, can contribute
to a strengthening of European identity in a search for what German Foreign Minister Joschka Fischer has called the right combination of a 'Europe of nation states
with a Europe of citizens' (Habermas, 2001: 25). Recognizing that environmental
challenges demand a larger sense of community, the Earth Charter prepared by
worldwide NGOs in 2000 exhorts that 'we must decide to live with a sense of universal responsibility, identifying ourselves with the whole Earth community, as well
as our local community' (quoted Glass, 2002: 99). The environmentalist writer
George Monbiot talks of how the notion of 'green citizenship' must take over the
ground that has been colonized by the commercially seductive drives of green con-
sumerism (Monbiot, 2000). The notion of 'civic environmentalism' has some currency in the United States in efforts to root environmental protection in a revival of
the body politic through broad public engagement in local issues (Warner, 2002:
35). A tripartite conversation pursued through an ongoing conference programme
linking Dublin, Belfast and Berlin explores the potential of 'environmental citizenship' to overcome socio-cultural barriers (Neill and Schwedler, 2002). Behind
all such appeals, however, is the need for basic human empathy. Kohler points to
the profound insight that

> all the divisive differences between tribes, religions, races and customs suddenly
> seem easy to disregard if we can recognise, be sure we recognise, in a strange
> face and in another fate, our own, often painful, sometimes joyful involvement in
> the unreasonable demands and possibilities of personal existence (Kohler,
> 2000: 32–3).

On the first anniversary of 11 September, Simon Schama appealed to such
impulses in the United States in the name of a 'tolerant secular pluralism' which he
argued is being suffocated by an atmosphere of 'reverent togetherness' against
'the other' (Schama, 2002), nauseatingly expressed by Bruce Springsteen's new
hymnal, 'The Rising'.

At a local, practical level the rebranding of Local Agenda 21 as Local Action
21 at the 2002 Earth Summit continues to offer some possibilities for using
common environmental consciousness as a kind of empathetic civic glue. As is
well known, Chapter 28 of Agenda 21 adopted at the Rio Earth Summit in 1992

exhorted every local authority to 'enter into a **dialogue** with its citizens and adopt a Local Agenda 21 promoting sustainable development' (emphasis added). This notion of local sustainable development as being a 'discursively created' rather than an authoritatively given product has always been central to at least the official rhetoric on Local Agenda 21 (Barry, 1996: 116). It is about feeling democratically involved in decision-making out of which common ethical concerns can potentially be a binding force in civic identification with and between places. Local Agenda 21, as the environmentalist David Korten puts it, 'has the potential to blunt the edges of cultural identity and special interest conflict by fostering a sense of shared values and civic responsibility. It has the potential through the engagement of free and active citizens to develop a "politics of the whole"' (Korten, 2000). In Belfast the work of the environmental action group 'Groundwork' proceeds with this philosophy to make small inroads into building a common civic sense based on shared environmental concerns, although such work rarely makes the media head-lines (Ellis *et al.*, 2003). In the words of Adlai Stevenson it is clearly better to 'light a candle than curse the darkness'. In the face of the shadows of the 'night country', however, where we come face to face with our common identity in human being, Paul Tillich has reminded us that 'the courage to take the anxiety of meaningless-ness upon oneself is the boundary line up to which the courage to be can go' (Tillich, 1952: 183). For some at this point, contemplating the fundamentally unset-tling groundlessness of Heidegger's 'Dasein' (Magee, 1987: 268), refuge can be sought in the saving power of 'small' things including dwelling and place connec-tions (ibid. 274). As it happened, the particular form of 'dwelling' to which Heideg-ger by association lent credence was based on the denial of a common humanity. For others, as Tillich put it:

> the courage to be is rooted in the God who appears when God has disappeared in the anxiety of doubt (Tillich, ibid. 183).

REFERENCES

Abel, Chris (1980) 'Architecture as identity', paper presented to the 5th annual meeting of the Semiotic Society of America, Lubbock, 16–19 October, in M. Herzfeld and M. Lenhart (eds) *Semiotics* (1981), New York: Plenum Press.

Adair, A., Berry, J. and McGreal, S. (1996) 'Regeneration processes in Northern Ireland: the public sector and partnership structures', *European Planning Studies* 4: 5, 527–43.

Adair, A.S., Berry, J.N., McGreal, W.S., Murtagh, B. and Paris, C. (2000) 'The local housing system in Craigavon: ethno-religious residential segregation, socio-tenurial polarisation and sub-markets', *Urban Studies* 37: 7, 1079–92.

Adams, Gerry (1986) *The Politics of Irish Freedom*, Dingle, Co Kerry: Brandon Books.

Adams, Gerry (2001) The equality agenda, *Belfast Telegraph*, 17 January.

Adamson, Ian (1982) The Identity of Ulster, Belfast: Pretani Press.

Adamson, Ian (1991) The Ulster People, Belfast: Pretani Press.

Albrechts, L. and Swyngedouw, U.W. (1989) 'The challenges for regional policy under a flexible regime of accumulation', in L. Albrechts, F. Moulaert, P. Roberts and U.W. Swyngedouw (eds) *Regional Policy at the Crossroads: European Perspectives*, London: Jessica Kingsley.

Allen, John (1999) 'Worlds within cities', in J. Allen, D. Massey and S. Pile (eds) *City Worlds*, London: Routledge.

Allen-Mills, Tony (1997) 'US blacks opt for school apartheid', *Sunday Times*, 21 December.

Allen-Mills, Tony (1998) 'Blacks package history their way', *Sunday Times*, 4 January.

Allen-Mills, Tony (1999) 'Rise of red ghosts taunts Schröder', *Sunday Times*, 10 October.

Allmendinger, Philip (2001) *Planning in Postmodern Times*, London: Routledge.

Allmendinger, Philip and Tewdwr-Jones, Mark (2002) 'The communicative turn in urban planning: unravelling paradigmatic, imperialistic and moralistic dimensions', *Space and Polity* 6: 1, 5–24.

Amis, Martin (2001) 'Fear and loathing', *Guardian*, 18 September.

Anderson, Kay (1998) 'Sites of difference: beyond a cultural politics of race polarity', Chapter 9 in Ruth Fincher and Jane M. Jacobs (eds) *Cities of Difference*, London: Guildford Press, 201–51.

Angelou, Maya (1984) *I Know Why the Caged Bird Sings*, London: Virago.

Ankeny, Robert (2000) '$6 billion forecast for downtown projects', *Crain's Detroit Business*, Spring. Special Edition.

Annan, Kofi (2002) 'Beyond the horizon', *Time*, 2 September, 20–1. Special Earth Summit supplement.

Anthony, Wendell (1999) Reverend and President, Detroit Chapter, NAACP. Interview, 9 July.

Archer, Dennis (1999) State of the City Report, City of Detroit.

Archer, Dennis (2001) State of the City Address, City of Detroit, Mayor's Office.

Ardagh, John (1995) *Germany and the Germans*, London: Penguin Books.

Arellano, Amber (2001) 'Detroit-only juries sought as an option', *Detroit Free Press*, 9 June.

Armstrong, Karen (2001) 'The war we should fight', *Guardian*, 13 October.

Arning, Matthias (1997) 'Bausenator will neuen Standort', 14 February.

Asante, Molefi Kete (1988) *Afrocentricity*, Africa World Press, Inc.

Asante, Molefi Kete (1998) *The Afrocentric Idea*, Philadelphia: Temple University Press.

Ash, Timothy Garton (2002) 'Our own bad Fortuyn', *Guardian*, 16 May.

Askari, Emilia (1999) 'School board gets viewed with caution', *Detroit Free Press*, 24 May.

Atkins, Elizabeth (1993) 'Grand Prix poster revs up race, marketing issues', *Detroit News*, 7 June.

Aughey, Arthur (2001) *Nationalism, Devolution and the Challenge to the United Kingdom State*, London: Pluto Press.

Awkward, Michael (1995) *Negotiating Difference: Race, Gender and the Politics of Positionality*, University of Chicago Press.

Babson, Steve (1986) *Working Detroit: The Making of a Union Town*, Detroit: Wayne State University Press.

Bachelard, Gaston (1994) *The Poetics of Space*, Boston: Beacon Press.

Balakrishnan, Gopal (2003) 'Overcoming emancipation', *New Left Review* 19: 115–28.

Balfour, Alan (1990) *Berlin: The Politics of Order*, New York: Rizzoli International Publications.

Barber, Benjamin R. (2002) 'An architecture of liberty? The city as democracy's force', Chapter 11 in Joan Ockman (ed.) *Out of Ground Zero: Case Studies in Urban Reinvention*, Munich: Prestel Verlag, 184–205.

Bardon, Jonathan (1992) *A History of Ulster*, Belfast: Blackstaff Press.

Bardon, Jonathan (1999) *Belfast A Century*, Belfast: Blackstaff Press.

Bärnreuther, Andrea (2000) 'Berlin in the grip of totalitarian planning. Functionalism in urban design between hostility to the city, megalomania and ideas of order on a new scale', in Thorsten Scheer, Josef Paul Kleihues and Paul Kahlfeldt (eds) *City of Architecture: Berlin 1900–2000*, Berlin: Nicolai, 201–11.

Barry, Brian (2001) 'The muddles of multiculturalism', *New Left Review* 8, Mar./April, Second Series.

Barry, J. (1996) 'Sustainability, political judgement and citizenship: connecting green politics and democracy', in D. Brian and M. de Geus (eds) *Democracy and Green Political Thought: Sustainability, Rights and Citizenship*, London: Routledge, 115–31.

Bartetzko, Dieter (1995) 'Synthesis of fragments', in Annegret Burg and Sebastian Redecke (eds) *Chancellery and Office of the President of the Federal Republic of Germany. International Architectural Competitions for the Capital Berlin*, Berlin: Birkhäuser Verlag, 9–21.

Bauman, Zygmut (1996) 'From pilgrim to tourist – or a short history of identity', Chapter 2 in Stuart Hall and Paul du Gay (eds) *Questions of Cultural Identity*, London: Sage, 18–36.

Baumert, Karin (1996) *Schlossplatz, Wohnen in Berlin-Brandenburg*, 6 December.

Beckett, J.C. (1971) *A Short History of Ireland*, London: Hutchinson.

Beckett, J.C. (1983) 'Belfast to the end of the eighteenth century', Chapter 1 in J.C. Beckett *et al.* (eds) *Belfast: The Making of the City*, Belfast: Appletree Press, 13–26.

Belfast Agreement (1998) *Agreement reached in the multi-party negotiations*, Belfast.

Belfast City Council (1997) Towards and beyond the Millennium: Vision Response, Belfast.

Belfast City Council (2000) Renaissance City, Belfast.

Belfast City Council (2002) Cultural Tourism: Developing Belfast's Opportunity.

Belfast City Council – Imagine Belfast (2002) One Belfast. Belfast Bid for European Capital of Culture 2008.

Belfast City Partnership Board (1998) What the People said. Belfast.

Belfast City Partnership Board (2000) Belfast City Vision, Belfast.

Belfast Telegraph (1999) 'Talking in tongues: Ulster-Scots. Is this the best use of public money?', 5 December.

Belfast Telegraph (2001) 'Apathy in Republic to Troubles', 6 February.

Belfast Telegraph (2002) 'Trimble in new swipe at Republic', 14 March.

Bell, Dawson (2002) 'Outgoing Engler lashes out once more at Detroit', *Detroit Free Press*, 24 December.

Benhabib, Seyla (2000) Democracy and Identity, in Swiss Federal Office of Culture, *Humanity, Urban Planning, Dignity*, 12–22.

Benveniste, Guy (1989) *Mastering the Politics of Planning*, San Francisco: Jossey-Bass Publishers.

Berkholz, Stefan (1990) 'Wohin mit Lenin?', *Die Zeit*, 17 August.

Berlin in Brief (1996) *Presse – und Informationsamt des Landes*, Berlin.

Berlin Kurier (1996) 'Senat beschützt den bronzenen Thälmann', 5 January.

Berliner Festspiele (1996) Topography of Terror. Guide to the Exhibition. Berliner Festspiele GmbH.

Berliner Zeitung (1995) 'Demonstrieren für den Palast der Republik', 31 July.

Bernard, Paul (1999) Director, Detroit Planning Department. Interview, 30 June.

Black's Guide (2001) *Directory for Commercial Real Estate*, Spring/Summer. Detroit.

Blease, Victor (2002) Developing Competencies for the Next Decade. Northern Ireland Housing Executive.

Bledsoe, Timothy (1990) *From One World, Three: Political Change in Metropolitan Detroit*, Wayne State University, Detroit: Center for Urban Studies.

Blight, David W. (1994) 'W.E.D. Du Bois and the struggle for American historical memory', Chapter 4 in Geneviève Febre and Robert O'Meally (eds) *History and Memory in African American Culture*, New York: Oxford University Press, 45–71.

Blom, Philipp (1998) 'The impossible monument', *Independent*, 4 September.

Blüm, Norbert (1991) Beitrag zur Hauptstadt debatte des Deutschen Bundestages vom 20 Juni in: Dokumente zur Bundeshauptstadt Berlin (1994), Presse-und Informationsamt des Landes Berlin, 12.

Boal, Frederick W. (1967) 'Contemporary Belfast and its future development', Chapter 15 in J.C. Beckett and R.E. Glasscock (eds) *Belfast: Origin and Growth of an Industrial City*, London: British Broadcasting Corporation, 169–82.

Boal, Frederick W. (1990) 'Belfast: hindsight on foresight – planning in an unstable environment', Chapter 1 in Paul Doherty (ed.) *Geographical Perspectives on the Belfast Region, Geographical Society of Ireland, Special Publications* 5: 4–14.

Boal, Frederick W. (1995) *Shaping a City: Belfast in the Late Twentieth Century*, Belfast: Institute of Irish Studies, Queen's University Belfast.

Boal, Frederick W. (1996) 'Integration and division: sharing and segregating in Belfast', *Planning Practice and Research* 11: 2, 151–8.

Boal, Frederick W. and Murtagh, B. (1998) Planning and Ethnicity in Northern Ireland: Comparative Experiences, Shaping our Future, Discussion Paper (unpublished).

Bockmeyer, Janice L. (2000) 'A culture of distrust: the impact of local political culture on participation in the Detroit enterprise zone', *Urban Studies* 37: 13, 2417–40.

Boddien, Wilhelm von (2001) 58% der Berliner wollen das Schloss! Berliner Extrablatt. Förderverein Berliner Stadtschloss e.v. October.

Bodemann, Y. Michal (1996) 'Reconstructions of History: From Jewish Memory to Nationalised Commemoration of Kristallnacht in Germany', in Y. Michal Bodemann (ed.) *Jews, Germans, Memory: Reconstructions of Jewish Life in Germany*, Ann Arbor: University of Michigan Press, 179–223.

Bodemann, Y. Michal (1998) Neues vom Reichsopferfeld. TAZ. 19 February.

Bodenschatz, Harald (1998) 'Berlin – Potsdam – Brandenburg an der Havel: Annäherungen an den historischen Stadtgrundriß'. Architektur in Berlin, Jahrbuch. Architektenkammer Berlin. Junius, Berlin, 10–19.

Bohy, Ric (1991) 'Dennis Archer interview', *Detroit Monthly*, 48–51.

Bollens, Scott A. (1999) *Urban Peace-Building in Divided Societies*, Colorado: Westview Press.

Bondi, Liz (1993) 'Locating identity politics', Chapter 5 in Michael Keith and Steven Pile (eds) *Place and the Politics of Identity*, London: Routledge, 84–101.

Bonfante, Jordan (1998) 'East of Eden', *Time*, 27 April, 22–6.

Bouchet, D. (1998) 'Information technology, the social bond and the city: Georg Simmel updated: about the changing relationship between identity and the city?', *Built Environment* 24: 2/3.

Boyes, Roger (1998) 'Bismarck legacy under scrutiny as Germans mark anniversary', *Times*, 31 July.

Boyes, Roger (1998) 'Memorial to Nazis' atrocities must be in the mind not in stone', *Times*, 17 August.

Boyes, Roger (1999) 'Holocaust museums oppose memorial', *Times*, 4 March.

Boyes, Roger (2000) 'Bismarck statue plan for Berlin polarises nation', *Times*, 17 August.

Boyes, Roger (2000) 'Germany's unhealed wounds', *Times*, 30 August.

Boyes, Roger (2001) 'Prussia is reborn – without goose-stepping this time', *Times*, 17 January.

Boyle, Robin (2000) Imagining the Impossible. Planning for Central City Decline. ACSP Annual Conference, Atlanta, Georgia, 1–4 November.

Boym, Svetlana (2001) *The Future of Nostalgia*, New York: Basic Books.

Brandt, Willy (1991) Beitrag zur Hauptstadt debatte des Deutschen Bundestages vom 20 Juni, in Dokumente zur Bundeshauptstadt Berlin (1994) Presse-und Informationsamt des Landes Berlin, 15.

Bratt, Heidi (1993) 'Prix poster leaves black Detroiters out of picture', *Detroit News*, 3 June.

Brett, C.E.B. (1985) *Buildings of Belfast*, Belfast: Friar's Bush Press.

Brett, C.E.B. (1986) Housing a Divided Community. Institute of Public Administration, Dublin.

Brown, Paul (2002) 'Peace but no love as Northern Ireland divide grows ever wider', *Guardian*, 4 January.

Brown, Stephen (1985) 'Central Belfast's shopping centre', *Estates Gazette*, 19 October.

Bruce, Steve (1986) *God Save Ulster! The Religion and Politics of Paisleyism*, Oxford: Oxford University Press.

Bruce, Steve (1994) *The Edge of the Union: The Ulster Loyalist Political Vision*, Oxford: Oxford University Press.

Bryson, L. and McCartney, C. (1994) *Clashing Symbols*, Institute of Irish Studies, Queen's University of Belfast.

Bubis, Ignatz (1997) 'Kommentar in Colloquium Dokumentation', *Denkmal füer die ermordeten Juden Europas*, Berlin: Senatsverwaltung füer Wissenschaft, Forschung und Kultur, 26–7.

Buckley, A (1991) 'Uses of history among Ulster Protestants', in (eds) Dawe, G and Foster, J. W. *The Poets Place: Ulster Literature and Society*, Belfast: Institute of Irish Studies.

Bude, Heinz (2000) Culture as a Problem, in Swiss Federal Office of Culture, *Humanity, Urban Planning, Dignity*, 35–43.

Bundesbaugesellschaft (1996) Das Unternehmen Parlaments–und Regierungsviertel, Berlin.

Bunting, Madeleine (1999) 'Fighting for their lives', *Guardian*, 15 November.

Bunting, Madeleine (2000) 'Diving into the unknown', *Guardian*, 12 June.

Burg, Annegret (1995) 'A new federal chancellery for Berlin', in Annegret Burg and Sebastian Redecke (eds) *Chancellery and Office of the President of the Federal Republic of Germany. International Architectural Competitions for the Capital Berlin*, Berlin: Birkhäuser Verlag, 25–47.

Bürgerinitiative Perspektive Berlin E.V. (1995) Ein Denkmal für die ermordeten Juden Europas. Documentation 1988–95, Berlin.

Buruma, Ian (1989) 'From Hirohito to Heimat', *New York Review of Books*, 26 October.

Buruma, Ian (1998) 'The rival spirits of Europe', *Sunday Times*, 29 November. Extract from an essay in *Prospect* magazine, 1998.

Business in the Community (1995) Pathway to Progress. Belfast.

Calle, Sophie (1996) Die Entfernung. Verlag der Kunst. Galerie Arndt and Partner.

Campbell, Heather (2002) 'Riverside Offers "Peaceful" Haven', *Belfast Telegraph*, 4 July.

Campbell, Joseph (1988) *The Power of Myth*, New York: Doubleday.

Camphausen, Gabriele (1999) 'The Monument of the Berlin Wall Memorial Site: A process of development', in (ed.) 'The Berlin Wall Memorial Site and Exhibition Center', *Association*, Berlin: Jaron Verlag, 18–22.

Camphausen, Gabriele (1999) 'The Berlin Exhibition Center', in (ed.) 'The Berlin Wall Memorial Site and Exhibition Center', *Association*, Berlin: Jaron Verlag, 27–30.

Cantle, Ted (2001) *Community Cohesion: Report of the Independent Review Team*, London: Home Office.

Casey, Edward S. (1993) *Getting Back into Place: Toward a Renewed Understanding of the Place-World*, Indianapolis: Indiana University Press.

Castells, Manuel (1989) *The Informational City*, Cambridge, MA: Basil Blackwell.

Castells, Manuel (1997) *The Power of Identity*, Malden, MA: Blackwell.

Caygill, Howard (1992) 'The futures of Berlin's Potsdamer Platz'. Discussion Paper No 9 in *Public Choice and Social Theory. Centre for Public Choice Studies*, Norwich: University of East Anglia.

Chafets, Zev (1990) *Devil's Night*, New York: Random House.

Cheyfitz, Kirk (1979) 'The incredible shrinking city', *Monthly Detroit*, July.

Christoff, Chris (2001) 'Race card leaves stain on Detroit mayoral campaign', *Detroit Free Press*, 5 November.

Christopher, Warren (1994) Speech at Farewell Ceremony for the Withdrawal of the Allied Troops from Berlin, 8 September. Presse-und Informationsamt der Bundesregierung-Auslandsabteilung-Bonn. Januar 1995.

Christy, Desmond (1999) 'Back to Nubia', *Guardian*, 26 July.

City of Detroit (1994) Jumpstarting the Motor City, *Detroit Empowerment Zone* 1, Detroit.

City of Detroit (1997) Building a World Class City II. A Progress Report on Economic Development in the City of Detroit, Detroit.

City of Detroit (1998) Community Reinvestment Strategy. Planning and Development Department, Detroit.

City of Detroit (2000) Building a World Class City III. A Progress Report on Economic Development in the City of Detroit, Detroit.

City of Detroit Downtown Development Authority (1997) Campus Martius. Redevelopment, Detroit.

Clarke, Liam (1999) 'Unionist leap of faith would bag a key prize', *Sunday Times*, 25 July.

Clarke, Liam (2001) 'Dying days of the 30 year war', *Sunday Times*, 28 October.

Clarke, Liam (2002) 'Deprive UDA of appeal to loyalist youth', *Sunday Times*, 20 January.

Clarke, Liam (2002) 'How St Patrick can help unite the North', *Sunday Times*, 3 February.

Clarke, Liam (2002) 'Maskey must box clever to get Sinn Féin off the ropes', *Sunday Times*, 9 June.

Clarke, Liam (2003) 'EU steps in to help save Ulster dialect', *Sunday Times*, 9 March.

Clarke, Timothy (1990) 'A Metropolis reborn', *Sunday Times*, 2 December.

Cockrel, Ken (1980) 'Politics in Detroit', interview in *Socialist Review* 49, January/February, 75–93.

Cohen, Roger (1999) 'Berlin Holocaust Memorial Approved by Parliament', *International Herald Tribune*, 26/27 June.

Collins, Martin (ed.) (1985) *Ireland after Britain*, London: Pluto Press.

Community Technical Aid, Queen's University Belfast, University of Ulster and Rural Community Network (1998) Shaping our Future: Public Consultation Report, Belfast: Stationary Office.

Connolly, Kate (2000) 'Swing hammer swing', *Guardian*, 1 December.

Conot, Robert (1974) *American Odyssey*, New York: William Morrow & Co.

Conradi, Peter (1997) 'Reich haunts new Berlin', *Sunday Times*, 9 November.

Conradi, Peter (1998) Denkmal für die ermordeten Juden Europas. Mitglied des Deutschen Bundestages Informationsbrief 7.

Cooke, Philip (1990) *Back to the Future: Modernity, Postmodernity and Locality*, London: Unwin Hyman.

Coulter, C. (1999) 'The absence of class politics in Northern Ireland', *Capital and Class*, Special Edition on Northern Ireland.

Cowan, Robert (1989) 'The man who built the Wall', *Architects' Journal*, 25 January, 50–2.

Cowan, Rosie (2001) 'Dublin State funeral for IRA men', *Guardian*, 15 October.

Craig, Gordon A. (1999) *The Germans*, London: Penguin Books.

Craig, Patricia (1999) *The Belfast Anthology,* Belfast: Blackstaff Press.

Cullen, Michael S. (1998) *The Brandenburger Tor*, Berlin: Quintessenz Verlags-GmbH.

Cullen, Michael S. (1999) *The Reichstag: German Parliament between Monarchy and Federalism*, Berlin: be.bra-Verlag.

Curtin, Deane (2002) 'Ecological citizenship', in Engin F. Isin and Bryan S. Turner (eds) *Handbook of Citizenship Studies*, London: Sage, 293–304.

Darden, Joe T., Hill, Richard Child, Thomas, June and Thomas, Richard (1987) *Detroit: Race and Uneven Development*, Philadelphia: Temple University Press.

Davidoff, Paul and Brooks, Mary E. (1976) 'Zoning out the poor', in Philip C. Dolce (ed.) *Suburbia: The American Dream and Dilemma*, Garden City, New York: Anchor Press/Doubleday, 135–66.

Davies, Nick (2001) 'Urban decline in Detroit', *Planning 1415*, 20 April, 22.

Davies, Norman (1996) *Europe. A History*, Oxford: Oxford University Press.

Davies, Richard O. (1975) *The Age of Asphalt: The Automobile*, the Freeway and the Condition of Metropolitan America, Philadelphia: J.B. Lippincott Co.

Davis, Mike (1993) 'Who killed LA? A political autopsy', *New Left Review* 197: 3–28.

De Botton, Alain (2002) *The Art of Travel*, London: Hamish Hamilton.

De Paor, Liam (1971) *Divided Ulster*, London: Penguin Books.

Delanty, Gerard (2002) 'Communitarianism and citizenship', in Engin F. Isin and Bryan S. Turner (eds) *Handbook of Citizenship Studies*, London: Sage, 159–74.

Democratic Unionist Party (1997) Belfast Electoral Communication.

Democratic Unionist Party (2001) Election Communication. Iris Robinson.

Department of the Environment (NI) (1997) Shaping our Future: Towards a Strategy for the Development of the Region. June.

Department of Economic Development (NI) (1999) Strategy 2010. March.

Department of the Environment (NI) (1990) *Belfast Urban Area Plan 2001*, Belfast: HMSO.

Department of the Environment (NI) (1996) *The Belfast City Region: Towards and Beyond the Millennium*, Belfast: HMSO.

Department of the Environment (NI) (1997) *Belfast City Region: Public Voices*, Belfast: HMSO.

Department of the Environment (NI) (1997) Shaping our Future. A discussion paper. November, Belfast.

Department of the Environment (NI) (1998) Draft Regional Strategic Framework for Northern Ireland. December.

Department of the Environment (NI) (1998) Shaping our Future: Towards a Strategy for the Development of the Region. June.

Department of the Environment (NI) (2001) Belfast Metropolitan Area Plan. Issues Paper.

Department for Regional Development (NI) 2001. Regional Development Strategy for N. Ireland. 2005.

Department for Regional Development (NI) (2001) Shaping our Future. Regional Development Strategy for Northern Ireland 2025. Belfast.

Department for Regional Development (NI) (2000) Response by the Department of Regional Development to the Report of the Independent Panel following the Public Examination. April.

Detroit 300 Inc. Publicity leaflet for Campus Martius Park, Detroit.

Detroit Economic Growth Corporation (2001) Information leaflet. Comerica Park, Detroit.

Detroit Economic Growth Corporation (2001) Information leaflet. Ford Field, Detroit.

Detroit Economic Growth Corporation (2001) Information leaflet. New Lions Stadium, Detroit.

Detroit Free Press (1993) 'Highlights of Twenty Years', 23 June.

Detroit Free Press (2001) 'Segregated kids', 10 May.

Detroit Free Press (2001) 'Racial divide', 8 June.

Detroit Free Press (2001) 'Diversity in Detroit', Supplement, June.

Detroit Museum of African American History (1999) *Information Brief*, Detroit.

Detroit Strategic Planning Project (1987) Final Report, Detroit Renaissance Inc.

Detroit Urban League (2001) 'What should be the qualities of Detroit's next mayor?', Detroit.

Dillard, Ernest (1988) 'Detroit perspectives', in Wilma Wood Henrickson (ed.), *Detroit Perspectives*, Detroit: Wayne State University Press, 565–7.

Dillard, Ernest (1991) 'Detroit perspectives', in Wilma Wood Henrickson (ed.), *Detroit Perspectives*, Detroit: Wayne State University Press, 565–7.

Diner, Dan (1996) 'Germany, the Jews, and Europe: history and memory and the recent upheaval', in Y. Michal Bodemann (ed.) *Jews, Germans, Memory: Reconstructions of Jewish Life in Germany*, Ann Arbor: University of Michigan Press, 263–79.

Dingel, F., Lutz, T., Hesse, K. and Sander, A. (1996) *Topography of Terror: Guide to the Exhibition*, Berlin: Berliner Festspiel GmbH.

Dixon, Melvin (1994) 'The black writer's use of memory', Chapter 2 in Geneviève Fabre and Robert O'Meally (eds), *History and Memory in African American Culture*, New York: Oxford University Press, 18–27.

Doherty, Paul (1990) 'Social contrasts in a divided city', Chapter 3 in Paul Doherty (ed.) *Geographical Perspectives on the Belfast Region*, Geographical Society of Ireland, Special Publications 5, 28–36.

Donald, James (1996) 'The citizen and the man about town', Chapter 10 in Stuart Hall and Paul du Gay (eds) *Questions of Cultural Identity*, London: Sage, 170–90.

Donaldson, Jeffery (2001) 'We're Brits and we're proud of it', *Guardian*, 22 August.

Doxiadis, Constantinos A. (1970) *Emergence and Growth of an Urban Region: The Developing Urban Detroit Area*, Three Volumes, Detroit: Detroit Edison Company.

Dubiel, Helmut (1994) 'The "Frankfurt School" – critical theory of society', in *Journal of the Deutsche Gesellschaft für Soziologie*. Special Edition 3, 127–34.

Dunlop, John, Adams, Roy and Toner, Tom (2002) North Belfast Community Action Project. Report of the Project Team, May, Belfast.

Dyson, Michael Eric (1997) *Race Rules: Navigating the Color Line*, New York: Vintage Books.

Eagleton, Terry (1996) *The Illusions of Postmodernism*, Oxford: Blackwell.

Earle, Jonathan (2000) *Atlas of African American History*, New York: Routledge.

Easthope, Antony (1997) 'The peculiar temporality of the national narrative', Paper delivered at Time and Value Conference. Institute for Cultural Research, Lancaster University, 10–13 April.

Eckert, Kathryn Bishop (1993) *Buildings of Michigan*, New York: Oxford University Press.

Economist (1989) 'West German survey', 28 October.

Economist (1993) 'Detroit's mayor: a job fit for heroes', 28 August.

Economist (1993) 'The Detroit mayor's race: she's catching up', 16 October.

Economist (1994) 'Detroit: a man, a plan', 12 March.

Economist (1997) 'Detroit: exorcising devils', 8 November.

Eiseley, Loren (1971) *The Night Country*, New York: Charles Scribner's Sons.

Eisenman Architects (1998) Denkmal für die ermordeten Juden Europas. New York, June.

Elfert, Eberhard (1993) *DENK MAL Positionen*, Berlin: Kulturamt Prenzlauer Berg.

Ellin, Nan (1999) *Postmodern Urbanism*, New York: Princeton Architectural Press.

Elliott, A , Forbes J. and Robins D. (2000) 'Report of the Panel Conducting the Public Examination on Shaping our Future'. Belfast.

Elliott, Marianne (2000) *The Catholics of Ulster*, London: Penguin Press.

Ellis, Geraint (2000) 'Planning and "Race" in Northern Ireland', in William J.V. Neill, (ed.) Planning and Cultural Pluralism. Report for Royal Town Planning Institute Irish Branch (N. Section), 63–73.

Ellis, Geraint, Neill, William J.V., Motherway, Brian and Hand, Una. (2003) *Towards a Green Isle? The future of Local Action 21 on the island of Ireland*, Centre for Cross Border Studies. Armagh.

Elrick, M. (2001) 'Detroit Mayor: Kilpatrick on path of purpose', *Detroit Free Press*, 30 October.

Endlich, Stefanie (1995) Der Blick nach Innen: Denkmal zur Erinnerung an die Bucherverbrennung vom 10. Mai 1933, in Architektur in Berlin Jahrbuch, Architektenkammer Berlin, Junius, 156–9.

Endlich, Stefanie (1998). 'Nach und Ferne'. in *Architektenkamer Berlin*, Jahrbuch, Junius 164–6.

Engel, Helmut (1992) Corporate Identity der Republik in Corporate Identity der Republik oder: Friedrich Wilhelm auf dem Pferde. Dokumentation einer Veranstaltung der Architektenkammer Berlin am 23.3.1992 im Hebbel-Theater, Berlin, Architektenkammer, Berlin, 7–30.

Etzioni, Amitai (2000) *The Limits of Privacy*, Basic Books (extract, *Guardian*, 19 September).

Evans, David and Patton, Marcus (1981) *The Diamond as Big as a Square: An Introduction to the Towns and Buildings of Ulster*, Belfast: Ulster Architectural Heritage Society.

Evans, E. Estyn (1973) *The Personality of Ireland: Habitat, Heritage and History*, Cambridge: Cambridge University Press.

Evans, E. Estyn (1984) *The Common Ground*, Mullingar, Ireland: Lilliput Press.

Ewen, Lynda Ann (1978) *Corporate Power and Urban Crisis in Detroit*, Princeton, New Jersey: Princeton University Press.

Fainstein, Susan and Fainstein, Norman (1993) *Urban Regimes and Racial Conflict: Economic and Political Consequences of Black Incorporation in the US*. Paper presented at the Fulbright Colloquium, Managing Divided Cities, University of Ulster, 6–8 September.

Farley, Reynolds, Danziger, Sheldon and Holzer, Harry J. (2000) *Detroit Divided*, Russell Sage Foundation, New York.

Farr, Michael (1992) *Berlin! Berlin! Its Culture, Its Times*, London: Kyle Cathie Ltd.

Faulkner, B. (1978) *Memoirs of a Statesman*, London: Weidenfeld and Nicolson.

Featherstone, Mike (1995) *Undoing Culture: Globalization, Postmodernism and Identity*, London: Sage.

Fessenden, Helen (2002) 'Immigration in Germany', *Prospect*, September, 38–41.

Fiedler, Carsten Von (2001) 'Wowereit und Gysi: Schnell an die Regierung', *Berliner Morgenpost*, 6 Dezember.

Finkelstein, Norman G. (1997) 'Daniel Jonah Goldhagen's "Crazy" thesis: a critique of Hitler's willing executioners', *New Left Review* 224, July/August, 39–88.

Finkelstein, Norman G. (2000) *The Holocaust Industry: Reflections on the Exploitation of Jewish Suffering*, New York: Verso.

Finn, Peter (2000) 'Germany in culture war against "immigrants"', *Guardian Weekly*, 30 November–6 December.

Fischer, Karin (1993) 'Thälmann-Koloß soll vor den Stasi-Knast', *Neue Zeit*, 6 March.

Fischer, Manfred (1999) 'The history of the "Chapel of Reconciliation"' in (ed.) 'The Berlin Wall Memorial Site and Exhibition Center', *Association*, Berlin: Jaron Verlag, 34–6.

Fitzgerald, Garret (1982) *Irish Identities*, London: BBC.

Flemming, Thomas (2000) *The Berlin Wall: Division of a City*, Berlin: be.bra-Verlag.

Flierl, Bruno (1994) Statement by the Moderator, Spreeinsel Initiative Forum, Stadtbibliothek, Berlin Mitte, 18 April.

Forbes Magazine (1995) 'Detroit: make it better for business', *Special Supplement*, 6 November.

Forester, John (1989) *Planning in the Face of Power*, California: University of California Press.

Foster, Roy F. (2002) *The Irish Story, Telling Tales and Making it up in Ireland*, London: Penguin.

Frick, Dieter (1995) 'Berlin: town planning under particular conditions', *European Planning Studies*, 3: 4, 427–39.

Fricker, Daniel (1999) 'Downtown Detroit wins major high-tech prize', *Detroit Free Press*, 10 April.

Fricker, Daniel (1999) 'Makeover of RenCen roads to begin', *Detroit Free Press*, 28 May.

Friedman, John (2002) 'Place-making as project? Habitus and migration in transnational cities', Chapter 16 in Jean Hillier and Emma Rooksby (eds) *Habitus: A Sense of Place*, Aldershot: Ashgate, 299–316.

Friedrich, Thomas (1999) *Wo die Mauer war*, Berlin: Nicolai.

Fukuyama, Francis (2002) *Our Posthuman Future*, New York: Farrar, Straus and Giroux.

Future of Multi-ethnic Britain, The Parekh Report (2000) London, Profile Books.

Gärtner, Andrea (1998) 'Bezirksamt Prenzlauer Berg von Berlin', *Kulturamt*. Interview September.

Gallagher, John (1999) 'Government choices speed Detroit's blight', *Detroit Free Press*, 10 April.

Games, Stephen and Nicoll, Ruaridh (1998) 'Missionary men', *Guardian*, 2 July.

Gates Jr, Henry Lewis (1997) 'Parable of the talents', Henry Lewis Gates Jr and Cornell West, *The Future of the Race*, New York: Vintage Books.

Garreau, Joel (1993) 'Detroit: the birthplace of edge city', *Detroit News*, 30 May.

Gavrilovich, Peter and McGraw, Bill (eds) (2001) 'The Detroit Almanac: 300 years of life in the Motor City', *Detroit Free Press*.

Gedenkstätte Haus der Wannsee-Konferenz (undated) Guide and Reader.

Geórgakas, Dan and Surkin, Marvin (1975) *Detroit: I Do Mind Dying*, New York: St Martin's Press.

Gerard, Jasper (2002) 'Moving where other citizens fear to tread', *Sunday Times*, 10 February.

Gibson, Katherine (1998) 'Social polarisation and the politics of difference: discourses in collision or collusion', Chapter 13 in Ruth Fincher and Jane M. Jacobs (eds) *Cities of Difference*, London: Guildford Press, 301–16.

Gill, A.A. (1999) 'Hunforgiven', *Sunday Times*, 11 July.

Gilloch, Graeme (1996) *Myth and Metropolis: Walter Benjamin and the City*, Cambridge: Polity Press.

Glass, Steven (2002) 'Sustainability and local government', *Local Environment*, 7: 1, 97–102.

Glazer, Nathan (1997) *We Are All Multiculturalists Now*, Cambridge, MA: Harvard University Press.

Goldhagen, Daniel Jonah (1999) 'Hitler's bunker', *Times*, 7 December.

Goldring, Maurice (1991) *Belfast: From Loyalty to Rebellion*, London: Lawrence and Wishart.

Gordon, David (2001) 'Trimble lashes Reid on emblems', *Belfast Telegraph*, 23 November.

Graham, B.J. (1994) 'Heritage conservation and revisionist nationalism in Ireland', in Chapter 8, G.J. Ashworth and P.J. Larkham (eds) *Building a New Heritage: Tourism, Culture and Identity in the New Europe*, London: Routledge, 135–58.

Graham, Steven and Marvin, Simon (1996) *Telecommunications and the City*, London: Routledge.

Graham, Steven and Marvin, Simon (2001) *Splintering Urbanism*, London: Routledge.

Grass, Günter (2002) (in conversation with Pierre Bourdieu) 'The "progressive" restoration', *New Left Review*, 14 March–April, 63–77.

Gray, Kathleen (2001) 'Rapid transit seeks a suburban fast lane', *Detroit Free Press*, 28 June.

Greater Downtown Partnership (1997) Lower Woodward District Reinvestment Strategy. Detroit, November.

Greer, Bonnie (2001) 'There is another America', *Observer*, 16 December.

Greer, John and Jess, Pat (1987) 'Town and Country Planning', Chapter 6 in R.H. Buchanan and B.M. Walker (eds) *Province, City and People: Belfast and its Region*, Belfast: Greystone Books, 101–24.

Grossberg, L. (1996) 'Identity and cultural studies: is that all there is?', in Stuart Hall and Paul du Gay (eds) *Questions of Cultural Identity*, London: Sage.

Guerra, Max Welch (1998) Hauptstadtplanung als Medium einer staedtischen Identitaetsfindung 69th Stadtforum Proceedings, Berlin.

Guerra, Max Welch (2001) 'Politische Macht am Berliner Spreebogen', in *Das Parlament*, Bonn: Wochenzeitung, 3–6.

Guratzsch, Dankwart (1996) 'Das Schloss, Leitartikel', *Die Welt*, 8 October.

HMSO (undated) Parliament Buildings Stormont, Belfast.

HMSO (1951) *The Second Report on Planning Proposals for the Belfast area*, Planning Commission. Cmd 302.

HMSO (1970) 'Northern Ireland Development Programme 1970–75'.

HMSO (1975) 'Northern Ireland Regional Physical Development Strategy 1975–95', Discussion Paper.

HMSO (1997) *Independent Review of Parades and Marches* (The North Report). Belfast.

HMSO (1998) *Shaping our Future: Public Consultation on a Regional Strategic Framework for N. Ireland*, Belfast.

Habermas, Jürgen (1998) *A Berlin Republic: Writings on Germany*, Cambridge, UK: Polity Press.

Habermas, Jürgen (1999) 'Der Zeigefinger. Die Deutschen' und ihr Denkmal, *Die Zeit*, 31 März.

Habermas, Jürgen (2001) 'Why Europe needs constitution', *New Left Review* 11, September/October, 5–26.

Hacker, Andrew (1992) *Two Nations: Black and White, Separate, Hostile, Unequal*, New York: Ballantine Books.

Hackney, Suzette (1999) 'Worried about safety? Don't be, cops say', *Detroit Free Press*, 10 April.

Hackney, Suzette (2001) 'Cops use new rule to move out of Detroit', *Detroit Free Press*, 9 July.

Hackney, Suzette (2001) 'An early exit for Napoleon: Detroit's top cop will retire', *Detroit Free Press*, 21 May.

Hain, Simone (2001) 'Struggle for the inner city – a plan becomes a declaration of war', in J.V. Neill William and Hanns-Uve Schwedler (eds) *Urban Planning and Cultural Inclusion*, Basingstoke: Palgrave, Macmillan.

Hall, Allan (2001) 'Achtung! And have a nice stay', *Sunday Times*, 23 December.

Hall, P. and Castells, M. (1994) *Technopoles of the World: The Making of the 21st Century Industrial Complexes*, London: Routledge.

Hall, Stuart (1996) 'Who needs "identity"?', Chapter 1 in Stuart Hall and Paul du Gay (eds) *Questions of Cultural Identity*, London: Sage, 1–17.

Hamilton, Hugo (1999) 'A longing for closure', *Irish Times*, 24 April.

Hampel, Harry and Friedrich, Thomas (1996) *Wo die Mauer war*, Berlin: Nicolai.

Harbinson, Joan (2001) 'A new house and a new focus for equality', *Belfast Telegraph*, 17 October.

Harlow, John (2001) 'Public Eminem No 1', *Sunday Times*, 4 February.

Harrington, Michael (1962) *The Other America: Poverty in the United States*, New York: Macmillan.

Harris, Eoghan (2001) 'Reaching into a sectarian past', *Sunday Times*, 11 February.

Hartung, Klaus (1999) 'Auf der Suche nach dem verlorenen Zentrum. Aus dem Berliner "Planwerk Innenstadt" wird ein politisches Projekt', *Die Zeit*, 17 June.

Hartung, Klaus (2001) 'Eine Stadt hofft auf Heilung', *Die Zeit*, 19 July.

Harvey, David (1996) *Justice, Nature and the Geography of Difference*, Oxford: Blackwell.

Harvey, David (2000) 'Reinventing geography', *New Left Review*, Second Series 4, July/August, 75–97.

Hauswirth, Iris, Herrschel, Tassilo and Newman, Peter (2000) Capital Regions: Berlin, London and the search for regional governance. Presentation to Cities in the Region, European Urban Research Association. Spring Workshop, University College Dublin, 13–15 April.

Hayden, Dolores (1997) *The Power of Place: Urban Landscapes as Public History*, Cambridge, MA: MIT Press.

Healey, Patsy (1993) 'The communicative work of development plans', *Environment and Planning B* 20: 83–104.

Healey, Patsy (1997) *Collaborative Planning: Shaping Places in Fragmented Societies*, Basingstoke: Macmillan.

Healey, Patsy (1999) 'Institutionalist analysis, communicative planning and shaping places', *Journal of Planning Education and Research* 19: 2, 111–21.

Healey, Patsy (2001) 'Towards a more place-focused planning system in Britain', Chapter 12 in Ali Madanipour, Patsy Healey and Angela Hull (eds) *The Governance of Place: Space and Planning Processes*, Aldershot: Ashgate, 265–86.

Healey, Patsy *et al.* (1982) 'Theoretical debates in planning: towards a coherent dialogue', in Patsy Healey *et al.* (ed.) *Planning Theory – Prospects for the 1980s*, Oxford: Pergamon.

Heaney, Mick (2001) 'New Ireland forgets its past imperfect', *Sunday Times*, 18 November.

Heimrod, Ute, Schlusche, Günter and Seferens, Horst (eds) (1999) Das Denkmal: Die Debatte um das 'Denkmal für die ermordeten Juden Europas'. Eine Dokumentation. Philo, Berlin.

Heinke, Lothar (1994) 'Passende Falle für die Maus auf dem Dachboden gesucht', *Der Tagesspiegel*, Berlin, 13 February.

Hemmens, George C. (1980) 'New directions in planning theory', *Journal of the American Planning Association* 46: 3, July, 259–84.

Henderson, Errol (1994) Interview in Robert H. Mast (ed.) *Detroit Lives*, Philadelphia: Temple University Press, 95–8.

Hendrickson, Wilma Wood (ed.) (1991) *Detroit Perspectives*, Detroit: Wayne State University Press.

Hendry, J. and McEldowney, J.M. (1987) 'Conservation in Belfast', Report to the Department of the Environment for Northern Ireland, Department of Architecture and Planning, Queen's University Belfast.

Henley, Jon and Hooper, John (2000) 'French minister sorry for "Nazi" jibe', *Guardian*, 23 May.

Henneke, Mechthild (1995) 'Thälmann trotzt dem Kapital', *Berliner Zeitung*, 7 May.

Higgins, Roisín (2001) 'Displacement: an historical perspective' in *No Place Like Home*, Belfast: Tinderbox Theatre Company, 27–33.

Hill, James G. (2001) 'Poll: Kilpatrick surges to the lead', *Detroit Free Press*, 31 August.

Hill, James G. (2002) 'Kilpatrick sworn in: new mayor pledges to better city', *Detroit Free Press*, 4 January.

Hillier, Jean (2001) 'Imagined value: the poetics and politics of place', Chapter 4 in Ali Madanipour, Patsy Healey and Angela Hull (eds) *The Governance of Place: Space and Planning Processes*, Aldershot: Ashgate, 73–106.

Hillier, Jean and Rooksby, Emma (2002) 'Introduction', Chapter 1 in Jean Hillier and Emma Rooksby (eds) *Habitus: A Sense of Place*, Aldershot: Ashgate, 3–26.

Hitler, Adolf (1971) *Mein Kampf*, Boston: Houghton Mifflin.

Hodgkiss, Rosalind (1999) 'The bitter tears of Fassbinder's women', *Guardian*, 8 January.

Hodgson, Godfrey (1997) 'Coleman Young: black hope in Motown', *Guardian*, 5 December.

Hoffmann, Wolfgang (1999) 'Das Festival der Demokratie', in Ulf Meyer (ed.) *Bundeshauptstadt Berlin*, Berlin: Jovis, 8–17.

Hoffmann-Axthelm, Dieter (2001) 'Der historische Staatsort', in *Ästhetik und Kommunikation* 114, Berlin, September, 68–83.

Hohendahl, Peter Uwe (1998) 'Introduction', in Jürgen Habermas, *A Berlin Republic: Writings on Germany*, Cambridge, UK: Polity Press, vii–xxiv.

Holbrooke, Richard (2001) 'Berlin's unquiet ghosts', *Newsweek*, 10 September, 33.

hooks, bell (1995) *Killing Rage: Ending Racism*, New York: Henry Holt and Company.

Hooper, John (1999) 'Berlin: the bitter sweet anniversary', *Guardian*, 10 November.

Hooper, John (1999) 'Divided by a now invisible wall', *Guardian*, 5 November.

Hooper, John (2000) 'Germany caught in far-right controversy', *Guardian*, 31 January.

Hooper, John (2000) 'Why can't we love the Germans?', *Guardian*, 28 January.

Hooper, John (2001) 'Fortress Germany', *Guardian*, 23 May.

Hooper, John (2002) 'Germans urged to revive banned state', *Guardian*, 23 February.

Hopkin's, Carol (1993) 'Reading, writing and Harambee', *Detroit Monthly*, May.

Hornbeck, Mark (2001) 'How to pay for Transit', *Detroit News*, 3 June.

Hughes, Joanne and Donnelly, Caitlin (2002) Life and Times Survey. University of Ulster, School of Policy Studies.

Hull, A. (1996) 'Strategic plan-making in Europe: institutional innovation', *Planning Practice and Research* 11: 3, 253–64.

Huntington, Samuel (1996) *The Clash of Civilizations*, New York: Simon and Schuster.

Huyssen, Andreas (1994) 'Monument and memory in a postmodern age', in James E. Young (ed.) *The Art of Memory: Holocaust Memorials in History*, Munich: Prestel-Verlag, 9–17.

Ignatieff, Michael (1994) *Blood and Belonging: Journeys into the New Nationalism*, London: Vintage.

Ignatieff, Michael (1999) *The Warrior's Honor: Ethnic War and the Modern Conscience*, London: Vintage.

Incirlioglu, Emine Onaran and Tandogan, Zerrin G. (1999) 'Cultural diversity, public space, aesthetics, and power', in Louise Nyström (ed.) *City and Culture: Cultural Processes and Urban Sustainability*, Karlskrona: Swedish Urban Environment Council, 135–47.

Inglis, Fred (2001) Universalism and Difference: the Separation of Culture and Politics. Paper presented to Canadian Studies conference. Centre for Canadian Studies, Queen's University Belfast, 19–20 October.

Internationale Expertenkommission. Historische Mitte Berlin. Abschlussbericht (2002) Bundesministerium für Verkehr, Bau- und Wohnungswesen und Senatsverwaltung für Stadtentwicklung, Berlin.

Isin, Engin F. and Turner, Bryan S. (2002) 'Citizen studies: an introduction', in Engin F. Isin and Bryan S. Turner (eds) *Handbook of Citizenship Studies*, London: Sage, 1–10.

Jacobs, Jane M. (1998) 'Staging difference: aestheticization and the politics of difference in contemporary cities', Chapter 11 in Ruth Fincher and Jane M. Jacobs (eds) *Cities of Difference*, London: Guildford Press, 252–78.

Jacobs, Jane M. and Fincher, Ruth (1998) 'Introduction', Chapter 1 in Ruth Fincher and Jane M. Jacobs (eds) *Cities of Difference*, London: Guildford Press, 1–25.

Jaenecke, Heinrich (1998) Bauplatz Zukunft. Merian Nr 6. Hamburg, 98–103.

Jaggi, Maya (2000) 'After the fall', *Guardian*, 4 November.

Jakubeit, Barbara (1995) 'Forward', in Annegret Burg and Sebastian Redecke (eds) *Chancellery and Office of the President of the Federal Republic of Germany. International Architectural Competition for the Capital Berlin*, Berlin: Birkhäuser Verlag, 25–47.

Jameson, Fredric (1991) *Postmodernism or the Cultural Logic of Late Capitalism*, London: Verso.

Jarman, Neil (1997) *Material Conflicts: Parades and Visual Displays in Northern Ireland*, Oxford: Berg.

Jencks, Charles (1995) *The Architecture of the Jumping Universe*, London: Academy Editions.

Jenkins, Richard (1996) *Social Identity*, London: Routledge.

Johnstone, Robert (1990) *Belfast: Portraits of a City*, London: Barrie and Jenkins.

Josar, David, Hunter, George, Grant, David (1999) 'Prosecutor blasts rising murder rate', *Detroit News*, 9 July.

Kachuk, P. (1993) *Irish Language Activism in West Belfast: A Resistance to British Cultural Hegemony*, PhD thesis, University of British Columbia.

Kähler, Gert (2000) 'As the steam began to rise...', in Thorsten Scheer, Josef Paul Kleihues and Paul Kahlfeldt (eds) *City of Architecture: Berlin 1900–2000*, Berlin: Nicolai, 381–8.

Karacs, Imre (2001) 'Wall casts long shadow over city's elections', *Independent*, 14 August.

Keith, Michael and Pile, Steven (1993) 'The politics of place', Chapter 11 in Michael Keith and Steven Pile (eds) *Place and the Politics of Identity*, London: Routledge, 1–21.

Kelly, John (2002) 'Reconstitute the Irish Provisional Republic', *Belfast Telegraph*, 4 March.

Kempe, Frederick (1999) *Father/land: A Personal Search for the New Germany*, New York: Penguin Putman.

Kennedy, Andy (2002) 'Housing and Sustainability across the divide in (ed.) Neill, William, J.V. and Schwedler Hanns-Uve, *Towards Environmental Citizenship: LA21 and overcoming socio-cultural barriers in Belfast*, Dublin and Berlin. European Academy of the Urban Environment. Berlin. 92–7.

Kennedy, Dennis (2002) 'Belfast, City of Culture? Does it stretch the imagination too far?', *Belfast Telegraph*, 8 January.

Kennedy, Liam (1986) *Two Ulsters. A Case for Repartition*, Belfast: Queen's University Belfast.

Keohane, Kieran (1997) 'Remembering the European Citizen: The Social Construction of Collective Memory in Weimar', Paper presented to Time and Value conference, Institute for Cultural Research, Lancaster University, 10–13 April.

Kiberd, Declan (2001) 'Strangers in their own country: multi-culturalism in Ireland', in Edna Longley and Declan Kiberd, *Multi-Culturalism: The View from the Two Irelands*, Cork: Cork University Press, 45–74.

Kiehn, Ute (1997) Historische Ausstellungen in den Rotunden des Stern. Berlin 2005 City Vision, Stern.

Kieren, Martin (1994) 'Which way to "Alex" please?', in (ed.) Verein Entwicklungsgemeinschaft Alexanderplatz und Senatsverwaltung für Stadtentwicklung und Umweltschutz. Alexanderplatz Urban Planning Ideas Competition. Ernst and Sohn, 30–69.

Kilmurray, Avila and McWilliams, Monica (1998) 'Republicanism revisited', Chapter 7 in Norman Porter (ed.) *The Republican Ideal*, Belfast: Blackstaff Press, 156–68.

King, Steven (2000) 'No clear-cut case in culture clash confusion', *Belfast Telegraph*, 27 April.

King, Steven (2001) 'Kevin Barry', *Belfast Telegraph*, 16 October.

Kleihues, Josef Paul (1990) 'New building areas, buildings and projects', *Internationale Bauausstellung Berlin 1987*, Project report, 6–9.

Kleihues, Josef Paul (1997) 'Der Ort an dem das Schloss stand', *Der Tagesspiegel*, 5 January.

Kleihues, Josef Paul (1998) 'Ein Fixpunkt des Stadtraums', interview in *Der Spiegel* 29, 162.

Klein, Bernard (1980) City of Detroit Comptroller under Mayor Cavanagh. Interview.

Klein, Naomi (2000) *No Logo*, London: HarperCollins.

Klemann, Jürgen (1997) Speech by Berlin Senator for Building, Housing and Transportation at the Official opening of the Prince of Wales' Urban Design Berlin Task Force, 28 August.

Knox, O. (1997) *Rebels and Informers: Stirrings of Irish Independence*, London: John Murray.

Kofman, E. (1998) 'Whose city?', in R. Fincher and J.M. Jacobs (eds) *Cities of Difference*, New York: Guildford Press.

Kohler, Georg (2000) 'The Demons of Difference and the Ethos of Understanding about Culture Policy', in Swiss Federal Office of Culture, Humanity, *Urban Planning, Dignity*, 23–34.

Kollhoff, Hans (1994) 'The 2nd phase design submission', in (ed.) Verein Entwicklungsgemeinschaft Alexanderplatz und Senatsverwaltung für Stadtenwicklung und Umweltschutz. Alexanderplatz Urban Planning Ideas Competition. Ernst and Sohn, 80–5.

Kontext: Informationen zum Umzug, Ausbau und Ausgleich (1996) Symbol für Offenheit und Transparenz. Nr. 1. Bundesregierung, Bonn, 3.

Kopp, Sheldon B. (1972) *If You Meet the Buddha on the Road, Kill Him*, New York: Bantam Books.

Korn, Salomon (1996) Der Tragödie letzter Teil – das Spiel mit der Zeit. *Frankfurter Rundschau*, 13 September.

Koselleck, Reinhart (1997) Vier Minuten für die Ewigkeit. *Frankfurter Allgemeine Zeitung*, 9 January.

Korten, D.C. (2000) 'The civilising of global society', in Rand Douthwaite and Jopling (eds) *FEASTA Review I*, Dublin.

Kramer, Jane (1995) 'The Politics of Memory', *New Yorker*, 14 August, 48–65.

Kramer, Jane (1999) 'Living with Berlin', *New Yorker*, July, 50–64.

Krätke, Stefan (1992) 'Berlin: the rise of a new metropolis in a post-Fordist landscape', Chapter 10 in M. Dunford and G. Kafkalas (eds) *Cities and Regions in a New Europe: the Global-Local Economy*, London: Belhaven Press.

Krätke, Stefan (2000) 'Berlin: the metropolis as a production space', *European Planning Studies* 8: 1, 7–27.

Krause, Martina (1996) *Brandenburg Memorials Foundation: An Overview*, Stiftung Brandenburgische Gedenkstätten.

Krumholz, Norman (2001) 'Planners and politicians: a commentary based on experience from the United States', *Planning Theory and Practice* 2: 1, 96–100.

Kugler, Anita (1997) Gegner waren nicht geladen. TAZ, 16 January, Berlin.

Kulturamt Prenzlauer Berg (1993) Denk Mal Positionen. Dokumentation zur Ausstellung vom 14 Juli–13 August 1993 im Prenzlauer Berg Museum, Berlin.

Kundnani, Hans (1999) 'German MPs back Jewish memorial', *Guardian*, 26 June.

Kundnani, Hans (1999) 'Schröder faces poll test over passports', *Observer*, 7 February.

Kurth, Joel (2001) 'Burbs shut checkbooks on 300 bash', *Detroit News*, 21 June.

Laabs, Rainer and Sikorski, Werner (1997) *Checkpoint Charlie and the Wall*, Berlin: Ullstein Buchverlag.

Lackman, Thomas (2000) *Jewrassic Park*, Berlin: Philo.

Ladd, Brian (1997) *The Ghosts of Berlin*, Chicago: University of Chicago Press.

Laduch, Kristina (1998) Director, Urban Planning Department, Bezirksamt Mitte, Berlin. Interview, 24 April.

Laird, Lord of Artigarvan (2002) 'How de Valera got it all wrong on Scotland', *Belfast Telegraph*, 25 July.

Larmour, Paul (1987) *Belfast: an Illustrated Architectural Guide*, Belfast: Friars Bush Press.

Le Roux, Martina (1999) 'Das Holocaust–Mahnmal: eine unendliche Geschichte', *Welt am Sonntag*, 7 February.

Leake, Jonathan (2002) 'The global ego trip', *Sunday Times*, 11 August.

Lean, Geoffrey (2002) 'Earth Summit: They came. They talked', *Independent on Sunday*, 8 September.

Leavitt, Helen (1970) *Superhighway–Superhoax*, Garden City, New York: Doubleday and Co.

Lefebvre, Henri (1991) *The Production of Space*, London: Blackwell.

Leonard, Mark (1997) *Britain: Renewing Our Identity*, London: Demos.

Lepik, Andres (2000) 'Die Alte Nationalgalerie' in Andres Lepik (ed.) *Masterplan Museumsinsel Berlin: Ein europäisches Projekt. Bundesamt für Bauwesen und Raumordnung*, Berlin: G & H Verlag, 81–4.

Levine, Herb (1994) 'The big move. Planning for Berlin as Germany's capital', *International Community* 1: 1, Berlin, 8–11.

Liggett, Helen (1995) 'City sights/sites of memories and dreams', Chapter 9 in Helen Liggett and David Perry (eds) *Spatial Practices*, California: Sage, 243–73.

Liggett, Helen and Perry, David (1995) 'Spatial practices: an introduction', Chapter 1 in Helen Liggett and David Perry (eds) *Spatial Practices*, California: Sage, 1–11.

Lipstadt, Deborah (1993) *Denying the Holocaust: The Growing Assault on Truth and Memory*, New York: Free Press.

Logue, Paddy (2000) *Being Irish*, Dublin: Oak Tree Press.

Longley, Edna (2001) 'Multi-culturalism and Northern Ireland: making differences fruitful', in Edna Longley and Declan Kiberd (eds) *Multi-Culturalism: The View from the Two Irelands*, Cork: Cork University Press, 1–44.

Low, Marsha (2001) 'From White to Black. Once an integration model, Southfield sees population shift', *Detroit Free Press*, 6 June.

Lowry, Ben (2002) 'Talks follow interface violence', *Belfast Telegraph*, 22 August.

Lynch, Kevin (1960) *The Image of the City*, Cambridge: MIT Press.

Mackie, Lindsay (1987) 'Baby, it's murder in Detroit', *Guardian*, 21 July.

Maćków, Jerzy (2001) 'Sowjetmenschen im Sozialstaat', *Die Zeit*, 22 March.

McAdam, Noel (2000) 'Councillor breaks ranks over name of RUC', *Belfast Telegraph*, 3 October.

McCarthy, Gerry (2001) 'Murals keep up their sects appeal', *Sunday Times*, 12 August.

McCartney, Clem and Bryson, Lucy (1994) 'Clashing Symbols?', A report of the use of flags, anthems and other national symbols in Northern Ireland. Institute of Irish Studies, Queen's University, Belfast.

McClure, Sandy (1981) 'Subway: no vote blamed on racism', *Detroit Free Press*, 14 January.

McConnell, Darci (1999) 'Archer may meet recall chiefs', *Detroit Free Press*, 25 June.

McConnell, Darci (1999) 'Group back with a vengeance: Black State revives fight against Archer', *Detroit Free Press*, 25 May.

McConnell, Darci (2001) 'Archer transformed Detroit', *Detroit News*, 18 April.

McConnell, Darci (2001) 'Family, political savvy paid off for Kilpatrick', *Detroit News*, 12 November.

McConnell, Darci (2001) 'Kilpatrick beats Hill for mayor of Detroit', *Detroit News*, 7 November.

McDonough, R. (1995) *A Partnership Approach to Regeneration: Some Guiding Principles*, Belfast: Dept of the Environment (NI).

McEldowney, M., Sterrett, K., Gaffikin, F. and Morrissey, M. (1998) 'Strategic planning in Northern Ireland: some reflections on contestation and consensus', *Pleanáil, Journal of the Irish Planning Institute* 14, 111–16.

McEldowney, M., Sterrett, K., Gaffikin, F. and Morrissey, M. (2000) 'Shaping our Future: Public Voices – a new approach to public participations – the Regional Strategic Framework for Northern Ireland', Paper presented to Planning Research 2000 Conference. London School of Economics, March.

McGovern, Mark and Shirlow, Peter (1997) 'Counter-insurgency, deindustrialisation and the political economy of Ulster loyalism', Chapter 9 in Peter Shirlow and Mark McGovern (eds) *Who are the People? Unionism, Protestantism and Loyalism in Northern Ireland*, London: Pluto Press, 176–98.

McGraw, Bill (1999) 'Computer chief puts people first', *Detroit Free Press*, 10 April.

McGraw, Bill (2001) 'Rooted in the air', *Detroit Free Press*, 15 May.

McGuinness, Martin (2000) 'What it means to be Irish', in Paddy Logue (ed.) *Being Irish*, Dublin: Oak Tree Press.

McKay, Susan (2000) *Northern Protestants: An Unsettled People*, Belfast: Blackstaff Press.

McKay, Susan (2001) 'Ulster Protestants and the Union', in Ronnie Hanna (ed.) *The Union, Essays on Ireland and the British Connection*, Belfast: Colourpoint Books, 138–50.

McWhirter, Cameron (1999) 'Detroit falls under 1 million', *Detroit News*, 30 June.

McWhirter, Cameron (2001) 'Broken Detroit. Life of one street mirrors city's fall', One of a series of articles on 'Broken Detroit', 17 June.

McWhirter, Cameron (2001) 'McNamara wins with Kilpatrick', *Detroit News*, 8 November.

McWhirter, Cameron and Josar, David (1999) 'Demolition outpaces building', *Detroit News*, 30 May.

Madanipour, Ali (1996) *Design of Urban Space: An Inquiry into Socio-Spatial Process*, Chichester: John Wiley and Sons.

Madanipour, Ali, Healey, Patsy and Hull, Angela (2001) 'Introduction', Chapter 1 in Ali Madanipour, Patsy Healey and Angela Hull (eds) *The Governance of Place: Space and Planning Processes*, Aldershot: Ashgate, 1–22.

Maeding, Heinrich (2000) 'Berlin 2000: a selective assessment of developments after German unification and prospects for the next decade', Presentation to European Urban Research Association, University College, Dublin, 13–15 April.

Magee, Bryan (1987) *The Great Philosophers*, London: BBC Books.

Maguire, W.A. (1983) 'Lords and Landlords – the Donegall Family', Chapter 2 in J.C. Beckett *et al.* (eds) *Belfast: The Making of the City*, Belfast: Appletree Press, 27–39.

Maitland, Sara (2001) 'Stanley and the woman', *Sunday Times*, 21 October.

Makiya, Kanan (2002) 'Jerusalem: the symbol of the dome of the rock from the seventh century to the present', Chapter 9 in Joan Ockman (ed.) *Out of Ground Zero: Case Studies in Urban Reinvention*, Munich: Prestel Verlag, 151–65.

Marcuse, Peter (1998) 'Reflections on Berlin', *International Journal of Urban and Regional Research*, 22: 2, 331–8.

Massey, Douglas S. and Denton, Nancy (1993) *American Apartheid: Segregation and the Making of the Underclass*, Cambridge, MA: Harvard University Press.

Mathewson, Kent (1975) *Looking at Regional Reality. Detroit: A Metropolis in History*, Detroit: Metropolitan Fund.

Matussek, Matthias (1998) 'Das Schloss als Symbol', *Der Spiegel* 29, 158–64.

Meier, Christian (1997) 'Zweierlei Opfer', *Die Zeit*, 11 April.

Mesecke, Andrea (2000) 'The specificity of prestige architecture in the Nazi period', in Thorsten Scheer, Josef Paul Kleihues and Paul Kahlfeldt (eds) *City of Architecture: Berlin 1900–2000*, Berlin: Nicolai, 187–98.

Meyer, Ulf (1999) 'Das Band des Bundes', in Ulf Meyer (ed.) *Bundeshauptstadt Berlin*, Berlin: Jovis, 18–30.

Meyer, Ulf (1999) 'Die Bundesbauten', in Ulf Meyer (ed.) *Bundeshauptstadt Berlin*, Berlin: Jovis, 31–75.

Millar, Peter (1999) 'After the fall', *Sunday Times*, 24 October.

Miller, David (1998) 'Colonialism and academic representations of the Troubles', Chapter 1 in David Miller (ed.) *Rethinking Northern Ireland*, London: Longman, 3–39.

Miller, Karen Lowry (2000) 'East loves West'. *Newsweek*, 25 September, 30–7.

Milner, Andrew (1994) *Contemporary Cultural Theory*, London: UCL Press.

Molam, M. (1997) *Introduction to DoE (NI) Shaping our Future: Towards a Strategy for the Development of the Region*, Belfast.

Monbiot, George (2002) 'For worse: world is suffering from broken promises', *Guardian* magazine in association with Action Aid (August).

Mongo, Adolph (1999) 'Detroiters deserve better than Archer', *Detroit Free Press*, 7 June.

Mönninger, Michael (2000) 'The political architecture of the capital', in Thorsten Scheer, Josef Paul Kleihues and Paul Kahlfeldt (eds) *City of Architecture: Berlin 1900–2000*, Berlin: Nicolai, 389–97.

Morley, David and Robins, Kevin (1995) *Spaces of Identity: Global Media, Electronic Landscapes and Cultural Boundaries*, London: Routledge.

Morrison, B. (2000) 'Staying ahead of the game on quality front', Special Irish Supplement, *Planning*, June, 8–9.

Moses, Alexandra (2001) 'Kilpatrick prepares to lead nation's 10th-largest city', *Detroit Free Press*, 29 December.

Moss, M. (1995) Opening remarks to a meeting of Belfast City Council on 11 May.

Moss, M. (1995) *A Strategic Vision for Belfast*, Belfast: Department of the Environment.

Mullally, G. (1998) 'Ireland: does the road from Rio lead back to Brussels?', Chapter 9 in M. Lafferty and K. Ekberg (eds) *From the Earth Summit to Local Agenda 21*, London: Earthscan.

Mumford, Louis (1964) *The Highway and the City*, New York: Mentor Books.

Munck, Ronnie (1992) 'The new Marxist revisionism in Ireland', *Capital and Class* 46: 95–110.

Murie, A. (1973) 'Planning in Northern Ireland: a survey', *Town Planning Review* 44, 337–58.

Murphy, Dervla (1979) *A Place Apart*, London: Penguin Books.

Murtagh, Brendan (2000) 'Life in a mixed religion area. Integration and division in South Belfast'. A research report to the Community Relations Unit, Belfast.

Murtagh, Brendan (2001) 'Integrated social housing in Northern Ireland', *Housing Studies* 16: 6, 771–89.

Museum der verbotenen Kunst (undated) Haus der Demokratie, Friedrichstraße, Berlin.

Museum of African American History (undated) Of the People: the African American Experience.

Nagel, Wolfgang (1994) Vorwort in, Kunst im Stadtraum. Senatsverwaltung für Bau – und Wohnungswesen, Berlin.

Nairn, Tom (2000) 'Ukania under Blair', *New Left Review* Jan./Feb., 1. Second Series, 69–103.

Nairn, Tom (2001) 'Farewell Britannia', *New Left Review* Jan./Feb., 7. Second Series.

Nasr, Joseph L. (1996) 'Beirut/Berlin: choices in planning for the suture of two divided cities', *Journal of Planning Education and Research* 16: 1, 27–40.

Needham, B. (1997) 'A plan with a Purpose: the regional plan for the province of Friesland in Healey, P., Khakee, A., Motte, A. and Needham, B. (eds) *Making Strategic Spatial Plans*, London, UCL Press.

Needham, Richard (1998) *Battling for Peace*, Belfast: Blackstaff Press.

Nesbitt, Dermot (2001) 'Open letter to Secretary of State for Northern Ireland', *Belfast Telegraph*, 3 December.

Neill, William J.V. (1987) 'The new plan for Belfast: a model for the future or dancing on a volcano?', *Journal of the Irish Planning Institute* 7, 45–55.

Neill, William J.V. (1988) 'Transportation planning in Detroit: conflict and the evolution of practice', *Planning, Practice and Research*, Winter, 13–19.

Neill, William J.V. (1991) 'Motown blues: no answer in privatised planning', *Town and Country Planning* 60: 3, 86–7.

Neill, William J.V. (1993) 'Physical planning and image-enhancement: recent developments in Belfast', *International Journal of Urban and Regional Research* 17: 4, 595–609.

Neill, William J.V. (1995) 'Lipstick on the gorilla? Conflict management, urban planning and image making in Belfast', in William J.V. Neill, Diana S Fitzsimons and Brendan Murtagh, *Reimaging the Pariah City: Urban Development in Belfast and Detroit*, Aldershot: Avebury.

Neill, William J.V. (1997) 'Memory, collective identity and urban design: the future of Berlin's Palast der Republik', *Journal of Urban Design* 2: 2, 179–92.

Neill, William J.V. (1999) 'Whose city? Can a place vision for Belfast avoid the issue of identity?', *European Planning Studies* 7: 3, 269–81.

Neill, William J.V. (2000) 'Planning and cultural pluralism. A report to the Royal Town Planning Institute', *Irish Branch (Northern Section)*, Belfast.

Neill, William J.V. (2001) 'Reflections on the place of fear in the promotional strategies of Belfast, Detroit and Berlin. *Urban Studies*, Vol 38: Nos 5–6, 815–28.

Neill, William J.V. (2002) 'Wider vision needed for the Belfast Area Plan', *Belfast Telegraph*, 18 January.

Neill, William J.V., Fitzsimons, D. and Murtagh, B. (1995) *Reimaging the Pariah City: Urban Development in Belfast and Detroit*, Aldershot: Avebury.

Neill, William J.V. and Gordon, Michael (2001) 'Shaping our future? The regional strategic framework for Northern Ireland', *Planning Theory and Practice* 2: 1, 31–52.

Neill, William J.V. and Schwedler, Hanns-Uve (2001) (eds) 'Towards environmental citizenship: LA21 and overcoming socio-cultural barriers in Belfast', Dublin and Berlin. *European Academy of the Urban Environment*. Berlin.

Neill, William J.V. and Schwedler, Hanns-Uve (eds) (2001) *Urban Planning and Cultural Inclusion: Lessons from Belfast and Berlin*, Basingstoke: Palgrave.

NIEC (1999) 'A response by the N.I Economic Council to Shaping our Future'. *NIEC Advice and Comment Series 99/2*, Belfast.

Niethammer, Lutz (2003) 'The Infancy of Tarzan', *New Left Review* 19, 79–91.

Nishen Kommunikation (1998) *Info-Box: The Catalogue* Nishen Kommunikation GmbH, Berlin.

Nora, Pierre (1994) 'Between Memory and History: Les Lieux de Memoire', in Genevieve Fabre and Robert O'Meally (eds) *History and Memory in African American Culture*, New York: Oxford University Press, 284–300.

Norberg-Schulz, Christian (1980) *Genius Loci: Towards a Phenomenology of Architecture*, London: Academy Editions.

North, Peter (1997) Independent Review of Parades and Marches, Belfast: Stationary Office.

Northern Ireland Housing Executive (1999) Towards a Community Relations Strategy, Belfast.

Northern Ireland Information Service (1978) *9 Point package to spell the rebirth of Belfast*, Belfast.

Nottmeyer, Karin (1998) Interview, 20 April.

Novick, Peter (1999) *The Holocaust and Collective Memory: The American Experience*, London: Bloomsbury.

Ockman, Joan (ed.) (2002) 'Introduction', Chapter 1 in *Out of Ground Zero: Case Studies in Urban Reinvention*, Munich: Prestel Verlag, 14–19.

O'Connor, Fionnuala (1993) *In Search of a State. Catholics in Northern Ireland*, Belfast: Blackstaff Press.

O'Dowd, Liam (1998) ' "New Unionism", British nationalism and the prospects for a negotiated settlement in Northern Ireland', Chapter 4 in David Miller (ed.) *Rethinking Northern Ireland*, London: Longman, 253–74.

Officer, David (1996) 'In search of order, permanence and stability: building Stormont, 1921–32', Chapter 8 in Richard English and Graham Walker (eds) *Unionism in Modern Ireland*, Dublin: Gill and Macmillan, 130–47.

O'Leary, Brendan (1999) 'The nature of the British–Irish agreement', *New Left Review* 233, 66–96.

O'Meally, Robert and Fabre, Geneviève (1994) 'Introduction', Chapter 1 in Geneviève Fabre and Robert O'Meally (eds) *History and Memory in African American Culture*, New York: Oxford University Press, 3–17.

Ó Muilleoir, Máirtín (1999) *Belfast's Dome of Delight. City Hall Politics 1981–2000*, Belfast: Beyond the Pale Publications.

O'Neill, Terence (1969) *Ulster at the Crossroads*, London: Faber and Faber.

Ormsby, Frank (1979) 'Introduction', in Frank Ormsby (ed.) *Poets from the North of Ireland*, Belfast: Blackstaff Press, 1–15.

Orr, Marion and Stoker, Gerry (1992) *Urban Leadership and Regimes in Detroit*, Detroit: Wayne State University, Centre for Urban Studies.

Osborne, Robert D. and Singleton, Dale (1982) 'Political processes and behaviour', Chapter 7 in Frederick W. Boal and Neville J. Douglas (eds) *Integration and Division: Geographical Perspectives on the Northern Ireland Problem*, London: Academic Press, 167–94.

PDS (1993) 'Gerechtigkeit für Thälmann', Press Release, 16 April.

Paba, Giancarlo and Paloscia, Raffaele (1999) 'The university and the city', in Richard Wolff *et al.* (eds) *Possible Urban Worlds*, Basel, Birkhäuser Verlag.

Paesler, Frau (1998) Senatsverwaltung für Bauen, Wohnen und Verkehr, Berlin. Interview, 23 September.

Partridge, S. (1999) *The British Union State: Imperial Hangover or Flexible Citizens' Home?* London: The Catalyst Trust.

Patterson, Tony (1999) 'Angry controversy engulfs Berlin's Wall celebration', *Guardian*, 4 November.

Patterson, Tony (1999) 'Berliners want their Wall back', *Sunday Telegraph*, 27 June.

Paulin, Tom (2000) 'It's a small step from cosy nationhood to ugly racism', *Sunday Times*, 16 July.

Peters, Günter (1994) 'ICC/West-Best=Sanierung, PdR/Ost-Best=Abriss?', *Berlin-Brandenburgische Bauwirtschaft* 7, April, 145–6.

Phillips, Duane (1997) *Berlin: A Guide to Recent Architecture*, London: Ellipsis.

Phillips, M. (2002) quoted in Ash, Timothy Garton (2002) 'Our own bad Fortuyn', *Guardian*, 16 May.

Phillips, Melanie (1999) 'Losing the battle in the Ulster peace', *Sunday Times*, 20 June.

Phillips, Melanie (1999) 'Losing the battle in the Ulster peace', *Sunday Times*, 20 June.

Poole, Michael A. (1997) 'In search of ethnicity in Ireland', Chapter 7 in Brian Graham (ed.) *In Search of Ireland: A Cultural Geography*, London: Routledge, 128–47.

Porter, M. (1990) *The Competitive Advantage of Nations*, New York: Macmillan.

Porter, Norman (1996) *Rethinking Unionism: An Alternative Vision for Northern Ireland*, Belfast: Blackstaff Press.

Pratt, Geraldine (1998) 'Grids of difference: place and identity formation', Chapter 2 in Ruth Fincher and Jane M. Jacobs (eds) *Cities of Difference*, London: Guildford Press, 26–200.

Purdy, M. (1996) 'Left out on a limb', *Belfast Telegraph*, 30 October.

Purdy, M. (1997) 'DUP in "Lundy" jibe over Ormeau', *Belfast Telegraph*, 2 April.

Rashid, Frank (1994) 'Interview', in Robert H. Mast (ed.) *Detroit Lives*, Philadelphia: Temple University Press, 146–9.

Range, Peter Ross (1996) 'Reinventing Berlin', *National Geographic* 190: 6, 96–117.

Rauterberg, Hanno (2000) 'Deutscher Nachlass', *Die Zeit*, 24 August.

Ravitz, Mel (1988) 'Perils of planning as an executive function', *American Planning Association Journal*, Spring 1988, 164–5.

Read, Anthony and Fisher, David (1994) *Berlin: The Biography of a City*, London: Pimlico.

Redmond, Sean (1985) in Martin Collins (ed.) *Ireland after Britain*, London: Pluto Press, 65–74.

Reichhardt, Hans J. and Schäche, Wolfgang (1998) *Von Berlin nach Germania*, Berlin: Transit.

Reinsch, Daniela (1994) 'Diebstahl im Staatsrat: Der Palast der Republik ist weg', *Foyer, Magazin der Senatsverwaltung für Bau und Wohnungswesen*, September, 16–18.

Reid, John (2002) 'Reply to Dermot Nesbitt', *Belfast Telegraph*, 4 February.

Rich, Wilbur C. (1989) *Coleman Young and Detroit Politics*, Detroit: Wayne State University Press.

Richie, Alexandra (1999) *Faust's Metropolis: A History of Berlin*, London: HarperCollins.

Robinson, Gloria (1999) Former Director Detroit Planning Department. Interview, 7 July.

Robinson, Guy M., Engelstoft, Sten and Pobric, Alma (2001) 'Remaking Sarajevo: Bosnian nationalism after the Dayton Accord', *Political Geography* 20, 957–80.

Robinson, Peter (2000) 'Department for Regional Development', *Executive Information Service*. 23 June.

Rödiger, Ulrich (1999) *The Olympic Stadium Berlin*, Berlin: Rödiger-Verlag.

Rolston, B. (1995) *Drawing Support 2: Murals of War and Peace*. Belfast: Beyond the Pale Publications.

Rolston, B. and Tomlinson, M. (1988) *Unemployment in West Belfast (The Obair Report)*, Belfast: Beyond the Pale Publications.

Rolston, Bill (1998) 'What's wrong with multiculturalism? Liberalism and the Irish conflict', Chapter 13 in David Miller (ed.) *Rethinking Northern Ireland*, London: Longman, 253–74.

Rolston, Bill (1992) *Drawing Support. Murals in the North of Ireland*, Belfast: Beyond the Pale Publications.

Rorty, Richard (2000) 'Globalisation, the Politics of Identity and Social Hope', in *Swiss Federal Office of Culture, Humanity, Urban Planning, Dignity*, 47–52.

Rose, Mathew D. (1998) *Berlin: Hauptstadt von Filz und Korruption*, Munich: Knaur.

Rose, Richard (1976) *Northern Ireland: A Time of Choice*, London: Macmillan.

Roseman, Mark (2002) *The Villa, The Lake, The Meeting: Wannsee and the Final Solution*, London: Allen Lane/Penguin Press.

Rosh, Lea (1999) Chair, Förderkreis zur Errichtung eines Denkmals für die ermordeten Juden Europas. Interview, 1 September.

Ross, Jan (1998) 'Aus Auschwitz lernen?', *Die Zeit*, Nr. 49, 26 November.

Roth, Andrew and Frajman, Michael (1998) 'Jewish Berlin', Berlin: Goldapple Publishing.

Roush, Matt (1993) 'City image: if you rebuild it will they come?', *Crain's Detroit Business*, 22 November, 17.

Roush, Matt (2000) 'What are we going to call this ballpark anyway?', *Crain's Detroit Business*, Spring, Special Edition.

Rowthorne, B. and Wayne, N. (1988) *Northern Ireland: the Political Economy of Conflict*, Cambridge: Polity Press.

Royal Town Planning Institute (2002) *A New Vision for Planning*. London.

Ruane, Joseph and Todd, Jennifer (1991) ' "Why can't you get along with each other?": culture, structure and the Northern Ireland conflict', Chapter 3 in Eamonn Hughes (ed.) *Culture and Politics in Northern Ireland 1690–1990*, Milton Keynes: Open University Press.

Rudwick, Elliott and Meier, August (1979) *Black Detroit and the Rise of the UAW*, New York: Oxford University Press.

Rumpf, Peter (2000) 'Developments in urban design and architecture 1990–2000', in Thorsten Scheer, Josef Paul Kleihues and Paul Kahlfeldt (ed.) *City of Architecture: Berlin 1900–2000*, Berlin: Nicolai, 361–70.

Rural Community Network (NI) (1999) 'Policy Change and Conflict Resolution in Rural Areas', Report on Feasibility (June).

Rusk, David (1993) *Cities Without Suburbs*, Washington, DC: Woodrow Wilson Center Press.

Rusk, David (1993) 'Remarks to the Greater Detroit Chamber of Commerce', Mackinac Conference, 3 June.

Rürup, Reinhard (1998) *Topography of Terror. Gestapo, SS and Reichssicherheitshauptamt on the Prinz-Albrecht-Terrain. A Documentation*, Berlin: Verlag Willmuth Arenhövel.

Ryder, Chris (2001) ' "Heroes" that Ireland doesn't need', *Sunday Times*, 30 September.

Sabel, C.F. (1989) 'Flexible specialisation and the re-emergence of regional economies', in P. Hirst and J. Zeitlin (eds) *Reversing Industrial Decline? Industrial Structure and Policy in Britain and her Competitors*, Oxford: Berg.

Said, Edward (2001) 'Islam and the West are inadequate banners', *Observer*, 16 September.

Samuel, Raphael (1994) *Theatres of Memory. Volume 1: Past and Present in Contemporary Culture*, London: Verso.

Sandercock, Leonie (1998) *Towards Cosmopolis: Planning for Multicultural Cities*, New York: John Wiley.

Schäche, Wolfgang (1998) Vom Umgang mit einem schwierigen Erbe: Das ehemalige Reichssportfeld in Berlin (unpublished paper).

Schama, Simon (2002) 'The dead and the guilty', *Guardian*, 11 September.

Schäuble, Wolfgang (1991) Beitrag zur Hauptstadt Debatte des Deutschen Bundestages vom 20 Juni in, Dokumente zur Bundeshauptstadt Berlin (1994) Presse-und Informationsamt des Landes Berlin, 14–15.

Schlusche, Günter (2001) Die Parlaments-und Regierungsbauten des Bundes im Kontext der Berliner Stadtentwicklung in Das Parlament, Wochenzeitung, Bonn, 17 August, 16–23.

Schmitt, Ben and Hackney, Susette (2002) 'Detroit's dilemma: children keep dying – solutions sought', *Detroit Free Press*, 26 December.

Schneider, Bernhard (1999) *Daniel Libeskind. Jewish Museum Berlin*, Munich: Prestel Verlag.

Schröder, Gerhard (1999) 'Eine offene Republik', Interview with Die Zeit, 4 February.

Schubert, Peter (2001) *The Government Quarter*, Berlin: Jaron Verlag.

Schulz, Bernhard (1997) 'Ruhe nach dem Sturm', *Der Tagesspiegel*, Berlin, 12 April.

Schwedler, Hanns-Uve and Neill, William J.V. (eds) (2001) *Towards Environmental Citizenship: LA21 and Overcoming Socio-cultural Barriers in Belfast, Berlin and Dublin*, Berlin: European Academy of the Urban Environment.

Schweitzer, Eva (1997) 'Abriss des Palastes ist offenbar doch teurer als die Sanierung', *Der Tagesspiegel*, Berlin, 7 January.

Seferens, Horst (1996) 'Der schmerzhafte Blick in den Spiegel. Die Spiegelwand in Steglitz', in *Architektur in Berlin Jahrbuch*, Architektenkammer, Berlin: Junius, 54–7.

Seferens, Horst (1995) *Ein deutscher Denkmalstreit: Die Kontroverse um die Spiegelwand in Berlin-Steglitz*, Berlin: Hentrich.

Selbourne, David (2001) 'Why Europe is destined to fall apart', *Sunday Times*, 13 May.

SEMCOG (1976) *Land use trends in Southeast Michigan, Southeast Michigan Council of Governments*, Detroit.

SEMCOG (1991) *The Business as Usual Trend Future: The Database*, Detroit: Southeast Michigan Council of Governments, January.

SEMCOG (1994) *Patterns of Diversity and Change in Southeast Michigan*, Detroit: Southeast Michigan Council of Governments.

SEMCOG (1999) *Land Use and Land Development in Southeast Michigan*, Detroit: Southeast Michigan Council of Governments.

SEMCOG (1999) *Residential Construction in Southeast Michigan, 1998*, Detroit: Southeast Michigan Council of Governments.

Senatsverwaltung für Bau-und Wohnungswesen (1994) *Kunst im Stadtraum*, Berlin: Denkmäler.

Senatsverwaltung für Bauen, Wohnen und Verkehr (1996) Künstlerischer Wettbewerb. Übergänge.

Senatsverwaltung für Bauen, Wohnen und Verkehr (1998) Liste der seit der Wiedervereinigung der beiden Stadthälften umbenannten bzw. benannten Straßen in den östlichen Bezirken Berlins. Berlin.

Senatsverwaltung für Stadtentwicklung des Landes Berlin und Ministerium für Landwirtschaft, Umweltschutz und Raumordnung des Landes Brandenburg (1999) Strategy Report: Metropolitan Region Berlin – Brandenburg.

Senatsverwaltung für Stadtentwicklung Umweltschutz und Technologie (1997) Planwerk Innenstadt Berlin.

Senatsverwaltung für Stadtentwicklung Umweltschutz und Technologie (1999) Planwerk Innenstadt Berlin: Ergebnis, Prozeß, Sektorale Planungen und Werkstätten. Berlin.

Senatsverwaltung für Verkehr und Betriebe (1994), Unabhängige Kommission zur Umbenennung von Straßen. Abschlussbericht, Berlin, March.

Senatsverwaltung für Wissenschaft, Forschung und Kultur (1997) Denkmal für die ermordeten Juden Europas. Colloquium. Dokumentation.

Senatsverwaltung für Wissenschaft, Forschung und Kultur (1997) Memorial to the Murdered Jews of Europe. Special Selection Procedure. Description of Brief and Procedural Conditions. Berlin.

Sennett, Richard (1990) *The Conscience of the Eye: The Design and Social Life of Cities*, New York: Norton.

Sennett, Richard (1999) 'The challenge of urban diversity', in Louise Nyström (ed.) *City and Culture: Cultural Processes and Urban Sustainability*, Karlstrona: Swedish Urban Environment Council, 128–34.

Shepardson, David and De Haven, Judy (1999) 'Judge considers blocking casino', *Detroit News*, 29 June.

Siedler, Wolf Jobst (1991) 'Das Schloss soll wieder her!', *Merian*, 13 September, 80–98.

Simms, Brendan (1998) 'City twinned with hell', *Times Higher*, 9 October, 23–4.

Singleton, D.A. (1987) 'Belfast: housing policy and trends', Chapter 8 in R.H. Buchanan and B.M. Walker (eds) *Province City and People: Belfast and its Region*, Belfast: Greystone Books, 151–68.

Sinn Féin (2001) Election communication. South Belfast.

Smith, Andrew (1997) 'Where did our love go?', *Sunday Times*, 2 March.

Smith, Suzanne E. (2000) *Dancing in the Street, Motown and the Cultural Politics of Detroit*, Cambridge, MA: Harvard University Press.

Smyth, Austin (2000) *The Implications of Segregation for Transport within Northern Ireland*, Edinburgh: Transport Research Institute, Napier University.

Soja, Edward W. (1996) *Thirdspace: Journeys to Los Angeles and Other Real-and-Imagined Places*, Malden, MA: Blackwell.

Sollors, Werner (1994) 'National identity and ethnic diversity: "of Plymouth Rock and Jamestown and Ellis Island"; or, ethnic literature and some redefinitions of "America"', Chapter 6 in Genevière Fabre and Robert O'Meally (eds) *History and Memory in African American Culture*, New York: Oxford University Press, 92–121.

Sontag, Susan (1979) *Introduction to Benjamin Walter, 'One Way Street and Other Writings'*, London: Verso, 7–28.

Sony Corporation (1998) 'Sony Centre am Potsdamer Platz', Publicity briefing in *Info-Box Catalogue*, Berlin: Nishen.

Sorges, Jürgen (1997) 'The red line through Berlin', *Berlin MAGAZIN*, 3, 20–2.

Speer, Albert (1995) *Inside the Third Reich*, London: Phoenix.

Spiegel (1995) 'Von New York Lernen', Nr 8, 42–78.

Spiegel (1996) 'Neues Leben im Ossi-Zoo', Nr 49, 2 December, 26.

Spiegel (1997) 'Die Zeit der Entscheidung', Nr 46, Hamburg.

Spiegel (1998) 'Die Macht der Mauern', Nr 22, 48–71.

Spreeinsel Initiative Berlin (1994) Proceedings of a Forum held on 18 April in the Stadtbibliothek, Breite Strasse in Berlin Mitte.

Stache, Rainer (2000) 'Internationale Expertenkommission', *Berliner Morgenpost*, 14 September.

Staunton, Denis (1994) 'Rebuilding Berlin', *Observer*, 6 November.

Staunton, Denis (1996) 'The voice for lost children', *Guardian*, 26 July.

Staunton, Denis (1998) 'Haunted still', *Guardian*, 12 August.

Staunton, Denis (1999) 'German politicians debate how to exorcise the Reichstag's ghosts', *Irish Times*, 9 March.

Steele, Jonathan (2000) 'Fortress Europe confronts the unthinkable', *Guardian*, 30 October.

Steele, Jonathan (2001) 'Berlin needs bridges, not walls, to end its cold war', *Guardian*, 17 August.

Steele, Shelby (1991) *The Content of our Character: A New Vision of Race in America*, New York: HarperCollins.

Stern (1995) 'Berlin 2005', Supplement to Nr 24. Hamburg.

Stern, Frank (1996) 'German-Jewish relations in the post-war period: the ambiguities of antisemitic and philosemitic discourse', in Y. Michal Bodemann (ed.) *Jews, Germans, Memory: Reconstructions of Jewish Life in Germany*, Ann Arbor: University of Michigan Press, 77–98.

Stewart, A.T.Q. (1989) *The Narrow Ground: Aspects of Ulster 1609–1969*, Belfast: Blackstaff Press.

Stiftung 'Topographie des Terrors', Berlin (2000) Internationales Dokumentations–und Besucherzentrum Berlin.

Stimmann, Hans (1995) City Centre Projects in City-Projekte. Büro-und Geschäftsbauten, Senatsverwaltung für Bau-und Wohnungswesen. Berlin, 7–12.

Stimmann, Hans D. (1996) Hauptstadt Berlin in Projekte für die Hauptstadt Berlin, Senatsverwaltung für Bau-und Wohnungswesen, Berlin, 7–11.

Stimmann, Hans D. (1996) 'Planwerk Berliner Innenstadt: Identität, Permanenz und Modernisierung, Stadtforum', *Journal der Senatsverwaltung für Stadtentwicklung, Umweltschutz und Technologie* 23, November, 14–17.

Stock, Gregory (2002) *Redesigning Humans*, London: Profile Books.

Stoker, G. (1995) 'Regime theory and urban politics', in D. Judge, *et al.* (eds) *Theories of Urban Politics*, London: Sage.

Stone, C.N. (1989) *Regime Politics: Governing Atlanta 1946–1988*, Lawrence: University Press of Kansas.

Strauss, Anselm L. (1961) *Images of the American City*, New York: The Free Press of Glencoe.

Strieder, Peter (1997) 'Creating the city's identity', in *Senatsverwaltung für Stadtentwicklung Umweltschutz und Technologie*, Innenstadt: Planwerk, 75–7.

Strieder, Peter (1997) ' "Haus der Demokratie" als Treffpunkt für alle', in Monika Zimmerman (ed.) *Der Berliner Schlossplatz: Visionen zur Gestaltung der Berliner Mitte*, Berlin: Argon Verlag, 118.

Strom, Elizabeth (1994) 'Planning in re-united Berlin: unification, post socialism and the redevelopment of the centre', Paper delivered at a conference entitled 'Shaping the Urban Future', sponsored by the Urban Affairs Association, School for Advanced Urban Studies, Bristol and Dept of City and Regional Planning, University of Wales College of Cardiff.

Stuart, Gisela (2000) 'Germans must think about redefining themselves', *Independent*, 12 July.

Süddeutsche Zeitung (1998) 'Hauptstadt der Reue', 20 March.

Sugrue, Thomas (1996) *The Origins of the Urban Crisis: Race and Inequality in Postwar Detroit*, Princeton: Princeton University Press.

Sullivan, Andrew (2000) 'United colours of America', *Sunday Times*, 15 October.

Sullivan, Andrew (2001) 'The beauty of a rainbow nation', *Sunday Times*, 11 March.

Sullivan, Kathryn (2002) 'A glimpse of home', *Time*, 2 September, 2–3. Special Earth Summit Supplement.

Sunday Times (1995) 'Profile of Louis Farrakhan'. 15 October.

Sunday Times (2001) 'Does Belfast hold clues to Britain's race crisis? Insight'. 15 July.

Swoboda, Hannes (2002) Vorwort. Internationale Expertenkommission. 'Historische Mitte Berlin', Abschlussbericht, Bundesministerium für Verkehr, Bau-und Wohnungswesen und Senatsverwaltung für Stadtentwicklung, Berlin, April, 4–5.

Tagesspiegel Berlin (1997) Wahrlich ein öffentlicher Platz, 7 January.

Tait, Paul (1999) Director, Southeast Michigan Council of Governments. Interview, 6 July.

Taylor, Carl S. (1990) *Dangerous Society*, East Lansing: Michigan State University Press.

Tepasse GmbH (1993) Die Asbestentsorgung des ehem. Palastes der Republik, March.

Tewdwr-Jones, M. and Allmendinger, P. (1998) 'Deconstructing communicative rationality: a critique of Habermasian collaborative planning', *Environment and Planning A, 1975–1989*, 30 pp.

Thieme, Wolf (1998) 'Der verschwundene Führer', *Merian*, Special Issue on Berlin, 6 June, 104–5.

Thierse, Wolfgang (1991) Beitrag zur Hauptstadt debatte des deutschen Bundestages vom 20 Juni in Dokumente zur Bundeshauptstadt Berlin (1994), Presse-und Informationsamt des Landes Berlin, 12–13.

Thomas, June Manning (1997) *Redevelopment and Race: Planning a Finer City in Postwar Detroit*, Baltimore: Johns Hopkins University Press.

Thompson, E.P. (1978) *The Poverty of Theory*, London: Merlin.

Thompson, John (1997) 'From Berlin to Belfast and Beirut: reconciliation and regeneration through community planning', *City*, Nr 8, 53–61.

Thornton, Chris (2001) 'Reid closely', *Belfast Telegraph*, 29 November.

Thrift, Nigel (2001) 'How should we think about place in a globalising world?', Chapter 2 in Ali Madanipour, Patsy Healey and Angela Hull (eds) *The Governance of Place: Space and Planning Processes*, Aldershot: Ashgate, 23–50.

Thurn und Taxis, Lilli (1995) 'Een stukje gebouwd geluk: Een pleidooi voor het Palast der Republik in Berlijn', *Archis* 4, 5–7.

Tillich, Paul (1952) *The Courage to Be*, Glasgow: Collins.

Töpfer, Klaus (1995) 'Forward', in Annegret Burg and Sebastian Redecke (eds) *Chancellery and Office of the President of the Federal Republic of Germany. International Architectural Competition for the Capital Berlin*, Berlin: Birkhäuser Verlag, 7.

Töpfer, Klaus (1996) Interview in *Der Tagespiegel*, Berlin, 23 December.

Traynor, Ian (1996) 'One people divided by a false dawn', *Guardian*, 19 November.

Traynor, Ian (1997) 'Kohl digs foundation of new Berlin powerhouse', *Guardian*, 5 February.

Traynor, Ian (1999) 'MPs pick holes in the new Reichstag', *Guardian*, 3 July.

Traynor, Ian (1999) 'Leader of Germany's Jews, he died a bitter man', *Guardian*, 16 August.

Treibel, Annette (1994) 'Theory of communicative action, discourse ethics and political practice. Notes on recent developments in Habermas', *Journal of the Deutsche Gesellschaft für Soziologie*, Special Edition 3, 135–48.

Trewsdale, Janet (1999) *Introduction to N. Ireland Economic Council , A Step Change in Economic Performance . A response to Strategy 2010 (Sept)*, Belfast.

Trimble, David (2000) 'My challenge to the DUP', *Belfast Telegraph*, 19 September.

Trimble, David (2000) 'There is so much at stake for us all', *Belfast Telegraph*, 6 October.

Trimble, David (2001) *To Raise Up a New Northern Ireland. Articles and Speeches 1998–2000*, Belfast: The Belfast Press.

Trotnow, Helmut (1999) 'Understanding the present by looking back at the past: Bernauer Strasse and the Berlin Wall Memorial site', in (ed.) 'The Berlin Wall Memorial Site and Exhibition Center', *Association*, Berlin: Jaron Verlag, 8–12.

Ullrich, Christiane (1993) 'Vom Umgang mit ungeliebten Symbolen', *Neue Zeit*, 16 July.

Ullrich, Volker (2002) 'Weltuntergang kann nicht schlimmer sein', *Die Zeit*, Nr 49, 28 November.

Vergara, Camilo José (1995) *The New American Ghetto*, New Brunswick, NJ: Rutgers University Press.

Vesilind, Priit J. (1982) 'Two Berlins – a generation apart', *National Geographic* 161: 1, 2–52.

Waldmeir, Pete (1999) 'Computer geek invasion a step toward to a real Detroit comeback', *Detroit News*, 12 April.

Walker, Brian (2002) 'Are we taking human rights too far?', *Belfast Telegraph*, 26 April.

Walker, Clarence E. (2001) *We Can't Go Home Again*, New York: Oxford University Press.

Walker, Gail (1999) 'Nothing to get up in arms about', *Belfast Telegraph*, 19 June.

Walker, Martin (1993) 'The mayor's race to the finish', *Guardian*, 30 October.

Walker, Richard A. (1981) 'A theory of suburbanization: capitalism and the construction of urban space in the United States', in Michael Dear *et al.* (eds) *Urbanization and Urban Planning in Capitalist Society*, London: Methuen.

Walker-Tyson, Joyce (1980) 'Gospel music: a race shares its sorrows and hopes', in Scott McGehee and Susan Watson (eds) *Blacks in Detroit*, Detroit Free Press, December, 86–8.

Warner, Alan (ed.) (1981) *The Selected John Hewitt*, Belfast: Blackstaff Press.

Warner, Kee (2002) 'Linking local sustainability initiatives with environmental justice', *Local Environment* 7: 1, 35–47.

Watson, Ronald and Monaghan, Elaine (2002) 'Race jibe hits black support for Bush', *Times*, 12 December.

Waugh, Eric (2002) 'Petty response to Maskey gesture', *Belfast Telegraph*, 3 July.

Waugh, Eric (2002) 'Changed times for the jubilee visit', *Belfast Telegraph*, 15 May.

West, Cornell (1993) *Race Matters*, Boston: Beacon Press.

West, Cornell (1997) 'Black strivings in a twilight civilization', in Henry Lewis Gates Jr and Cornell West, *The Future of the Race*, New York: Vintage Books.

Wheatcroft, Geoffrey (1993) 'The disenchantment of Ireland', *Atlantic Monthly*, July, 65–84.

White, Barry (2001) 'Northern Ireland Inc.', *Belfast Telegraph*, 17 November.

Whyte, John (1991) *Interpreting Northern Ireland*, Oxford: Clarendon Paperbacks.

Widick, B.J. (1989) *Detroit: City of Race and Class Violence*, Detroit: Wayne State University Press, revised edition.

Widmer, Ted (2002) 'In shadow of the greats, president proves he's no Berliner', *Guardian*, 24 May.

Wiedemann, Charlotte (1996) 'Die Palast–Intrige', *Der Tagesspiegel*, Berlin, 9 August.

Wiehler, Stephan (1992) 'Sympathien für Honni-Horror-Picture-Show', *Berlin Tagesspiegel*, 7 October.

Wiener, Ron (1980) *The Rape and Plunder of the Shankill*, Belfast: Farset Co-operative Press.

Wiesel, Elie (2001) 'Palestinians' rights do not include the right to Jerusalem', *Guardian*, 25 January.

Wilhelm, Karin (2001) Demokratie als Bauherr. Überlegungen zum Charakter der Berliner politischen Repräsentationsbauten in Das Parlament Wochenzeitung, Bonn, 7–15.

Will, Detlef (1996) Building Director, Steglitz, Berlin. Interview, 4 September.

Williams, Raymond (1983) *Towards 2000*, Middlesex: Pelican Books.

Williamson, Nigel (1997) 'A ghost town called Motown', *Independent*, 13 December.

Willis, Daniel (1999) *The Emerald City and Other Essays on the Architectural Imagination*, New York: Princeton Architectural Press.

Wise, Michael Z. (1998) *Capital Dilemma*, New York: Princeton Architectural Press.

Wood, Michael (1999) 'Rewriting history', *Guardian*, 19 August.

Woodhead, Michael (1998) 'Angel of death haunts Germany again', *Sunday Times*, 18 October.

Woodhead, Michael and Cleaver, Hannah (1999) 'Thatcher haunts cold war reunion', *Sunday Times*, 7 November.

Woodward, Kathryn (1997) 'Concepts of identity and difference', Chapter 1 in Kathryn Woodward (ed.) *Identity and Difference*, London: Sage Publications in association with the Open University, 7–62.

Wright, Oliver (2001) 'Children walk a gauntlet of Belfast hatred', *Times*, 4 September.

Wroe, Nicholas (2002) 'Literature's Loose Cannon', *Guardian*, 23 March.

Wulf-Mathies M, (1997) 'Shaping our Future: the European Perspective'. Paper at Shaping our Future Conference 27 November, Belfast.

Wyatt, Caroline (1997) 'Honecker's ghost made welcome in Berlin', *Sunday Times*, 27 April.

Young, Coleman (1987) 'Personal Observations on Race Relations in Detroit', in Detroit Strategic Planning Project, Conference on Race Relations, *Proceedings*, 25 July, 1–8.

Young, James E. (1993) *The Texture of Memory. Holocaust Memorials and Meaning*, New Haven: Yale University Press.

Young, James E. (1994) 'The art of memory', in James E. Young, (ed.) *The Art of Memory: Holocaust Memorials in History*. Munich: Prestel-Verlag, 9–17.

Young, James E. (1997) *Memorial for Europe's Murdered Jews: The Next Stage, May 1997*, Department of English and Judaic Studies, University of Massachusetts at Amherst.

Young, James E. (1998) Assessment of Peter Eisenman's Revised Design for Berlin's 'Memorial for the Murdered Jews of Europe'. Statement as spokesman for the Findungskommission.

Young, James E. (2000) *At Memory's Edge: After-Images of the Holocaust in Contemporary Art and Architecture*, New Haven: Yale University Press.

Younge, Gary (2001) 'A nation expects', *Sunday Times*, 20 October.

Zander, Peter (1995) 'Weiter Diskussion um Mauer-Markierung', *Die Welt*, 16 June.

Zimmer, Dieter and Paeschke, Carl-Ludwig (1991) Das Tor. Deutschlands berühmtestes Bauwerk in zwei Jahrhunderten. Deutsche Verlags–Anstalt, Stuttgart.

Zimmerman, Monika (1997) 'Nachdenken über den Schlossplatz', *Der Tagesspiegel*, 7 January.

INDEX

Note: Page references in *italic* refer to captions.

eBooks – at www.eBookstore.tandf.co.uk

A library at your fingertips!

eBooks are electronic versions of printed books. You can store them on your PC/laptop or browse them online.

They have advantages for anyone needing rapid access to a wide variety of published, copyright information.

eBooks can help your research by enabling you to bookmark chapters, annotate text and use instant searches to find specific words or phrases. Several eBook files would fit on even a small laptop or PDA.

NEW: Save money by eSubscribing: cheap, online access to any eBook for as long as you need it.

Annual subscription packages

We now offer special low-cost bulk subscriptions to packages of eBooks in certain subject areas. These are available to libraries or to individuals.

For more information please contact webmaster.ebooks@tandf.co.uk

We're continually developing the eBook concept, so keep up to date by visiting the website.

www.eBookstore.tandf.co.uk